RECONSIDERING
FLANNERY
O'CONNOR

RECONSIDERING FLANNERY O'CONNOR

EDITED BY ALISON ARANT AND JORDAN COFER

AFTERWORD BY MARSHALL BRUCE GENTRY

UNIVERSITY PRESS OF MISSISSIPPI / JACKSON

The University Press of Mississippi is the scholarly publishing agency of the Mississippi Institutions of Higher Learning: Alcorn State University, Delta State University, Jackson State University, Mississippi State University, Mississippi University for Women, Mississippi Valley State University, University of Mississippi, and University of Southern Mississippi.

In Monica C. Miller's essay, "Country People: Depictions of Farm Women in Flannery O'Connor's Short Fiction," quotes from three letters by Flannery O'Connor and unpublished drafts from *Wise Blood* appear. These quotes and drafts are © 1947 Flannery O'Connor, © renewed by Regina Cline O'Connor. Reprinted by permission of the Mary Flannery O'Connor Charitable Trust via Harold Matson Co., Inc. All rights reserved.

www.upress.state.ms.us

The University Press of Mississippi is a member of the Association of University Presses.

First printing 2020
∞

Library of Congress Cataloging-in-Publication Data available

Hardback ISBN 978-1-4968-3179-8
Trade paperback ISBN 978-1-4968-3180-4
Epub single ISBN 978-1-4968-3181-1
Epub institutional ISBN 978-1-4968-3182-8
PDF single ISBN 978-1-4968-3183-5
PDF institutional ISBN 978-1-4968-3184-2

British Library Cataloging-in-Publication Data available

Contents

PART 3: STRANGE BEDFELLOWS

PART 4: O'CONNOR'S LEGACY

Acknowledgments

We would like to begin by thanking the National Endowment for the Humanities (NEH) for their support for much of this research. Any mistakes or inaccuracies are our own.

Thanks too to those who not only made the NEH support possible but also made it an absolute pleasure to experience: Marshall Bruce Gentry, Robert Donahoo, James Owens, Laura Martin, Nancy Davis Bray, and Special Collections staff in the Georgia College Library.

We would also like to acknowledge all of our tremendous scholar-colleagues who participated in the 2014 NEH Institute. There are too many to list individually, and some have work included in the collection, but a greater group of scholars could not be found. They offered such wonderful company and such great music, laughter, and conversation. Specifically, thanks to Sticky, who taught us all about telos.

We would also like to thank the anonymous readers who reviewed our manuscript and offered thoughtful and thorough feedback to us and to our contributors. This collection benefited greatly from your generosity.

Also we thank Matt McCullough for the expertise and good humor he brought to the project as our editorial assistant, as well as the willingness to sacrifice his time and energy amid the demands of graduate school.

ALISON:

My thanks to Wagner College for support in developing my essay and in promoting the collection as a whole at various conferences. Thanks to my colleagues in the English department for their encouragement and especially to Susan Bernardo, who first suggested to me that a good edited collection could come out of the NEH Institute. Additional thanks to my students for their kind inquiries as to the book's progress and for their patience when my work on this project delayed my engagements with their work.

Closer to home, I would like to thank my family. I would also like to thank the Whealy family for their hospitality as I worked on parts of this collection, both in Beaver Creek and in Omaha. And thanks especially to my husband, Tyler Coquillard, for his good cheer and patience in living with this project along with me. I'm so glad it's you.

Finally, thanks to Jordan Cofer, my coeditor, for his generosity, curiosity, and good-natured collaboration. Your deep knowledge of O'Connor criticism and commitments to collegiality rounded out the project in ways I so appreciate.

JORDAN:

I would like to offer my thanks to my family, especially Rebecca Cofer, for encouragement and working around my schedule so that I could finish this project.

I would also like to thank the institutions of Abraham Baldwin Agricultural College, Georgia College & State University, and the good people at Emory University's Woodruff Library, specifically, Kathleen Shoemaker in the MARBL Special Collections, and Nancy Davis Bray in Georgia College's Ina Dillard Russell Library for all the assistance. Finally, thank you to all my colleagues who helped me talk out this project (Joe Brown, Brian Yost, Herbert Shippey, Tamatha Lambert, etc.).

Finally, I'd like to thank my co-contributor, Alison Arant, for giving up so many weekends on the phone working on this project. You are a keen reader and sharp editor and I will forever be grateful for the *MEAL* method of approaching an essay.

RECONSIDERING
FLANNERY
O'CONNOR

Recovering Interpretative Possibilities in the Fiction of Flannery O'Connor: An Introduction

ALISON ARANT AND JORDAN COFER

The project of reconsidering Flannery O'Connor is one that returns to the wide range of interpretations her work received in the early days of publication. For some of her initial readers, O'Connor's fiction was a puzzle, a sort of false bottom. At first, certain features of her fiction seemed to invoke familiar interpretive frameworks, but read a little further and weird things happened. In the end, her stories upset those same frameworks that at first promised to make sense of them, and the effect was unsettling for some. Though O'Connor's profile traits—white, southern, Catholic, woman—gave her a characteristic or two in common with many other contemporary writers, her combination of all these features together made her and her writing unlike most of them too. Her fiction was uncanny, at once familiar and unfamiliar. It resisted easy classification, despite some readers and critics who have tried simplifying her work as a way of resolving the discomfort it can generate.

As we will demonstrate, several critical habits have contributed to reductive readings of the fiction and person of Flannery O'Connor, and one goal of this collection is to challenge those habits and recover the interpretive breadth O'Connor's work invites. As the collection's editors, we grant the strength of a great deal of O'Connor scholarship and recognize how our work and that of others is indebted to it; however, we also maintain that a persistent strand in O'Connor criticism seeks not just to understand but to overly resolve the weirdnesses of Flannery O'Connor. Rather than seeing interpretive possibility as a problem in need of resolution, we work from the premise that such tensions can be productive for both readers and scholars. Our purpose is not to deliberately misread O'Connor or erase her commitments or historical situatedness. Rather we want her fiction to receive the most robust readings possible, plausible readings that explore all the meanings her work engenders.

Though detailed chapter summaries are included later, it is worth mentioning here the basic structure of this volume. The first three sections seek to open up interpretations of O'Connor's work by applying new methodologies, drawing on new contexts, and putting her in conversation with unlikely or neglected counterparts. Lastly, the collection's fourth section comes full circle, returning to some of the conventional concerns regarding O'Connor's legacy that are due for reevaluation. We hope this form can stoke creativity in approaches to Flannery O'Connor, build on the body of lively scholarship that currently engages her work, and course correct where the field risks calcification.

In order to demonstrate the range of interpretation O'Connor's work enables and assess the strengths and weaknesses of O'Connor studies to date, a more detailed overview of O'Connor's reception is helpful. For many members of Flannery O'Connor's early audience, her fiction was easy to read, but hard to understand. On one level, it was straightforward enough. Readers found her prose lucid and concrete, unlike the work of her more experimental contemporaries. Her plots, frequently set in the US South, were quite linear. A pattern seemed to characterize much of O'Connor's work: though the main characters could be anyone from familiar farm mothers to reluctant prophets to pensive serial killers, the action often culminates in some kind of horrible accident. Upon reaching the conclusion of these works, competent readers would have no trouble summarizing them.

On another level, however, the meaning of O'Connor's fiction was elusive. Nested within the works' apparent simplicity was an engagement with some transcendent but shadowy reality. Writing in 1970, just six years after the death of O'Connor, Miles D. Orvell imagines the typical O'Connor reader as a man who perceives but cannot comprehend O'Connor's work. He is a "dumb witness to some terrible accident; he has had the experience—he is sure of that—but he has missed the meaning" (184–85). In this formulation, the extremity of the experiences in O'Connor's stories makes their elusiveness especially puzzling. Surely such strange and striking works must mean something. Orvell detected "the quality of a mysterious reality that is the heart of her best stories" (184), but sensed that the average reader felt obstructed in comprehending it. This difficulty resulted in unsatisfying criticism of O'Connor's work, according to Orvell. Scholars approached her fiction with confidence, but finally failed to account for its larger significance (184).

To make sense of O'Connor's fiction in the early days, some critics latched onto one feature or another of her work that felt reminiscent of other writers and often proceed to assess her work on the basis of comparison. Logical as it was to read O'Connor alongside other women writers or Catholic writers or southern writers, the effects of applying such frameworks could be more reductive than expansive in their approach. Some readers found her prose taut, dry, and blunt (*New Yorker*), too masculine for a woman writer ("Such

Nice People"). Her work was too religiously preoccupied for some secular readers (Rosenfeld 21), but also too violent and impious for some religious readers (Simons 20). Her work was not especially flattering in its representation of the South, as local boosters would have liked (Streight xx). Rather than grappling with her work in its complexity, some of these approaches mitigate discomfort by applying genre formulas and then writing off those aspects of her work that failed to conform to the pattern in question.

This left a gap in critical interpretations that could more fully account for the complexity of O'Connor's work. To address that gap, some critics centered O'Connor's theology, which had an indelible effect on her fiction. Some scholars emphasize her engagement with the work of Thomas Aquinas (Andretta; Edmondson, *Return*; Montgomery) while others explore her connections to the work of Jacques Maritain (Gordon, Lewis). Some debate the extent of her obedience to or subversion of official church dogma. Jordan Cofer, a coeditor of this volume, authored a study on O'Connor's indebtedness to the Bible itself. Still others, noticing her affinity for certain strains of fundamentalism, examine how her fiction locates Catholic concerns in protestant forms (Milder, Peede, Wood). At their best, these treatments of O'Connor's theology offer tools for considering the interplay of elements in O'Connor's fiction that can sometimes appear to be in opposition—violence, grace, humor, damnation, and redemption. In their less productive forms, they verge on hagiography or become redundant, amounting to what Robert Donahoo identifies as "simply another slightly rephrased argument that O'Connor is indeed Christian and Catholic" (246). Rather than deepening the mysteries of O'Connor's fiction, such arguments threaten to short-circuit them.

Another tension in the field of O'Connor studies involves the interpretive influence the author herself can or should exercise over her work. In English studies more generally, debates regarding the role of the author have a history we will review here briefly in order to clarify the stakes of the question, to discuss its role in O'Connor studies, and to identify the position of this collection in relation to it. Broadly speaking, the debate exists between those critics John Farrell identifies as "intentionalist" on the one hand and those he calls "textualists" on the other (6). Farrell uses intentionalism to name a range of interpretive assumptions including the belief that the author's intentions are discernable in the work, that the best practice is to read according to the author's intentions, and that the author's intentions could provide a standard for judging the work's value. In the mid-1940s, several writers including T. S. Eliot, C. S. Lewis, and William Wimsatt and Monroe Beardsley offered critiques of these assumptions. Wimsatt and Beardsley famously argued "that the design or intention of the author is neither available nor desirable as a standard for judging the success of a work of literary art" (468). Together they ushered in a modernist paradigm of interpretation that centered the text itself and displaced the author as the key to interpretation. The textualist critique was later extended by postmodern theorists like Roland Barthes and Michel Foucault, who respectively saw the author as a function of capitalist ideology and of discourse. Declaring the death of the author, arguments like theirs helped popularize textualism among literary critics, though in practice, the author often remains very much alive.

This is especially true in O'Connor studies, where the author looms large, and intentionalists far outnumber the textualists for a few reasons. First, O'Connor did more in her essays, lectures, and extensive correspondence to name her intentions than most artists will. It is also worth noting, however, that she personally seemed "willing to accept heathen or 'misreadings'" if they highlighted the artistry of her work (Donahoo 242). O'Connor's explanations, in addition to being numerous and often irresistibly quotable, can also shed light on otherwise confounding questions that attend her writing. Furthermore, in the years after her death, the more her biographical details, personal correspondence, and nonfiction writing have become available, the more scholars have used them as a major interpretive lens for reading her short stories and novels. The temptation to rely on the interpretation of the author is perhaps especially strong for those who share O'Connor's religious beliefs since her stature in American letters can feel vindicating amid narratives of Christianity in decline.

The results of this prevailing authorial approach have been varied. Certainly some indispensable scholarship on O'Connor has taken its interpretive cues from the writer herself. In one strong vein, access to O'Connor via her nonfiction and her published correspondence has helped critics map narrative strategies within her fiction. For example, Bruce Gentry invokes the views of the author to explore how O'Connor's work approaches the grotesque degeneration of an ideal as a key aspect in the process of redemption and not as an obstacle. Robert Brinkmeyer works from the starting point of O'Connor's devout Catholicism to argue that her fiction engages a range of voices, including those that challenge faith. More recently, Christina Bieber Lake uses the doctrine of the incarnation, a tenet of O'Connor's faith, as a lens for understanding the grotesque bodies that appear in her fiction and to especially emphasize the centrality of embodiment for human personhood. In these and other fine works of scholarship, the views of the author herself function as one way of probing interpretive possibility, illuminating the tensions that structure her stories and not necessarily seeking to foreclose them.

Following O'Connor's lead, however, can have its hazards too, as Daniel Moran, Robert Brinkmeyer, and Timothy Caron demonstrate. In his study of the creation of Flannery O'Connor's literary reputation, Moran notes a critical tendency toward reading for "watchwords" that enable a form of confirmation bias: "Once an author's style, content, and favorite issues [...] have been agreed upon, anything from his or her previous life can be read as evidence for the dominant critical opinion" (4). In addition to these self-fulfilling acts of interpretation, Robert Brinkmeyer points out the risks that come from following O'Connor's lead around her casual attitude toward acts of violence as long as the characters' experiences of trauma promote their spiritual growth ("Murder and Rape," 100). He points out the misguided lengths some scholars go to in defending fictional actions they would never condone in real life (108). Yet another danger involves recapitulating O'Connor's blind spots, especially around issues of race, as Timothy Caron argues. He uses the term "True Believers" to name critics who share Flannery O'Connor's theological understanding of the world and who read her fiction accordingly. In his view, O'Connor elevates spiritual concerns about regeneration over social concerns about racial justice, and many critics accept those terms as she establishes them, thus reproducing the religious rhetoric that characterized the white southern church in the 1950s and '60s (139). In their admiration for O'Connor, some of these scholars speak as if her faith functioned as a perfect guard against internalizing the white supremacist status quo that organized the world she inhabited. Would that it were so, but when numberless black and white people within the church and without testify to their lifelong struggle to unlearn white supremacy, an ideology that seeks to naturalize itself, this defense is much too simple.

In serving as the collection's editors, we aim to avoid these pitfalls of intentionalism, on the one hand, without going so far as to erase the author on the other. Here we return to the work of John Farrell, whose recent reassessment of the intentional fallacy names a realistic middle ground between intentionalism and textualism that informs our approach to Flannery O'Connor. We recognize that even as O'Connor often revealed aspects of her intentions, intentions are always complex and layered. They might succeed on one level while miscarrying on another—in the same way that someone might understand a joke, but not find it funny (Farrell 37). We recognize that while a total ban on intention is unnecessary and impossible to maintain, it is also a mistake to imagine the text can only mean what an author might intend. We see the fiction of Flannery O'Connor as a human creation, carried out in a specific historical context toward an audience that is potentially identifiable. Thus, we practice an intentionalism that avoids the intentional fallacy in its classic form while also fully recognizing the role of the reader in constructing the text (Farrell 6). In sum, our premise is that author, text, and audience all play roles in the process of meaning making.

We are by no means the first O'Connor critics to deny sovereign status to the author, nor are we the first to call for reconsiderations of O'Connor (see May, Kreyling, Donahoo). Even as intentionalism has constituted the majority position in O'Connor studies, there have always been critics who read against the grain and seek to diversify the range of approaches to Flannery O'Connor. From John Hawkes's argument that O'Connor was of the Devil's party more than not to Carol Shloss's study of O'Connor and the limits of inference to Timothy Caron's self-described "apostasy" as an O'Connor critic, the scholarship of doubters has had a vibrant impact on O'Connor studies. So too have the contributions of O'Connor critics who take up other subjects altogether. Influential works like Jon Lance Bacon's study of O'Connor and the Cold War or Patricia Yaeger's engagement with O'Connor and feminism, along with more recent works like Henry Edmondson's political companion to O'Connor all testify to the vitality that comes from a broad range of critical frameworks.

In that spirit, *Reconsidering Flannery O'Connor* pursues questions that productively complicate the commonplaces of O'Connor studies while also circling back to some old questions that are due for new attention: How can O'Connor's fiction be a site for creating and not just applying literary theory? What has an awareness of O'Connor's priorities kept us from seeing in her work? What surprising insights might we gain if we put O'Connor in conversation with writers other than the usual suspects? How does our understanding of O'Connor change as a result of access to newly released or previously overlooked archival material? How do we assess O'Connor's influence on American literature and her role in the rise of the creative writing workshop? What accounts for the limits on scholarly access to O'Connor's archives? In addressing these and other questions, our contributors each offer their own reconsiderations of Flannery O'Connor. Some essays are loud and startling, while others are subtler; however, we argue that if the shape of the collection on the whole should be ungainly, it is fitting, not only in light of our goals, but also in light of O'Connor's penchant for misfits.

At the same time, we have tried to lend order to the collection, and although a few options were promising, we ultimately decided on four sections, each with a different type of reconsideration. The volume opens with "New Methodologies," featuring writers who either take original approaches to O'Connor or develop new angles on established theories of interpretation. Their innovations often work in two directions—using new theories to read the fiction of O'Connor and considering how the fiction of O'Connor talks back to these theories. Their work thus points the way for further applications of and innovations in the methodologies scholars use to understand her work.

Gina Caison coins "feather method," an object-oriented ontology that considers the feather itself as a lens for reading several of O'Connor's stories. Rather than seeing the peacock feather as a metaphor for the author's work or as a religious symbol, as many readers have, Caison takes the feather as a meaning-making object in its own right and uses its characteristics to reconsider O'Connor. Caison argues that O'Connor's writing both upholds and challenges an object-oriented ontology that rejects status hierarchy. Thus, her essay uses O'Connor's work to further theorize object-oriented ontology.

Drawing on disability studies and queer theory, Bruce Henderson uses a "crip-queer" lens to read "A Temple of the Holy Ghost" and "The River." Henderson argues that while O'Connor rarely writes non-heteronormative characters, there are, in fact, several "queer" figures in O'Connor's fiction, who don't play into normative roles. Furthermore, Henderson notes that despite the number of disabled characters who populate O'Connor's stories, few scholars write about O'Connor from a disability studies lens. Henderson recognizes the complications that most likely contribute to this critical gap, ranging from O'Connor's orthodox Catholic beliefs about sexuality on the one hand, to the uneasy relationship between associating queerness and crip-ness on the other. However, he argues that a crip-queer approach provides a useful way into understanding the function of nonnormative bodies and souls in O'Connor's work.

Using the framework of praxis, Alicia Beeson offers a new way to think about the misguided acts of charity in "The Lame Shall Enter First" and "The Comforts of Home." Beeson defines praxis as the balance of action and reflection that informs disciplines like education and philosophy. She points out that for O'Connor's religious and nonreligious characters alike, charitable action without productive reflection often leads to tragic outcomes. Beeson pays particular attention to the power hierarchies that undergird acts of charity, and she shows that while overconfidence discourages critical reflection, self-examination of motives and consequences can be transformative.

Finally, Doreen Fowler takes a new approach to O'Connor by showing how her fiction both anticipates and revises the work of Jacques Lacan. Though others have used Lacan to read O'Connor's fiction, this chapter is the first to note that both authors' explorations of mystery (psychological for Lacan and theological for O'Connor) center around language, which they recognize as an obstacle to transcendent meaning. Fowler ultimately rereads the Lacanian Real as O'Connor's encounter with the Divine Life, arguing that what Lacan sees as coming to the end of meaning making is what O'Connor sees as the precondition for grace.

The volume's second section, "New Contexts," demonstrates how fruitful it can be to think about O'Connor's work in new surroundings or from a different perspective. While some of these new contexts provide more strik-ing reconsiderations than others, all three essays offer alternatives to popular interpretations of O'Connor's work. These essays stretch expectations on liter-ary genre, on popular archetypes in her stories, and on which of her characters deserve readerly sympathy. These essays also rely on new archival material, as well as previously unconsidered or unpublished material, to frame their reconsiderations and situate aspects of her work in a new context.

Where convention categorizes southern literature as especially preoccupied with the past, Doug Davis reads O'Connor's stories as science fiction, highlighting the surprising extent of her engagement with futurism. From time travelers to space cadets to cyborgs, O'Connor's stories are filled with images and characters that appear in popular science fiction. Davis argues that for O'Connor, the vocabulary of science fiction provides a way to both explore and critique the promises and effects of technological progress in the context of Cold War America.

In dialogue with Eric Bennett and Mark McGurl's work on the Iowa Writers' Workshop, as well as Tara Powell's work on archetypes, Jordan Cofer uses new information from the Emory Archive and *A Prayer Journal* to contextualize one of O'Connor's most famous comedic devices: the antagonistic intellectual. Cofer argues that although this device may have roots in southern fiction, O'Connor's anti-intellectual trope derives from her time in the Iowa Writers' Workshop. This chapter examines some of O'Connor's juvenilia, the drafts of *Wise Blood* she was writing in Iowa (while simultaneously writing in her journal), and some of the short stories she wrote while enrolled at the Workshop. Finally, Cofer reconsiders the origins of O'Connor's anti-intellectual as a potential outgrowth of her own anxieties during this time.

Monica Miller recuperates O'Connor's female farmers and mothers, women whose labor keeps their dependents financially stable but whose complaints and unhappiness often invite censure from other characters as well as readers and critics. Miller offers a more sympathetic reading of these women, suggesting that their preoccupations might stem less from pettiness than from practical concerns about managing farms and finances. To support her argument, Miller draws on archival material newly acquired by Emory University's Manuscript, Archives, and Rare Book Library. These materials, excerpted here for the first time, provide context about the realities of managing Andalusia, the O'Connor family farm. Ultimately, Miller argues that through these women farmers and mothers, O'Connor's stories offer a realistic representation of farm life that corrects the romantic depictions that appear in the fiction of many of O'Connor's contemporaries.

The third section, which we lovingly called, "Strange Bedfellows," puts Flannery O'Connor in dialogue with overlooked or neglected conversation partners. This section is—on some level—our attempt to reclaim the oddness, the unsettling capacity of O'Connor's fiction. Some of these pairings might be more surprising than others while other pairings raise the question: why hasn't she been put in conversation with these authors more often?

William Murray finds surprising continuity regarding the purpose of art in the works of Flannery O'Connor and Friedrich Nietzsche. Although these two are often mentioned together (based on the famous "wingless chickens" quotation), few writers other than Henry Edmonson III have offered any extended critique of the pair. Although the two writers differed in nationality, language, and most obviously, in their beliefs about religion, Murray reconsiders the notion that Nietzsche and O'Connor were fundamentally at odds with each other. He argues that O'Connor's fiction engages with Nietzsche's early work, in particular on the influence of art and myth on a culture. By putting these two writers in conversation, Murray challenges prevailing approaches that reduce them both to their most memorable quotes about God and instead foregrounds their shared belief that art can be a powerful tool for challenging calcified cultural knowledge.

Recognizing O'Connor's relevance as a political thinker, political scientist Alison Staudinger puts O'Connor in dialogue with Hannah Arendt in order to explore O'Connor's approach to fascism, a pressing subject in the author's Cold War context, as well as in our contemporary political moment. By engaging Arendt, Staudinger examines O'Connor's relationship with fascism on three levels—as the practice of the artist, as the worldview of some fictional characters, and as an approach to her personal friendships. Staudinger argues that while O'Connor sees the temptations of fascism, she finally rejects it as a totalizing denial of human plurality. Staudinger suggests that O'Connor falls short of depicting an earthly community that could accept this plurality, especially regarding racial equality; at the same time she points out that O'Connor's fiction demonstrates how it is the country's deep-seated racial hierarchy that makes it vulnerable to fascism.

Rachel Watson also takes up O'Connor's role as a political thinker and writer by examining issues of racial hierarchy in O'Connor's fiction and putting her work in conversation with that of Richard Wright. Watson notes that although O'Connor invokes the "manners" of the Jim Crow South, she does not offer a sentimental or abject form of pity for her characters, regardless of their race. It is in this pity, so often connected with Cold War totalitarianism, that Watson finds a connection between the work of Flannery O'Connor and Richard Wright. This chapter shows the commonality between two authors whose work had previously seemed disparate, as Watson highlights their mutual fear of a racial and economic hegemony.

Alison Arant uses the zoot suit—an outfit that is simultaneously conspicuous and difficult to interpret—as a way to put the fiction of Flannery O'Connor in conversation with that of Toni Morrison. In their fiction set in the 1940s and '50s, including one unpublished story by O'Connor, both authors create zoot-suited figures who are not quite visible to those around them. By focusing on the object of the zoot suit, Arant's essay in some ways connects to the materiality of Miller's approach to the farm as well as to Caison's object-oriented analysis of the peacock feather. Arant reads O'Connor's and Morrison's works in the context of the zoot suit riots of 1943 and argues that both writers use these inscrutable zoot suiters as a way of exploring the

fears, promises, and limits of racial integration. Together these texts demonstrate the persistence of white ideology, which lingers both in individual
minds and in social systems that purport to be free of it.

The last essay in the "Strange Bedfellows" section reconsiders the form of
the academic essay itself while also examining Flannery O'Connor alongside
Sylvia Plath. In an approach that is closer to a work of creative writing than
to conventional criticism, poet Lindsey Alexander compares O'Connor's and
Plath's reception as women writers. This essay is something of an anomaly in
the collection since it relies on elements of the personal essay, asks more questions than it answers, and uses anecdotal evidence. However, we see it as an
essential demonstration of the volume's commitment to a broad reconsideration of O'Connor, which includes exploring how she affects current writers
and their work and practices. Alexander examines O'Connor and Plath as
a way to consider how female authors are received by a male readership
and identifies several similarities between the two authors—who are rarely
regarded in tandem—and one striking difference: the perceived masculinity
of O'Connor's violent subject matter and the assumed femininity of Plath's
subject matter. Alexander uses these two gendered designations to raise the
question: why one and not the other?

The book's final section, "O'Connor's Legacy," reconsiders the long-term
impacts of Flannery O'Connor. As we noted above, the majority of the
essays in this collection set aside issues of authorial intent when it comes to
O'Connor's fiction; however, the essays in this final section recuperate the
intentions of the author when it comes to her personal views on creative
writing and her wishes regarding the handling of her estate upon death. With
these essays, the collection comes full circle, attesting to the hazards that
come from overly relying on O'Connor but also from ignoring her views and
desires.

Eric Bennett examines O'Connor's legacy in an influential but often-over-
looked venue: the creative writing workshop. Bennett argues that creative
writing programs have benefited from O'Connor's success story, but they
have also mischaracterized her method as a writer. Bennett demonstrates how
manuals and instruction in creative writing laud the practice of not knowing
where one's fiction is going during the writing process, and often some of
O'Connor's words get marshaled in support of this approach. Bennett claims
that such uses of O'Connor both distort who she was and demonstrate how
impoverished current theories of fiction often are.

In the last essay in this section, Carol Loeb Shloss takes a literal approach
to the subject of legacy by exploring and questioning the legal nature of
Flannery O'Connor's literary estate, a hot topic among many O'Connor scholars. Using "A Circle in the Fire" as a structural metaphor, Shloss argues that the
disputes over ownership and property that are present in O'Connor's fiction

echo the reality of Flannery O'Connor's personal literary estate. Shloss draws on extensive archival research in order to trace the history of O'Connor's literary estate since the author's death, while exploring the meaning of property in O'Connor's work and positing how O'Connor's writing itself becomes a type of property. Following the succession of O'Connor's literary executors, Shloss identifies a tendency to move away from creativity about O'Connor and toward an enshrinement of her image by a small number of people. Shloss argues that in the end, relaxing the copyright restrictions on O'Connor's archive would best carry out the wishes of the author.

Finally, it seems apropos that this collection should end with an afterword from Bruce Gentry, the editor of *Flannery O'Connor Review* and a driving force behind both the 2007 and 2014 NEH institutes. The germ for *Reconsidering Flannery O'Connor* started with Gentry in collaboration with Robert Donahoo, and this collection was put together with their blessing. During Gentry's tenure at Georgia College, he has maintained critical vitality around the work of O'Connor. We hope this volume can further that project, and we are continually grateful for his outstanding work and personal generosity.

WORKS CITED

Andretta, Helen R. "The Hylomorphic Sacramentalism of 'Parker's Back.'" *Inside the Church of Flannery O'Connor: Sacrament, Sacramental, and the Sacred in Her Fiction*, edited by Joanne Halleran McMullen and Jon Parrish Peede, 41–63. Macon, GA: Mercer University Press, 2007.

Bacon, Jon Lance. *Flannery O'Connor and Cold War Culture*. New York: Cambridge University Press, 1993.

Bennett, Eric. *Workshops of Empire: Stegner, Engle, and American Creative Writing during the Cold War*. Iowa City: University of Iowa Press, 2015.

Brinkmeyer, Robert H., Jr. *The Art and Vision of Flannery O'Connor*. Baton Rouge: Louisiana State University Press, 1989.

Brinkmeyer, Robert H., Jr. "Murder and Rape: Reading Flannery O'Connor alongside Eudora Welty." *Eudora Welty Review* 10 (Spring 2018): 89–111.

Caron, Timothy P. "'The Bottom Rail Is on the Top': Race and 'Theological Whiteness' in Flannery O'Connor's Short Fiction." In *Inside the Church of Flannery O'Connor: Sacrament, Sacramental, and the Sacred in Her Fiction*, edited by Joanne Halleran McMullen and Jon Parrish Peede, 138–64. Macon, GA: Mercer University Press, 2007.

Cofer, Jordan. *The Gospel according to Flannery O'Connor: Examining the Role of the Bible in Flannery O'Connor's Fiction*. New York: Bloomsbury, 2014.

Donahoo, Robert. "Everything That Rises Does Not Converge: The State of O'Connor Studies." *Flannery O'Connor in the Age of Terrorism*, edited by Avis Hewitt and Robert Donahoo, 241–58. Knoxville: University of Tennessee Press, 2010.

Edmondson, Henry T., III. *A Political Companion to Flannery O'Connor*, edited by Henry T. Edmondson III. Lexington: University Press of Kentucky, 2017.

Edmondson, Henry T., III. *Return to Good and Evil: Flannery O'Connor's Response to Nihilism*. Lanham, MD: Lexington Books, 2002.

Farrell, John. *The Varieties of Authorial Intention: Literary Theory beyond the Intentional Fallacy.* New York: Palgrave, 2017.

Gentry, Marshall Bruce. *Flannery O'Connor's Religion of the Grotesque.* Jackson: University Press of Mississippi, 1986.

Gordon, Sarah. "Seeking Beauty in Darkness: Flannery O'Connor and the French Catholic Resistance." *Flannery O'Connor's Radical Reality,* edited by Jan Nordby Gretlund and Karl-Heinz Westarp, 68–84. Columbia: University of South Carolina Press, 2006.

Hawkes, John. "Flannery O'Connor's Devil." *Sewanee Review* 70 (1962): 395–407. EBSCO-host, search.ebscohost.com/login.aspx?direct=true&db=mzh&AN=1962006251&site=eh ost-live&scope=site.

Kreyling, Michael. "Introduction." *New Essays on Wise Blood,* edited by Michael Kreyling, 1–24. New York: Cambridge University Press, 1995.

Lake, Christina Bieber. *The Incarnational Art of Flannery O'Connor.* Macon, GA: Mercer University Press, 2005.

Lewis, Stephen E. "Mysterious Heart: Maritain, Mauriac, Chrétien, and O'Connor on the Fictional Knowledge of Others." *Revelation and Convergence: Flannery O'Connor and the Catholic Intellectual Tradition,* edited by Mark Bosco and Brent Little, 78–98. Washington, DC: Catholic University of America Press, 2017.

May, John R. "The Methodological Limits of Flannery O'Connor's Critics." *Flannery O'Connor Bulletin* 15 (1986): 16–28.

McDonald, Henry. "Backwoods Manichaen." *American Scholar* 58, no. 4 (September 1989): 622–25.

McGurl, Mark. *The Program Era.* Cambridge, MA: Harvard University Press, 2009.

Milder, Robert. "The Protestantism of Flannery O'Connor." *Southern Review* 11 (1975): 802–19.

Montgomery, Marion. *Hillbilly Thomist: Flannery O'Connor, St. Thomas, and the Limits of Art, Volume 2.* Jefferson, NC: McFarland, 2006.

Moran, Daniel. *Creating Flannery O'Connor: Her Critics, Her Publishers, Her Readers.* Athens: University of Georgia Press, 2016.

New Yorker, 14 June 1952, 106.

Orvell, Miles D. "Flannery O'Connor." *Sewanee Review* 78 (1970): 184–97.

Peede, Jon Parrish. "Inside the Church of Flannery O'Connor: An Introduction." *Inside the Church of Flannery O'Connor: Sacrament, Sacramental, and the Sacred in Her Fiction,* edited by Joanne Hallern McMullen and Jon Parrish Peede, 1–13. Macon, GA: Mercer University Press, 2008.

Powell, Tara. *The Intellectual in Twentieth-Century Southern Literature.* Baton Rouge: Louisiana State University Press, 2012.

Robillard, Douglas, Jr. "Introduction." *The Critical Response to Flannery O'Connor,* edited by Douglas Robillard Jr., 1–18. Westport, CT: Praeger, 2004.

Robillard, Douglas, Jr. "Preface." *The Critical Response to Flannery O'Connor,* edited by Douglas Robillard Jr., ix–xx. Westport, CT: Praeger, 2004.

Rosenfeld, Isaac. "To Win by Default." *The Critical Response to Flannery O'Connor,* edited by Douglas Robillard Jr., 21–22. Westport, CT: Praeger, 2004.

Shloss, Carol. *Flannery O'Connor's Dark Comedies: The Limits of Inference.* Baton Rouge: Louisiana State University Press, 2012.

Simons, John W. "A Case of Possession." *The Critical Response to Flannery O'Connor,* edited by Douglas Robillard Jr., 20–21. Westport, CT: Praeger, 2004.

Streight, Irwin H. "Introduction." *Flannery O'Connor: The Contemporary Reviews,* edited by R. Neil Scott and Irwin H. Streight, xv–xlvi. New York: Cambridge University Press, 2009.

"Such Nice People." *Time,* 6 June 1955, 114.

Wimsatt, W. K., Jr., and M. C. Beardsley. "The Intentional Fallacy." *Sewanee Review* 54, no. 3 (1946): 468–88. EBSCOhost, search.ebscohost.com/login.aspx?direct=true&db=edsjsr&AN =edsjsr.27537676&site=eds-live.

Wood, Ralph C. *Flannery O'Connor and the Christ-Haunted South*. Grand Rapids, MI: Eerdmans, 2004.

Yaeger, Patricia. "Flannery O'Connor and the Aesthetics of Torture." *Flannery O'Connor: New Perspectives*, edited by Sura P. Rath and Mary Neff Shaw, 183–206. Athens: University of Georgia Press, 1996.

PART I

NEW METHODOLOGIES

Feather Method: Rereading O'Connor in the Age of the Object

GINA CAISON

You couldn't hurt an angel but I would have been happy to know that I had dirtied his feathers—I conceived of him in feathers.
—FLANNERY O'CONNOR TO BETTY HESTER, 17 January 1956

The peacock feather remains a frequently employed symbol associated with Flannery O'Connor's life and work. In several instances she mentions sending peacock feathers to her friends and their families, and feathers appear on the covers of several editions of her works, including *The Complete Stories* (2008 edition), *Everything That Rises Must Converge* (FSG Classics edition, 1965), *The Habit of Being* (1988), and *A Prayer Journal* (2013).[1] A peacock feather also graces the cover of several biographies, critical works, and films about the author such as Jordan Cofer's *The Gospel According to Flannery O'Connor* (2015), Brad Gooch's *Flannery: A Life* (2010), Jonathan Roger's *The Terrible Speed of Mercy: A Spiritual Biography of Flannery O'Connor* (2010), and Bridget Kurt's documentary *Uncommon Grace: The Life of Flannery O'Connor* (2000). This association makes sense. After all, O'Connor raised peacocks, and she was a noted lover of birds from even her earliest childhood when she appeared on a Pathé newsreel, "Do You Reverse?" with her backward-walking chicken. In this chapter, however, I take up the feather as more than a talisman of the author's creative legacy, and I attempt to think about the feather as more than a metonym of the bird. Rather than read the feather as a metaphor for the author's work or life, or offer a cultural approach that might read feathers as only religious symbols, I attempt to use the feather *as* method— as a way to reconsider the author's work. In short, I explore how and why feathers are continually associated with O'Connor, and I examine feathers as objects in their own right: as items that carry meaning, causality, and ways of understanding the world. I use these ways of meaning attached to the feather in order to reread several of O'Connor's most popular short stories from across her oeuvre, including "The Displaced Person," "Good Country People," "Parker's Back," and "Everything That Rises Must Converge."

To pursue this line of inquiry, I outline four characteristics of peacock feathers that might open up new approaches to these texts. These include ptilochronology (feather-time), coversion, sexual selection versus natural selection (and within this the "handicap principle"), and the use of structural coloration rather than pigment. I use these feather characteristics to outline a speculative approach to these selected short stories, and I explore how understanding a common and persistent object of O'Connor's universe—the feather—offers an imaginative way into the works that a traditional narrative analysis may not. To begin, ptilochronology allows me to offer a reconsideration of the pacing of O'Connor's stories such as "The Displaced Person" where biblical time seems to crash up against calendar time. While the story is marked by the appearance of regimented time via calendars, a more fluid temporality of what I call biblical time also pervades the text. This biblical time includes, but may not be limited to, the wildly productive temporality of the six days of creation, the cyclical order of the liturgical calendar, and eschatology. These competing temporal frameworks from secular calendars to biblical cycles exist in friction with the biological ptilochronology of the text. Furthermore, I consider how aesthetic coversion (the use of "covering" feathers for either physical or aesthetic purposes) offers a new way to consider O'Connor's pairing of O. E. Parker's audacious tattoos with the structure of his physical body in "Parker's Back," where his tattoos are like the peacock's covert feathers. Following this, I turn to sexual selection, which, unlike natural selection, is the term for when females of a species seemingly choose males based on physically attractive, but evolutionarily detrimental, traits (e.g., a peacock's tail). Using this concept, I consider how O'Connor's women characters find men such as Parker and Pointer attractive despite their obvious flaws, and how O'Connor might have recognized the "handicap principle," which is the term for when an animal is healthy enough to sustain the evolutionary drag of the supposedly useless trait. Given O'Connor's frequent attention to disability, I pause on that phrasing, the handicap principle—the idea that the "useless" trait is not a signal of liability but of added health and strength over and above what may be initially diagnosed as weakness—to reconsider how various prostheses indicate characters' relationships to ability and one another. I close by putting these readings in dialogue under the principle of structural coloration, which is when color appears to the human eye by refraction rather than reflection and is the mechanism by which peacock feathers appear as having iridescent colors beyond their brown pigment. This thinking calls on numerous other recurring O'Connor themes including illumination and the limitation of human sight in texts such as "Everything That Rises Must Converge." This feather knowledge allows readers to consider the reality of what is seen and known within O'Connor's works, and this, I posit, we might apply across numerous texts. My consideration of these O'Connor texts does not follow publication chronology. Rather, I think of the texts as reactive to one another via the act of reading. Just as I posit that the feather as object does work and achieves causality within the philosophical universe of the story, my method forgoes the assumption that meaning follows biographical development of the human author. Therefore, I move from questions of time through matters of structure into considerations of perception to demonstrate a recurrent and recursive possibility for reading O'Connor via a focus on a singular object.

The feather method I outline in this chapter draws from emergent ideas in object-oriented ontology. O'Connor's writings both adhere to and trouble an object-oriented ontology that posits that all things—human, animal, mineral, natural, synthetic, et cetera—exist without any particular hierarchy of status. As Graham Harman outlines within this approach:

> What emerges in its place is a ghostly cosmos in which humans, dogs, oak trees, and tobacco are on precisely the same footing as glass bottles, pitchforks, windmills, comets, ice cubes, magnets, and atoms. Instead of exiling objects to the natural sciences (with the usual mixed emotions of condescension and fear), philosophy must reawaken its lost talent for unleashing the enfolded forces trapped in the things themselves. (*Tool-Being* 2)

In other words, this object-oriented approach within O'Connor attempts to step around anthropocentrism into a philosophical space that might enliven critical possibility within O'Connor studies, or as Harman writes of philosophy, "a thought experiment, a process of smashing fragments of reality together to see what emerges" (*Tool-Being* 5). Object-oriented ontology attempts to imagine the interactions and causality transmitted by objects to objects. Within this view, humans, lamps, paintings, and trees all transmit causality into the world, and they bump up against one another, making meaning out of interactions that do not require a human recognition at the center.[2] This approach follows the logic that "Object-oriented philosophy proclaims that any relation between any two objects automatically produces distortion," and it is this distortion that my readings of O'Connor's feathers attempts to chart (Harman *Speculative Realism* 168). While this chapter uses an object-based approach to reconsider the author's writing via the peacock feather, it also considers how O'Connor's work may help us further theorize object-oriented ontology, particularly if twenty-first-century readers begin to approach O'Connor with an eye toward the objects of her work without imagining them as only symbols or metaphors. O'Connor continually challenged the construction of realism alongside religious thinking, and her work seems like a particularly robust place to consider the vibrations between real objects within a universe that is not entirely divorced from magical thinking.

While there are several veins of thought within object-oriented ontology, this chapter proceeds most directly from Timothy Morton's work, which engages objects in their ecological capacity while eschewing ideas of romantic "nature."[3] As most scholarship in object-oriented ontology argues, objects are not merely metaphorical representations of reality determined by human phenomenology nor are they merely the sum of their parts or observable qualities. In fact, objects are precisely not their qualities. Rather, they produce effects and affects within and among themselves. The objects of O'Connor do work and create causality beyond our beliefs in authorial intent or reader response. Just as O'Connor continually questioned human arrogance and folly, a focus on reading for the causality of a singular object within her fiction—without reducing that object to mere symbol—pushes us toward a consideration of her work that imagines all objects as simultaneously linked to and imminently alienated from one another. In other words, object readings open up space to reconsider O'Connor beyond the biographical or religious without negating the importance of those two approaches. It asks that we pay attention to the meanings that detailed objects carry in the story without simply reapplying standards of "symbolism" or imagining that an object is only the sum of its parts or associations, focusing instead on what every object *does*—what distortion or vibration it might carry—within the carefully crafted universe of her work. As Morton outlines, "To say that existence is coexistence is not to say that things merely reduced to their relations. Rather, it is to argue that because of withdrawal, an object never exhausts itself in its appearances—this means there is always something left over, as it were, and an excess that might be experienced as a distortion, gap, or void" (113). This chapter reads with the distortion of one particularly common object of O'Connor, the feather, in order to reconsider the space between realism and what we might alternately call "religion," "grace," "theology," or even "magic," within her work.

If we think with the peacock feather, we see larger questions about aesthetics and use-value, questions that O'Connor herself queried in "King of the Birds," when she says: "Many people, I have found, are congenitally unable to appreciate the sight of a peacock. Once or twice I have been asked what the peacock is 'good for'—a question which gets no answer from me because it deserves none" (836). In other words, O'Connor finds the question of the object's perceived use-value in human terms as nonsensical. In her view, the bird does aesthetic work that one can either understand or not. Such a sentiment is largely consistent with Morton's brand of object-oriented ontology that argues "causality is wholly an *aesthetic* phenomenon," which is not simply "limited to interactions between humans or between humans and painted canvases or between humans and sentences in dramas" (19). While O'Connor might find such a philosophy incongruent with her religious beliefs or overly theoretical, I argue that this focus on the radical materiality of the universe of her writing creates new areas for investigation. Rather than imagine that each item in every story is merely a symbol that carries an abstract idea via its concrete reality, this reading highlights the concrete reality that each object inhabits on its own terms. That is to say, while my feather-reading may verge on the speculative, I am not interested in the abstracted associations of the objects as much as their embedded knowledge as physical objects with their own meanings that create their own potential distortions or reveal a void of knowing within the story. Indeed, O'Connor famously quipped that if the Eucharist was only a symbol then "to hell with it" (*Habit* 125). Of course, for the Catholic O'Connor the Eucharist may enjoy a special status, but its power, perhaps like any designated object, lies beyond its symbolic function. I propose, then, that we take O'Connor at her word, and consider the objects of her writing as neither pure metaphors nor symbols but as real things that have causal effect within her works that create meaning and open up possibility in their invocation.

One such place of possibility exists in the recognition that physical feathers record their own time. As Thomas C. Grubb explains, ptilochronology is the study of "feather-time," which "concerns daily intervals" (i). Along the shaft of a feather, an observer will see bands, and each of these bands represents roughly twenty-four hours of feather growth. Much like the rings of a tree, these bands reveal information about the relative nutritional health of the individual. According to ptilochronology, wider bands indicate an overall more robust nutritional picture for the animal while thinner bands may indicate some deficiencies or stresses. Regardless of band size, however, the temporal concept remains the same: feathers count the days. Indeed, like many other species, birds operate primarily on seasonal time. However, when considering the fact that each feather on the bird reveals information about daily factors, including health and nutrition, and that this information is visible to both the human and avian eye, a speculative object-oriented ontology of the feather should ask us to consider a temporality where the daily and hourly intervals take precedence over historical scales of calendar months, years, or decades.

"The Displaced Person" represents one O'Connor story in which feather-time reveals itself as potentially significant for examining how competing temporal orders subtend the text's action. The main characters in "The Displaced Person" frequently appeal to time as a measure of adaptation and change. Much of the text works within and against what Elizabeth Freeman calls "chrononormativity," which she outlines as "the use of time to organize individual human bodies toward maximum productivity" and "is a mode of implantation, a technique by which institutional forces come to seem like somatic facts" where "schedules, calendars, time zones, and even wristwatches inculcate what the sociologist Evitar Zerubavel calls 'hidden rhythms,' forms of temporal experience that seem natural to those whom they privilege" (3) The text showcases the battle of temporal experience as each character competes to earn more privilege in their respective roles on the farm. However, while they seem caught up in human ideas of chrononormativity, the narrative consistently bends and adjusts temporal scales. The story occurs on a seemingly more extended time frame, at once both incredibly slow *and* action packed much like the first six days of Christian creation, than other O'Connor works, which often operate on daily intervals. In this way, one might argue that "The Displaced Person" is not the most obvious place to begin a feather-method reading of the author's narrative timing. However, the story demonstrates both a preoccupation with the peacock feather and a continual referral to shifting temporalities. The story begins and ends with the farm's lone peacock. O'Connor's opening sentences recount, "The peacock was following Mrs. Shortley up the road to the hill where she meant to stand. Moving one behind the other they looked like a complete procession" (285). Somewhat paradoxically, this forward momentum of the opening hurls the reader into the slow-moving action of the story where silent observation characterizes many of the interactions of the characters. Following this introduction of the peacock, along with an extended description of his tail, the story proceeds to move simultaneously quickly and slowly as Mrs. Shortley and her husband Mr. Shortley (the white farmhands), the farm owner Mrs. McIntyre, the priest, the black farmhands, and the Polish "displaced person" Mr. Guizac, collide with one another in the most minute ways. And while on its face, the story might seem mostly preoccupied with a spatial geographic scale as the characters consider race and nationality, I argue that the continual appearance of feathers in the story might also signal its preoccupation with scales of time.

Throughout the text, time and feathers intrude into the narrative. The temporal scales at work in the first part of the story reveal the ways in which the various narrative orders compete across the text. Almost halfway through the story, Mrs. Shortley skeptically observes the priest's behavior: "His visits irked her more and more. On the last one, he went about picking up feathers off the ground. He found two peacock feathers and four or five turkey feathers and an old brown hen feather and took them off with him like a bouquet" (300). Notably, the priest, who seems to have an obsession with the peacock across the whole story, does not only collect peacock feathers. In fact, the peacock feathers account for just a fraction of his entire bouquet. If we read the feathers as temporal indicators, the priest's collection of them suggests not so much a bouquet as him assembling an alternate calendar to the secular one that Mrs. Shortley considers later in the story.

The priest's feather-collecting scene occurs exactly between Mrs. Shortley's resolve to be a more devout Christian and her apocalyptic vision. Immediately following her religious revelation, she sees the priest visiting with Mrs. McIntyre again and in order to avoid meeting them, she slips into the feed house where the walls are covered with old calendars. While hiding out, she overhears Mrs. McIntyre tell the priest that she will be giving Mr. Shortley his thirty-day notice the following day. As Mrs. Shortley processes this news she stares at a "gentleman on the calendar" across the wall. There is a human-dictated, secular calendar time that seeks to confine her as it papers the walls of her hideout where she learns of her husband's impending dismissal, notably thirty days away. Her intervening end-times vision is interspersed with these scenes, and it leads the reader to question which temporality commands the action of the story: the human-delineated secular calendar time, the biblical time, or the twenty-four-hour index cataloged in the intruding object of the feather. Immediately following the revelation of her husband's dismissal, she forces her family to pack their belongings overnight. As they leave before dawn, Mrs. Shortley has a convulsive episode where she seems again to be possessed by an eschatological vision, and only later in the story (three months within the narrative time), we learn that Mrs. Shortley has died, suggesting her unsuccessful attempt to reconcile the chrononormative time of the calendar (literally represented with a nondescript [hu]man) with her biblical vision.

This appeal to time occurs across the plot. Earlier in the story Mrs. Shortley remembers a newsreel covering the Holocaust and hears its final directive that "Time marches on!" (287). Mrs. McIntyre tells one of the black farmhands, "Times are a changing," and when she expresses her frustration with Mr. Guizac, the priest suggests that she "Give him time" (307, 316). Just after this counsel, as the priest stands to leave, the peacock brandishes his tail, which O'Connor describes as "Tiers of small pregnant suns float[ing] in a green-gold haze over his head" (317). This display causes the priest to exclaim, "'Christ will come like that!'" (317). This reaction to the peacock's tail feathers again places the narrative into relation with a specific temporal uncertainty of the second coming. Rather than seeing the peacock as a symbol of the divinity of Christ, I want to consider the effect that the feathers have on the priest as objects carrying their own meaning. The revelation of the bird's covert feathers causes the priest to murmur to himself, "The Transfiguration," revealing his own thought process as the object of the feather acts on him (317). This reaction to the object appears in a narrative universe where time picks up, slows down, marches inevitably, and ultimately suspends as each character confronts the vision of an end of days. Whereas the feathers of the priests' bouquet log a "real" daily index of health, the humans in the story cannot seem to agree on a temporal scale that governs their collective lives.

In many ways, the feather object brings with it a causality of staring into time and the attempt to brace oneself against the resulting distortion of that act. Morton links this disorientation to Heidegger's ultimate attraction to Nazi-ism as he mistakes this broad object-based causality for his theories of correlationism. Notably, this is also the abyss on which "The Displaced Person" stands, but the story presses on what Morton calls the "protective gear at precisely the point of 'seeing truth'" (225). The feather allows the reader into the distortion at this moment. As Morton writes, "Since all causal relationships, including seeing, happen in an aesthetic dimension, there is no way at all to see the 'real' thing 'underneath' the illusion. Heidegger fails to see that the illusoriness is where all the action is" (225). O'Connor's story makes a similar argument. It is the appearance of the object, carrying its own temporality, that protects the story as it leans over into the abyss of Nazi-ism to "see truth," but that appearance does not rescue the human characters as they negotiate the temporal distortion of their own concerns.

If the feathers of the story point toward an awareness of competing temporalities or challenges to a secular chrononormativity from an eschatological vision, then Mrs. McIntyre by contrast is almost entirely consumed with humans competing for material and economic resources. She consistently accounts for people as "extra," suggesting that the world, or she herself, cannot feed so many humans. In biological terms, she is obsessed with nutritional index and scarce resources. Once she decides that Mr. Guizac is "extra," she continually delays informing him of his own thirty-day notice. Here again the story returns to the small unit of time as its most important measurement. This temporal smallness informs the story's climax, where the inaction of the characters as they exchange looks allows a tractor to roll slowly over Mr. Guizac, breaking his spine. During the scene, Mr. Shortley even "turn(s) his head with incredible slowness" as the others are suspended in the silent, fateful seconds (325). The story then ultimately reaches a climactic point in drawn-out seconds, again focusing the reader's attention on flexible temporalities that move neither quite in step with biblical time nor secular chrononormativity. Rather, we read a slow abyss of causality. Following the death of Mr. Guizac, Mrs. McIntyre enters into her own suspended animation, slowly suffering a paralysis that inches up her body. The priest becomes her only consistent visitor, and O'Connor narrates a veritable description of ptilochronology: "He came regularly once a week with a bag of breadcrumbs and, after he had fed those to the peacock, he would come in and sit by the side of her bed and explain the doctrines of the Church" (327). This regular feeding of the bird ensures the consistent continuation of its nutritional index, and we can assume creates wide bars on the shaft of its feathers, logging a different time over and above the bodily and spiritual reality that the two remaining characters are locked into for eternity or until the second coming.

Beyond "The Displaced Person," O'Connor frequently considered the peacock's tail. These famous feathers are known as covert feathers, which are designed primarily to cover over the bird's structural feathers. O'Connor noted the structural feathers, or what Andalusia's visiting first-grade children called the bird's "underwear"—"a stiff gray tail, raised to support the larger one, and beneath it a puff of black feathers that would be suitable for some really regal woman—a Cleopatra or a Clytemestra—to use to powder her nose" ("King" 835). Coverts are simply feathers that cover other feathers, and they can be located on different parts of the bird's body. While wing coverts are designed to aid in airflow for flight, the peacock's tail coverts are a more apparently aesthetically purposed object. This relationship between the structural and covert feathers offers a way to think about the relationship between structure and aesthetics in "Parker's Back," where the main character continually attempts to cover over the functional skin and muscles of his body with colorful displays of ink. I argue that the tension between Parker's un-inked, functional body and his desire to cover over this with an aesthetic apparatus mimics the relationship between the structural and covert feathers of the peacock. Again in this story, the aesthetics exist in the causality rendered by the feather as object.

Parker and Sarah Ruth's first meeting occurs because he has injured his hand, and the ensuing tension reveals the underlying issue of functional structure and aesthetic covering. While Parker imagines his hand as broken, Sarah Ruth takes a hard eye to it, examining it for deformity. As she does, she notices that "every space on the skin of Parker's arm, from wrist to elbow, was covered in some loud design" (657). She expresses disgust and drops both his hand and the consideration of his bodily injury. In this initial encounter, we see that Sarah Ruth begins with concern for the physical structure of Parker, but she becomes distracted and expressly repulsed by the covering over his body. Parker too struggles with the incongruence of his bodily structure and the outward expression of his aesthetic goal via tattooing. His initial inspiration for his project was "a man in a fair, tattooed from head to foot" (657). However, perhaps without even being aware, Parker is compelled by the man's ability to use his structural body to highlight his inked covering. O'Connor writes: "The man, who was small and sturdy, moved about on the platform, flexing his muscles so that the arabesque of men and beasts and flowers on his skin appeared to have a subtle motion of its own" (657). While Parker is moved by the scene, the resulting application of tattoos to his own body seems to lack the beauty of the man who inspired his endeavor. Parker's disappointment in his own attempts at aesthetic transcendence through tattooing seems related to his inability to support his inked covering with the same muscular understructure as the man at the fair. There are virtually no images in the story of Parker's own muscular movement or control. If anything, he is doughy. His mouth is often described as agape, and his body is described as "heavy and earnest, as ordinary as a loaf of bread" (658). After his five years in the navy, "his mouth ceased to hang open. His features hardened into those of a man [...] and seemed a natural part of the grey mechanical ship, except for his eyes" (658). Parker's structural body is as plain as he accuses Sarah Ruth of being, and despite his physical labor, he seems to lack the musculature to support the aesthetic choices of his tattoos.

Parker's back, the one remaining blank space on his body, initially does not interest him as a space for a tattoo because he does not see the point of having an inked image that he cannot view himself. However, once he makes the decision to have the Byzantine Christ image tattooed on his back for Sarah Ruth, we see him use his muscles for the first time in the story. After washing his back following the tattoo artist's instructions, he "returned to pace back and forth across the room, nervously flexing his shoulders" (658). This exercise of the physical structure of his back changes the effect and meaning of his covert aesthetic adornment. Like the peacock, Parker cannot view his own most compelling trait. The other tattoos served as aesthetic adornment without active musculature beneath them. This image, however, is etched on a back that has flexed its muscles. Perhaps the Christ-image back tattoo is a symbol of something, but it only achieves its meaning because there is a structural body beneath it able to hold it up for full viewing. In this way, the aesthetic covert image creates meaning because of the structure beneath it.

Like the peacock's covert tail feathers, Parker's tattoos might initially be considered as aesthetic adornments aiding in sexual selection. Repeatedly, his tattoos are referred to as colorful items that attract the attention of women. Plumage has long been attached to sexual selection in birds, but for many years the selection of mates for presumably aesthetic traits has troubled evolutionary theorists. As Charles Darwin wrote to Asa Gray in 1860, "The sight of a feather in a peacock's tail, whenever I gaze at it, makes me sick!" Seemingly, Darwin puzzled over the questions of female choice and the existence of beauty without a corollary material or evolutionary benefit. Against prevailing Victorian notions of beauty as created by God, Darwin struggled to account for why sexual selection seemed to rely upon the aesthetic. In his follow-up to On the Origin of Species (1859), The Descent of Man (1871), he spends a considerable amount of time on birds and plumage. We might understand Darwin's conundrum over sexual selection and peacock tail feathers as an object-oriented concern. Why does this object exist? What effect does it have on the other objects it encounters? Should there be a reason for something to exist purely for aesthetic purposes?[4] In the world of O'Connor's text, Sarah Ruth would seemingly be uninterested in the supposedly useless peacock tail feather, as she was "against color" (655). And yet, Sarah Ruth is attracted to Parker for reasons that neither she nor Parker seems to understand fully.

Parker's tattoos repeatedly aid in his ability to attract potential mates, but they do not seemingly impress Sarah Ruth. Upon first meeting her, "He did not for a minute think that she didn't like the tattoos. He had never yet met a woman who was not attracted to them" (657). From his very first tattoo, Parker "found out that the tattoos were attractive to the kind of girls he liked but who had never liked him before" (658). Despite marrying him, Sarah Ruth remains resistant to the aesthetic embellishments to his body: "When he attempted to point out especial details of them, she would shut her eyes tight and turn her back as well. Except in total darkness, she preferred Parker dressed and with his sleeves rolled down" (663). Sarah Ruth refuses to see the colorful covering of Parker's skin. If we imagine the tattoos, particularly the one of Christ on Parker's back, as aesthetic objects (whose very nature requires questioning the boundary of where one object—the skin—begins and another—the ink—ends) meant to achieve sexual attraction, then Sarah Ruth defies that principle. She is, we might say, not fooled by covert feathers. She is unswayed by the seemingly aesthetic causation that Parker imagines. However, the fact remains that Sarah Ruth *does* select O. E. Parker for a mate.

Within this feather-reading, it seems that the tattoos signal some other desirable factor to Sarah Ruth over and above an aesthetics that merely exists on the surface of an object. As Grubb explains, "In the peacock, presumably, sexual selection for longer, heavier coverts has been stopped by natural selection opposing longer coverts. Perhaps, production of even longer, heavier coverts would leave insufficient energy and nutrients for body maintenance" (98). This tension between natural and sexual selection is often discussed in terms of what is called "the handicap principle." Or, as Grubb summarizes, "All else being equal, a peacock with longer, heavier feathers possesses a handicap making him more subject to predation or starvation" (98). However, Amotz Zahavi posits that sexual ornamentation such as the peacock's covert tail feathers presents an honest signaling of an animal's health, demonstrating that the animal is healthy enough to sustain the evolutionary drag of the useless trait. In other words, a peacock that has a large, decorative tail proves to the peahen that he is strong enough to support the excessive covert feathers. Ptilochronology studies have indeed confirmed that the growth bars on "advantageously" plumed birds indicate a strong nutritional index, further suggesting that the seemingly purely aesthetic object can work as an honest signal of a species' ability to survive and acquire food. This biological understanding of feathers' indicative factors bears an uncanny resemblance to the plot of "Parker's Back."

Significantly, Parker's opening move in courting Sarah Ruth involves bringing apples for her and her entire family. The next day he returns with peaches. And although this feather-reading of "Parker's Back" is something of a thought experiment, it pushes us to consider the story in ways that draw upon an object's material effect in the world. Like the peacock's covert feathers, Parker's tattoos do work above and around the characters' (in)abilities to make meaning of them. Importantly, however, Sarah Ruth and Parker *are not birds*, and such a reading of the story should not be understood as a biologically determinate one. Assigned sex and gender are just as complicated in other species as they are in humans, and I do not mean to suggest that Sarah Ruth's motivations are reducible to "animal attraction" or gendered ideals around masculine "providing." Instead, I seek to open a conversation about how aesthetics, causation, and sexual attraction trouble an O'Connor world in which many central characters struggle with their object-oriented bodies.

The conundrum of sexual selection as imagined within the context of feathers extends to other O'Connor works, particularly if we think through the idea of the handicap principle. The specter of sexual selection hovers above "Good Country People" as the reader is first told about Mrs. Freeman's daughters, one of whom is beset by suitors and the other of whom is pregnant by the age of sixteen. These characters foil Joy-Hulga, Mrs. Hopewell's intentionally plain and "ugly" daughter, who seemingly has no prospects for finding a mate. Joy-Hulga has both a heart condition and a prosthetic leg, and either *despite* or *because* of her extensive schooling, to her mother she seems ill-equipped for the world. For all of her attempts to irritate others with her awkward dress and harsh style of interpersonal interaction, Joy-Hulga finds some sort of seemingly mutually based attraction with the Bible salesman, Manley Pointer. As it turns out, he claims that he too has a heart condition, and he manages to use his conversational abilities to get a meal out of his visit with Mrs. Hopewell as well as a return picnic outing with Joy-Hulga. The night before their date, Joy-Hulga imagines herself as some sort of beacon of knowledge for the young man, and during their romantic encounter, she waxes philosophical about her ability to "see through to nothing" (280). In the O'Connor universe, a reader should remain skeptical about such "enlightened" pronouncements as the author consistently points out such hubris of insight as little more than human folly. However, these mounting details—physical disabilities, intellectual arrogance, and baseless charm—do not in and of themselves allow the story to open up to a feather-reading.

Joy-Hulga is an ideal character to examine in this feather-reading not simply because she possesses disabilities that might be colloquially thought about as "handicaps." Instead, O'Connor's brief description of Joy-Hulga's attitude toward her prosthetic leg, one of the few moments that accounts for Joy-Hulga's interiority about her own body, pushes the reader to think about the handicap principle of sexual selection: "But she was as sensitive about the artificial leg as a peacock about his tail" (281). This fact is revealed to the reader during Joy-Hulga's sexual encounter with Manley Pointer, and the context underscores the relative presumed use-value of each object in relation to the perception of its aesthetic appearance versus its effect as an object that allows insight to a more causally based aesthetic dimension. However, Pointer makes off with Joy-Hulga's leg as well as her glasses, and these two objects bear a relationship to her perceived physical deficiencies. In their value as stolen objects, or objects worth stealing, we might understand them as honest signals that indicate Joy-Hulga's actual health. Pointer, by contrast, offers no honest signals, and his behavior indicates that he is healthy in neither mind, body, nor spirit. He even confesses to stealing another woman's prosthesis, a glass eye, with the same seductive techniques. Over and above the recognition of the leg as a potential object signifying the supposed handicap of the peacock's tail, there seems to be more work to do in Pointer's desire to steal objects that signal their original owner's actual strength. These objects are valuable because they are honest signals that, although they might at first glance represent deficiency, indicate added strength, a strength that Pointer cannot ever fully attain by his own accord. The peacock then is sensitive about his tail, his own covert prosthesis if you will, because it conceals and reveals his fitness. When human observers wonder about its use, they fall into a phenomenological trap where they imagine objects as only acting upon their own human consciousness and use-value needs. Where humans, including Darwin, see a lie in the peacock's tail, O'Connor's works see honesty. In the stolen prosthetics, Pointer indeed sees the strength that he himself lacks, but because his body does not have the same object-relationship with these items, they can never be more than a continuation of his own dishonesty. His own anthropocentrism undoes the causality among the objects themselves. Or put another way, he possesses the covert feathers, but unlike Parker, he lacks the structural feathers to support them.

In addition to querying ideas of aesthetics, causality, and use-value, peacock feathers also call up other matters of seeing and knowing. Or simply put, peacock feathers are not what they appear to be. Rather than work on the basis of pigment reflection, peacock tail feathers achieve their appearance through the use of structural coloration. In pigment terms, peacock feathers are brown, but they appear to us as iridescent in their blues, greens, and purples. Their brilliant-appearing colors do not come from carotenoids, melanins, and porphyrins. Rather, the appearance of the feather lies within its isotropic nanostructure, which refracts light in an ordered pattern to produce the prismatic effect humans perceive. In simpler terms, what we see is only how the light refracts—rather than reflects—off the object. Moreover, almost all blue and blue-necessary hues (greens, purples, etc.) in feathers are achieved through some combination of structural coloration.[5] Or as some recent popular scholarship has summarized: a blue bird is never blue.[6] While these mechanisms of coloration have been confirmed with the advent of microscopic technologies that allow us to view feather structures, even early ornithologists such as Alexander Wilson perceived the prismatic nature of some feathers as reacting to light in ways that seemed more complex than pigment-based reflection.[7] In short, almost any careful observer of feathers might have noticed the tricks that light plays in one's perception of color.

One initial place for inquiry along these lines might be "Everything That Rises Must Converge" as the use of perception and sight when thinking about "color" pervades the action. The use of the feather as method, particularly when we think about the appearance of structural coloration within the story, creates critical possibilities beyond arguments that position race against grace. From the mother's initial looks in the mirror to her inability to "see" what Julian sees, and from her confrontation with her doubled image in the African American woman and to her game of peek-a-boo with the woman's young son, the short story keeps the questions of sight and color perception at the forefront. As Julian's mother worries about race and societal structures, the reader is pointed toward a consideration of the appearance of difference in phenotype and the relative class similarities among the black and white characters. Neither his mother nor Julian, despite his claims to "see her with complete objectivity," seem capable of understanding how their vision is limited by their human perception of color (491). The very fact that O'Connor makes so many mentions of Julian's ability to "see" cues her readers to know that he cannot see at all.

Notably, the matching hats the women wear do not include feathers (or at least O'Connor does not mention if they do). However, the young African American boy wears a "Tyrolean hat with a blue feather" (495). Indeed, the appearance of the blue feather seems significant because in order for a feather to appear blue it must have some degree of structural coloration. However, given that this story takes place nearly half a century after the passage of the Migratory Bird Treaty Act of 1918 (United States and Canada), which made it illegal to possess, collect, or trade numerous species' feathers, there is a distinct possibility that this young boy's hat feather is dyed rather than "naturally" blue, as it is likely a goose or game bird feather rather than plumage from a blue songbird. In short, the feather may appear blue because of its nanostructure, or it may appear blue because of artificially imposed pigment. This double possibility of the feather's color, I argue, might be the crux of O'Connor's story.

Are Julian and his mother merely reacting to the simple reflection of the world they see around them, or are they having their perceptions constantly adjusted by the bouncing of light off of deeper structures of a white supremacist society? Does either character know when they are seeing "color" or when they are seeing the creation of racialized reality refracted through the deeper structural inequality of transportation infrastructures, generational wealth, and continued white privilege? These are not questions that critics always imagine that O'Connor addresses. And if we think she is addressing them, sometimes it's natural to fall back on either what we know about her offensive statements on James Baldwin and Dr. Martin Luther King Jr. or her consistent Catholic orthodoxy around "moments of grace."[8] I argue that careful attention to the objects of O'Connor might help us think outside of these two approaches, which constitute the heart of many existing arguments about the story. If each object becomes a method rather than just a metaphor, we might open up inquisitive space for what O'Connor considered and reconsidered herself.

Indeed, "Everything That Rises Must Converge" is not a story about feathers, but it is a story that asks how we know what we know when it comes to color and structure. While "Good Country People" might very well be a story about something akin to the "handicap principle," it takes this question into what we might call refracted territory, where what we see in Manley Pointer and Joy-Hulga is not simply a reflection of the author, but a refraction of the larger issues around them. Similarly, "Parker's Back" is not a story about a biological nutritional index, but it does ask questions about aesthetics and use-value. Likewise, "The Displaced Person" is not a story about ptilochronology, but I would argue that it is a text about the pace of life and the ways that secular and biblical time bump up against each other and the temporality of every object on the farm. Feathers help us think about these stories in new ways, and I advocate for more object-oriented approaches to the author's work beyond simply the feather.

Following the feather trail of O'Connor asks us to walk backward a bit, like her Pathé chicken, through causality into an object-oriented universe. Along this reverse walk we find an image from Timothy Morton that could very well be from O'Connor: "Reality, on the [object-oriented ontology] view, is a dense thorn bush spiked with diamond tipped thorns that dig into my flesh from every angle—that *are* my flesh. To find oneself in an [object-oriented ontology] universe is to allow the thorns to sting you, a little more each day" (30). This is where the "minute particulars" (as Morton quotes William Blake) of O'Connor's deeply imagined universe take on meanings that scholars have only begun to consider. What if every object of O'Connor is acting on every other object, not as a hell-bound symbolic Eucharist, but as diamond-tipped thorns of a reoriented reality?

NOTES

1. In letters to Maryat Lee (4 April 1957), Catherine Carver (18 February 1959), Robert Lowell (10 January 1960), Sister Julie (17 June 1962), Elizabeth McKee (3 January 1963), and Janet McKane (25 February and 19 June 1963), O'Connor mentions sending peacock feathers to her correspondents. She also references wanting to send feathers to Elizabeth Bishop via Ashley Brown on 15 June 1964. All letters cited come from *The Habit of Being*. The feather research for

this chapter was made possible in large part from a Jay and Deborah Last Fellowship from the American Antiquarian Society.

2. For example, see work in object-oriented ontology, including Jane Bennett's *Vibrant Matter: A Political Ecology of Things* (2010), Ian Bogost's *Alien Phenomenology, or What It's Like to Be a Thing* (2012), and Levi R. Bryant's *The Democracy of Objects* (2011).

3. See Morton's *Ecology without Nature: Rethinking Environmental Aesthetics* (2009) and *Realist Magic: Objects, Ontology, and Causality* (2013).

4. Morton, too, identifies Darwin as interested in questions of what defines an object, for as he points out, "the punchline of [On the Origin of Species] is that there are no species and they have no origin" because what Darwin lays out is that "You can't just specify when one species ends and another begins" and thus the work "is based on paradoxes that involves dialethias—contradictions, 'double truths'" (*Realist Magic* 29).

5. See Richard O. Prum, "Anatomy, Physics, and Evolution of Structural Colors," in *Geoffrey Hill and Kevin McGraw's Bird Coloration, Volume I* (2006) and chapter 12 of *Thor Hanson's Feathers: The Evolution of a Natural Miracle* (2011).

6. See "Blue Birds Aren't Blue, and This Is How They Fool You" by Josh Bloom.

7. Wilson notes of the Indigo Bird in Wilson's *American Ornithology* that the bird's color is similar to that of the peacock's tail and that "There is one singularity which, as it cannot be well represented in the figure, may be mentioned here, viz. that, in some certain lights, his plumage appears of a rich sky blue, and in others a vivid verdigris green; so that the same bird, in passing from one place to another before your eyes, seems to undergo a total change of color. When the angle of incidence of the rays of light, reflected in his plumage, is acute, the color is green; when obtuse, blue. Such, I think, I have observed to be uniformly the case, without being optician enough to explain why it is so. From this, however, must be expected the color of the head, which, being a very deep blue, is not affected by a change of position" (67). And he notes that the Purple Grackle appears differently when "near a good light" (220).

8. See O'Connor's letter To Maryatt Lee (21 May 1964).

WORKS CITED

Bennett, Jane. *Vibrant Matter: A Political Ecology of Things*. Durham, NC: Duke University Press, 2010.

Bloom, Josh. "Blue Birds Aren't Blue, and This Is How They Fool You." *American Council on Science and Health*. 30 June 2016. http://www.acsh.org/news/2016/06/30/blue-birds-arent-blue-this-is-how-they-fool-you.

Bogost, Ian. *Alien Phenomenology, or What It's Like to Be a Thing*. Minneapolis: University of Minnesota Press, 2012.

Bryant, Levi R. *The Democracy of Objects*. Ann Arbor, MI: Open Humanities Press, 2011.

Darwin, Charles. *The Descent of Man*. (1871). New York: Penguin Books, 2004.

Darwin, Charles. "To Asa Gray," 3 April 1860. *Darwin Correspondence Project*.

"Do You Reverse?" (1932). *YouTube*. uploaded by *British Pathé*, 13 April 2014. https://www.youtube.com/watch?v=dtnV-iD2QlI.

Freeman, Elizabeth. *Time Binds: Queer Temporalities, Queer Histories*. Durham, NC: Duke University Press, 2010.

Grubb, Thomas C., Jr. *Ptilochronology: Feather Time and the Biology of Birds*. New York: Oxford University Press, 2006.

Hanson, Thor. *Feathers: The Evolution of a Natural Miracle*. New York: Basic Books, 2011.

Harman, Graham. *Tool-Being: Heidegger and the Meta-Physics of Objects*. Chicago, IL: Open Court, 2002.

Harman, Graham. *Towards Speculative Realism: Essays and Lectures*. Hampshire, UK: Zero Books, 2010.

Morton, Timothy. *Ecology without Nature: Rethinking Environmental Aesthetics*. Cambridge, MA: Harvard University Press, 2009.

Morton, Timothy. *Realist Magic: Objects, Ontology, and Causality*. Ann Arbor, MI: Open Humanities Press, 2013.

O'Connor, Flannery. "The Displaced Person." *Collected Works*. New York: Library of America, 1988. 285–327.

O'Connor, Flannery. "Everything That Rises Must Converge." *Collected Works*. New York: Library of America, 1988. 485–500.

O'Connor, Flannery. "Good County People." *Collected Works*. New York: Library of America, 1988. 263–84.

O'Connor, Flannery. *The Habit of Being: Letters*. Edited by Sally Fitzgerald. New York: Farrar, Straus and Giroux, 1979.

O'Connor, Flannery. "The King of the Birds." *Collected Works*. New York: Library of America, 1988. 832–42.

O'Connor, Flannery. "Parker's Back." *Collected Works*. New York: Library of America, 1988. 655–75.

Prum, Richard C. "Anatomy, Physics, and Evolution of Structural Colors." *Bird Coloration Volume I: Mechanisms and Measurements*, edited by Geoffrey E. Hill and Kevin J. McGraw. Cambridge, MA: Harvard University Press, 2006.

Wilson, Andrew, and T. M. Brewer. *Wilson's American Ornithology: with notes by Jardine; to which is added a synopsis of American birds, including those described by Bonaparta, Audubon, Nuttall, and Richardson*. New York: Charles L. Cornish, 1854. American Antiquarian Society. Worcester, Massachusetts.

Zahavi, Amotz. "Mate Selection—A Selection for a Handicap." *Journal of Theoretical Biology* 53 (1975): 205–14.

"God Made Me Thisaway": Crip-queer Perspectives on Flannery O'Connor

BRUCE HENDERSON

In his recent (2016) memoir of his time in a Christian ex-gay "therapy" program, *Boy Erased*, Garrard Conley prefaces his narrative with two epigraphs, one from an ex-gay leader, John Smid, the other from a less obvious source: Flannery O'Connor's penultimate story, "Revelation." It is the ironic, yet soulful story of pig-farmer Ruby Turpin, who sorts categories of people by race and class, only to find to her horror, in an apocalyptic vision with which O'Connor ends the story, that she sees that she and her husband, "good country people" she believes them to be, have no more place of pride in the march to salvation than those upon whom she looks down. Conley simply cites one sentence, near the end of the story, "Yet she could see by their shocked and altered faces that even their virtues were being burned away" (*CS* 508). Conley makes no additional references to O'Connor in his harrowing book, but her place at the start of it suggests the power this writer of outcasts—whether "crips," "queers," or other groups—has in Conley's own self-reflection on his road to self-acceptance as a gay man.

While O'Connor's fiction is filled with characters whose bodies and minds are "grotesque," non-heteronormative characters are less frequently found. There are a handful of unmarried men whose sexuality may be open to speculation, but homosexuality per se is rarely visible in a definitive way: the man in the car who rapes Tarwater near the end of *The Violent Bear It Away* is the rare "coded" homosexual—and even this act occurs "off-stage," the man's almost-certain homosexuality only implied by his appearance and by the aftermath and its effect on Tarwater. One could argue that, using contemporary parlance, there are far more "queer" figures in O'Connor's fiction, if we include sexual and, very occasionally, romantic relationships that defy, by body or mind, what the typical reader might imagine as "normative" sexuality.

The encounter between Hulga-Joy and Manley Pointer, for example, involves the removal of the woman's prosthetic leg, thus "queering" expectations of the typical female body, as does the confederate Bible salesman's paraphilia for such devices, which he carries with him from town to town, "trophies," to use the language of profilers of serial killers and other violent offenders. Desire shows itself in "queer" ways in such tales as O'Connor's novel *Wise Blood*, where the inspiration of erotic attraction pushes borders of "the norm."

O'Connor, who does indeed sit in judgment on such characters, but perhaps, it is important to remember, no more so than many other characters, whose sins may be less exotic and visible, but deeper and more mortal, and who also reminds us in her "Introduction to *A Memoir of Mary Ann*," that the "face" of good "too is grotesque, that in us the good is something under construction" (*MM* 226). Thus, while O'Connor's own theological commitments might keep her from embracing sexual queerness as acceptable in act, her spiritual sense of the "pilgrim's progress" might not condemn those who sin in this way as any worse or any less available to God's grace than, say, Ruby Turpin—perhaps more so, in some ways, as they may come from a place of love, humility, and "construction."

While there has been some writing on O'Connor through the lens of disability studies, such as Timothy Basselin's 2013 book *Flannery O'Connor: Writing a Theology of Disabled Humanity*, given the simple frequency of disabled characters and images in her writing, there has been less than one might expect. This may be in part because it may be difficult to know what to do with O'Connor in the identity-politics-based scholarship of disability studies. While there is, of course, a political consciousness in O'Connor's writing, her representation and rhetoric of disability is more theological and, in ways this essay will argue, aesthetic. The "beauty" she finds in Mary Ann's face of goodness, for example, is consonant with one of the earliest pieces on disability aesthetics, Harlan Hahn's 1990 interrogative essay, "Can Disability Be Beautiful?" There is even less from a queer theory/queer studies perspective, again, in part, because O'Connor's orthodox Catholicism would seem to preclude any openness to nonheterosexual acts, though she is accepting and even loving of her nonheterosexual friends, as many of her letters to Betty Hester, "A" in *The Habit of Being*, attest.

The "reconsideration" of Flannery O'Connor in this essay will focus on two of her best-known stories through what can be called a "crip-queer" critical perspective. The term "queer-crip" was coined by the theater/performance scholar Carrie Sandahl in her 2003 *GLQ* article, "Queering the Crip or Cripping the Queer?: Intersections of Queer and Crip Identities in Solo Autobiographical Performance," in which she examined four performance artists who identify as both "queer" and "crip" and focused especially on what Kimberle Williams Crenshaw and others have identified as "intersectional" moments when multiple axes of identity meet and produce something more complicated than the simple additive plurality of categories. Building on Sandahl's work and those of others in disability and queer theory, Robert McRuer offered, in his 2006 book, *Crip Theory: Cultural Signs of Queerness and Disability*, an expanded discussion of how the two areas might work together. McRuer uses case studies such as the case of Sharon Kowalski, the closeted lesbian who became disabled after an accident, and whose custody battle, carried out between her partner and her parents, exposed the uneasy relationship between nonnormative sexuality and nonnormative bodies and, for a time, nonnormative cognitive abilities. This essay follows in the path of the work of both Sandahl and McRuer.

Both Sandahl and McRuer combine the critical perspective of disability studies with the somewhat-amorphous set of approaches often grouped under the heading "queer theory." The term "queer theory" itself is typically seen as originating in the issue of the feminist journal *Difference*, bearing the name "queer theory" and edited by film and cultural scholar Teresa de Lauretis. While its usage varies, queer theory begins from the post-structuralist deconstruction of binary oppositions (such as heterosexual and homosexual) and from the decentering of what may be considered "normative" as the unmarked position from which experiences and texts may be read and understood. In its narrowest sense, queer theory has been used to reorient (in the words of Sara Ahmed) the phenomenology of the consciousness of the non-heteronormative subject. In broader terms, it has produced such work as that of Judith Butler, who famously argued, in her landmark *Gender Trouble*, that all gender and all sexuality is constructed, performative in the sense in which speech act theorists Austin and Searle use the latter term—Butler denaturalizes heterosexuality and gender binary. Similarly, Eve Kosofsky Sedgwick, in *Between Men* and *Epistemology of the Closet*, interrogates the boundaries of sexual and gender identity, especially in her examination of "the closet" as a liminal, often-porous site. Thus, while such broadening runs the risk of being so inclusive of difference that all "deviations" from the "norm" become queer, it is useful to observe that "queer theory," while still marked by an interest in analysis and theorizing of sexual and gender categories and the inherent problems in marking such borders in any way that implies natural categories, has expanded to encompass a wider spectrum of difference. Thus, it finds itself grouped with and overlapping with critical race studies and intersectionality in its commitment to challenging readers and writers to reconsider the nature of difference itself.

Given the scarcity of both disability studies–based scholarship and queer scholarship on O'Connor's work, it is no surprise that there has not been a body of "crip-queer" or "queer-crip" approaches to her writing. In addition to the reasons given for the comparatively little amount of O'Connor scholarship emerging from either theoretical perspective, it is perhaps also the case that this particular intersectional axis may be uncomfortable for some scholars, as it puts the positions of "queerness" and "cripness" in metonymic relationship. On the one hand, there is the potentially "dangerous" potential of making the two terms synonymous by such a reading, though intersectional criticism exists to make the very point that it is the meeting of the two related, but significantly different identity positions that produces unique experiences and points of view. A less nuanced use of intersectionality can make it seem as if queerness is a disability, which it has often been depicted as by mental health professionals, and, similarly, that disability places individuals outside of "sexual citizenship." A more socially and politically radical stance might respond that it is exactly the stigmatizing implications of dissociating queerness and cripness from each other, and viewing the productive potential not only of each, but of the intersection of the two that such a reading might offer.

CRIP QUEERING "A TEMPLE OF THE HOLY GHOST"

In his 1993 book, *Making Things Perfectly Queer: Interpreting Mass Culture*, the late critic-scholar Alexander Doty examines a number of twentieth-century mediated texts (such as television series *Laverne and Shirley*, *The Jack Benny Show*, and the various performances by Pee Wee Herman) through what might be called "queer lenses": while he is attuned to queer content in these texts and performances, he is also interested in leading readers through what might be called "queer seeing"—ways in which the perspectives of queer subjectivity offer alternative or complicated readings of the familiar and usually unremarked-upon. Limitations of space preclude a close and detailed reading of the stories *in toto*, but I hope to suggest what it might mean to read O'Connor in a sustained crip-queer fashion.

Both stories feature at their center child protagonists, neither of whom are identified in any manifest or overt way as either "queer" in the traditional sense of homosexual or bisexual, in part because both seem to be prepubertal, and, hence, outside of sexual identity, at least in the mindset of the stories, or "crip" in the standard senses of physical or intellectual disabilities. Indeed, invoking "queer" in relation to a child character may indeed push us into areas of discomfort and the forbidden or unspeakable, as they may be aligned with narratives of pedophilia on the one hand, and children's sexual desires, latent in Freud's terms at this stage, on the other; similarly, to view children who are represented as able-bodied and of normative or typical intelligence as "crip" requires some thinking or rethinking about what "crip" might encompass in the popular imagination.

The contemporary critic Kathryn Bond Stockton's 2009 book, *The Queer Child or Growing Sideways in the Twentieth Century*, offers an entry into the former. In this book, Stockton leads the reader through some canonical texts associated with childhood sexuality, from Henry James's novella "The Pupil" to Nabokov's *Lolita*. She makes a number of moves in her invocation of "queer" with regard to childhood, including an argument that, in some sense, *all* children are queer children, outside active heteronormativity, though being presented with lessons designed to lead them into a "proper" adult sexuality even at this age. Stockton also sees an important literary and other cultural alignment with narratives of the nonhuman in the depiction of children, especially with dogs in various popular texts (think of all the children's literature that focuses on the close relationships between children and their pets, for instance, with the child-dog bond often more meaningful than that between children and adult humans, from Nana in *Peter Pan* to such more recent examples as Beverly Cleary's *Ribsy* books, Gipson's *Old Yeller*, and Naylor's *Shiloh*, just to name a few). She argues that children, by virtue of psychological development and by social position and control, serve both as queer objects and queer subjects. Rather than embracing the post hoc narratives of childhood lesbian or gay male identity that circulate in everyday life, Stockton takes a stronger and perhaps more controversial position, and that is the child—by which she means *all* children—by definition stands "queerly" outside normative sexuality.

Stockton's concept of the "queer child" offers an analogous possibility for the child as "crip" figure. If "crip" refers, by comparison to "queer," a position of disability or handicap in terms of adult power/knowledge and social position, as theorized by Michel Foucault, for example, then all children have some degree of "cripness" through which they view and engage with their worlds. Just as most children grow out of social queerness, in Stockton's argument, so most children grow out of "cripness": one is reminded of the first sentence of J. M. Barrie's beloved, if uncannily troubling story of a kind of eternal childhood of cripness, *Peter Pan*—"All children, except one, grow up." In O'Connor's fiction, *many* children "never grow up," either because the Misfit and his band shoot them, they drown, or they are abandoned in other ways.

The two protagonists in the stories discussed in this section, the unnamed little girl in "A Temple of the Holy Ghost" and Harry/Bevel in "The River," are children who may or may not "grow up" in a normative sense of that phrase, and are "crip queered" within the worlds of their story. In the case of "Temple," the female child stands outside sexual knowledge—though not outside of desire of such knowledge. Indeed, by the end of the story, she may have achieved a profounder spiritual knowledge of the meaning of "queer" sexuality as embodied through the "freak" she learns about secondhand from her adolescent cousins Joanne and Susan, and both are given names. This simple difference, that the protagonist is left unnamed and the cousins, otherwise flat characters, have names suggests that in the public sphere in which the story takes place, they have identities that are on their way to permanence. The cousins are described as "positively ugly, particularly Joanne who had spots on her face anyway" (*CS* 236), but they also have access to a world of sexuality not yet available to the little girl. They have been permitted to go to the fair and, perhaps acting *sub rosa*, to enter the realm of the freak show, where they view and listen to the spiel of the "you-know-what," the phantasmic figure who in O'Connor's day would have been called a "hermaphrodite," and today an "intersex" person. Such a "forbidden" room is evocative of a lineage of fairy and folk tales, but particularly the "Bluebeard" tradition where the entrance of the young female into a forbidden room of dismembered bodies is a violent initiation into sexual relations. It is a sign of the disdain in which O'Connor (or her narrator) holds these cousins that they never seem moved or transformed by their audience with the "you-know-what."

The first half of the story is occupied with the arrival of the cousins from their convent school, Mount St. Scholastica, quickly changing from the drab, sexless brown uniforms to more secular garb. They parrot and parody the lessons of chastity—hence, their bodies as "temples of the holy ghost"—and, as part of a kind of religio-erotic mating ritual with local Protestant boys, sing the "Tantum Ergo" in Latin, in response to the masculine hymns "I've Found a Friend in Jesus" and "The Old Rugged Cross." In this sense, the little girl witnesses a kind of simultaneity of Christian gendering, in which the performance forms a kind of "androgynous" reiteration of heteronormativity. The little girl, while educated in the typical catechism of her age and upbringing and hence, aware of a kind of theology of the Eucharist, is both a/theistic and a/gnostic with regard to the mysteries and manners of sexual distinctions (and processes and organs of reproduction), except at the broadest reaches she would have observed in her child's phenomenology. Wendell's response to Joanne and Susan's performance, "That must be Jew singing," suggests a different kind of ignorance, one based in narrowness of perspective and pointing to the kind of bigotry O'Connor may be critiquing in the unearned religiosity, practiced in "bad faith" by the two pairs of adolescents as part of their short-term "courting."

The little girl may be viewed as Stockton's "queer child" in her lack of understanding, let alone participation, in matters of sexuality and reproduction. It takes multiple efforts by the cousins to explain what the specifics of the freak's anatomical "queerness" are, and, when she bargains with them to exchange her "observation" of a reproductive act (a rabbit giving birth), what she describes belies her lack of any authentic knowledge of the processes involved: she blurts out, "It spit them out of its mouth . . . six of them," reinforcing Stockton's concept that the Child is aligned with the nonhuman. She does not know (agnosis) what the cousins know about sex and therefore is epistemologically "asexual" in some sense: in this sense, as Stockton might argue, she stands in a "queer" position—outside the world of heteronormativity. O'Connor ends the story with the disappearance of the cousins and with report of the shutting down of the fair by town fathers—whether the girl grows up into heterosexuality or not is immaterial to the story.

In this regard, a comment made by O'Connor in a letter to "A" (Betty Hester, the woman with whom O'Connor developed a friendship, serving as a mentor, and who revealed her lesbianism to O'Connor later in their relationship), dated 11 February 1956 may be relevant in viewing the child queerly: "What you say about there being two [sexes] now brings it home to me. I've always believed there were two but generally acted as if there were only one" (*HOB* 136, bracketed word provided by editor Sally Fitzgerald). The comment is made in response, presumably, to a query or observation made by Hester about "the bride-bridegroom analogy" (, that Christ is the groom of all confirmed Catholic). While biography may suggest more complex interpersonal levels of sexual/erotic desires on O'Connor's part, though, as best as can be told, directed toward men, not women, as she makes clear elsewhere to Hester, on a theological level, O'Connor is, in a sense, offering an "a/gender" (and, perhaps, celibacy-based) understanding of the spiritual union as marriage. In this sense, the little girl in "Temple" is in a state of grace, not yet an initiate into sexual desire and potential sin, but she is also "atheistic" as well, or at least "agnostic." Her "atheism" and her "agnosis" not only "queer" her, but they "crip" her—while she may, even will presumably grow into knowledge and, if the story is viewed as hopeful, into experience of God, at the moment she is "disabled"—spiritually "handicapped," spiritually and cognitively unable to fulfill the everydayness of religious experience.

Where the turn to viewing the child through "crip-queer" eyes is useful is in what is the most moving and powerful section of the story: the reverie as the child drifts off to sleep and imagines, caught somewhere in that liminal zone between consciousness and dream, a space where one might argue the potential for knowledge and experience beyond the material world most exists. She ventriloquizes internally the voice of the freak, in a liturgy in which the freak serves as witness and communicant, saying,

> God made me thisaway and I don't dispute hit . . . God done this to me and I praise Him . . . He could strike you thisaway . . . But he has not . . . Raise yourself up. A temple of the Holy Ghost. You! You are God's temple, don't you know? Don't you know? God's spirit has a dwelling in you, don't you know? . . . If anybody desecrate the temple of God, God will bring him to ruin and if you laugh, He may strike you thisaway. A temple of God is a holy thing. He may strike you thisaway. A temple of God is a holy thing. Amen. Amen. (*CS* 246)

In her half-dream, the child imagines a congregation injecting its "amens" between each of the freak's testimonies and the dream is so real to her that the description, by the third-person narrator, ends the section with the observation that "The people began to slap their hands without making a loud noise . . . as they knew there was a child near, half asleep." The form and content of the freak's speech is a combination of the descriptions of it given in oblique form by the cousins, as well as the little girl's own memories of her own experiences sitting through church services, but it is or at least may be more than that. The theology expounded is a complex one, almost aporic in its self-turning. In some sense, it gets at the mysteries, still debated, around sexual queerness and corporeal disability, that God-believing Christians must face: if God is perfect and everything he creates is perfect, then how can a figure such as the hermaphrodite be anything but part of God's own plan? Yet, the freak stands outside social acceptability, with a body and a sexuality that cannot serve the reproductive "plan" assumed by Catholic theology in particular (at least as understood in everyday terms). The hermaphrodite, as imagined by the little girl, asserts its rightful and righteous place, indeed in a sermonic fashion different from standard carnival spiels, which tended to focus more on the sensual and erotic possibilities or complexities of such bodies. At the same time, the freak warns its audience that they too can be "struck" into this neither/nor/both/and body, if they dare to laugh at one of God's creations. The threat that they may be "struck" suggests that the hermaphrodite both does and does not view its identity and its place in creation as part of perfection—for why would such a fate be a "threat" if not at some level viewed (and experienced by the freak) as punishment?

Of course, one explanation for the seeming contradiction in the freak's warning is that it is, in the world of the story, the creation of the child's imagination—and therefore, a kind of performance of her own queerness and her own cripness—one we may all share, in striving, never wholly successfully to make sense of the seeming contradictions in the founding principle that God is perfect and Christ is all-loving and yet also creates/allows the (re)production of bodies like the freak's and the abject roles to which it is assigned. While O'Connor does not engage the performance of homosexuality or other forms of non-procreative sex, and, hence, may be seen as bracketing the sexual act from the bodily fact of "queerness," her child, who remains "disabled" in terms of her ability to reconcile intellectual and spiritual matters as she drifts off to sleep, may indeed be the most authentic "temple of the Holy Ghost" in the story, certainly more so than her "ugly" cousins, who may be able to perform the holy rites they have been taught with a Chomskyian "competence," but who lack the "inscape," in the sense Jesuit poet Gerard Manley Hopkins used it to mean a kind of individual spirituality, experienced through the "instress" of her poetic imagining of the freak's speech, that the little girl does have. In this sense, she may maintain, maybe not unlike O'Connor herself, a queerness and cripness that will serve as the "blessing" she can take "with one eye squinting."

PASSING DOWN "THE RIVER": TRANS THEORY AND HARRY/BEVEL'S JOURNEY

"The River," also published in *A Good Man Is Hard to Find*, features another child protagonist, though in this case the child is a boy and has one, arguably two names: Harry, who rechristens himself as Bevel, in an act of identification with the preacher whose sermon and ceremony of baptism will lead to the child's death by drowning in the story. Because Harry/Bevel is also under the age of responsibility in most interpretations of Christian doctrine, he is not to be held as guilty of either the venial sin of lying, as in misstating his name to Mrs. Collin, his "minder," or the mortal sin of suicide, and O'Connor depicts his final immersion into the deadly waters in such a way that it can surely also be interpreted as an accident. Like the child in "Temple," Harry/Bevel is "agnostic," though in this case not only in his knowledge of the world and its natural processes, but in any kind of exposure to spiritual knowledge. In that sense, both children are "intellectually disabled," crippled by both their youth and the social structures around them that keep essential understanding from them: in the case of the little girl in "Temple," it is not a "developmental" handicap, as she might be considered too young to have been taught the "facts of life." It may be more complicated for Harry/Bevel: O'Connor establishes a milieu of a neglectful set of parents, who seem to acknowledge their child's presence in the most desultory of ways. They are not outright abusive of him, but simply prioritize their adult pleasures—their drinking, smoking, late parties—over any conscious raising of their son. That they are willing to hand him over, in fairly casual fashion, to the odd Mrs. Collin, mainly to get Harry out of the way while the mother recovers from her hangover, speaks to their lack of skills or agency. Indeed, Harry is not only, then, lacking guidance that would give him the knowledge to understand what will take place on this day and to distinguish between baptism as a rite of initiation and drowning as an end to worldly life, he also lacks a kind of identity in general, of what it means, in the words of Reverend Bevel, who baptizes him, "to count." That he discards the name his parents gave him to adopt that of the preacher he has been told he will meet suggests that, if only at an unconscious level, he is seeking "to count."

While there is no overt "queerness" tied to sexuality in "The River," as one can argue there is in "A Temple of the Holy Ghost," a subset of queer theory is useful in trying to understand the journey of Harry in the hotel to Bevel at the river (and back again, where his mother insists on "rechristening" him as Harry, though the narrator then refers to him as Bevel once he has returned from the revival meeting): "trans" theory. Indeed, trans theory has expanded its reach, in recent years, beyond sexual or gender identity, as in the case of arguments by such writers as Rogers Brubaker that raise the challenge of considering the analogies between transgender and transracial possibilities of identity. While "The River" is one of O'Connor's least racially inflected stories, Brubaker's taxonomy of "trans" variations provides a useful set of lenses through which to "queer" Harry/Bevel.

Brubaker suggests that there are three principal ways of conceptualizing the "trans" move in identitarian terms: trans of migration, a permanent state from one category to another, such as "moving" or asserting that one has always "authentically" been a member of a category different from that assigned or assumed—from male to female or vice versa, or from white to black. The second is trans of between, where there is a strategic impermanence to identification with some category or class of people, where liminality is asserted as a genuine state of fluidity, and the identification as male, female, or other, or black, white, or other, may change, depending on life narrative or the context in which an individual finds themselves at a given moment. The third in Brubaker's classification is "trans of beyond," in some ways the most mysterious (in O'Connor's sense) and the one that might provide the most insights into O'Connor's story. The "trans of beyond," as Brubaker describes it:

> may take the form of an assertion of a new category—like genderqueer, trans, or multiracial—that is not situated within the conceptual space defined by established categories. It may entail personal or political opposition to being categorized at all, or the categorization of others. Or it may involve a normative vision or empirical diagnosis of a social world no longer organized—or no longer organized so deeply—by gender or racial categorization. (113)

"The River" presents, in the mind, body, and soul of Harry/Bevel, an allegory of "the trans of beyond." Because the protagonist remains a child, and will remain so forever, given the fatal climax of the story, he is not mindfully, consciously, or deliberately living a "trans of beyond" in the sense that Brubaker emphasizes in discussing adult subjects, but he is living in a "spiritual trans" that goes beyond typical binary categories—saved/unsaved, alive/dead, Christian/atheist, and so forth.

With her typical irony and compassion, O'Connor depicts the child Bevel (as her narrator has come to call him once he has enunciated his own "rechristening" at the revival) just at a state of becoming as he is about to leave his earthly life. Bevel has misunderstood the preacher's explanation of the meaning of the baptism he has experience and, as a child is likely to do, has mistransferred one piece of knowledge, the spiritual meaning of baptism and the metaphorical location of the Kingdom of God in the river, to a literal, if incorrect second instance. While the baptism itself is not merely metaphoric, the idea that there is a geographical Kingdom of God in the river, which Bevel can access by returning to it, is a deadly error. In a sense produced not only by Bevel's youth, but by the neglect of anyone charged with the responsibility of caring for him to provide him with the education that would equip him with the intelligence to distinguish between them.

Only as he struggles against the current does Bevel come to the knowledge he needed to make his way in the world, post-baptism, only then does he achieve something like "accountability" intellectually, though too late to save himself: "This was the way it had been when the preacher held him under—he had to fight with something that pushed him back in face. He stopped and thought suddenly: it's another joke, it's just another joke! He thought how far he had come for nothing and he began to hit and splash and kick the filthy river" (*CS* 173). His last sensations are of the well-meaning, but feckless (and ironically named) Mr. Paradise vainly trying to save him. But at the very moment of death, Bevel experiences something that O'Connor might identify as God's grace: "For an instant he was overcome with surprise: then since he was moving quickly and knew that he was getting somewhere, all his fury and fear left him" (*CS* 174).

It would be easy and not unreasonable to read this final moment as a bitter one on the part of the narrator, as one of O'Connor's many children seem destined for bad ends, usually because of the sins of the adults around them, such as the grandmother's culpability in the execution by the Misfit of John Wesley and June Starr in "A Good Man Is Hard to Find," but a "trans" reading of Bevel may offer redemption for him. While we may stand in horror at his belief that "he was getting somewhere"—that somewhere being death—in the world of the story, his "trans" journey is to a place "beyond" that of ordinary and everyday life. Indeed, having been baptized, albeit not under his "assigned" name, which also suggests a "trans move" on Bevel's part, he is surely heading to Christian paradise, even if the "good Christian" Mr. Paradise lacks the agency to restore him to mortal life. While the renaming of self from the everyday "Harry" to the less common "Bevel" is a matter of chance, the implication being that Harry would have called himself by whatever name was that of the preacher, there is also a kind of fittingness to it. A "bevel" is a carpenter's tool, which allows the artisan to create a "slope," something not simply flat, something that might "count" by having an individuality to it; famously, Cash Bundren explains the process by which he built his mother Addie's coffin in Faulkner's *As I Lay Dying*, another family narrative in which flooding waters play a tragic role: "I made it on the bevel."

The name may also evoke the image of a "beveled mirror," one "with edges cut at an angle, so that it gives the appearance of a mirror with a framed edge around it" (https://www.hunker.com/13412227/what-is-the-meaning-of-a-beveled-mirror). As the home furnishings website (Hunker.com) from which this definition is taken goes on to say, "The slant of a beveled mirror catches and refract the light, acting like a **prism**, causing a **rainbow effect**." While the website's intention is to describe the aesthetic and practical benefits of a beveled mirror (it may save the buyer from the extra expense and trouble of having such a mirror framed), there is a sense in which the qualities of framing and refracting may also serve to align Harry/Bevel with a sense of spiritual reflection, and of diffusion of the "colors" of being saved. On the one hand, prisms appeal to the human sense of wonder at light and its properties; indeed, prisms are used by some practitioners in working therapeutically with people on the autistic spectrum; adherents to this form of therapy assert that their patients, after using prismatic glasses, are better able to perform fine motor skills and exhibit greater confidence and well-being in general (https://covdblog.wordpress.com/2011/04/05/the-power-of-lenses-and-prisms-saving-stellas-toes/). At the same time, purely from the standpoint of physics, prisms always involve some kinds of displacement of light, which may be experienced as distortion. So, a beveled mirror may, on the one hand, give the viewer a sense of framing and enhancement of perceived appearance of self; at the same time, like all mirrors, it may distort "reality" (whatever that means in a particular instance)—it can "queer" the image and the perception. While it is not made explicit in the story, it may be the case that Harry's rechristening of himself as "Bevel" (not unlike the echolalia performed by some autistic persons, here echoing the name of the preacher, told to him by Mrs. Connin before they arrive at the revival) is both an attempt to see himself in a mirror, a beveled one, "through a glass darkly."

His baptism saves him from limbo, insofar as that term has a place in the theology of the story, his lack of will and formal accountability keeps his self-administered death from being a suicide in the religious sense. While he has little knowledge of Jesus and is described as not recognizing an image of him earlier in the story, his "trans"-ition from the godless Harry, arguably a trans of migration, as conversions usually are, to the baptized Bevel, though the return to his parents and his mother's hailing him as Harry suggests a "betweenness" he has acquired, by death a "trans of beyond."

Ironically, though it ends in his death, Bevel's final moments provide a more beatific vision of the "trans" identity than that of the freak in "A Temple of the Holy Ghost." Both his "cripness," his lack of knowledge and social structures to accommodate this "handicap" and his "queerness," that of not initially "counting," which is followed by death as a result of having transitioned into the salvation offered by Christ, allow us to view his death, however tragic in our "sentimental" experience of narratives of the death of children, as a story with a spiritually queer and crip, what might best be described as a "spiritual sublime"—an ecstasy in the midst of dissolution into something beyond individual identity. The river, the agent of death, also provides a way to deliverance.

CONCLUSION

Scholarship on O'Connor and disability has focused either on representation of disabled characters, usually as "freaks" or "the grotesque," or on her theological perspectives, both implicitly in her fiction and explicitly in her essays, especially, "An Introduction to *A Memoir of Mary Ann*." Similarly, because O'Connor's own relationship to sexuality, especially homosexuality, in her life has focused on either her own identity or on her friendships and romances or the often-disastrous sexual activities and fantasies of her characters, a "crip-queer" perspective, provides a useful way into understanding the function of nonnormative bodies and souls in O'Connor's work. Though this essay has focused exclusively on child figures in two of O'Connor's best-known stories, the enfreakment with which her pages are filled offers opportunities for more sustained and individual "crip-queer" readings, from Enoch's complex "relationship" with the gorilla in *Wise Blood*, perhaps another example of the queer child (for Enoch seems as childlike in many respects as the girl in "A Temple of the Holy Ghost") as contiguous with the "nonhuman" or animal (or pseudo-animal, in this case) to the final confrontation between the grandmother and the Misfit, in which her speech act of declaring that "Why, you're one of my babies," intended as a moment of revelation and forgiveness on her part, perhaps, but interpreted as a hailing of the killer as child, presexual, developmentally impaired, leads him to pull the trigger.

Because critical analysis of "crips" and "queers" in O'Connor's writing has either tended to focus on the representational or the allegorical (the "symbolic," which O'Connor memorably scorned in Mary McCarthy's comments on the Eucharist), there has either been relative silence on these subjects (perhaps a discomfort in reading too facile into O'Connor's biographical relationship with her narratives) or too literalist readings. The "crip-queer" (or "queer-crip," as Sandahl and McRuer would have it) approach focuses more on ways of reading and experiencing O'Connor's writings from nonnormative perspectives—"habits of reading," so to speak, which may offer as useful and valid an entry in her work as do those who precede Mrs. Turpin and her husband in the final procession in O'Connor's penultimate masterpiece, "Revelation." That, in this essay, (two) little children lead the way may indeed be fitting, both narratively and scripturally.

WORKS CITED

Basselin, Timothy J. *Flannery O'Connor: Writing a Theology of Disabled Humanity*. Waco, TX: Baylor University Press, 2013.

Brubaker, Rogers. *Trans: Gender and Race in an Age of Unsettled Identities*. Princeton, NJ: Princeton University Press, 2016.

Conley, Garrad. *Boy Erased: A Memoir*. New York: Riverhead Books, 2016.

Doty, Alexander. *Making Things Perfectly Queer: Interpreting Mass Culture*. Minneapolis: University of Minnesota Press, 1993.

Hahn, Harlan. "Can Disability Be Beautiful?" *Social Policy* 18, no. 3 (1988): 26–32. https://covd blog.wordpress.com/2011/04/05/the-power-of-lenses-and-prisms-saving-stellas-toes/.

https://www.hunker.com/13412227/what-is-the-meaning-of-a-beveled-mirror.

O'Connor, Flannery. *The Complete Stories*. New York: Farrar, Straus and Giroux, 1991.

O'Connor, Flannery. *The Habit of Being: Letters of Flannery O'Connor*, edited by Sally Fitzgerald. New York: Farrar, Straus and Giroux, 1979.

O'Connor, Flannery. *Mystery and Manners*, edited by Sally and Robert Fitzgerald. New York: Farrar, Straus and Giroux, 1969.

Sandahl, Carrie. "Cripping the Queer or Queering the Crip? Intersections of Queer and Crip Identities in Solo Autobiographical Performance." *GLQ: A Journal of Lesbian and Gay Studies* 9, no. 1–2 (2003): 25–56.

Stockton, Kathryn Bond. *The Queer Child, or Growing Sideways in the 20th Century*. Durham, NC: Duke University Press, 2009.

The "Failure of… Compassion": Problematic Redemption and the Need for Praxis in "The Lame Shall Enter First" and "The Comforts of Home"

ALICIA MATHENY BEESON

In Flannery O'Connor's short story "The Lame Shall Enter First," Sheppard, the father of young Norton, takes Rufus, whom he met at a juvenile delinquent facility, to get a new shoe to accommodate his clubfoot. Their distinct physical demeanors reflect their contrasting attitudes about the experience. Sheppard's face is "flushed" and his heart is beating rapidly, while Rufus slumps down into his seat (470). Despite Rufus's lack of interest or pleasure, Sheppard is overly pleased with himself; as the narrator explains, "It was as if he had given the boy a new spine" (470). When Rufus explains that he is not going to wear the shoe because he does not need one, Sheppard blames the boy, saying that "he's not mature enough for it yet" (471). In his eagerness to practice what he sees as good charitable work to inflate his own sense of self, Sheppard disregards what Rufus actually wants or needs. Additionally, Sheppard does not adequately reflect on the impact that his actions, such as leaving Norton home alone while he takes Rufus to the brace shop, will have on his son. Sheppard illustrates the potential negative outcomes that charitable action without reflection can have on the charitable individual, the person receiving charity, and even surrounding family members.

In this chapter, I reconsider O'Connor's work by discussing her characters' attempted charity outside of a religious framework. More specifically, I explore praxis—or the careful balance of action and reflection—in "The Lame Shall Enter First" and "The Comforts of Home." Praxis has been discussed in a variety of fields including philosophy, theology, and education; as a theoretical construct it is easily applied in a variety of areas, including charity. Praxis relates to charity because the latter involves acting on a thought about helping someone that one perceives is in need. While this is often motivated by and associated with religious belief, I am interested in considering the concept of charity—or aiding others—more broadly. Charity is typically not an impulsive action; it often requires some preparation, though some are more deliberate and socially responsible than others in their planning. To practice the most effective charity, it is imperative to balance charitable action with reflection on the receiving individual's actual needs, rather than the giver's perception of their needs or a fulfillment of their own desire to be charitable. My argument applies this concept of praxis in a manner that moves the conversation away from O'Connor's characters' need for faith and toward their need for thought and reflection.

The theme of charity is exhibited in many of O'Connor's short stories including "The Comforts of Home," "Everything That Rises Must Converge," "The Lame Shall Enter First," "A Circle in the Fire," and "The Turkey." O'Connor scholars such as Carter Martin, David Eggenschwiler, and Henry Edmonson have considered charity within O'Connor's work but primarily from a Christian perspective that emphasizes the characters' need for a stronger faith in God. Vikki Bell joins this conversation in her article "On the Critique of Secular Ethics," in which she discusses "The Lame Shall Enter First" and reads O'Connor's critique of Sheppard's actions as a pronouncement of his lack of faith. I offer the alternative view that Sheppard lacks productive praxis rather than religious faith. Religious belief would not make Sheppard inherently better at interacting with and caring for Rufus; however, reflecting more on the impacts of his actions could, potentially, better all of his relationships.

Considering "The Lame Shall Enter First" and "The Comforts of Home" through the lens of praxis illuminates the idea that charitable action without productive reflection leads to disastrous consequences despite the unexpected, even tragic, redemption as reconciliation that occurs. In both "The Lame Shall Enter First" and "The Comforts of Home," the conclusion of each story forces the protagonists to confront the disastrous consequences of not critically considering their acts of charity. Rather than helping those they perceive are in need, the givers of charity damage their relationships with their children who reconnect with a deceased parent, which, in both cases, causes a troubling death. O'Connor's upsetting stories implicitly advocate for praxis, including productive reflection, in familial and charitable relationships. In this chapter, I will discuss Sheppard and Thomas's challenged position of power, the unexpected redemption of a child with a deceased parent, and finally the need for praxis that these short stories emphasize. My argument encourages readings of O'Connor's stories beyond religious considerations, and perhaps even reminds us of our own need to balance our action and reflection, including in our charitable efforts.

RELATIONSHIPS OF POWER

In "The Lame Shall Enter First" and "The Comforts of Home," the familial and charitable relationships include complicated struggles for power, autonomy, and meaning that impact the characters' sense of self and relationships to others. In the former, Sheppard invites Rufus Johnson to come live with them. Norton's mother passed away about a year prior to the opening of the story, and both he and his father have been struggling to connect and cope with the loss. Sheppard largely overlooks Norton, Rufus's behavior disappoints Sheppard, and Norton eventually hangs himself to be reunited with his mother. In "The Comforts of Home," Thomas's mother tries to aid Sarah Ham, who has been arrested for bad checks, by getting her an attorney and finding a boardinghouse for her. But when she is kicked out for drunkenness, she invites Sarah to live with them, much to her adult son Thomas's dismay. Eventually, Thomas's deceased father's voice either literally enters his mind or influences his thinking, and in a scramble with the sheriff and Sarah Ham, Thomas tries to shoot Sarah and kills his mother, who steps in front of her. The parental figures from "The Lame Shall Enter First" and "The Comforts of Home," Sheppard and Thomas's mother, respectively, are middle class and position themselves as capable of charitable action. They both feel that they have something to offer to someone they deem as lesser than themselves in multiple ways. Thomas's mother focuses on Sarah Ham's economic need and morality, while Sheppard concentrates on Rufus Johnson's economic need, intellectual development, and physical disability.

The familial relationships within these stories are also complicated. Sheppard views himself as superior to his son Norton, and Thomas views himself as better than his mother. While gender contributes to both Thomas and Sheppard's sense of identity and social position, Thomas's position of authority above his mother is also influenced by his education, and Sheppard's power over his son is affected by his intelligence and his notion that he is selfless. Thomas and Sheppard's inflated sense of self leads them to criticize and dismiss their immediate family members to such an extent that readers begin to question their integrity.

As many critics have noted, Flannery O'Connor does not allow the hierarchies of power in her fiction to stand unchallenged. The givers of charity, and especially the adult male characters in these short stories, do not endure the narrative without challenges to their perceived superior position. Laura Behling explains of O'Connor's social order, "readers expect disabled characters to be ugly people, both metaphorically and literally. But O'Connor suggests that . . . the characters who are not physically whole are, in fact, not the ugliest characters in these texts" (94). Rather than reinforcing cultural hierarchies, O'Connor draws our attention to the problematic actions and thoughts of those traditionally placed in power: in these short stories, Sheppard and Thomas. As the stories develop, it becomes clear that the integrity of those in power is not superior to those positioned below them, and that productive praxis would be incredibly beneficial. Brian Abel Ragen suggests that the "simple distinction between the bad people and the good people will not hold" in O'Connor's short stories (106). Though Thomas and Sheppard position themselves well above Rufus and Sarah, who are deemed in need of saving, this dichotomy of good and bad is certainly complicated by the close of the narrative.

Sarah Ham and Rufus Johnson's entries into the homes challenge Thomas and Sheppard's perceived superiority. Natalie Wilson notes, "The outsider status allows [O'Connor's] characters to question, subvert, and transgress patriarchal authority. And, significantly, this outsider status is often tied to being a *body* that patriarchy defines as inferior or abnormal" (96; emphasis in original). In these short stories, Sarah Ham and Rufus Johnson are outsiders to the family and to dominant society because of their low socioeconomic status. Additionally, their bodies are viewed as inferior because of Sarah's sexual transgressions and Rufus's clubfoot. However, both characters are able to place tension on the patriarchal authority of Thomas and Sheppard. Rufus and Sarah frustrate and confuse the protagonists, revealing the ugly underbelly of their seemingly superior status and making it clear to the reader that despite their inflated sense of self, Thomas and Sheppard have much room for improvement. For instance, Sheppard gets so frustrated with Rufus that he wishes, "If he would only leave now of his own accord," challenging Sheppard's self-conception as a giving, charitable provider (O'Connor 474). Similarly, Thomas becomes so frustrated with Sarah Ham that he gives his mother an ultimatum: "If you bring that girl back into this house, I leave. You can choose—her or me" (383). But when his mother decides to bring Sarah Ham back again to the house, Thomas's position as an authority figure in the household is challenged, making him lash out at Sarah in ways that undermine his integrity. Thus, Sarah and Rufus serve as the catalysts to the challenging of traditional hierarchies in these short stories; ironically, those who receive charity in the story show the reader that the individuals offering it are not as capable and superior as they think.

Though Thomas is established as the authority figure and positions himself as superior to the other characters, O'Connor challenges his position above others in "The Comforts of Home." Edward Kessler provides a framework for Sarah Ham's impact on Thomas: "Sarah Ham defies conventional decorum and shatters the passivity of her well-established superior. She is the individual who will not conform" (89). But rather than slut-shaming or ridiculing the nonconformist Sarah, O'Connor "chastises [Thomas] because of his pride-filled arrogance" (McDermott). Thomas refers to Sarah Ham as a "moral moron" (*CS*

385), though by calling Sarah a "dirty criminal slut" (403) and by treating her with such disdain, Thomas reveals himself as the insensitive, even immoral, character. Additionally, Sarah Ham is labeled as a "psychopathic personality" by society, but it is Thomas who starts to have psychotic episodes, hearing the voice of his deceased father, which eventually drives him to try to shoot Sarah (388). He chastises Sarah Ham for her moral laxity but then becomes a murderer when he shoots his mother. Though he compares the blast of the gun to "a sound meant to bring an end to an evil in the world," his actions seem like a result of evil rather than an end to it (403). Thomas thinks of himself as better than the other characters in the story, but it quickly becomes apparent that he is not as morally or psychologically superior as he thinks, thus challenging the hierarchies established in the beginning.

Similarly, Sheppard starts in a position of authority, but his actions and integrity are eventually called into question through his neglect of his son. Repeatedly Sheppard places his own selfish need to feel as if he is doing good, charitable acts for Rufus over the needs of Norton. For instance, when Sheppard climbs to the attic and finds his son looking through the telescope, he does not even greet his grieving son but instead abruptly asks, "Where's Rufus?" and then repeats the question even louder (O'Connor 463). He tells Rufus, "I have every confidence in you" and "I believe that you can make anything of yourself that you set your mind to" (468). However, he never encourages his son throughout the story. Sheppard also leaves Norton at home when he takes Rufus to the brace shop because he "did not want his attention divided" (469). If the reader is not aware of Sheppard's neglect of Norton throughout the story, O'Connor draws attention to the fact when Sheppard himself realizes that he "did more for [Rufus] than [he] did for [his] own child" (480). Sheppard's oversight emphasizes the need for praxis, not just in the charitable relationships but also in the familial. As James Wilson remarks, "Sheppard is hardly the 'good shepherd' his name ironically calls to mind; though he pretentiously preaches the abstract ethic of charity to his child, Sheppard withholds the warmth and devotion the child naturally commands" (161). While Sheppard is positioned as the intellectual and class superior, his position of power and his integrity are questioned as a result of his treatment of Norton. Ultimately, the actions of Sheppard, Thomas, and Thomas's mother lead to destruction and a problematic form of redemption; thus, the unfolding of the story reveals a need for praxis.

REDEMPTION AS RESTORATION

In "The Lame Shall Enter First" and "The Comforts of Home," the damaged familial relationships cause the children to reconnect, or be redeemed, not with their living parent but with their deceased one. The *Oxford English*

Dictionary defines redemption, from a Christian perspective, as "Deliverance from sin and damnation, esp. by the atonement of Christ; salvation" ("Redemption, *1a*"). However, the term can also refer to "The action of saving, delivering, or restoring a person or thing; deliverance or restoration" ("Redemption, *5a*"). In Charles Taylor's discussion of secularization, he explores the movement from "a society in which it was virtually impossible not to believe in God, to one in which faith, even for the staunchest believer, is one human possibility among others" (3). I see secularizing redemption along similar lines; it is not that Christian redemption is nonexistent, but that there are other, secular ways of understanding redemption. In other words, there are forms of restoration among humans that operate outside of and perhaps alongside of religious salvation. These short stories emphasize redemption between living and dead family members rather than between a redeemer and the redeemed.

Most scholars agree that redemption occurs in much of O'Connor's fiction, or at least that her novels and short stories often raise the possibility of redemption, but the majority of these scholars consider redemption from a Christian perspective because of O'Connor's Catholic roots. For instance, Susan Srigley considers the connection between penance and relationships, as well as the possible result of redemption in *Wise Blood*. Srigley notes that her reading of redemption in the novel is "a religiously grounded critique" (96). In contrast, I argue that some of O'Connor's stories seem to be less about the "atonement of Christ" ("Redemption, *1a*") and more about a "saving, delivering, or restoring [of] a person or thing" ("Redemption, *5a*"), often saving them from their own problematic thoughts and actions or restoring a broken relationship. In line with this secular conceptualization of redemption, Diane Prenatt considers redemption to be a "collaps[ing] of the distance between . . . simulated and authentic selves," reconciling parts of one individual (46). The reader may expect the protagonists Sheppard and Thomas to reach a moment of redemption, either theologically with Christ or from a secular perspective with the healing of a broken relationship to their son or mother. While neither of these characters receives salvation nor restores these broken relationships, a secular form of troubling redemption occurs through the child's restoration of a relationship with a deceased parent.

Though it briefly seems as though Sheppard will experience redemption with his son in "The Lame Shall Enter First," in actuality Norton is reconciled with his deceased mother. Sheppard finally reaches the realization that he "had stuffed his own emptiness with good works like a glutton. He had ignored his own child to feed his vision of himself" (O'Connor 481). Sheppard then experiences a "rush of agonizing love for the child [that] rushed over him like a transfusion of life," and he hurries to tell Norton that "he loved him, that he would never fail him again" (482). If Sheppard had been able to actualize this plan, he would have experienced redemption with his son. Marshall Bruce Gentry points out that Sheppard's realization is "chilling" because he still "believes, inaccurately, that he has redeemed himself" (158). Gentry fairly depicts Sheppard's inaccuracy because by the time Sheppard arrives in the attic to mend their relationship, Norton has already "launched his flight into space" (O'Connor 482). Norton hangs himself in the beams to be with his mother, a result of Rufus Johnson's teaching that if he died right now he would "go where she is" in heaven (462). The location of Norton's suicide is significant because earlier in the story, Norton looks through the telescope in the attic at the stars and tells Sheppard, "I've found her . . . Mamma!" (478). Norton believes that through his death he will be reunited with his mother, the individual whose loss he has been mourning for the length of the story. As Gentry observes, "Norton works out his redemptive reunion with his dead mother on the story's margin; Sheppard ignores him, while Rufus uses him to attack Sheppard . . . Norton takes over his own redemption when the other characters leave him alone" (Gentry 159). Though the protagonist's redemption is not actualized, his son's suicide symbolizes his own redemption as he joins his mother in the afterlife.

Ironically, redemption in "The Comforts of Home" also occurs between a child and a deceased parent: Thomas and his father. After Sarah Ham enters their home, Thomas's father "took up a squatting position in his mind" and tells Thomas, "you ain't like me. Not enough to be a man" (O'Connor 393). Repeatedly throughout the story, the voice of Thomas's father challenges Thomas's male authority and calls him an "idiot," a "moron," and an "imbecile" (O'Connor 402). Even his actions are influenced by the voice. For instance, "Thomas, as if his arm were guided by his father . . . snatched the gun" from Sarah Ham (403). When the voice of his father encourages Thomas to fire at Sarah, he obeys. However, his mother throws "herself forward to protect her," so Thomas actually kills his own mother (403). Thus, redemption between Thomas and his mother is impossible, and reconciliation between Thomas and Sarah Ham seems unlikely.

O'Connor writes about the story, "If there is any question of a symbolic redemption, it would be through the old lady who brings Thomas face to face with his own evil—which is that of putting his own comfort before charity (however foolish)" (*The Habit of Being* 434). While this may be true, the story does not demonstrate this realization or allow us to see the results of this potential redemption. However, the story does describe another form of redemption between Thomas and his deceased father. By obeying the voice of his father, Thomas experiences a reconnection with his deceased parent, even if it is an imagined one. Thomas "inherited his father's reason without his ruthlessness and his mother's love of good without her tendency to pursue it," but in the end of the short story Thomas becomes ruthless and divorces his love of good, bringing him closer to his father and allowing redemption with the deceased parent to occur (388).

While redemption and reconciliation usually have positive connotations, the reconciliations that occur in these short stories seem troublesome. Rather than a living child and a living parent being reconciled, at least one individual in the equation is dead. In some ways, this reflects Christian redemption: a reconciliation between humanity and the divine after the crucifixion. However, in these short stories, there is no connection to the divine, only humans attempting to connect with other humans both living and dead. These reconciliations lack the permanency and positivity associated with salvation. The redemptions in these short stories happen through suicide and murder, which draws attention to the potentially tragic results of action without reflection. However, it is through these terrible circumstances that the protagonists are presented with the opportunity to transcend their present circumstances and productively reflect on their thoughts and actions. The narratives do not include this reflection after tragedy but imply that this reflection could have been beneficial earlier in the story. The traumatic loss at the end serves as a starting point for the protagonist's reflection beyond the bounds of the short story. Though it is too late for the protagonists to prevent what has occurred, perhaps O'Connor intends for her stories to spur readers to reflect on their own actions and relationships.

A NEED FOR PRAXIS

Through the disastrous, yet surprisingly and unconventionally redemptive, consequences of O'Connor's short stories, they implicitly argue a need for praxis. Theorists such as Aristotle, Kant, and Marx considered the concept of praxis,[1] and though some use the term synonymously with practice, here I emphasize its quality in combination with theory or reflection. In *The Human Condition* (1958), Hannah Arendt enters the centuries-long conversation about praxis when she challenges the hierarchical position of contemplation over action; she suggests that the *vita activa* "is neither superior nor inferior to the central concern of the *vita contemplativa*" and that they are best when combined (17).[2] Even more recently, Steven Vogel builds from Marx's argument that humans are always changing their environments through normal activity. In "What Is the 'Philosophy of Praxis?'" (2017), he argues that humans "can also transform the things around them purposefully, in accordance with plans" (20).

Contemporary discussions in education and spirituality also employ the concept of praxis. For instance, Roman Catholic theologian Clodovis Boff writes that "[e]xisting liberation theology is a theology directed upon praxis—precisely a praxis of social transformation. Thus, it is at once critical and utopian" (65). Though, as Boff suggests, the concept can be utilized in a religious context, the theory is not inherently spiritual and has broader applications for theists, agnostics, and atheists in every sector of life. For example, Paulo Freire considers praxis in relation to education. He writes, "praxis is not blind action, deprived of intention or of finality. It is action and reflection" (qtd. in hooks 48). Though definitions of praxis shift across time and disciplines, a central tenet remains true: action is best when combined with contemplation. As charity typically involves some kind of action, praxis theorists would advocate careful consideration of the circumstances before proceeding with attempted goodwill. Applying the theory of praxis to "The Lame Shall Enter First" and "The Comforts of Home" emphasizes that "blind action" can lead to destruction within familial and charitable relationships.

Throughout the stories, Thomas, Thomas's mother, and Sheppard lack productive reflection on how their actions will impact their family members. Here, I make a distinction between productive and unproductive reflection to emphasize the characters' problematic usage of the latter. Productive reflection suggests an ability to view a situation (somewhat) objectively and consider consequences that your own actions and thoughts will have on others. Unproductive reflection indicates a cyclical thought process that reinforces previously held opinions without critically examining them, which can lead to delusional thinking. In these short stories, the characters' perspectives differ: Sheppard is a humanitarian atheist, Thomas is primarily concerned with his own personal comfort, and Thomas's mother is a Christian. By including the failed charitable attempts of individuals from both Christian and non-Christian worldviews, O'Connor's stories imply that it is not the alignment with Christian values or the lack thereof that causes the destruction. However, in her introduction to *A Memoir of Mary Ann*, O'Connor insists that tenderness "without faith," "cut off from the person of Christ," and "wrapped up in theory" leads to terror (Introduction 18). She frames Christ as the "source of tenderness," but while some characters such as Sheppard lack faith, others like Thomas's mother who have faith and attempt to live by Christian teachings are still unable to practice responsible and successful charity (Introduction 18). While some might argue that the characters must seek a deeper connection with the divine in order to practice "tenderness" successfully, I argue instead that the stories suggest a need for productive reflection. Thomas, Thomas's mother, and Sheppard all practice unproductive reflection in which their problematic views and actions are simply reinforced by their unique perspectives, which consequently leads to destruction.

Through the death of a family member, Sheppard and Thomas do reach a moment of awareness and potential transcendence, but it comes too late in these short stories: the problematic behaviors and attitudes have already occurred. Therefore, praxis does not seem to be necessary at the end of the story, but rather at the beginning or in the reader's reality. If Sheppard, Thomas, and Thomas's mother had been able to simultaneously act and productively reflect, if they had been able to transcend their current view in order to consider the situation more objectively before the death of a loved one, the disastrous consequences would likely have been avoided. However, Sheppard, Thomas, and Thomas's mother seem incapable of productive reflection within the story; the characters are not cognizant of the possible ramifications of their actions. Therefore, O'Connor's stories imply that the concept of praxis is needed in familial and charitable relationships, and though her characters are not able to put this idea into practice, perhaps her readers can.

Sheppard's motivation for his interaction with Rufus is selfish rather than altruistic; he does not reflect on his son and Rufus's true need, but instead focuses on his own need. Sheppard wanted Rufus to learn not about math, science, or language, but instead "that his benefactor was impervious to insult and that there were no cracks in his armor of kindness and patience where a successful shaft could be driven" (O'Connor 461). Sheppard paints himself as a soldier of charity—strong and invulnerable. O'Connor describes Sheppard as "a man who thought he was good and thought he was doing good when he wasn't" (*The Habit of Being* 490). His motivation for taking Rufus in and teaching him is egotistical; he wants to be seen as a kind, patient, charitable hero. The irony of Sheppard's motivation comes in his treatment of his son, as he constantly emphasizes his son's selfishness despite the fact that it is he himself who is selfish. However, Sheppard does acknowledge his problematic motivation later when he considers that "he had been over-lenient, too concerned to have Johnson like him. He felt a twinge of guilt. What difference did it make if Johnson liked him or not?" (O'Connor 464). But even after this brief moment of reflection, Sheppard suggests that he's trying to "impress the boy"; thus, Sheppard's focus again becomes pleasing Rufus (466). Sheppard finally recognizes the "failure of his compassion"—his inability to practice effective humanitarianism—and he reaches a full awareness of his selfish motivation through true reflection spurred on by his son's death at the end of the story, immediately prior to the disastrous consequences of his unreflective charity (475). Because Sheppard's egocentric actions (disguised as kindness toward Rufus) and neglect of his son lead to his son's suicide, "The Lame Shall Enter First" demonstrates the potentially disastrous consequences of selfish actions without reflection, even when disguised as charity.

Thomas's mother may seem to have better intentions in her charitable relationship with Sarah Ham, but she plunges into superficial charity without productively reflecting on her actions or Sarah's need. The destruction that her charity will bring is directly forecasted at the start of the short story: "His mother, with her daredevil charity, was about to wreck the peace of the house" (383). According to Frederick Asals, Thomas's mother seems "addicted to helping the 'unfortunate'" (109). She takes Sarah a box of candy in jail, which Carter Martin refers to as "blind charity" (39–40). He explains, "Sarah Ham is a thoroughly depraved person, and the mother's failure to acknowl- edge that condition is one measure of her tragically shallow nature"; she does not reflect on Sarah Ham's true need (Martin 39–40). Thomas's mother's primary motivation for helping Sarah seems to be her conflation of her son with Sarah. Repeatedly she asks her son, "suppose it were you?" (O'Connor 385). Her question implies that she would want her son to receive charity if he were in the same position as Sarah. Thus, Thomas's mother misplaces her love for her son on others, such as Sarah Ham, without recognizing their need or the need of her son. Thomas tells his mother that he "won't put up with this another day" and that he will leave if Sarah Ham is brought back into their home (384). However, Thomas's mother ignores the requests of her son and continues with her "useless compassion" toward Sarah (387). If she had been better able to reflect and evaluate the needs of both her son and Sarah Ham, positive change could have occurred. Though Thomas, as an adult, is not dependent on his mother in the same way that Norton, a child, is depen- dent on Sheppard, Thomas's mother similarly ignores her child's needs and preferences. She could have consulted with Thomas about the possibility of boarding Sarah Ham and could have collaborated with Sarah Ham to identify the best way to address her needs. Thomas's mother does not practice produc- tive praxis; she acts without reflecting, and the subsequent chain of events leads to her son's unraveling and her own death.

These stories highlight a need for praxis, or a balance of productive reflec- tion and action, in the stories as well as in society. Sheppard and Thomas's mother are positioned above Rufus Johnson and Sarah Ham, both from soci- ety's perception and their own. As they are in a position of power due to their class, they are considered capable of providing for and teaching those from a lower socioeconomic status. However, by not carefully considering and reflecting on their actions, the parental figures demonstrate ineffective charity in need of praxis. If Thomas's mother and Sheppard had appropriately and adequately considered their perceptions and actions, they may have been bet- ter able to meet the needs of their children as well as those they brought into their home. The stories never allow us to see what might happen if praxis had occurred; they only show us the consequences of it not occurring. However, given the tragic events at the close of each narrative, O'Connor leaves readers questioning their own actions and relationship with others and encourages praxis regarding familial and charitable relationships. In *A Secular Age* (2007), Charles Taylor suggests that, regardless of religious belief or nonbe- lief, humans seek fullness, and certainly familial and charitable relationships are primary methods to reach that end. The concept of praxis is relevant in an increasingly secularized world—for those religious and nonreligious—and through productively reflecting on thoughts and actions, people can move toward the fullness that Taylor describes.

O'Connor's stories emphasize the problematic result of unthinking charity and implicitly argue for the need for praxis—the careful balance of thinking and acting—in order to most effectively transform your relationships or your community. By considering the motivation and consequences of charitable actions, while also learning the recipient's true need, hierarchies can break down, true relationships can form, and effective change can occur. Expanding our understanding of power dynamics in O'Connor's works, as well as exploring secular understandings of redemption and praxis, can illuminate O'Connor's ideas about human interactions and maybe even give us as readers a moment to reflect before we act, as it would have been helpful for her characters to do. My analysis approaches the text from a more humanist than religious perspective; it places power with the individual to negotiate the improvement of their own lives and relationships with others rather than relying on a higher power. My argument moves the conversation about these short stories outside the realm of O'Connor's religious background or biography, which allows for new understandings of the stories' implicit argument regarding troubling redemption and the need for more critical reflection. "The Lame Shall Enter First" and "The Comforts of Home" encourage readers to employ reason and reflection, balanced with action, to better familial and charitable relationships.

NOTES

1. Aristotle asserted that praxis (doing) was one of three basic human activities that also include theoria (contemplating) and poiesis (making). Greeks often associated the term praxis with free political action, and later theorists expanded on this notion. In the eighteenth century, Immanuel Kant advocated the relevance of philosophy when he emphasized that ethical principles could and should be enacted. Kant argued that morality should guide action more than self-interest or economics. In the following century, Karl Marx described the relationship between one's understanding of the world and ability to change it, leading philosophers such as Antonio Labriola and Antonio Gramsci to call Marxism the philosophy of praxis. In *Theses of Feuerbach*, Marx famously argues, "Philosophers have merely interpreted the world in various ways; the point is to change it."

2. Vikki Bell considers Hannah Arendt and ethics in "The Lame Shall Enter First," even pointing out that O'Connor read and admired Arendt. However, Bell focuses more on goodness than the *vita activa*, which is the more relevant concept to my argument regarding praxis.

WORKS CITED

Arendt, Hannah. *The Human Condition*. Chicago: University of Chicago Press, 1958.
Asals, Frederick. *Flannery O'Connor: The Imagination of Extremity*. Athens: University of Georgia Press, 1982.

Behling, Laura L. "The Necessity of Disability in 'Good Country People' and 'The Lame Shall Enter First.'" *Flannery O'Connor Review* 4 (2006): 88–98.

Bell, Vikki. "On the Critique of Secular Ethics: An Essay with Flannery O'Connor and Hannah Arendt." *Theory, Culture, & Society* 22, no. 2 (2005): 1–27.

Boff, Clodovis. "Epistemology and Method of the Theology of Liberation." *Mysterium Liberationis: Fundamental Concepts of Liberation Theology*, edited by Ignacio Ellacuría and Jon Sobrino, 57–85. Maryknoll, NY: Orbis Books, 1993.

Edmonson, Henry T. *Return to Good and Evil: Flannery O'Connor's Response to Nihilism*. Lexington: University Press of Kentucky, 2002.

Eggenschwiler, David. *The Christian Humanism of Flannery O'Connor*. Detroit, MI: Wayne State University Press, 1972.

Gentry, Marshall Bruce. *Flannery O'Connor's Religion of the Grotesque*. Jackson: University Press of Mississippi, 1986.

hooks, bell. *Teaching to Transgress: Education as the Practice of Freedom*. New York: Routledge, 1994.

Kessler, Edward. *Flannery O'Connor and the Language of Apocalypse*. Princeton, NJ: Princeton University Press, 1986.

Martin, Carter W. *The True Country: Themes in the Fiction of Flannery O'Connor*. Nashville: Vanderbilt University Press, 1968.

McDermott, John. "Blameless Versus Blameful Corruption in Flannery O'Connor's 'The Comforts of Home.'" *Notes on Contemporary Literature* 35, no. 5 (2005): 6–7.

O'Connor, Flannery. Introduction. *The Memoir of Mary Ann*, by the Dominican Nuns of Our Lady of Perpetual Help Home. New York: Farrar, Straus and Giroux, 1961. 3–23.

O'Connor, Flannery. *The Complete Stories of Flannery O'Connor*. New York: Farrar, Straus and Giroux, 1971.

O'Connor, Flannery. *The Habit of Being*. Edited by Sally Fitzgerald. New York: Farrar, Straus and Giroux, 1979.

Prenatt, Diane. "Simulation and the Authentic Self: Issues of Identity in Works by Flannery O'Connor and Mary Gordon." *Flannery O'Connor Review* 3 (2005): 39–48.

Ragen, Brian Abel. "Daredevil Charity: Love and Family in O'Connor's 'The Comforts of Home.'" *Northeast Regional Meeting of the Conference on Christianity and Literature* edited by Joan F. Hallisey and Mary-Anne Vetterling, 102–7. Weston, MA: Regis College, 1996. *ProQuest*, 15 October 2013.

"Redemption, 1a." *OED Online*. September 2009. Oxford University Press. Accessed 4 December 2013.

"Redemption, 5a." *OED Online*. September 2009. Oxford University Press. Web. 4 December 2013.

Srigley, Susan. "Penance and Love in *Wise Blood*: Seeing Redemption?" *Flannery O'Connor Review* 7 (2009): 94.

Taylor, Charles. *A Secular Age*. Cambridge, MA: Belknap Press of Harvard University Press, 2007.

Vogel, Steven. "What Is the 'Philosophy of Praxis?'" In *Critical Theory and the Thought of Andrew Feenberg*, edited by Darrell P. Arnold and Andreas Michel, 17–45. New York: Palgrave Macmillan, 2017.

Wilson, James. "Luis Bunel, Flannery O'Connor, and the Failure of Charity." *Minnesota Review* 5 (1973): 158–62.

Wilson, Natalie. "Misfit Bodies and Errant Gender: The Corporeal Feminism of Flannery O'Connor." In *On the Subject of the Feminist Business*, edited by Teresa Caruso, 94–119. New York: Peter Lang, 2004.

"The Words to Say It":
Using Flannery O'Connor to Reconsider Lacan

DOREEN FOWLER

Flannery O'Connor is a mysterious writer. She never tired of saying that the express goal of her fiction is to render "the mystery of man's encounter with God" (*Mystery* 161), and she acknowledged that when the writer "finishes there [is] always left over that sense of Mystery which cannot be accounted for" (*Mystery* 153). In this essay, I propose to read O'Connor's fiction together with Lacanian theory and to argue that Lacan and O'Connor are engaged in parallel projects—to explore the mystery of human existence—and, while they use different methods, one, psychological, the other, theological, for both, language is the obstacle to be overcome in the pursuit of Mystery. Whereas other scholars who have applied Lacan to O'Connor have overlooked religious meanings, my project is to show that Lacan's theory of language can help us to penetrate more deeply the elusive mystery that O'Connor's fiction is always tracking.[1] My project, then, is an intertextual reading that aims to read reciprocally; that is, I read O'Connor through Lacan and Lacan through O'Connor.

Flannery O'Connor of course predates Lacan, whose works were not translated into English until after her death. But, while O'Connor had no direct knowledge of Lacan, her fictions nonetheless anticipate Lacanian theory, because, as Freud frequently observed, poets often discover what philosophers and others come to theorize about many years later.[2] The subject of both Lacan's theory and O'Connor's remarkable fiction is a search for transcendental meaning or an ultimate authority, and the works of both thinkers examine the same dilemma: that language, which is a closed system, can never know a meaning that lies outside of the system.

Lacan's theory introduces us to a post-structural world, where, according to Lacan, the word takes precedence over the thing. To designate this power relationship, Lacan uses the formula S/s, with the uppercase S standing for the signifier, the name by which we know a person, place, or thing, and the lower-case *s* representing what Lacan calls the signified, the actual person, place, or thing. According to Lacan, the signifier assigns a meaning to the signified, but there is no real relation between the assigned identity and the subject (lower-case s) it identifies; rather, the cultural meaning assigned is arbitrary. Despite this arbitrary, baseless relation between the name and the thing, Lacan insists that the word sign or signifier exerts a terrible power over the signified. He goes so far as to say that "the world of words . . . creates the world of things" (*Écrits* [Norton] 66) and that "the subject disappears under the being of the signifier" (*Écrits* [Seuil] 709).

In this essay, I argue that O'Connor's works explore and expose the subject-subverting power of the cultural signifier (the arbitrary assigned meaning) over the signified (the actual thing in the world); and that her fiction both anticipates and revises Lacan's theory. "Judgment Day," for example, reveals the power of the signifier to dominate and even create in its image the subject of signification; and "A Late Encounter with the Enemy" exposes the signifier as an empty, artificial social construction, without basis or foundation; even as other O'Connor stories push beyond Lacanian theory to make the case that, in contrast to culture's free-floating signifiers, which only point to other signifiers in an endless chain of signification, material existence in the world is grounded in what Lacan calls the Real, that which exists outside of symbolization and the cultural order. For Flannery O'Connor, the Lacanian Real is our participation in the Divine Life, and it is accessed through the body in the world.

O'Connor's late story, "Judgment Day," reads like a textbook illustration of the Lacanian theory that we exist as creatures in a realm of symbols where the name assigned to a material entity subordinates the entity named. For Lacan, the importance of language cannot be overstated. Lacanian interpreter James Mellard explains the power of language: "while Lacan—and we after him—may posit a primal real apart from words or signs or even perception itself, there is for Lacan another real, a symbolic real that comes to have priority over the first because of its being available to apprehension by the subject. That apprehension occurs only through signs and symbols" (167). What Mellard means is that we locate meanings and we locate ourselves as subjects through language, but words do not designate meanings already existing; rather, they arbitrarily assign a meaning to what was unknown to us before the advent of the sign. Jane Gallop describes the subject as trapped in language: "There is no place for a 'subject,' no place to be human, to make sense outside of signification" (168).

In "Judgment Day," a man of color finds himself caught in the catch-22 of language theory: he must choose between incomprehension or culture's fictional, unstable, foundationless meanings. The choice appears in a flashback that is narrated through white eyes—the eyes of an old feeble white man whose name, Tanner, associates him with a tan skin color that suggests the instability of a white identity. Tanner recalls an occasion some thirty years earlier when he was the boss of a crew of African American men working for a sawmill and a dark-skinned giant of a man starts hanging around the edge of the sawmill, watching and sleeping in full view of the working men. After the strange man loafs about for a second day, modeling insubordination, Tanner's crew quits working, and he needs to find a way to assert his social status as the white boss. Given that the crew Tanner "is working" is "in the middle of a pine forest fifteen miles from nowhere" (*CS* 536), he has no cultural back-up to help him assert white authority. Far from civilization's centers of power that enforce the dominant cultural order, Tanner is "one yellow-faced, scrawny white man with shaky hands," trying to subordinate to his will six men of color and a giant "twice his own size" (537). In other words, in a natural state, Tanner has no real, material power over these men, so he turns to the power of signification, that is, the power of the symbol to assign a name that identifies the subject named.

It is important to note that the insubordinate man is unnamed and unknown: "None of them knew who he was" (537). Another telling detail is the description of the stranger's eyes, which are "bloodshot," "muddy," and "liquor-swollen" (538). These descriptors point to the stranger's inability to apprehend or identify himself and the world about him. Tanner's seemingly instinctive response to the stranger's clouded vision is formulated as a parable or allegory that invites a symbolic reading. Tanner picks up a piece of bark and whittles a toy pair of spectacles, which he then hands to the stranger, and says: "You can't see so good, can you, boy?" … "Put these on," … "I hate to see anybody can't see good" (538). When the African American man puts on the carved spectacles, Tanner asks him: "What you see through those glasses?" and the man answers: "See the man make theseyer glasses." To which, Tanner responds, "Is he white or black?" and the stranger responds, "as if only at that moment was his vision sufficiently improved to detect it, 'Yessuh, he white'" (539). Clearly, O'Connor means us to read the fake spectacles symbolically. The whittled wooden frames symbolize culture's frames, the white-dominant social order's way of making sense of a world that eludes us. Like the toy pair of spectacles, which are a mere representation of real eyewear, words are only representations of the real thing, and O'Connor's parable points out that culture's meanings are just as fake as the pretend spectacles. But even though culture's meanings are arbitrary, changing, and foundationless, they nevertheless provide the man with blurred vision with a way to identify himself and others in the world. Because the Tanner-made spectacles represent a vision of the world devised by the dominant white culture, the price of cultural intelligibility for this man of African heritage is high. Accepting the

Tanner-constructed spectacles symbolizes submitting to a white-constructed system of hierarchical meanings that privileges white over black. We see his acceptance registered when he looks through the Tanner-made spectacles and acknowledges that Tanner is white. Once the man identifies Tanner as white, Tanner is quick to remind him of the white-dominant culture's assigned meaning for whiteness: "Well, you treat him like he was white" (539). It is also significant that after the unnamed man accepts Tanner's whittled spectacles, he identifies himself as Coleman, a name that signifies his black identity in a white-dominant culture. And, from the time that he labels "the yellow-faced" (537) Tanner as white and himself as Coleman, that is, a coal-dark man, Coleman becomes, as Tanner puts it, "[his] nigger" (535).[3]

As if to indicate that Coleman's subordination to the rule of the signifier is not an isolated incident but representative, O'Connor includes in "Judgment Day" yet another example of the power of the signifier to determine the identity of the subject. This second illustration of the word sign's preeminence takes place in the time present, thirty years after the subjection of Coleman, and Tanner is an old man who has been reduced to living with his daughter in a tenement in New York City. The old man, who longs for his home in the South and thinks New York is "no place for a sane man" (541), is immensely cheered when a new neighbor—an African American man—moves into the apartment next door. Tanner is certain the man of color "would like to talk to someone who understood him" (543).

Soon thereafter it becomes evident that, when Tanner describes himself as "someone who understood" a man of color, he means that he, a white southerner, knows the identity of black men, and can tell the man who he is; in Lacanian terms, he can assert the power of the signifier. When Tanner meets the African American on the stairs, he attempts to define the man in terms of white racial stereotypes about people of color. Tanner calls the man "Preacher"; identifies him as from south Alabama; and is certain that the black man knows some ponds where they can fish together.

What is most telling about Tanner's representations is that the young black man, who is a well-dressed and well-spoken New Yorker, cannot simply shrug them off. Rather, O'Connor is at pains to show that the old southerner's attributions have the power to diminish the New Yorker, just as, some thirty years earlier, Tanner diminished Coleman. Throughout the scene on the stairs, the New Yorker acts like a man who feels threatened. His voice, as he tries to counter Tanner's vision of him, is "high and piercing and weak" (545); under Tanner's gaze, "some unfathomable dead-cold rage seemed to stiffen and shrink him" (544); and finally he runs from the old white man "as if a swarm of bees had suddenly come down on him out of nowhere" (545). When Tanner ambushes the black man on the stairs a second time, again calling him "Preacher," the imagery of diminishment culminates with a reference to the black man's "crotch" that points to the threat of emasculation: "a tremor racked him from his head to his crotch" (545). The old white man, with his false racial stereotype, threatens to unman the black man. Significantly, in trying to refute the identity Tanner imputes to him, the New Yorker asserts a self-identification. He says, "I'm not no preacher. I'm an actor" (545). The man's way of identifying himself—as an actor—is the way Lacan characterizes all identity; that is, for Lacan, we are all actors, acting roles scripted for us by culture. Every subject, Lacan writes, "is inserted into a symbolic order that pre-exists the infantile subject and in an accordance with which he will have to structure himself" (*Écrits* [Norton] 234). What Lacan means is that we exist as creatures in language who must "structure" ourselves in accordance with culture's preexisting definitions in much the same way that an actor loses herself in the role she is given to play. Tanner is profoundly threatening to the actor because the white man has cast him as the subordinate black man in the dominant culture's drama of white supremacy. It is a measure of how menacing Tanner's racist vision is to the actor's sense of self that the actor twice pulls down Tanner's wool hat over the white man's eyes as if to guard himself from the white's defining gaze.

In "Judgment Day," we see illustrated the Lacanian tenet that "the world of words . . . creates the world of things" (*Écrits* [Norton] 65); but Lacan's theory of language also holds that, while a culture's representations have the power to transform and even determine the subject named, nonetheless a culture's signifiers are mere unstable, fabricated, arbitrary representations or interpretations. As Terry Eagleton explains, "there is no harmonious one-to-one set of correspondences between the level of the signifiers and the level of the signifieds in language" (111). Most importantly, there is no ultimate authority that guarantees a culture's assigned meanings; rather, signifiers only point to other signifiers in an endless chain of signification. We look to what Lacan variously calls the Other, the phallus, or the paternal signifier to secure culture's assigned meanings, but Lacan writes that "there is no Other of the Other" (*Écrits* [Norton] 311). In a gloss on Shakespeare's *Hamlet*, he expresses the same idea in less obscure language. He writes that when Hamlet says, "'The king is a thing—Of nothing,' we should replace the word *king* with the word *phallus*" ("Desire" 52). What Lacan means is that there is no fixed or transcendental meaning, "nothing," that stands outside the chain of signifiers and authorizes it. Jacqueline Rose sums up the status of the transcendental signifier this way: "the subject has to recognize that there is . . . lack in the place of the Other, that there is no ultimate certainty or truth, and that the status of the phallus is a fraud" (40).[4]

O'Connor's story, "A Late Encounter with the Enemy" exposes the fraudulence of empty signifiers. Whereas "Judgment Day" (1964) is a very late story, possibly the last story O'Connor wrote before her death, "A Late Encounter with the Enemy" is an early story, written in 1953. "A Late Encounter with the Enemy" is usually read as a scathing critique of southern romanticization of the heroic "Lost Cause," but I propose that the story's larger purpose is to expose the lack of any underpinnings to authenticate a culture's assigned meanings. The story is about southerners' celebrations of their Confederate past, and the exhibit A at these celebrations is General Sash. At a premiere in Atlanta of a film about the glorious Lost Cause, for example, General Sash is displayed as the touchstone, the reality behind southern history. His presence, as someone who actually fought and bled in the Civil War, is supposed to be the basis to legitimize the meanings in the fictional film. In other words, Sash's role is very much like the role of a transcendental or fixed signifier in Lacanian theory. Just as Sash is supposed to be a real vestige of a heroic southern past that gives credence to all the Hollywood artifice, so also a transcendental signifier or the phallus would be the guarantor of a culture's hierarchal meanings; and just as the concept of a supreme signifier is fraudulent, so also General Sash is a sham.[5]

Sash's fraudulence is the central meaning of the story. A 104-year-old veteran of the Civil War, dead from the waist down, "as frail as a dried spider" (140), he is displayed in his wheelchair at the local museum on Confederate Memorial Day and at events like the Hollywood premiere. Sash, as his name suggests, is all outward show. He loves to sit on a stage and be viewed in his full-dress general's uniform, with his sword across his lap. The problem is that Sash was not a general in the war—"he didn't remember what he had been; in fact, he didn't remember the war at all" (135)—and the uniform and the sword, the signifiers of his war experience, are not authentic; rather, they were given to him to wear at the Hollywood premiere. In other words, Sash, who is displayed as the token or foundation that supports Hollywood's illusions, is himself an artificial production of Hollywood. The circularity of this authentication—that Sash is a product of the Hollywood artifice that he is supposed to authenticate—perfectly mirrors the Lacanian tenet that there is no signifier that is not an artificial human construct.

The lack of any ultimate authority to authorize man-made constructions seems also to be the message of the central event of the story, the college graduation of the old man's sixty-two-year-old granddaughter, Sally Poker Sash, who ardently desires to display her grandfather at her graduation at the state teacher's college. She wants to receive her diploma with Sash in his wheelchair behind her on the stage: "She wanted the General at her graduation because she wanted to show what she stood for, or as, she said, 'what all was behind her'" (135). Once again this allusion ties Sash to the transcendental signifier: like the fixed signifier, which supposedly backs up our meanings, Sash's granddaughter feels that her relationship to the war veteran imbues her with status. But this supposed authorization is undercut by a dream Sally Poker

Sash has. One night she dreams that she is standing on the platform with her grandfather in his wheelchair on the stage behind her and in her dream "she screamed, 'See him! See him!' And turned her head and found him sitting in his wheel chair behind her with a terrible expression on his face and with all his clothes off except the general's hat" (135). The dream suggests the false status of the General and likewise the paternal signifier: the uniform, the signifier of the General's authority, is our own fabrication, and what lies behind the artificial construct is no supreme authority, but material existence in the world; in the General's case, what is behind the uniform is the nearly dead body of a very old man.

As the story moves toward its climax, the old man, in his uniform with his sword across his lap, is positioned on the stage, while the procession of graduates in black robes files by. At this point in the narrative, the story focuses on words. As one commencement speaker after another orates, Sash feels as if "the slow black music" has put a hole in his head, and the hole is "letting the words he heard into the dark places of his brain. He heard the words, Chickamauga, Shiloh, Johnston, Lee, and he knew he was inspiring all these words that meant nothing to him" (142). With this focus on words, the text seems to point again to the falseness of the status of a transcendental or phallic signifier. Like the phallic signifier, which, according to Lacan, "is bound to nothing: it always slips through your fingers" ("Desire" 52), Sash is set up to validate their words, but instead the words "meant nothing to him."

The climax of the story seems to literalize Lacan's pronouncement that "the phallus is a ghost" ("Desire" 50). At the end of "A Late Encounter with the Enemy," General Sash dies while on stage during the graduation ceremony. His death goes unnoticed by all, including Sally Poker Sash, who, as she proudly crosses the stage to accept her diploma, steals a glance at her grandfather. Seeing "him sitting fixed and fierce, his eyes wide open . . . , she turn[s] her head forward again and held it a perceptible degree higher and received her scroll" (144). We recall that she had dreamed about this moment as an opportunity to show "what she stood for, or as she said, 'what all was behind her,' and not behind them" (135). What is literally "behind" her as she receives her diploma is a corpse. In other words, the validation she seeks eludes her, and, like the dead General seated on stage in his fake uniform, so also the supreme signifier is just another dead and empty symbol, or, in Lacan's words, "a ghost."

Thus far in this essay, I have argued that we find exemplified in O'Connor's fiction Lacan's theory of language. I want to propose now that O'Connor pushes beyond Lacanian theory to offer her own vision of what Lacan calls the Real. For Lacan, the Real always eludes us, because we exist as creatures of the symbolic order (the order of language and culture), and the Real exists outside of this register. Lacanian commentator Madan Sarap writes that the

Real "is the domain that subsists outside symbolization. It is what is outside the subject" (109). What is important about the Real is that it posits the possibility of meaning outside of the arbitrary cultural designations of the symbolic order. The Real may be the transcendental meaning that we desire, but it is not to be confused with the phallus, which, it must be remembered, is a symbol, a construct of the symbolic order. For Lacan, as creatures trapped in our signing system, we can never know the Real; it is always a mystery. But, for Flannery O'Connor, the mystery that lies beyond human apprehension is the Divine Life, and her fiction hints that we access it, not through culture's system of hierarchical meanings, but through the body in the world.

In O'Connor's stories, bodies matter. Repeatedly in her fiction, the same paradigm plays out: her weak and erring characters achieve a moment of grace through bodily contact. In "Everything That Rises Must Converge," Julian experiences the possibility for grace when the African American woman on the bus strikes his mother with her purse; in "Revelation," Mrs. Turpin is touched by grace when the aptly named Mary Grace strikes her with a book; and in "A Good Man Is Hard to Find," the grandmother feels God's grace when she reaches out and touches the Misfit. Even O'Connor's definition of grace evokes the body. She writes that grace is made possible by a "gesture which somehow made contact with [the] mystery" of the Divine Life (*Mystery* 111). Her words here, "gesture" and "contact," suggest that it is through the physical that we connect with the spiritual, and, more often than not in O'Connor's fiction, the gesture that makes contact with grace is violent. When asked about her use of violence, O'Connor steadfastly averred that violent bodily contact was a pathway to grace: "in my own stories I have found that violence is strangely capable of returning my characters to reality and preparing them to accept their moment of grace. Their heads are so hard that almost nothing else will do the work" (*Mystery* 112). The operative word here is "strangely." How, we ask, does bodily violence prepare us for grace? O'Connor seems to point to the answer when she writes that violence "return[s] [us] to reality." As I understand O'Connor's words, she means that violence breaks through the artifice and illusion of symbolization and exposes what underlies human constructs—corporeal existence. She seems to allude again to this effect of violence when she writes: "It is the extreme situation that best reveals what we are essentially" (*Mystery* 113). In other words, a near-death situation strips us of conceptualization and opens us up to what is "essential." In what follows, I make the case that, in O'Connor's story, "Revelation," bodily injury enables a moment of grace by shattering Ruby Turpin's socially constructed self and making her aware of what she is "essentially."

"Revelation" begins with a scene that identifies Ruby Turpin as a creature of the symbolic order. The story opens in a doctor's waiting room, where Ruby is passing the time by assigning the other patients a position in a class and racial hierarchy. Categorizing people, we are told, is a frequent occupation of hers. She even puts herself to sleep at nights "naming the classes of people": "On the bottom of the heap were most colored people, ... next to them—not above, just away from—were white trash; then above them were the home-owners, and above them the home-and-land owners, to which she and Claud belonged" (491). Ruby is quite certain of her secure place in the social order, and the work of the story is to unsettle Ruby's smug satisfaction with herself and with a social caste system.

The deconstruction of the symbolic order's artificial constructs begins even as Ruby names the categories of people at night, because real existence has a way of blurring her neat social divisions. No sooner does Ruby line up her tidy, exclusive classifications than "the complexity of it would begin to bear in on her, for some of the people with a lot of money were common and ought to be below she and Claud and some of the people who had good blood had lost their money and had to rent and then there were colored people who owned their homes and land as well" (491). But such subtle indications that her sense of a social order is a house of cards are lost on Ruby, and it takes bodily injury to shake up her secure sense of who she is within a cultural hierarchy. Sig-nificantly, the bodily harm is perpetrated by a character named Mary Grace, a patient in the waiting room, who fumes visibly as she listens to Ruby extol herself and condescend to those whom she deems inferior. And when Ruby's self-congratulation culminates in a loud shout-out to Jesus—"When I think who all I could have been besides myself, ... I just feel like shouting, Thank you, Jesus" (499)—Mary Grace responds violently: she hurls a thick book, suggestively titled *Human Development*, and then herself at Ruby. After the attack, as Mary Grace lies subdued on the floor, Ruby senses "that the girl did know her, knew her in some intense and personal way, beyond time and place and condition," that is, outside of the social order; and she looks to the girl for a "revelation." The revelation that follows is an identification of Mrs. Turpin with a wart hog: "Go back to hell where you came from, you old wart hog" (500). This identification, I think, is a key to understanding what O'Connor means when she says that violence has the potential to reveal to us "what we are essentially."

Disturbed by Mary Grace's message to her, later that day as the sun is set-ting, Ruby marches down to the pig parlor to demand answers from heaven. Even as she addresses God, Ruby clings to culture's signifiers: "'Go on,' she yelled, 'call me a hog! Call me a hog again. From hell. Call me a wart hog from hell. Put that bottom rail on top. There'll still be a top and bottom!'" (507). Ruby is arguing the Lacanian position that signifiers signify; that is, culture's meanings, albeit unstable and foundationless, are the only mean-ings we, as creatures of the symbolic order, have. Ruby is allowed to make the Lacanian case, but, at this point in the narrative, O'Connor uses a series of images of a fiery red sun to advance beyond Lacan and postulate a theological position, namely, that as long as we are locked into our own system of fabricated meanings we can never access the Real, which, for O'Connor, is our participation in the Divine Life. The first of these images notes that "in the deepening light everything was taking on a mysterious hue" (507). In O'Connor's lexicon, the word "mysterious" is usually code for Divine existence. Fiery images are foregrounded again—"the color of everything, field and crimson sky, burned for a moment with a transparent intensity"—as Ruby shakes her fist at heaven and "roar[s]": "Who do you think you are?" When her question carries over the field and the echo "returned to her clearly like an answer from beyond the wood" (508), O'Connor's meaning is clear—God is asking Ruby to question and even surrender her notion of a socially constructed self. This message seems to profoundly affect Ruby Turpin, who stares into the pig pen at the hogs while "a red glow suffused them" and "they appeared to pant with a secret life" (508). The hogs, O'Connor's imagery suggests, are a clue to understanding the mystery of the Divine Life: Ruby stares at them "as if at the heart of mystery," and she seems to be "absorbing some abysmal life-giving knowledge" (508).

When asked about the mystery of grace, O'Connor always said that grace is earned "at considerable cost" (*Mystery* 112). In my reading, the "abysmal life-giving knowledge" that Ruby intuits as the story ends is the "considerable cost" of grace. And the price Ruby has to pay is pictured in the vision she sees as she lifts her head from the pig pen to the sky where the setting sun has left "a purple streak in the sky" that looks like "a vast swinging bridge extending upward from the earth through a field of living fire" (508). Upon this swinging bridge Ruby sees "a vast horde of souls . . . rumbling toward heaven":

> There were whole companies of white-trash, clean for the first time in their lives, and bands of black niggers in white robes, and battalions of freaks and lunatics shouting and clapping and leaping like frogs. And bringing up at the end of the procession was a tribe of people whom she recognized at once as those who, like herself and Claud, had always had a little of everything and the God-given wit to use it right. She leaned forward to observe them closer. They were marching behind the others with great dignity, accountable as they had always been for good order and common sense and respectable behavior. They alone were on key. Yet she could see by their shocked and altered faces that even their virtues were being burned away. (508)

The previous images of burning light have moved inexorably to this vision of souls who are able to cross the "bridge" between the human and the Divine only by passing through "a field of living fire." What exactly is being burned away? The answer lies, I think, in a parallel O'Connor draws here.

This concluding image of a procession of souls marching to heaven bookends with Ruby's earlier classification of people—"white trash," "colored people," and "respectable" people like her and Claud—as the story opens. In that earlier image, Ruby was doing the work of the symbolic order, assigning socially constructed identities to people. In this image, that work is undone. Even the characteristics Ruby admires in herself and others like her—"dignity," "good order," "common sense," and "respectable behavior"—are "being burned away." In other words, all cultural markers are being incinerated, returning these souls to a pre-cultural, natural state, allied to the hogs and the chirping crickets. And, when O'Connor writes in the last sentence of the story that what Ruby hears as the "invisible cricket chorus" strikes up are "the voices of the souls climbing upward into the starry field shouting hallelujah," O'Connor points yet again to a natural, unacculturated state as the necessary condition to bridge the gap between the human and the Divine.[6]

Ultimately, I am arguing that the experience of what Lacan calls the Trauma of the Real prepares O'Connor's characters for an encounter with the Divine Life. According to Lacan, the Trauma of the Real is the realization that the meanings by which we identify ourselves and the world around us are merely the artificial fabrications of society, supported by nothing. It is the experience of meaninglessness, analogous to what Julia Kristeva calls abjection: the "place where meaning collapses" at "the edge of non-existence" (2). The Trauma of the Real can perhaps best be described as seeing through to nothing, and not coincidentally, I think, in "Good Country People," Joy/Hulga describes herself to Manley Pointer as "one of those people who see *through* to nothing" (287). The story reveals that Joy/Hulga is not unillusioned; that, much as she thinks she rejects cultural ideologies, she herself is also culturally made; but, by the story's end, when the Bible salesman, whom she thought was so simple and innocent, robs her of her eye glasses and her prosthetic leg and abandons her in a barn loft, Joy/Hulga *is* stripped of all illusions. When Manley Pointer steals her artificial leg and her corrective lenses (reminiscent of the fake spectacles Tanner carves for Coleman), at a literal level, he takes away her cultural crutches that enable her to function in the world. These artificial aids enable her just as a culture's representations construct for us a meaningful world. Without her corrective lenses, a symbol for cultural lenses, and her artificial leg, Joy/Hulga is reduced to what she is "essentially": she is lost and helpless in a world she cannot decipher; but, the ending of the story suggests that it is only in this culturally unmade state that God's grace can touch her. In the last paragraphs of the story, as the Bible salesman retreats, Joy/Hulga blindly looks out from the loft and sees a "blue figure struggling successfully over the green speckled lake" (291). What she mis-sees is of course Manley walking across the field, but the girl's lack of visual acuity carries a symbolic meaning: the phony Bible salesman seems to be walking on water. In my reading, this puzzling use of Christ imagery for this fetishist is warranted because Manley has been the instrument of her salvation. Earlier in the story Joy/Hulga had said that "some of us have taken off our blindfolds and see that there's nothing to see. It's a kind of salvation" (288). Her statement proves prophetic. Manley saves her by taking off her blindfolds and opening her eyes to nothingness.

From a Lacanian point of view, what O'Connor posits as the necessary precondition for grace is nothing short of the annihilation of subjectivity. While Lacan admits that the structures of the symbolic order dominate us, maim us, and alienate us, he also maintains that we exist as speaking subjects only within symbolization. "Man speaks," he writes, "but it is because the symbol made him man" (*Écrits* [Norton] 65). Translated, Lacan means that there is no place to be human outside of symbolization. At the same time, however, Lacan admits that the Real exists outside of the register of the symbolic. For that reason, Lacan calls the Real "unspeakable," "impossible" (Mellard 160), and always beyond our apprehension. To an extent, O'Connor agrees with Lacan; her fiction also suggests that we can never approach the Real as a speaking subject within the cultural order. But, in O'Connor's theological vision, the Real is the Divine Life, and to participate in it, we must surrender to a kind of death of the socially constructed ego and experience what we are "essentially," a condition prior to alienation and socialization, a terrifying, primal, boundaryless existence "beyond time and place and condition." This, I think, is what O'Connor refers to when she says that grace is earned at "considerable cost" (*Mystery* 112), and the cost is indeed high. For O'Connor, we can "make contact with mystery" (*Mystery* 111) only when "we see that there is nothing to see" (288).

NOTES

1. Three published essays interpret Flannery O'Connor's fiction though a Lacanian lens. James Mellard reads "A View of the Woods" through Lacan's Law of the Father; André Bleikasten uses Lacan's notion of mirror stage narcissism to interpret Parker's tattoos in "Parker's Back"; and David Knauer's objective is to challenge Frederick Crews's assertion that O'Connor's works are "intractable" to post-structural approaches.

2. O'Connor was conversant with Freudian theory, and Lacan rewrites Freud in terms of language theory that O'Connor, who was widely read, might well have knowledge of. While O'Connor was dismissive of Freudian readings of her work, her dismissal was qualified. She writes: "As to Sigmund, I am against him tooth and toenail but I am crafty: never deny, seldom confirm, always distinguish. Within his limitations I am ready to admit certain uses for him" (*Habit* 110).

3. Suzanne Paulson notes that "the glasses force Coleman to 'see' and 'accept' the master-servant relationship" (74). I discuss the significance of the Tanner-made spectacles in an earlier article, "Writing and Rewriting Race: Flannery O'Connor's 'The Geranium' and 'Judgment Day,'" that compares and contrasts "The Geranium" with "Judgment Day" to show the evolution of O'Connor's representation of race.

4. While post-structuralist theory builds on Lacanian theory, Lacan cannot be read as strictly a post-structuralist. Lacan and post-structuralists agree that there is no one-to-one correspondence between the signified and the signifier. According to Lacan, the "subject disappears under the being of the signifier," and, for post-structuralists, there is no language that "would function as a purely transparent medium for the designation of a pre-given reality" (Zizek 36). However, as Zizek points out in his essay, "Why Lacan Is Not a Post-structuralist," whereas post-structuralists hold that language is always saying something other than what it means to say and there is no authority that guarantees the meanings of our words, Lacan maintains that the phallus is the signifier of lack; that is, it stands for what is not there, but nonetheless Lacan equivocates about the authority of the transcendental signifier. It is Jacqueline Rose who calls the phallus a fraud. As my essay notes, Lacan often suggests that the phallus is fraudulent, but he also sometimes seems to complicate this position, saying of the phallus, for example, "you are so powerful, but for all that, you are impotent" (Zizek 35). In her story, "The Late Encounter with the Enemy," O'Connor seems to take a more Derridean position about the false status of a transcendental or phallic signifier, but in my essay I use Lacan rather than Derrida to illustrate post-structuralist meanings in O'Connor largely because Lacan's concept of the Real, for which there is no equivalent in Derridean theory, corresponds to O'Connor's notion of the mystery of our participation in Divine Life.

5. In his reading of "A Late Encounter with the Enemy," David J. Knauer makes the case that the General represents the Lacanian phallus; however, his Lacanian reading, unlike mine, does not focus on the story's exposure of the phallus or Symbolic Father as fraudulent. Rather he writes about the General as representing an Oedipal threat that Sally Poker Sash's graduation "neutralizes" (6).

6. John Duvall, Ralph C. Wood, and Dan Wood have noted that Mrs. Turpin insists on a class and racial hierarchy. In Ralph Wood's reading, the fact that "she and Claud are at the rear of the train is meant as a positive spur to a new kind of excellence" (115). Dan Wood finds that her final vision "alludes to the ethical priority of the Other over the Same" (43). Duvall argues that stories like O'Connor's "Revelation" "create ruptures in culture's normative structures of identity" (xv), and expose racial categories as a social performance. In "Aligning the Psychological with the Theological: The Black Double in Flannery O'Connor's Fiction," I briefly discuss "Revelation." I argue that all of Ruby Turpin's attempts to establish exclusive race and class categories deconstruct in the text and that the appearance of the black double is another figure for the blurring of culture's divisions.

WORKS CITED

Bleikasten, André. "Writing on the Flesh: Tattoos and Taboos in 'Parker's Back.'" *Southern Literary Journal* 14, no. 2 (Spring 1982): 8–18.

Duvall, John N. *Race and White Identity in Southern Fiction: From Faulkner to Morrison.* New York: Palgrave Macmillan, 2008.

Eagleton, Terry. *Literary Theory: An Introduction.* 2nd ed. Minneapolis: University of Minnesota Press, 1996.

Fowler, Doreen. "Aligning the Psychological with the Theological: The Black Double in Flannery O'Connor's Fiction." *Flannery O'Connor Review* 13 (2015): 78–89.

Fowler, Doreen. "Writing and Rewriting Race: Flannery O'Connor's 'The Geranium' and 'Judgment Day.'" *Flannery O'Connor Review* 2 (2003–2004): 31–39.

Gallop, Jane. *The Daughter's Seduction: Feminism and Psychoanalysis.* Ithaca, NY: Cornell University Press, 1985.

The Holy Bible: New International Version. Grand Rapids, MI: Zondervan, 1984.

Knauer, David J. "A Late Encounter with Poststructuralism." *Mississippi Quarterly* 48, no. 2 (Spring 1995): 277–90.

Lacan, Jacques. "Desire and the Interpretation of Desire in *Hamlet*." Translated by James Hulbert. *Yale French Studies* 55–56 (1977): 11–52.

Lacan, Jacques. *Écrits*. Paris: Seuil, 1966.

Lacan, Jacques. *Écrits: A Selection*. Translated by Alan Sheridan. New York: Norton, 1977.

Mellard, James M. "Flannery O'Connor's *Others*: Freud, Lacan, and the Unconscious." *American Literature* 61, no. 4 (December 1989): 625–43.

Mellard, James M. *Using Lacan, Reading Fiction*. Champaign: University of Illinois Press, 1991.

O'Connor, Flannery. *The Complete Stories*. New York: Farrar, Straus and Giroux, 1971.

O'Connor, Flannery. *The Habit of Being*. New York: Farrar, Straus and Giroux, 1979.

O'Connor, Flannery. *Mystery and Manners: Occasional Prose*. Edited by Sally and Robert Fitzgerald. New York: Farrar, Straus and Giroux, 1969.

Paulson, Suzanne Morrow. *Flannery O'Connor: A Study of the Short Fiction*. Boston: Twayne, 1988.

Rose, Jacqueline. Introduction II to Jacques Lacan, *Feminine Sexuality*. Edited by Juliet Mitchell and Jacqueline Rose. Translated by Jacqueline Rose. New York: Norton, 1982.

Sarup, Madan. *Jacques Lacan*. Toronto: University of Toronto Press, 1992.

Wood, Dan. "Misfits, Anarchy, and the Absolute: Interpreting O'Connor through Levinasian Themes." *Literature and Theology* 29, no. 1 (2015): 33–46.

Wood, Ralph C. "Climbing into the Starry Field and Shouting Hallelujah: O'Connor's Vision of the World to Come." *Flannery O'Connor: Modern Critical Views*, edited by Harold Bloom. New York: Chelsea House Publishers, 1986.

Zizek, Slavoj. "Why Lacan Is Not a Post-structuralist." *Newsletter of the Freudian Field* 1, no. 2 (Fall 1987): 31–39.

PART 2

NEW CONTEXTS

Flannery O'Connor's Gothic Science Fiction

DOUG DAVIS

A woman dreams that the man she wants to marry is traveling thousands of years back in time to Bethlehem. A serial killer longs to traverse millennia to witness the miracles of Jesus Christ. A young boy lost in a city full of strange dark inhabitants learns that its massive sewer system leads all the way down to hell. A young man escapes the anonymity of the urban jungle by becoming a gorilla. A schoolteacher turns his head on and off with a switch. A mechanic abandons his wife to share a life with a car he has lovingly rebuilt. A farmer is dazzled by the mechanized future of dairy production. A woman stores her personality in her artificial leg. A farm owner hires a cyborg to work in her fields, eventually killing him with a runaway machine. A father tries to rebuild a human being, promising him bus rides to the moon. Stories like these have been told throughout the history of science fiction. Midcentury fans of the genre would expect to find such tales in an issue of *Astounding Science Fiction* or an episode of *The Twilight Zone*. Yet every one of them can be found in a story by Flannery O'Connor. From time travelers and astronauts to cyborgs and strangers in strange alien lands, Flannery O'Connor's stories are imbued with science fiction's ideas and imagery.

Boldly going where no reader of O'Connor has gone before, in this essay I show how O'Connor strategically deploys science fictional imagery and scenarios in her tales. Recognizing the science fiction in O'Connor's stories not only reveals a hitherto neglected element of her craft but also clarifies the author's relationship to history and modernity alike, foregrounding the struggle between the forces of the past and the agents of the future that drives many of her stories. O'Connor's characters fight and die over the shape of things to come in their modernizing South. This struggle plays out as a science-fictional contest in O'Connor's tales that pits the technosocial optimism of her era against the author's own gothic pessimism about American technoculture's eagerness to remake itself in the name of progress. The popular genre of science fiction is the only genre that regularly entertains both of these attitudes, and as such it gives O'Connor a vocabulary with which to dramatize the fraught progress of both her region and the nation in a way that is at once familiar and productively estranging. By deploying what science fiction scholar Robert Adams describes as a "gothic science fiction" style, O'Connor can realistically chronicle the social, technological, and scientific progress of her Cold War American Age while making her characters' blinkered faith in that kind of progress look monstrous. The science fiction references in her fiction shine a spotlight on the mortal dangers that await those who, on their hurried way to the future, fail to grant the endurance of old histories, folkways, and faiths.

This project is very much a part of an ongoing endeavor within the O'Connor studies community to explore the author's relation to American popular culture. Such scholars have uncovered some startling affinities between O'Connor's work and a range of popular texts from slapstick comedies (Saunders) to noir fiction (Brevda) to the films of Alfred Hitchcock (King). Jon Lance Bacon has discussed O'Connor's engagement with her cultural moment in no fewer than four studies, reading *Wise Blood* in dialogue with the "contemporary critique of consumerism" found in both the mainstream and Christian press in the 1950s ("Fondness" 33) and her entire body of work as expressive of the sentiments and imagery found in horror comics ("Gory Stories"), Jack Chick's doomsday pamphlets and end-time paperback novels ("Jesus Hits"), and the constellation of cultural narratives about invasion and identity that defined the Cold War for Americans (*Cold War Culture*).

If O'Connor made strategic use of the horror comics, crime novels, and Hollywood movies that were popular during her writing career, it simply makes sense to explore how she used the massively popular multimedia phenomenon of science fiction as well. As literary historian Edward James discusses in *Science Fiction in the 20th Century*, the period that comprises O'Connor's mature writing career was also a so-called golden age for science fiction in print and film alike. At the genre's peak of popularity in the 1950s, over forty magazines were dedicated to publishing works of science fiction (86) while Hollywood filled movie theaters with "creature features" about monsters "unleashed by science" (81). Given the growing visibility of the themes and iconography of science fiction in print and film over the course of her writing career, if O'Connor wanted to see what Americans thought the future would be, she wouldn't have far to look.

However, what she would find in the genre, from the covers of magazines and movie posters to the characters, creatures, and plots of the stories themselves, would be two very different attitudes toward the relations of science, technology, and society. As Edward James discusses, science fiction of this period championed science and rationality and dramatized how new and improved worlds could be built only by forsaking traditional ways of living:

> In most respects the two media [print and film] were worlds apart, the attitudes of the average Hollywood SF film being diametrically opposed to those which predominated in the written medium. On the whole, written SF liked to believe that humanity, through science and rationality and by abandoning old social conventions (or re-establishing an imagined golden age), could build a better world. (James 82)

Fabled editor John Campbell set the tone for golden-age print science fiction with his industry-leading magazine, *Astounding Science Fiction*. Campbell replaced the garish pulp covers of his predecessors with a new scientific style of magazine cover that celebrated the adventure of space exploration "somber in color, with slick modernistic machinery, plausible human beings, and sometimes with realistic astronomical paintings which illustrated the theme of the human conquest of the solar system rather than a particular story" (James 56) (Fig. 1). Within *Astounding*'s pages, stories by Isaac Asimov, Robert A. Heinlein, and Arthur C. Clarke dramatized the challenges of space exploration and social progress alike, introducing readers to a panoply of scientific discoveries and engineering marvels from computers to robots that promised to transform human civilization as it spread to the stars. Even cautionary tales about future wars and technological tyranny by *Astounding* authors such as Judith Merrill and Ray Bradbury sought to humanize scientific and technological advancements, treating disaster and dystopia not as failures of science, reason, or progress but as tragedies about flawed societies that misused their advanced sciences and technologies for war and oppression.

While science fiction literature at this time dramatized humanity's inevitable technosocial progress into the future, Hollywood often told a different, more grotesque kind of story akin to the gothic tale of terror, depicting scientists as coldly rational intellectuals meddling with forces best left alone and outer space as full of evil forces bent on humanity's destruction (James 82). Scientists cannot be trusted in creature features, and the advanced technology in these films is often a source of terror and destruction. *The Thing from Another World* (1951) is raised by a foolishly rational scientist; the great brains behind the nation's nuclear weapons program unwittingly create a monstrous colony of *Them!* (1954); and researchers in the arctic testing atomic bombs accidentally revive a prehistoric *Beast from 20,000 Fathoms* (1953). Even scientific exploration to other planets is a threat to humanity. Explorers to the planet Venus recklessly ferry a rampaging monster *Twenty Million Miles to Earth* (1957), and the rescue team sent to distant Altair IV in *Forbidden Planet* (1956) learns that technologically advanced alien planets should, indeed, stay forbidden. With a handful of

Fig. 1 Note the realistic tiny astronauts gamboling about
Phobos that give this scene a sublime sense of scale.

notable exceptions such as Robert A. Heinlein's own *Destination Moon* (1950),
which portrays a heroic first trip to the moon, Hollywood films of the 1950s
don't depict the peaceful conquest of space or successfully transformed high-
tech tomorrows. For midcentury Hollywood, the future is filled with frights
and space is a realm where mostly monsters dwell:

> the films preached that there were things that humanity should not dabble in,
> that the status quo should be defended against all attempts to change it, that
> emotion is more important than reason, and that the cold and essentially
> unwise scientist cannot be trusted. Written sf tended to think of the human
> species as being on the brink of a great new adventure on the frontier of outer
> space; Hollywood sf generally portrayed outer space as somewhere from which
> only evil could come. (James 82)

O'Connor reproduces these two contrasting science-fictional attitudes
throughout several of her stories, moving from the technosocial optimism
and imagery found in the paperback novels and digest magazines to the more
pessimistic attitudes and much more gothic themes and terrifying imagery
common to her era's creature features. A close reading of "The Lame Shall
Enter First," written in the early 1960s (Driggers and Dunn xxi), reveals the
extent to which O'Connor incorporates the optimistic and terrifying themes

and images found in both the print and Hollywood science fiction of her lifetime. O'Connor's narrative motion from technosocial optimism to gothic terror in this story turns the ideology of Cold War America against itself, casting the champions of the nation's most celebrated scientific and technological accomplishments as Frankensteinian monster-makers. The story's protagonist, Sheppard, is brimming with technosocial optimism and eager to leave old social conventions behind. Sheppard's name is a telling pun, evoking both America's first astronaut, Alan Shepard (Gooch 340), and his own self-proclaimed mission to shepherd young miscreants into modern, space-faring civilization. A firm believer in technological fixes to humanity's ills, Sheppard tries to turn the sinisterly devout Rufus Johnson into an enthusiastic inhabitant of the space age by taking him on imaginary adventures through both inner and outer space:

> He roamed from simple psychology and the dodges of the human mind to astronomy and the space capsules that were whirling around the earth faster than the speed of sound and would soon encircle the stars. Instinctively he concentrated on the stars. He wanted to give the boy something to reach for besides his neighbor's goods. He wanted to stretch his horizons. He wanted him to *see* the universe, to see that the darkest parts of it could be penetrated. (601, emphasis in original)

Of course, nothing will sway Rufus from his belief that "Satan . . . has me in his power" (600). The aptly named Rufus *refuses* to think like an inhabitant of a space capsule. Yet Sheppard keeps trying to (re)build Rufus into the spaceman he thinks he should be. He buys the boy a telescope and points it at the moon. "Some day you may go to the moon," he tells Rufus and his own indifferent son, Norton. "In ten years men will probably be making round trips there on schedule. Why you boys may be spacemen. Astronauts!" (611). Rufus remains unimpressed, so Sheppard then purchases a microscope. "If he couldn't impress the boy with immensity," he reasons, "he would try the infinitesimal" (617). Rufus is not impressed with the infinitesimal either. The promises of scientific exploration do not inspire him at all.

By introducing Rufus to telescopes and microscopes and attaching to those things the promises of great technosocial advancements to come, Sheppard is striving to produce an emotional response in the boy that science fiction scholars and fans have long identified as the genre's "sense of wonder" (James 103). Trying one last time to imbue a sense of wonder in Rufus about space travel, Sheppard frames spaceflight within the sublime expanse of deep geological time: "Man's going to the moon," he tells Rufus, "is very much like the first fish crawling out of the water onto land billions and billions of years ago. He didn't have an earth suit. He had to grow his adjustments inside. He developed lungs" (612–13). Man's traveling to the moon fills Sheppard with a sense of wonder about the future evolution of the human species.

Yet wonder can take two wildly different forms in science fiction, just as it does in O'Connor's story. While Sheppard feels awestruck when thinking about humanity's future in outer space, Rufus sees outer space as a place where only the dead dwell (612). In his study of the aesthetics of the genre, *The Seven Beauties of Science Fiction*, Istvan Csicery-Ronay identifies two opposed kinds of wondrous experiences that are produced by works of science fiction: the science-fictional sublime and the science-fictional grotesque. Both are forms of "imaginative shock" stemming from encountering something more awe-inspiring and/or terrible than ever previously comprehended (146). The *science-fictional* sublime is itself an imaginary projection of the "technological sublime," a feeling described by historian David Nye as "the awe induced by seeing an immense or dynamic technological object" such as a mighty dam, towering rocket, or great radio telescope array that then becomes "a celebration of the power of human reason" (in Csicery-Ronay 156). It is this very sense of the technosublime that *Astounding* editor John Campbell sought to produce through his new magazine cover designs that celebrated the conquest of space, and that Sheppard wants Rufus to feel when he peers through his telescope and contemplates his future commute to the moon.

Rufus, however, is repulsed by the future Sheppard shows him, finding in it not a sublime thrill but a grotesque threat. "I ain't going to the moon and get there alive," he tells Sheppard, "and when I die I'm going to hell" (*Collected* 611). As Csicery-Ronay discusses, repulsion can be a science-fictional feeling too, for there is another imaginative shock commonly offered by science fiction that is the polar opposite of the technological sublime: the science-fictional grotesque. "The grotesque is a response to another sort of imaginative shock," writes Csicery-Ronay, "the realization that objects that appear to be familiar and under control are actually undergoing surprising transformations, conflating disparate elements not observed elsewhere in the world" (146). "The grotesque brings the sublime to earth," Csicery-Ronay elaborates, "making it material and on our level, forcing attention back to the body" (182). Instead of impressing the reader or viewer with the limitless power of human reason to conquer space and time, "The modern forms of the grotesque are . . . constrained and suffused with threat, precisely because they call into question the physical foundations of the new materialism of science and technology" (184). Within the science-fictional grotesque on display in Hollywood's numerous creature features, science and technology become agents of terror responsible for "releasing and revealing the uncontainable metamorphic energies of the world and its discrete things" (188).

In "The Lame Shall Enter First," O'Connor continually counters Sheppard's technosublime visions of space travel with the grotesque bodily spectacle of his efforts to repair Rufus's clubfoot. In doing so, she aligns Sheppard less with his namesake, the astronaut Alan Shepard, and more closely with the embodiment of bad science himself, Dr. Victor Frankenstein. Rufus, for his part, is already a monster by the time he first meets Sheppard. During their initial meeting, Sheppard is struck by the grotesque spectacle of Rufus's decrepit shoe, a vision that evokes the massive iconic shoes worn by the monster (Fig. 2) ever since James Whale's 1931 film, *Frankenstein*: "[Rufus] leaned back in his chair and lifted a monstrous clubfoot to his knee. The foot was in a heavy black battered shoe with a sole four or five inches thick. The leather parted from it in one place and the end of an empty sock protruded like a grey tongue from a severed head" (*Collected* 599). Sheppard immediately identifies Rufus's clubfoot as the source of his misbehavior and vows to fix it (600).

As if possessed of its own "uncontainable metamorphic energies" (Csicery-Ronay 188), Rufus's foot refuses to stay within his shoe, and the shoe itself changes shape. Rufus creates his own patchwork monstrosity around his clubfoot by reassembling the pieces of the original shoe: "What was roughly the toe had broken open again and he had patched it with a piece of canvas; another place he had patched with what appeared to be the tongue of the original shoe. The two sides were laced with twine." The new shoe that Sheppard purchases for Rufus in the brace shop is even more monstrous than the one it replaces: "It was a black slick shapeless object, shining hideously. It looked like a blunt weapon, highly polished" (*Collected* 620). Rufus refuses to wear the new shoe.

The brace shop where Sheppard takes Rufus to be fitted with his new shoe is a house of horrors filled with artificial body parts reminiscent of Frankenstein's grisly laboratory. While Victor Frankenstein collects "bones from charnel-houses and disturbs, with profane fingers, the tremendous secrets of the human frame" (Shelley 36), the brace shop offers an equally disturbing display of "[a]rtificial limbs . . . stacked on the shelves, legs and arms and hands, claws and hooks, straps and human harnesses and unidentifiable instruments for unnamed deformities" (O'Connor *Collected* 620). Sheppard further echoes his science-fictional predecessor in that his attempt to play God only highlights his failure as a father. While Victor Frankenstein's failure to parent his creation leads to the death of all the women in his life, Sheppard's failure leads to the death of his own biological son.

Sheppard realizes at story's end that because he has spent so much time rebuilding Rufus he has neglected his own son, Norton. In Sheppard's parental absence, Rufus has devilishly convinced Norton that he can see his deceased mother's soul through the telescope. The ever-practical Norton then decides to take the next logical step into space to be reunited with his mother. Upon rushing to the attic to begin life anew with his son, Sheppard finds instead that "The tripod had fallen and the telescope lay on the floor. A few feet over it, the child hung in the jungle of shadows, just below the beam from which

Fig. 2 A close-up of the huge, battered black shoe worn by the monster in James Whale's 1931 film, *Frankenstein*. Note its similarity to the thick-soled shoe worn by Rufus Johnson.

he had launched his flight into space" (632). The final image of the story turns Sheppard's technosublime dream of space exploration on its head, landing him squarely within the grotesque realm of gothic science fiction.

In contrast to Victor Frankenstein, Sheppard's failure as both science enthusiast and parent ultimately stems not from his willful rejection of society and its mores, but from his unwillingness to appreciate the presence of history. Sheppard thought the new ideology of the space race had replaced the ancient ideology of devils and souls. It had not. Sheppard's refusal to appreciate the presence of history was a common attitude in the midcentury science fiction literary community, which had few ties to southern literature and little interest in regional cultural traditions. In his article, "The South and Science Fiction," Alabama-born science fiction author Gregory Benford discusses the reasons why there is not a visible tradition of science fiction in the American South. The region has a remarkable literary history, after all, and is also home to the nation's space program. However, with the exception of alternate histories that posit the South's winning the Civil War, there are not very many expressly *southern* science fiction stories. Benford attributes this lack of literary production to the genre's attitude toward history, an attitude that is much like Sheppard's. "We Americans are embedded in a rich and fruitful past," he writes, "none more deeply than Southerners; but the genre keeps its beady gaze firmly fixed on the plastic futures we authors so glibly devise. Yet much of history is dominated by inertia, not by the swift kinetics of technology" (386). Science fiction writers, Benford argues, generally do not have "an appreciation for the magnitude" of "social inertia" that one finds in much southern literature. Rather than recognize that "[t]he past isn't over," the genre's authors instead prefer to dream of "freedom from both history . . . and from our own bodies" (390). These are Sheppard's dreams too, yet they aren't Rufus's, who has no interest in freeing himself from his own troubled family history, from Christian orthodoxy, or from his clubfoot.

Many of O'Connor's characters share Sheppard's science-fictional dreams of technosocially transformed tomorrows; but just as many do not, preferring instead to champion traditional ways of living and believing. O'Connor's fiction often dramatizes the struggle between these two kinds of inhabitants of her modernizing South: those who want to boldly break from history and those who don't. She commonly sets her stories within spaces of progress, from desegregated busses and gleaming milking parlors to new concrete pig pens and developing lakefronts. O'Connor certainly does not celebrate the modernizing South's future in her fiction, but neither does she valorize the region's past. Instead, she dramatizes the terrible things that happen to characters who, in their eagerness for a new future, ignore the presence of the past.

Science fiction contains both technologically sublime representations of futures freed from the past and grotesque representations of scientific and technological progress gone wrong. It should be hardly surprising that the genre serves in O'Connor's fiction as a ready source of narrative devices and images with which to describe—as science fiction historian Adam Roberts writes of Hollywood's gothic science fiction itself—"the eerie copresence of undead past and contaminated future" (Roberts xii). The way Roberts describes gothic science fiction can also describe many of O'Connor's stories, for each dramatize how "the dereliction of the past always inflects the shiny new spaces of the present and future" (Roberts xii).

Consider O'Connor's science-fictional treatment of time itself. O'Connor uses the science fiction trope of time travel to locate the origins of good and evil in her characters' attitudes toward the properties of time. Both Mrs. Flood in *Wise Blood* and the Misfit in "A Good Man Is Hard to Find" dream a science-fictional dream of traveling through time. While seemingly good and charitable people, neither feels the presence of the past. The past for them is a distant place to be traveled to, and as they ponder that trip to a long-dead place they do terrible things. In the concluding pages of *Wise Blood*, Mrs. Flood is so perplexed by Hazel Motes's medieval monkish behavior that she imagines he is a time traveler:

> How would he know if time was going backwards or forwards or if he was going with it? She imagined it was like you were walking in a tunnel and all you could see was a pin point of light; she couldn't think of it at all without that. She saw it as some kind of a star, like the star on Christmas cards. She saw him going backwards to Bethlehem and she had to laugh. (*Collected* 123)

Mrs. Flood has no personal use for anything from the time of Bible-era Bethlehem. As she tells Hazel, "time goes forward, it don't go backward and unless you take what's offered you, you'll find yourself out in the cold pitch black and just how far do you think you'll get?" (*Collected* 129). Only her future marriage to Hazel Motes concerns Mrs. Flood.

The Misfit also thinks about traveling back in time, but in this case because he doesn't believe in anything unless he actually sees it. After the grandmother mentions that Christ may not have raised the dead in the story's final scene, the Misfit explains that he is a murderer precisely because he was not present to see what Christ actually did:

> "I wasn't there so I can't say He didn't," the Misfit said. "I wisht I had of been there," he said, hitting the ground with his fist. "It ain't right I wasn't there because if I had of been there I would of known. Listen lady," he said in a high voice, "if I had of been there I would of known and I wouldn't be like I am now." (*Collected* 152)

The Misfit thinks like an empirical scientist. The thing that pains him most is his lack of hard evidence. Lacking evidence upon which to base his behavior, he treats murder like a thought experiment. He creates his morality in response to a series of speculative "what if" scenarios—what "if I had of been there," what if Christ "didn't raise the dead" (152)—that the empirical world alone cannot resolve.

Science fiction writers and filmmakers have long used the device of time travel to explore the far future and prehistoric past, variously pondering the paradoxical "metaphysics of time" ("Time Travel"). O'Connor uses the narrative device of time travel in these two stories to describe not the paradoxical nature of time but the paradoxical nature of her characters, making a grotesque spectacle of seemingly good people who don't feel the living presence of the (sacred) past: Mrs. Flood turns a blind man (a man she wants to marry!) out onto the cold wet streets in a gambit to secure his love and the polite, thoughtful Misfit murders children.

Modern urban and agricultural spaces receive a science-fictional treatment in O'Connor's stories as well. In "The Artificial Nigger," Mr. Head's traditional racism contaminates his view of the modern city and leads him to experience the city streets of Atlanta and its inhabitants as a grotesque spectacle of subterranean terrors and strange dark denizens that is reminiscent of the cosmic horror of H. P. Lovecraft. O'Connor's Atlanta and Lovecraft's city of Innsmouth feel similarly alien and unsettling. Much as the narrator of Lovecraft's "The Shadow over Innsmouth" "could not escape the sensation of being watched from ambush on every hand by sly, staring eyes that never shut" as he travels through the fishy titular city, "Nelson's skin began to prickle" as he senses that "[b]lack eyes in black faces were watching them from every direction" while he and his uncle walk through Atlanta (*Collected* 221).

Like Lovecraft's narrator, Mr. Head and Nelson are strangers in strange lands where even human bodies appear oddly exaggerated and grotesque. Lovecraft's narrator catalogs the abnormal physical details of a strange inhabitant of Innsmouth, noting how "his hands were large and heavily veined, and had a very unusual greyish-blue tinge. The fingers were strikingly short in proportion to the rest of the structure, and seemed to have a tendency to curl closely into the huge palm" (Lovecraft, "Shadow over Innsmouth"). Nelson likewise doesn't know what he is looking at as he asks a black woman—the first black women he has ever seen up close—for directions. He "stood drinking in every detail of her. His eyes traveled up from her great knees to her forehead and then made a triangular path from the glistening sweat on her neck down and across her tremendous bosom and over her bare arm back to where her fingers lay hidden in her hair" (*Collected* 223). The sight of these two city dwellers is so unsettling that neither can be comprehended whole but must be described in pieces.

O'Connor's Atlanta resembles both Lovecraft's dark, tunnel-riddled Innsmouth and his otherworldly city of R'lyeh, a lost alien capital that, as described in "The Call of Cthulhu," is both futurist marvel and ancient terror. Lovecraft's characters describe "great Cyclopean cities of titan blocks and sky-flung monoliths" carved from green stone, covered in odd hieroglyphics, and full of strange sculptures. Mr. Head is similarly struck by the novel names painted on Atlanta's businesses, beyond which, in the distance, "a line of blue buildings stood up" (*Collected* 218). Yet a horrific subterranean realm undergirds each city. Entering a black "aperature" opening to R'lyeh's hidden depths, Lovecraft's adventurer finds that "[t]he odour arising from the newly opened depths was intolerable, and at length the quick-eared [adventurer] thought he heard a nasty, slopping sound down there" (Lovecraft, "Call of Cthulhu"). An ancient, demonic horror soon emerges from those depths. To convince Nelson that Atlanta is a grotesque realm of technosocial horror, Mr. Head also reveals the city's depths, holding the boy's head into a sewer: Nelson "drew it back quickly, hearing a gurgling in the depths under the sidewalk." After learning from his uncle how the sewer is "full of rats and how a man could slide into it and be sucked along down endless pitchblack tunnels," Nelson "connected the sewer passages with the entrance to hell and understood for the first time how the world was put together in its lowest parts" (*Collected* 220). The futurist modern skylines of each city belie the eldritch realms of horror that comprise their foundations.

Even though Mr. Head's traditional racism contaminates his and Nelson's experience of modern-day Atlanta, the two do not meet a grotesque fate because Nelson does not ignore their past together. Nelson may have been born in Atlanta, but he learns over the course of the story that the city is not where he is from. "Let's go home," the gracious Nelson tells his terrible uncle at story's end, "before we get ourselves lost again" (*Collected* 230). He vows never to return to Atlanta again.

While Mr. Head and Nelson are shocked by the science-fictional grotesque, in "Greenleaf" Mrs. May is shocked by the science-fictional sublime. The sight of the Greenleaf boy's new dairy barn—"built to the latest specifications" (*Collected* 514)—takes her breath away:

> She opened the milking room door and stuck her head in and for the first second she felt as if she were going to lose her breath. The spotless white concrete room was filled with sunlight that came from a row of windows head-high along both walls. The metal stanchions gleamed ferociously and she had to squint to be able to look at all. She drew her head out the room quickly and closed the door and leaned against it, frowning. (515)

Blinded by the future she sees in the Greenleafs' new barn, Mrs. May still insists on believing that she alone is responsible for her former tenants' success. Her traditional southern class biases contaminate her view of postwar social mobility, leaving her unable to reconcile her once-prosperous past with the Greenleaf boys' prosperous future. Rejecting a gleaming future that contains the Greenleafs, Mrs. May meets a grotesque technological fate, killed by a resident of the Greenleafs' own farm, a rogue bull that "don't like cars and trucks" and accordingly rams them (512). The bull confuses Mrs. May with the car whose bumper she is sitting next to and gores her, fusing woman, animal, and machine together. Mrs. May may have failed to embrace the Greenleafs in life, but as the bull "buried his head in her lap, like a wild tormented lover" (523), she finally embraces one of them in death.

While old-fashioned Mrs. May is forced into a grotesque posthuman fusion of woman, bull, and car at her story's end, many of O'Connor's most modern characters—her nimble mechanics, social scientists, and philosophical nihilists—seek this hybrid condition out willingly, using machines, artifacts, and even animals to grotesquely complete their bodies and spirits. When Enoch Emery—a young man pining to be "THE young man of the future" (*Collected* 108)—seeks a new destiny for himself in *Wise Blood*, he becomes "Gonga!" (100), a creature from an imaginary science fiction film based on *King Kong*, one of the most famous science fiction films of all time. Other characters who are eager to leave their pasts behind conjoin themselves to machines much like the cybernetic warriors featured in the comic books of the 1940s and '50s, fusions of man and technological apparatus inspired by the Second World War's military research and development such as Marvel's Captain America, whose super strength is sustained by an energizing liquid cooked up in a wartime laboratory, and DC's Robotman, a superhero with the body of a robot and the brain of a human scientist (Wasielewski 64–67). Tom Shiftlet from

"The Life You Save May Be Your Own," Rayber in *The Violent Bear It Away*, Hulga Hopewell from "Good Country People," and the Displaced Person all evoke science fiction's image of the part-human, part-machine cyborg. For example, Tom Shiftlet discourses on modern medicine's ability to remove a human heart like a mechanical part and eventually augments his incomplete body with a machine that he loves more than his wife: a car. In a similar vein, Hulga augments her mind with a piece of wood. O'Connor herself explains how Hulga's wooden leg contains her nihilistic personality: "when the Bible salesman steals it, the reader realizes he has taken away part of the girl's personality" (*Mystery* 99). Both Tom and Hulga use their posthuman appendages to distance themselves from their families and their pasts: Tom drives away in the family car from the mother who had taken him in and the daughter he had married while Hulga dreams of walking away from her family farm— with Manley Pointer—on her wooden leg.

In an even more shocking use of science-fictional cyborg imagery, O'Connor depicts Rayber as a literal man-machine who has to assemble himself when he first meets his nephew:

> He came back almost at once, plugging something into his ear. He had thrust on the black-rimmed glasses and he was sticking a metal box into the waist-band of his pajamas. This was joined by a cord to the plug in his ear. For an instant the boy had the thought that his head ran by electricity. (*Collected* 386)

When Rayber does not want to hear something (such as Lucette Carmody's sermon), he simply turns his head off (415). Not only is Rayber part machine, but he also does the job of an information-processing machine at his school where he is "the expert on testing" (402). Old Mason Tarwater had originally kidnapped his nephew from Rayber's household to prevent him from becoming a cyborg: "I saved you to be free, your own self!" he tells young Tarwater, "and not a piece of information inside his head! If you were living with him, you'd be information right now . . ." (339). Like Sheppard, Rayber even tries to use the technologically sublime experience of manned flight to convince Tarwater of the value of technoculture. "Flying is the greatest engineering achievement of man," he tells Tarwater. "Doesn't it stir your imagination even slightly?" Flying does not stir Tarwater's imagination at all (438). Much as Tom's and Hulga's posthuman appendages enable their grotesque flights from their pasts, Rayber's prosthesis and technoscientific mindset disconnect him from his own family's past.

Where Rayber, Hulga, and Tom embody the alienating and inhuman aspects of science fiction's grotesque cyborgs, the Displaced Person is a more radical cyborg, a mechanic whose prowess with machines and whose global kinships promises/threatens to transform the traditional social order of Mrs.

McIntyre's farm. Mrs. McIntyre praises how efficiently the Displaced Person works in the same awestruck tones that Sheppard uses to describe spaceflight. "That man is my salvation!" she describes the Displaced Person atop one of his machines (294). Inspecting the fields the Displaced Person has recently plowed with "a new drag harrow and a tractor with a power lift," she exclaims, "That's been done beautifully!" (298).

Mrs. McIntyre's science-fictionally sublime dreams for her farm become a science-fictionally grotesque nightmare when she realizes just how much socially mutagenic force she has accidentally released by employing a cyborg. Like Sheppard, Mrs. McIntyre initially ignores the presence of the past; she simply does not think about how thoroughly a new kind of mechanical worker will destroy her farm's traditional race-based social order. Yet much as the racist views of old Mr. Head contaminated his and Nelson's experience of modern-day Atlanta, the racist past of the McIntyre farm contaminates its gleaming future. While the Displaced Person does not care about the farm's traditional racial order, Mrs. McIntyre actually does. She realizes, too late, that she does not want to break entirely from the past but wants instead to preserve her farm's traditional racial order.

Learning of the Displaced Person's plans to marry his white cousin to a black farmhand, Mrs. McIntyre's technological "salvation" becomes an integrating monster: "You would bring this poor innocent child over here and try to marry her to a half-witted thieving black stinking nigger! What kind of a monster are you!" She even repeats the term to herself: "Monster!" (313). Rather than suffer the monstrous fate of having races blend on the farm, Mrs. McIntyre and her farmhands arrange a grotesque, machinic death for the cybernetic Displaced Person, watching silently while he is crushed by a runaway tractor (325). Unable to reconcile her farm's future with its past, Mrs. McIntyre destroys it completely.

In her essay, "The Fiction Writer and His Country," O'Connor explains why her stories are often so shocking, violent, and grotesque:

> When you can assume that your audience holds the same beliefs you do, you can relax a little and use more normal means of talking to it; when you have to assume that it does not, then you have to make your vision apparent by shock— to the hard of hearing you shout, and for the almost-blind you draw large and startling figures. (*Mystery* 34)

What she leaves unsaid is that, sometimes, those shocks come in the form of science fiction. Science fiction enables O'Connor to become the prophetic "realist of distances" that she aspires to be, a writer who is both the chronicler and critic of her age (44). The realism of the prophetic writer must span distances across space and time. "The writer of grotesque fiction," she elaborates in "The Grotesque in Southern Fiction," is "looking for one image that will connect or combine or embody two points; one is a point in the concrete, and the other is a point not visible to the naked eye, but believed in by him firmly, just as real to him, really, as the one that everybody sees" (42). Sometimes those points are in the past. Sometimes they are in the future. The imagery of science fiction combines those two points, embodying in O'Connor's stories the technosublime promises of tomorrow and the grotesque perils of shiny new futures sundered from their pasts.

WORKS CITED

Bacon, Jon Lance. *Flannery O'Connor and Cold War Culture*. New York: Cambridge University Press, 1993. Print.

Bacon, Jon Lance. "A Fondness for Supermarkets: *Wise Blood* and Consumer Culture." *New Essays on "Wise Blood,"* edited by Michael Kreyling, 25–50. New York: Cambridge University Press, 1995. Print.

Bacon, Jon Lance. "Gory Stories: O'Connor and American Horror." *Flannery O'Connor in the Age of Terrorism: Essays on Violence and Grace,* edited by Avis Hewitt and Robert Donahoo, 89–112. Knoxville: University of Tennessee Press, 2010. Print.

Bacon, Jon Lance. "'Jesus Hits like the Atom Bomb': Flannery O'Connor and the End-Time Scenario." *Flannery O'Connor Review* 10 (2012): 19–54. Print.

Benford, Gregory. "The South and Science Fiction." *Science Fiction Studies* 27, no. 3 (November 2000): 385–90. Print.

Brevda, William. "All the Dead Bodies: O'Connor and Noir." *Flannery O'Connor in the Age of Terrorism: Essays on Violence and Grace,* edited by Avis Hewitt and Robert Donahoo, 113–24. Knoxville: University of Tennessee Press, 2010. Print.

Csicsery-Ronay, Istvan, Jr. *The Seven Beauties of Science Fiction*. Middleton, CT: Wesleyan University Press, 2008. Print.

Driggers, Stephen G., and Robert J. Dunn. *The Manuscripts of Flannery O'Connor at Georgia College*. Athens: University of Georgia Press, 1989.

Gooch, Brad. *Flannery: A Life of Flannery O'Connor*. New York: Little, Brown and Company, 2009.

James, Edward. *Science Fiction in the 20th Century*. New York: Oxford University Press, 1994. Print.

King, David A. "Hitched: The Similar Legacies of Flannery O'Connor and Alfred Hitchcock." *Flannery O'Connor Review* 11 (2013): 50–69. Print.

Lovecraft, H. P. "The Call of Cthulhu." 1926. Accessed 6 February 2018. http://www.hplovecraft .com/writings/texts/fiction/cc.aspx. Online.

Lovecraft, H. P. "The Shadow over Innsmouth." 1931. Accessed 6 February 2018. http://www .hplovecraft.com/writings/texts/fiction/soi.aspx. Online.

O'Connor, Flannery. *Mystery and Manners: Occasional Prose*. New York: Farrar, Straus and Giroux, 1961. Print.

O'Connor, Flannery. *The Habit of Being*. New York: Farrar, Straus and Giroux, 1979. Print.

O'Connor, Flannery. *Collected Works*. New York: Library of America, 1988. Print.

Roberts, Adam. "Foreword." *Gothic Science Fiction 1980–2010,* edited by Sara Wasson and Emily Adler, xi–xiv. Liverpool: Liverpool University Press, 2014 (2011). Print.

Saunders, Lisa. "'Slapstick, Two-Dollard Up': Thinking about Flannery O'Connor and W. C. Fields." *Flannery O'Connor Review* 6 (2008): 1–10. Print.

Shelley, Mary. *Frankenstein*. New York: Bantam Books, 1981 (1818).

"Time Travel." *The Encyclopedia of Science Fiction*, 3rd ed. Eds. John Clute, David Langford, Peter Nicholls, and Graham Sleight. Accessed 5 July 2017. http://www.sf-encyclopedia.com /entry/time_travel. Online.

Wasielewski, Marek. "Golden Age Comics." *The Routledge Companion to Science Fiction*, edited by Mark Bould, Andrew M. Butler, Adam Roberts, and Sherryl Vint. New York: Routledge, 2009.

The Trouble with "Innerleckchuls": Flannery O'Connor, Anti-Intellectualism, and the Iowa Writers' Workshop

JORDAN COFER

In his biography, *Flannery: A Life*, Brad Gooch jokingly observes that Flannery O'Connor has become a one-woman academic industry. The fact is . . . he's right. O'Connor has been the subject of well over one hundred book-length critical studies, tens of thousands of dissertations and theses, articles, book chapters, and essays. Not to mention the multiple biographies, a journal, a society, a newsletter, and even a Flannery O'Connor studies program, all faithfully devoted to a writer who published two novels and a collection of short stories in her lifetime. Posthumously, she has achieved the enviable position of being both embraced by the academy and remaining one of America's most famous writers, a rare feat. Yet, while few writers occupy such a position—revered by the general public, the *literati*, and the academy—this immense popularity certainly asks the question: why are academics so drawn to a writer who is so critical of them?

Ad nauseum, academics, intellectuals, and artists are the target of O'Connor's wrath. In her fiction, these characters' condescension isolates them from society—stuck in their respective ivory tower and unable to relate to the world around them. Often these characters' intellect becomes the very embodiment of their isolation (Coles 49). This pattern occurs so frequently that readers are not surprised when an academic is the subject of folly, or when the intellectual elite are outsmarted by an undereducated character because O'Connor has prepared us for this—she has trained us how to read her fiction. From her earliest stories, we are taught to associate academics with antagonism, whether it's the Misfit in "A Good Man Is Hard to Find," whose glasses "gave him a scholarly look," or "the old goat teacher," Mr. Jerger, who plays comic relief in "A Stroke of Good Fortune" (*CW* 146, 196). Even the naïve Sally Poker Sash, who finally graduates from the teacher's college and is upstaged by General Sash, literally, dying on stage during her commencement in "A Late Encounter with the Enemy." In fact, this trend—as others have pointed out—extends even earlier. Biographers, friends, and even her godson, William Sessions, have all recounted stories, early writings, drawings, et cetera, to demonstrate the intelligence and preciousness of her youth,[1] such as *The Colonnade* cartoon,[2] she drew as a college student, set at a school dance where one lonely young lady sitting alone comments, "Oh well, I can always be a Ph.D." (Gentry 50).

This common thread, parodies of those who ought to be wise but are made to look foolish, continues throughout her work. In fact, O'Connor's humor trains us to laugh when Manley Pointer steals the solipsistic Hulga's leg and tells her off: "You ain't so smart. I been believing in nothing ever since I was born!" (*CW* 283). We cheer when, as the police haul Rufus Johnson to jail, Sheppard realizes that he had told the police that he would be responsible for Rufus's actions and that Rufus has outsmarted Sheppard. We snicker (derisively) when we read O'Connor's letter to Dr. Ted Spivey detailing her reading at Wesleyan College where a young professor asked a series of inane questions to O'Connor, such as "what is the significance of the Misfit's hat?" to which she replied, "to cover his head," before she concludes "that's what's happening to the teaching of literature" (*CW* 1098). So many of her works focus on failed academics.

Part of this humor comes from O'Connor's own biography. Much like Mark Twain,[3] O'Connor played the role of the interloper, poking fun at the ivory tower. In her introduction to the second edition/FSG reissue of *Wise Blood*, she writes that the novel: "was written by an author congenitally innocent of theory, but one with certain preoccupations." Someone unfamiliar with O'Connor's biography might think of her as an outsider artist. This was a joke that delighted O'Connor, who writes, "Everybody who has read *Wise Blood* thinks I'm a hillbilly nihilist" (*HB* 81). Yet, O'Connor was anything but an outsider. She attended the top creative writing school in the country, the Iowa Writers' Workshop, rubbed elbows with great literary minds from Robert Penn Warren to Robert Lowell, was a regular book reviewer for multiple publications, a frequent speaker on the college circuit, penned many critical essays, and received the prestigious Yaddo fellowship. O'Connor was an academic, and a fine one at that, which might seem at cross purposes with her satire of intellectuals.

From the outside, O'Connor's anti-intellectual pose seems to be part of her regional identity. Tara Powell, Robert Coles, Fred Hobson, and many others have argued that O'Connor's parody of academics follows a longstanding southern tradition. For years, this has seemed a suitable, if unsatisfying answer. However, the last decade has given O'Connor scholars a more complete picture of Flannery O'Connor as a writer and a person.[4] By capitalizing on these new materials, this essay reconsiders the popular thesis that O'Connor's anti-intellectual archetype is purely a product of regionalism as an oversimplification and argues that O'Connor's critique is more complicated. By exploring how her archetype emerges as a byproduct of the Cold War era, heavily indebted to her time attending the Iowa Writers' Workshop, and highlighting a time when her initiation into academia challenged the beliefs and orthodoxy she had held dear, readers discover a writer whose use of parody is as much a self-defense mechanism as a literary device. To avoid psychobiography, this essay will look at some recently released archival information from O'Connor's time at the Iowa Writers' Workshop, as well as some previously unpublished drafts she was writing at the time. These materials will help paint a fuller portrait of a writer whose works will always be tied to her southernness, yet demonstrate that O'Connor was a writer whose critique of the academy is as much a self-critique—as an intellectual, academia, and an artist—as it was of intellectuals at large.

On 28 October 1960, Flannery O'Connor stood in front of a southern audience at Wesleyan College in Macon. In her talk, which was never published during her lifetime, but was edited and later published as "Some Aspects of the Grotesque in Southern Fiction," O'Connor quips, "I used to think it should be possible to write for some supposed elite, for the people who attend the universities and sometimes know how to read" (*CW* 820). It seems a risky move, to make fun of the academics in an audience filled with professors, but by 1960, this might as well have been O'Connor's trademark (*CW* 820). While Powell notes "the South has never been noted for its deference to the intellectual," perhaps O'Brien's more forceful declaration is in order: "The Southern intellectual has had to look over his shoulder; he has often been poor; he has been fired for critical independence; he has been pilloried by press or pulpit; he has been harried by state legislatures more interested in corn than poetry . . . One consequence is clear: the southern intellectual has masked his intellectuality in order to survive" (1, 213).[5]

It comes as no surprise, as others have noticed, that O'Connor, who came of age internalizing this southern anti-intellectual zeitgeist, creates fiction that follows in much the same line as her predecessors. Yet, despite evidence to the contrary, the southern influence on O'Connor's anti-intellectual archetype seems to be overstated, while the influence of the Iowa Writers' Workshop on her trademark satirical target has been overlooked. New research, such as Mark McGurl's *The Program Era* and Eric Bennett's *Workshops of Empire*, as well as new archival material from O'Connor's time at Iowa, helps shape this reconsideration of O'Connor's anti-intellectual archetype. Both the spiritual and cultural forces she encountered in Iowa are absolutely essential for understanding this trope and that the anti-intellectual theme is as much personal as it is provincial. Perhaps O'Connor said it best when asked by Harvey Breit[6] whether her work appealed merely to southern audiences, "When you're a Southerner and in pursuit of reality, the reality you come up with is going to have a Southern accent, but that's just an accent; it's not the essence of what you're trying to do," which is to say that O'Connor's anti-intellectual theme transcends its own southern accent (qtd. in Magee 8).

THE IOWA WRITERS' WORKSHOP, 1945

Encouraged by professors at GCW to attend the University of Iowa to study journalism, Flannery O'Connor found herself in a fortuitous position arriving at the school that housed the nation's first graduate program in creative writing, which was still in its infancy. Looking back, it seems appropriate that O'Connor, who loved to mock PhDs, enrolled in the university that, at the time, had "the highest percentage of full-time, resident PhDs in the country" (Gooch 119). Although the Iowa Writers' Workshop was originally conceived by Wilbur Schramm (1939–1941) as a summer writing program, by the time of O'Connor's arrival in 1945, director Paul Engle had developed the most influential creative writing program in the country.

The Iowa Writers' Workshop's rise to prominence, occurring before and during Flannery O'Connor's time in the program, came largely from circumstances beyond her control, but would benefit her immensely. As with all aspects of American life, the Cold War had its impacts on the arts. While the pendulum swung away from the Popular Front and American artists distanced themselves from the socialist movements of the 1930s, World War II cemented nationalism around the country.[7] This nationalism, and fear of the Soviet Union's courting of artists into academia as a means of indoctrination, led to increased support for the arts.[8] After all, the WPA Writer's Project had already set a precedent for supporting these programs. Both private and public funding, ranging from the Rockefeller Foundation's Humanities wing to the CIA, emerging as unlikely benefactors for the Iowa Writers' Workshop[9] and creative writing materialized as "a new academic discipline created by men who not only loved literature but also reacted to the pressure of political anxieties, felt the lure of philanthropic money and placed enormous faith in the role literature could play in the peace that followed World War II" (Bennett 32).

Whether by fate or fortune, O'Connor's participation in the Iowa Writers' Workshop during this influential time meant that her "fiction was more overly shaped by the institutionalization of painstaking craft in graduate creative writing programs in the postwar period. From her time at Iowa until her death in 1964 at the age of thirty-nine, O'Connor never once wavered from a disciplinary aesthetic regime" (McGurl 129). The workshop, being the first graduate creative writing program for an emerging academic discipline, while simultaneously serving as the cultural benefactor of Cold War paranoia, was under an immense pressure to produce both commercial and academic success. It had to prove itself among doubters. In turn, creative writing programs rationalized "their presence in a scholarly environment by asserting their own disciplinary rigor," which lead to creating new methods of critique and an extreme emphasis on the act of revision. The birth of New Criticism, heralded as a scientific approach to texts, which became the foundation for the Iowa Writers' Workshop pedagogy. Thus, the New Critical approach offered a method to replicate *literary fiction* and "in part to give academic legitimacy to something as soft as creative writing" (Bennett 41).

Hence, during her time at Iowa, New Critical practices became immensely influential on O'Connor's fiction since she internalized these practices for the rest of her career (McGurl 129). By institutionalizing creative writing during O'Connor's time as a student, the Workshop "stabilized a set of literary values even as it put them in circulation throughout the U. S. educational system," a set of values that emerge throughout her fiction (McGurl 132). As Mayers notes, many of the "aesthetic preferences and practices encouraged in the creative writing workshop (especially a preference for concreteness over abstraction) have deep roots within the turbulent swirl of competing Cold War ideologies" (14). Yet, even in her earlier fiction at Iowa, in stories like "The Crop," O'Connor demonstrates her tendency to lash out against academics in her satire of literary fiction.

The problem, however, of pinning O'Connor's academic parodies to her southern heritage lies in the fact that during her time at Iowa, O'Connor was surrounded and embraced by the southern intelligentsia. During O'Connor's time in the workshop, she was surrounded by many of the top New Critical and southern writers of the era, including John Crowe Ransom, Allen Tate, Andrew Lytle, who served as O'Connor's thesis advisor, and visits from Robert Penn Warren. Higher education's embrace of creative writing as a new academic discipline offered many artists professional status, luring established writers and potential students into the academy with "the dream of a nuclear family and a steady job" (Bennett 37). O'Connor's very approach to writing— as well as the DNA of writing programs across the country—was shaped by academics and writers from the South, especially from the Southern Literary Renaissance. *Understanding Fiction*, a textbook fundamental to the workshop, was written by southern writers (Cleanth Brooks and Robert Penn Warren), featured many stories from southern writers (Poe, Caroline Gordon, William Faulkner, Thomas Thompson, Eudora Welty, and Katherine Anne Porter). The same could be said about many of the celebrity faculty members. Not only did Engle stack the deck with southern authors (Warren, Tate, Ransom, Lytle), but Andrew Lytle served as the interim director while Engle was away.

Rather than being indoctrinated in anti-intellectualism, the southern intellectual was *en vogue* at Iowa. "People who were favored in the Writers' Workshop at that time were Southern Writers," Eugene Brown, one of O'Connor's fellow students, noted (qtd. in Gooch 137). In fact, some participants believed that both O'Connor and fellow southerner James B. Hall found favoritism among many of the faculty due to their regional identity. When John Crowe Ransom first visited the Iowa Writers' Workshop, he "chose one of O'Connor's stories to read to the class" and Robert Penn Warren "selected a story of hers from a pile of student work during a visit" (Gooch 124, 128). When Andrew Lytle joined the staff of the Iowa Writers' Workshop, again, it was O'Connor's story that he chose to read out loud. Being a southerner in the early days of the Iowa Writers' Workshop brought a distinct advantage.

O'Connor arrived at a moment in history when the stakes were the highest for the merger of creative writing and academia, and she became Engle's— and the creative writing workshop's—bellwether celebrity. Although she gains fame skewering the academy—seemingly biting the hand that fed her—the success of the Writers' Workshop would be forever entangled with her writing career. At the same time, Engle has been depicted as a tireless promoter, working hard to secure accolades for his students and gain publicity for the workshop.[10] Engle knew that the Iowa Writers' Workshop's success was tied to its ability to produce a literary celebrity. For the workshop, "publicity raised consciousness; consciousness inspired donations; donations bankrolled famous writers; famous writers raised the profile of the program" (Bennett 98). Engle worked with Rinehart Publishers to secure "two one-year fellowships of $750 each to students whose manuscripts showed promise of publishing success," O'Connor was the first winner of the Rinehart book contract (qtd. in Cash 79). Of course, Engle capitalized on this partnership with a newspaper announcement in the *Des Moines Sunday Register*.[11]

For her part, the role of Iowa Writers' Workshop success story was not one that O'Connor willingly embraced. Dismissing much of the fiction she encountered in workshops, she writes "with the exception of one story, they might all have originated in some synthetic place" (*MM* 56). Rather than fall into what she saw as formulaic system for writing literary fiction, others have suggested that O'Connor explicitly tried to resist the academic influence of the Iowa Writers' Workshop by doubling down on her own southern identity. However, as more evidence of O'Connor's time at Iowa becomes available, the more apparent it becomes that her critique of academia grew out of the tension between her southern identity and the changing Cold War embrace of writers, both of which came to a head while she was in Iowa City.

Despite these anxieties that benefits, for O'Connor, extend beyond just the discipline of practice, attending the Iowa Writers' Workshop jumpstarted her literary career. Before she left, Engle advocated for O'Connor's Yaddo fellowship, where she would befriend Robert Lowell. In 1952, *Kenyon Review* editor, and former mentor at the Iowa Writers' Workshop, John Crowe Ransom, invited her to apply for *Kenyon Review* fellowship, which she won. In 1954, Paul Engle was selected to serve as the judge for the O. Henry Prize, which honors the best short story published in a given year, and in 1956, he selected O'Connor's "Greenleaf." This is not to suggest that O'Connor's success is solely the product of nepotism, far from it, but rather that she certainly owes a lot to the Iowa Writers' Workshop, and the faculty who championed her work—not bad for a writer who complained that universities weren't doing enough to "stifle" writers (*MM* 84).

It seems antithetical that O'Connor would turn against those who aided in her success, although, ironically, this anti-intellectual theme was pivotal to much of her later success. This parody shows up consistently during her time at Iowa, starting with her first semester, where in an assignment for her news writing class with William Porter, she mockingly describes the level of education in Iowa City, even claiming that their building's janitor was working on his dissertation.[12] Yet, outwardly, O'Connor's impulse is to parody the intellectual atmosphere—in much the same way she parodies the W. A. V. E. S. training at Georgia College for *The Colonnade*—of Iowa City, reflected her own inner turmoil. While privately she kept her prayer journal, her fiction during this time was highly influenced "at a formative stage by the norms of a discipline trying to justify its right to be academic" (Bennett 164). Ironically, one of Engle's chief pieces of advice for his students was not to overintellectualize their writing, to ground it in the concrete. This, too, was a key for O'Connor's own fiction. While she openly argued for simplicity in fiction, O'Connor herself wants readers to engage on an intellectual level. In multiple letters and essays, she complains of readers misunderstanding her work, arguing that she never intended for her writing to "satisfy the tired reader" (*CW* 821). O'Connor famously mentioned that she intended to clobber readers, to hit them in the eye the way that Mary Grace accosts Ruby Turpin. Hence, O'Connor's ideal reader is one who can engage with the complexity to which O'Connor was so drawn. So when O'Connor writes, "When people think they are smart—even when they are smart—there is nothing anybody else can say to make them see things straight," she hopes for an engaged and intellectual audience to laugh at the self-deprecating humor (*CW* 551).

Without making too much of the autobiographical impulse, O'Connor's repeated parody of academics reads very much as a self-parody. Many scholars, starting with Jean Cash, have pointed out how some of O'Connor's intellectuals, who might seem like southern stereotypes, also read as modified forms of O'Connor—in fact, there are enough similarities that it is worth noting. Both Thomas in "The Comforts of Home" and Julian in "Everything That Rises Must Converge" are academics/writers who live at home and have an uncomfortable relationship with their mothers, much like O'Connor. Mary Grace, in "Revelation," has left the South for Wellesley, Hulga Hopewell returns home from graduate school to live with her mother, and Asbury Fox in "The Enduring Chill" leaves for New York, returning only because he is sick. In fact, in an early draft, Fox is described as being stuck on his mother's farm, which is located twenty miles outside of Macon, which sounds curiously like Andalusia, which is in reality about thirty miles from Macon.[13]

The anti-intellectual theme, nascent in her juvenilia, becomes prominent during her time in Iowa, appearing in drafts, early stories, letters, and her journals,[14] all of which suggests that O'Connor's participation in the Writers' Workshop heightened her engagement with these tensions. In many ways, enrolling at the University of Iowa challenged her in ways she could not have anticipated—not just academically, but holistically. While she may have skewered intellectuals and academics in her assignments and stories, privately, she seemed to undergo serious spiritual turmoil during this time. Her attack on academia feels extremely personal, indicative of an internal struggle between faith and intellect.

Perhaps the best way to understand how this anti-intellectual trope develops, even in her undergraduate and high school days—simultaneously mocking, yet feeling an attraction to education—is to understand the real threat intellectual seduction posed for O'Connor. In *A Prayer Journal*, O'Connor details her own fears of the effects that academia would have on her faith. In her first (undated) entry, O'Connor asks, "Oh God please make my mind clear. Please make it clean," adding, "My intellect is so limited, Lord, that I can only trust in You to preserve me as I should be" (*PJ* 4). The O'Connor of *A Prayer Journal* shows vulnerability and insecurity as her fears of losing her faith are paralleled by her prayers for success: "Please help me dear God to be a good writer and to get something else accepted" (*PJ* 10).

It seems that during her time in the Iowa Writers' Workshop she felt that her faith was under attack. She writes, "At every point in this educational process, we are told that it [faith] is ridiculous and their arguments sound so good it is hard not to fall into them. The arguments might not sound so good to someone with a better mind, but my mental trappings are as they are" (*PJ* 15). This balance between her faith and fiction continues during her time at Iowa as she fluctuates between reason and emotion, writing, "I cannot comprehend the exaltation that must be due You. Intellectually, I assent: let us adore God. But can we do that without feeling?" (*PJ* 8). It's a problem she continued to work out and this conflict manifests itself in several of her writings during this time period. For instance, in one assignment, O'Connor writes about the Italian philosopher, Benedetto Croce, and his positioning of intellect versus intuition in *Aesthetic*. Although privately she claimed, "I am not a philosopher or I could understand these things," her essay certainly demonstrates an innate understanding of Croce's argument (*PJ* 7).

As she continued to take graduate classes, she became anxious that her fiction might cause this same insecurity she was personally experiencing, a fear of corrupting her readers: "Please let the story, dear God, in its revisions, be made too clear for any false & low interpretation, because in it, I am not trying to disparage anybody's religion" (*PJ* 11). This possibility bothered O'Connor so much, she finally visited "one of the local Iowa City priests and carefully explain[ed] the problem" (Gooch 126). The priest responded by telling her "that she didn't need to write for fifteen-year-old girls" and sending her on her way with "one of those ten cent pamphlets that they are never without" (qtd. in Gooch 127). Perhaps, corresponding with this visit, O'Connor writes, "The Msgr. Today said it was the business of reason, not emotion—the love of God" (*PJ* 13). The priest's advice comforted a young O'Connor, although his pamphlet did not. However even as her anxiety of corrupting her readers subsides, her critique of intellectualism, especially of modern psychology, seems to center on thinking, specifically the types of thinking of which she approves and disapproves.

It is clear from O'Connor's writings during this period, especially in her subsequent drafts of *Wise Blood*, that the intellectualism she encounters in graduate school, namely, the presence of Freud in the zeitgeist of the academy threw her for a loop. Evidently O'Connor did not agree with her character, Hoover Shoates, who complains, "That's the trouble with you innerleckchuls . . . you don't never have nothing to show for what you're saying" since she took the academics around her quite seriously (*WB* 159). She did not merely dismiss the new ideas she was encountering, as this entry demonstrates:

> Dear God, I don't want to have invented my faith to satisfy my weakness. I don't want to have created God to my own image as they're so fond of saying. Please give me the necessary grace, oh Lord, and please don't let it be as hard to get as Kafka made it. (*PJ* 16)

O'Connor's fear of psychological and intellectual seduction manifests itself in her early work, such as in one story fragment where O'Connor's narrator tells of a female novelist who knew that her problem was Freudian[15] or in her March 1947 in-class essay, "Falkner's Children," which begins with a discussion of modern psychology's role in interpreting child characters in fiction and continues into her mature fiction.

Long before she skewered Hulga Hopewell, the nihilist PhD, in her story "Good Country People," O'Connor's early unpublished stories in the Iowa Writers' Workshop expose a personal vendetta with psychologists, intellectuals, and social scientists, ironic since her baccalaureate was in the social sciences. With plenty of insider knowledge about the banality of academia, O'Connor's critique comes from inside the academy—she knew her subject well, and perhaps, that is why academics, who can often be gluttons for punishment, enjoy her satire as much as everyone else. While "Ready Writer" and "A Summer Story" focus on solipsistic writers, her story "The Cock" features a social science professor, Mr. McCoy, who teaches a criminology class designed for schoolteachers, similar to the program in which Sally Poker Sash matriculates in "A Late Encounter with the Enemy." Mr. McCoy believes all the teachers are stupid and is humiliated when a student, Ms. Finly, who Mr. McCoy believes is infatuated with him, reveals she is only interested in her grade.

Of course, this approach, targeting an institution from the insider perspective is fairly common among her fiction. For example, as an academic, she mocks academics, and though a practicing Catholic, Christians, whether Catholic or Protestant, are often the target of her wrath. To account for this tension, I argue that targeting academics so publicly in her fiction becomes O'Connor's way of dealing with her own internal struggles. In one undated entry, she writes, "Please do not let the explanations of the psychologists about this make it [her faith] turn suddenly cold" (*PJ* 4). Moreover, her next entry continues, "I dread, Oh Lord, losing my faith. My mind is not strong. It is a prey to all sorts of intellectual quackery" (*PJ* 5). This quackery became the source material she uses to parody academics, and at Iowa, she found plenty of "quackery" to parody.

THE *WISE BLOOD* DRAFTS AND MA THESIS, 1947

Although it would not be finished in earnest for another four years, at the same time that O'Connor was chronicling her own spiritual anxieties, her earliest drafts of her debut novel, *Wise Blood*, reflect these same projections: fear of psychology, fear of intellectual abstraction, even the fear of losing her faith.[16] As she was working on *Wise Blood* in Iowa City, she writes:

> Oh dear God I want to write a novel, a good novel. I want to do this for a good feeling & for a bad one. The bad one is uppermost. The psychologists say it is the natural one. Let me get away dear God from all things thus "natural" . . . I would like to be intelligently holy. I am a presumptuous fool. (*PJ* 18)

In these early drafts[17] of *Wise Blood*, this same anxiety of education superseding her faith show up in many different characters. In one such draft, Hazel remembers the principal, Slatum, an atheist "who had taken over the school at Eastrod" (Driggers and Dunn 47). In others, Hazel moves to Taulkinham to live with his sister Ruby Hill and her husband, Bill, who sells "MIRACLE" products, a brand which deeply disturbs Motes.[18] However, this angst of intelligence versus faith is most palpable in the later excised character of Henry Caulder, a PhD student in psychology, who appears prominently in early versions of the novel. Caulder, nicknamed Chin, shares a striking resemblance to Sigmund Freud. Chin is bald with a mustache, speaks of time spent in Berlin, smokes a pipe, and often defaults to observations on religion and sex. Chin is a psychologist, atheist, pseudo-intellectual who is writing a dissertation in direct response to B. F. Skinner and who frequently demeans "those child psychology dopes," while claiming that Hazel's problems are related to sex and his obsession with religion (Drafts).

It is during this time that the drafts of *Wise Blood* seem to line up with O'Connor's belief that intellectualism was an assault on her faith, especially as Chin confuses Hazel for a "divinity student—he thinks Haze looks intelligent," and continually mocks Motes's belief in God (Driggers and Dunn 56).[19] Chin attempts to "educate" Hazel, yet, throughout these conversations, all Hazel can do is respond that "he does not understand," and repeats that "he only finished 7th grade" (Driggers and Dunn 56). Throughout these drafts, Chin assures Hazel that sin is a manufactured concept. Yet, as she was writing these early drafts of *Wise Blood*, in 1947, O'Connor writes in her journal that "Sin is a great thing as long as it's recognized. It leads a good many people to God who wouldn't get there otherwise. But cease to recognize it or take it away from devil as devil & give it to devil as psychologist, and you also take away God. If there is no sin in this world there is no God in heaven" (*PJ* 26–27). At this point, we can only speculate; however, it seems that the secularism she encountered at Iowa (at least from her reading list) threatened to undo her entire belief system, which might explain why she humiliates academics for their ability to "take away God."

In these drafts, her critique of academe emerges in subtler ways, such as, through two characters whose roles shift drastically in the finished *Wise Blood*. The first, Leora Watts, the prostitute who is also mentioned in "A Stroke of Good Fortune," who, in the earliest drafts of the novel, was a much more developed character. O'Connor gives Watts's backstory in prostitution, starting at the age of fourteen. O'Connor compares Watts to a "kind of graduate student" of the sex trade who was "beginning to specialize" (Drafts). For Watts, her *beducation* in the sex trade is equated with the specialization found in graduation school, an irony of which O'Connor, a then-graduate student herself, was quite aware. The second character, Enoch Emory, is an early version of her later autodidact characters. In the published *Wise Blood*, Emory has run away from "Rodemill Boys' Bible Academy," his lack of intellectual prowess and sophistication may be more a comment on fundamentalist education than on academe itself (*CW* 25). However, in the drafts, Enoch tells Hazel that he went to the Rodemill Boys' Academy "and came out educated. I ain't no dupe for Jesus crap" (Drafts).

In this early incarnation of *Wise Blood*, O'Connor uses both Enoch and Chin to demonstrate how education erodes faith. If Watts is a satire of the inanity and overspecialization that O'Connor found in graduate school, Enoch's education has had the effect of which O'Connor most fears—his faith is killed by his intellect (although it is safe to say that even in the drafts, Enoch must not possess much of it either). The Enoch of the early drafts who left school not believing is the very incarnation of the anxieties that Haze has of education in his discussions with Chin (the academy erases belief). The theme was autobiographical for O'Connor, who at the time wrote, "Now how am I to remain faithful without cowardice when these conditions influence me like they do . . . Dear God, please let it be that instead of that cowardice the psychologists would gloat so over & explain so glibly" (*PJ* 15).

This trend of satirizing the academy while she is enrolled in the Iowa Writers' Workshop is not limited to the drafts of *Wise Blood*, rather this pattern shows up in the stories collected in her thesis. Of all the short stories she produced as a student at the Iowa Writers' Workshop, the most well known are perhaps the six stories from her MA thesis: "The Geranium," "The Barber," "Wildcat," "The Crop," "The Turkey," and "The Train" (a chapter from *Wise Blood*). Of these stories, "The Barber" and "The Crop," neither of which are highly praised, highlight an early version of O'Connor's archetypical anti-intellectual approach.

"The Crop" is an early prototype of what will become familiar territory for O'Connor readers: the failed writer/artist/intellectual as the object of ridicule. A rewriting of an earlier story, "A Summer Story," which she also wrote while at Iowa and which includes many of the same events, "The Crop" centers around the comical protagonist, Ms. Willerton or Willie, as she is known in the story. She is a graduate of Willowpool Female Seminary and serves as an "early shade of the artist intellectuals who come to dominate O'Connor's later fiction" in stories such as "Everything That Rises Must Converge" and "The Enduring Chill" (Powell 51). Regardless, Ms. Willerton imagines herself a serious writer, although no one takes her seriously. Satirizing her peers in the MFA program, O'Connor's protagonist sets out to find the perfect muse, something important with "social tension" or a "social problem" (*CW* 733). She decides sharecroppers "would make as arty a subject as any, and they would give her that air of social concern which was so valuable to have in the circles she was hoping to travel!" (*CW* 733). The searing critique of writers only continues as it becomes clear that Ms. Willerton does not know her subject, "she decided that not only was 'Lot Motun' a good name for a sharecropper, but also having him call his dog was an excellent thing to have a sharecropper do" (*CW* 734). The story comically follows Miss Willerton's arbitrary writing process and ends with her deciding that sharecroppers were not a good subject for literary fiction, "She needed something more colorful—more arty" before deciding on "the Irish!" (*CW* 740).

"The Crop" read in context of her time in the Iowa Writers' Workshop can tell us a lot about O'Connor's own feelings on literary fiction at the time, and perhaps even the writers with whom she was interacting. The fact that such a simplistic and superficial O'Connor character has graduated from a "female seminary" is a clear stab at education, especially since these qualifications would hardly qualify her as a professional writer. Interestingly, in the story, the single Ms. Wilterton has changed her name to the more masculine, Willie, something that Flannery O'Connor, who changed her name from Mary Flannery to Flannery upon enrolling at the Iowa Writers' Workshop, would know something about. There is also the contrived subject matter, as Ms. Willerton wants to make her story a stinging class-conscious attack when combined with poverty tourism, as her authorial intent seems to drift into a parody of James Agee and Walker Evans's *Let Us Now Praise Famous Men*.

Others have dismissed this story as just another example of the writing about writing cliché or an unsuccessful early parody of southern busybodies, "The Crop" (and its predecessor) satirize both intelligensia and the writing process—a process to which she was very much committed. It reflects the later statements that O'Connor makes about the writing process: "I find that most people know what a story is until they sit down to write one. They find themselves writing a sketch with an essay woven through it, or an essay with a sketch woven through it, or an editorial with a character in it" (*MM* 66). If O'Connor loathed writers with an axe to grind, ironically, "the Crop" is a story that reads as a writer with an axe to grind. However, it is useful as another, more polished, example of how O'Connor was developing this theme while she was in graduate school.

"The Barber," on the other hand, features a different type of archetype, which will be quite common in O'Connor's later fiction: the ineffectual intellectual. "The Barber" is a class-coded story in which the local working-class barbers best the elitist outsider, Rayber, an out-of-touch progressive-minded professor, who cares more about being right than advocating for desegregation. Every time that Rayber visits his barber, the professor is humiliated for supporting Darmon—and by extension desegregation—in the upcoming gubernatorial race. After undergoing his barber's public harassment, Rayber becomes frustrated that neither the barber nor his clients are swayed by Rayber's own well-reasoned convictions and harangues. "Nossir . . . big words don't do nobody no good. They don't take the place of thinkin'," the barber tells Rayber (*CW* 716). As both sides argue over the issue of segregation, the humor comes at both parties' expense, since neither hears the other. In one instance, the barbershop patrons dismiss Rayber, "He's a college teacher, ain't he" (*CW* 718). Meanwhile, Rayber cannot accept the fact that he is unable to persuade these men while "defending myself against barbers," eventually questioning a colleague, "you ever tried to argue with a barber[?]" (*CW* 720). Powell notes that, "during each encounter with the barbers, it is not his intellectual frustration that bothers him but mockery he has to endure" (Powell

39). So, when a patronizing Rayber tries to make his stand, promising "I won't say anything you can't understand," he finds himself completely ineffective, as one patron tells Rayber, "just because you teach doesn't mean you know everything" (*CW* 721). The barbers heckle Rayber until he finally explodes, "Do you think I'd tamper with your damn fool ignorance[?]" (*CW* 724). The story ends as Rayber, who "jumps out the barber chair and pushes through the doors, running into the street," as "lather began to drip" from his face and the "barber's bib, dangling to his knees" (*CW* 724).

What's intriguing about reading "The Barber," as an early version of her satire on the academy is that her protagonist, Rayber, is a model for many of her later failed academics. In fact, he seems like a character who will be later fleshed out in stories in *Everything That Rises Must Converge* and *The Violent Bear It Away*. In his bad faith of good politics, Rayber reminds readers of Thomas the Historian in from "The Comforts of Home," Rayber, the social worker/academic do-gooder in "The Lame Shall Enter First," or even as a model for the professor/antagonist—Rayber of *The Violent Bear It Away*. In the story's end, Rayber, the academic, is infantilized, reduced to a child or raving lunatic, foaming at the mouth, with a bib hanging down, running away. The joke is on the intellectual who can neither explain himself nor function outside the academy.

While neither of these stories quite highlight the theological tension that shows up in *Wise Blood*, both stories from O'Connor's MA thesis produce two different archetypes of her trope of the intellectual as the target of satire. In "The Crop," the target is the inanity of the failed artist, yet, "The Barber" is perhaps the earliest model of her academic whose own superiority complex, and underestimation of the less educated, leads to their own downfall.

IOWA'S LEGACY

It is easy to look at the satire of O'Connor's juvenilia and her later fiction and draw a straight line to her southern heritage; however, doing so overlooks just how deeply the Iowa Writers' Workshop impacted O'Connor, not just her writing, but her habits, her faith, and even her psyche. For one thing, it's hard to place the anti-intellectual archetype solely at the feet of her southern upbringing. Although there is a long history of an anti-intellectual sentiment in the South, O'Connor's own southernness played to her advantage. The southern influence on the DNA of creative writing programs after Iowa is unmistakable. Iowa's textbook *du jour*, Brooks and Warren's *Understanding Fiction*'s second edition, included O'Connor's "A Good Man Is Hard to Find."[20] Furthermore, many of her southern influences were *anything but* anti-intellectual. Even Warren himself had a positive impact on O'Connor. *All the King's Men*, Warren's opus published in 1946, features a protagonist, Jack

Burden, who dropped out of a history graduate program to be a journalist, while Judge Irwin, who, revered as an academic, serves as the moral center of the work. If anything, Warren's Pulitzer Prize–winning novel honors a south-ern intellectual. Finally, even O'Connor's own statements on southern fiction show a writer who is not interested in "reproducing the tropes associated with the region," especially since O'Connor says, "Don't be a Southern writer; be an American writer" (Hoberek 103, *MM* 29).

Rather, it is during her time at the Iowa Writers' Workshop, and her own initiation into academia, that O'Connor's fears of the institutionalization of her art and the destruction of her faith begin in earnest. This explains her reactionary and biographical need to create these academics in her own image. The crux of this autobiographical urge can be found ten years later (1956) in a letter to her friend, Betty Hester, where writing about Hulga Hopewell, O'Connor states, "It's not said that she has never had any faith, but it is implied that her fine education has got rid of it for her, that purity has been overridden by pride of intellect through her fine education" (*HB* 170). And though O'Connor tells Hester, "I have thrown you off myself by inform-ing you that Hulga is like me," perhaps O'Connor believed that she had gotten better at burying her own biographical impulses (*HB* 170).

NOTES

1. See *Cash* 18.

2. Published 3 April 1943.

3. Kenneth Lynn's *Mark Twain and Southwestern Humor* outlines this concept as the *cordon sanitaire*.

4. Brad Gooch's biography, *Flannery: A Life of Flannery O'Connor*, the 2013 release of Flannery O'Connor's *A Prayer Journal*, Emory's acquisition of their Flannery O'Connor collec-tion to name a few recent releases.

5. See Michael O'Brien's *Conjectures of Order* for a detailed discussion.

6. Breit was the assistant editor of the *New York Times Sunday Book Review* and host of the show *Galley Proof*.

7. John Crowe Ransom, who taught at the Iowa Writers' Workshop, wrote a series of edi-torials for the *Kenyon Review*, arguing "that it is just as much a patriotic duty in our present short-of-war economy to the arts going—or for that matter the sciences going, and the colleges and the homes—as to attend the military effort" (240).

8. "Julian Huxley, promoting the United Nations Educations, Scientific, and Cultural Organ-ization (UNESCO), heralded in 1946 the danger of a widespread decline in cultural excellence" (Bennett 2).

9. Not only did the CIA funnel money into creative writing programs, but they also sup-ported creative writing journals, "Also benefiting from CIA largesse that year was a group of journals invited to take advantage of the Congress's clearing house . . . These included *Partisan Review, Kenyon Review, Hudson Review, Sewanee Review, Poetry, The Journal of the History of Ideas* and *Daedalus*" (Saunders 333).

10. See Stephen Wilbers's *The Iowa Writers' Workshop* (1980).

11. *Des Moines Sunday Register*, 28 December 1947.

12. See "Tracking the Sectional Differences," Box 7, Emory Special Collections.

13. See "The Enduring Chill" Draft 194b in the Flannery O'Connor Collection at Georgia College.

14. "Ready Writer," "A Summer Story," and "The Cock" are all unpublished stories that O'Connor wrote during her time at Iowa that feature this theme. All three are available in the Emory University archive.

15. Emory Archives, MSS1305.

16. The previously unpublished excerpts of the *Wise Blood* drafts are quoted with permission from Harold Matson Co., Inc.

17. Dating the *WB* drafts is difficult. Many fragments do not have dates. Her outlines were sent to Rinehart & Co. in late 1946 and she began working on the novel in earnest in 1947, where she also used "The Train" as part of her MA thesis. Many of the excised plots were written in late 1947. She started working on the novel under the direction of Andrew Lytle in spring 1948.

18. The Hills' plot, written in fall 1947, is excised from the novel and later becomes the plot of "A Stroke of Good Fortune."

19. In the drafts, Hazel seems a prototype of Tarwater, who "knew that escaping school was the surest sign of his election" (*CW* 340).

20. This is one of several creative writing anthologies around this time which included O'Connor's work, including the next edition of Caroline Gordon and Allen Tate's *House of Fiction*, which became another famous creative writing textbook edited by southern writers.

WORKS CITED

Bennett, Eric. *Workshops of Empire: Stegner, Engles, and American Creative Writing during the Cold War*. Iowa City: University of Iowa Press, 2015.

Brinkmeyer, Robert. *The Fourth Ghost: White Southern Writers and European Fascism, 1930–1950*. Baton Rouge: Louisiana State University Press, 2009.

Brooks, Cleanth, and Robert Penn Warren, eds. *Understanding Fiction*. New York: F. S. Crofts & Co., 1943.

Cash, Jean. *Flannery O'Connor: A Life*. Knoxville: University of Tennessee Press, 2002.

Coles, Robert. "Flannery O'Connor: A Southern Intellectual." *Southern Review* 16 (1980): 46–64.

Driggers, Stephen, Robert J. Dunn, and Sarah Gordon. *The Manuscripts of Flannery O'Connor at Georgia College*. Athens: University of Georgia Press, 1989.

Engle, Paul. "How Creative Writing Is Taught at the University of Iowa Workshop." *Des Moines Sunday Register*, 28 December 1947.

Gentry, Marshall Bruce, ed. *The Cartoons of Flannery O'Connor at Georgia College*. Milledgeville: Georgia College, 2010.

Gooch, Brad. *Flannery O'Connor: A Life*. New York: Little, Brown and Company, 2009.

Hoberek, Andrew. *The Twilight of the Middle Class: Post–World War II American Fiction and White-Collar Work*. Princeton, NJ: Princeton University Press, 2005.

Hobson, Fred. *The Southern Writer in the Postmodern World*. Athens: University of Georgia Press, 1991.

Magee, Rosemary. *Conversations with Flannery O'Connor*. Jackson: University Press of Mississippi, 1987.

Mayers, Tim. "(Re)Figuring the Future: Lore, Creative Writing Studies, and Institutional Histories." *Can Creative Writing Really Be Taught: Resisting Lore in Creative Writing Pedagogy*. New York: Bloomsbury, 2017.

McGurl, Jerome. *The Program Era: Postwar Fiction and the Rise of Creative Writing*. Cambridge, MA: Harvard University Press, 2011.

O'Brien, Michael. *Rethinking the South: Essays in Intellectual History*. Athens: University of Georgia Press, 1993.

O'Connor, Flannery. *A Prayer Journal*. Edited by William A. Sessions. New York: Farrar, Straus and Giroux, 2013.

O'Connor, Flannery. *O'Connor: Collected Works*. New York: Library of America, 1988.

O'Connor, Flannery. *Mystery and Manners: Occasional Prose*. Edited by Sally and Robert Fitzgerald. New York: Farrar, Straus and Giroux, 1970.

O'Connor, Flannery. *The Complete Stories*. New York: Farrar, Straus and Giroux, 1971.

O'Connor, Flannery. *The Habit of Being*. Edited by Sally Fitzgerald. New York: Farrar, Straus and Giroux, 1979.

Powell, Tara. *The Intellectual in the Twentieth-Century South*. Baton Rouge: Louisiana State University Press, 2012.

Ransom, John Crowe. "Muses and Amazons." *Kenyon Review* 3 (1941): 240.

Saunders, Frances Stonor. *The Cultural Cold War: The CIA and the World of Arts and Letters*. New York: New Press, 2000.

Country People: Depictions of Farm Women in Flannery O'Connor's Short Fiction

MONICA CAROL MILLER

When scholars and fans of Flannery O'Connor alike consider the mother-daughter relationships in her work, they tend to assume that the dynamics in the stories have their basis in O'Connor's relationship with her mother, Regina Cline O'Connor. To be fair, much of this interpretation is based on Flannery's own descriptions of their relationship. Often referring sardonically to Regina[1] as "the parent" in her letters, Flannery seems at times to chafe at living her adult life with her mother who disapproved of anything remotely inappropriate. Such biographical readings of O'Connor's work have been further encouraged by Louise Westling's foundational 1978 article on the "sour, deformed daughters and self-righteous mothers" who appear in O'Connor's work. Westling argues that "their distortions express a passionate but inadvertent protest against the lot of womankind. Flannery O'Connor can make these women live because she is one of them" (511).

However, these psychobiographical readings distract from what I see as a striking current of critique of both earlier depictions of southern pastoralism as well as the retrogressive idealism of her contemporary southern Agrarians. I propose that the mother characters in these stories have often been misread, and I want to reconsider several mother figures—Mrs. McIntyre in "The Displaced Person," Mrs. May in "Greenleaf," and Asbury's mother in "The Enduring Chill"—who often run farms and are known for their constant complaints and unhappiness with life. Typically, such women (who resemble Regina to varying degrees in their dedication to their work) are understood as ridiculous. Their preoccupation with money, appearances, and appropriate behavior is generally read as indicative of their own failings—albeit failings that prepare them for shocking moments of grace.

I suggest a different approach. Given O'Connor's own affect, which often eschewed pretentiousness for a more down-to-earth practicality, I propose reading such characters' preoccupation with material matters more generously. Indeed, the tension in "The Enduring Chill" between Asbury's condescension toward his mother's circumscribed concerns and the realities on which these concerns are based—to be specific, his defiance of her rule not to drink unpasteurized milk and his resultant undulant fever—exemplifies the shift in perspective for which I am advocating. Reading their concerns about the material matters of running a farm more sympathetically allows a fuller understanding of the grace they receive. By considering the realities of farm life and taking seriously the difficulties which these characters face, we see a more complex picture of characters such as Asbury's mother. Rather than reading them simply as comic relief or burdens for their children to bear, instead, they gain agency, and through this shift, are themselves candidates for grace.

And further, such a shift in perspective illuminates what I am identifying as O'Connor's initiation of a counternarrative to the prevailing movement of the southern Agrarians, which is generally seen as holding sway in southern literature of the time. Specifically, O'Connor's farm women provide an important counternarrative to earlier depictions of agrarian[2] southern life, from Erskine Caldwell to William Faulkner. Unlike characters such as Jeeter Lester in *Tobacco Road* or Anse Bundren in *As I Lay Dying*, subsistence farmers whose tragedies are to a great extent a result of their own ignorance and sloth, O'Connor's female farmworkers "prove tough and resourceful in their dealings with the outside world, providing comfortable if modest homes for their children. The side effects of their struggle are a degree of stinginess and smugness, wariness of strangers, and determination to see things in a cheerful light" (Westling 511). Not only do O'Connor's depictions of farm life stand in contrast to these earlier examples, but they also belie the romantic (and myopic) Agrarian vision of the South mythologized by writers such as the "Twelve Angry Southerners" in 1930s *I'll Take My Stand*. This foundational work in traditional southern studies established a long-prevailing understanding of the rural South as "an agrarian civilization which had strength and promise for a future greatness second to none" (Owsley 71). As Frank Lawrence Owsley wrote in his *I'll Take My Stand* essay "The Irrepressible Conflict," "The life of the South was leisurely and unhurried for the planter, the yeoman, or the landless tenant. It was a way of life, not a routine of planting and reaping merely for gain" (71). Importantly, the farm stories in O'Connor's work—and the women who run and work on these farms—provide a much more realistic, unsentimental account of actual agrarian life. O'Connor's farm stories demonstrate, in fact, that this "way of life" was primarily a routine of planting and reaping, complicated by the arbitrary whims of weather and human nature. Ultimately, I argue that the characters in

O'Connor's stories and their pragmatic attachment to the land, which eschews romantic identification for an accounting of balance sheets, demonstrate a counter-nostalgic vision of the mid-twentieth-century South.

Taking this view also challenges the prevailing notion of the nature of O'Connor's relationship to the Agrarians. Generally, scholars have seen O'Connor's relationship with the southern Agrarian philosophy as being one of sympathy and influence. Katherine Hemple Prown, for example, analyzes the "strong . . . kinship [O'Connor felt] with the Fugitive/Agrarians, whose conservative vision of southern culture she shared" (19). It is true that many of these writers, including Allen Tate, Andrew Lytle, and Robert Penn Warren played various roles in the development and publication of her work, and indeed, the foundational textbook *Understanding Fiction* edited by *I'll Take My Stand* authors Cleanth Brooks and Robert Penn Warren was one which O'Connor herself often referred to as being "of invaluable help to me" (*Mystery and Manners* 83).[3] Prown argues that O'Connor's work shares "a common artistic vision with these writers—particularly in regard to the importance of the southern past and the traditions it inspired" (20). Specifically, Prown identifies the Agrarians' rejection of the southern "genteel tradition" as an aesthetic strategy that O'Connor shared: "based on sentimental and domestic conventions," this "genteel tradition" functioned "as a code for anything hinting of the feminine and came finally to embody the antithesis of every aesthetic principle they sought to establish" (26).

Indeed, most scholarship that contemplates the role of women in O'Connor's work concurs with this understanding, that her stories represent a consistent rejection of the feminine. For example, in her introduction to *On the Subject of the Feminist Business: Re-Reading Flannery O'Connor*, Teresa Caruso concludes that O'Connor's female characters are trapped in a world in which women's value is defined solely in terms of their relationships with men. According to Caruso, even "those women who are given a voice are nevertheless silenced in the face of the patriarchy that controls them, a control that extends beyond the merely physical and into the unconscious, manipulating their actions and rendering them grotesque in ways that do not affect O'Connor's males" (3). However, there is not a completely monolithic interpretation of O'Connor's female characters. Within this same collection, Robert Donahoo argues that "reading an anti-female bias into O'Connor's plots and characters overlooks the limitations imposed by the reality of the visible, historical universe her writings seek to render" (15). Indeed, I believe that by more fully taking into account the realities of the "visible, historical universe" that O'Connor was both influenced by as well as seeking to render—particularly the material realities of running a farm—we see less of an antifemale bias and more of an antisentimental bias.

Contemplating the real-life Andalusia farm and the ways in which O'Connor understood its material realities provides a more comprehensive foundation for O'Connor's personal understanding of the lives of the rural characters she created. Indeed, the most significant influence on my reading that visiting Andalusia has had has been to highlight the reality of Andalusia as a working dairy farm during O'Connor's life.[4] By 1951, after O'Connor's lupus diagnosis, she and her mother moved to Andalusia full-time, where Flannery could write (without having to negotiate steps, as she did in their family's home in town), and Regina took over running the family farm while caring for her daughter.

Understanding Andalusia as a functioning farm, I have been struck by what strength Regina Cline O'Connor must have possessed.[5] Widowed at forty-four, she raised a precocious daughter and ran a functioning dairy farm during the 1950s in rural central Georgia, all of which were formidable responsibilities. She inherited the farm from her brother, Dr. Bernard Cline, who originally purchased the farm in the early 1930s as a weekend getaway from his home in Atlanta. Hiring workers to operate the farm as he expanded his acreage, Cline trained his sister to keep the books for what by the 1940s was a growing, productive farm. When Bernard Cline died in 1947, he left the farm jointly to his sister Regina and their brother Louis Cline. Regina and Louis expanded the operation, establishing two hundred acres of pasture and several hay fields while keeping the rest of the property for timbering. As Louis continued to work and live in Atlanta, the day-to-day operations of the farm lay primarily with Regina in the 1950s and 1960s. After Louis's death in 1973, Regina became the farm's sole owner until her death in 1995.[6]

The financial and emotional stress that running Andalusia exerted on Regina has been made even more real to me by reading through the letters that Flannery sent to her mother while she was in graduate school in Iowa. Written during the time that Regina was in the process of taking over the running of the farm, these letters not only demonstrate that Flannery understood the difficulties that her mother faced in running Andalusia but also provide a different picture of the relationship between the two women than is generally understood. Reading through this correspondence, I have found not the contentious mother-daughter relationship seen so often in her fiction, but rather daily letters home in which Flannery is grateful for care packages and chats about her roommates. And upon learning that her mother is taking over running Andalusia, Flannery expresses concern for the difficulties she expects her mother to face in taking on this arduous responsibility. In one letter, she says she hopes that the farm will not increase her mother's worries (1 February 1947); two days later, she writes that she hopes Regina will be able to make the farm pay—"that is, come out even"—and suggests that Regina might rent out the house (3 February 1947). The archive does not contain Regina's side of the correspondence, but a few days later, Flannery wrote:

> Didn't mean to imply any lack of enthusiasm over your having the farm. I think he knew you were the only one in the family who could & would handle it like it ought to be done; however, my doubts are simply in the line that it may increase your worries without increasing your pocket book. It always seemed to be eating up his. I presume that you are going to cut it down to such an extent however you will be able not to loose [sic] anything on it. (8 February 1947)

Flannery's remarks to her mother in this correspondence highlight the fact that Flannery understands that the expenses and troubles of running a farm are real and significant.

This understanding led her, I believe, to create characters in Regina's likeness who are tough negotiators and driven businesswomen. However, while scholarship has generally focused on the friction that such determination leads to, I believe we should shift our focus to the need for such determination itself. While it's true that Regina had a reputation for penny-pinching and being a savvy businesswoman, Flannery herself was aware of the practical difficulties of farm life. Realizing that Flannery understood that running a farm was a difficult, financially precarious endeavor has prompted me to reread her stories that feature women who run farms in a more sympathetic light.

In stories such as "The Displaced Person," "Greenleaf," and "The Enduring Chill," these women are alone. Their attempts at companionship, whether the "friendship" between Mrs. McIntyre and Mrs. Shortley in "The Displaced Person" or the many failed attempts at intimacy between mother and child in stories such as "Greenleaf" or "The Enduring Chill," all fall short. In considering these relationships, Carole K. Harris analyzes these characters' use of clichés, particularly the phrase "good country people," which these farm-owning women so often invoke for what Harris describes as "white 'trash' workers whom they have hired and with whom they interact on a daily basis, as if they were family." Harris observes, "The fact that O'Connor keeps rewriting this relationship in her letters and stories reveals that something beyond a mere comic effect is at stake in their cliché-filled speech: she records the politics of the farm for future readers and, through the cautionary violent endings of her stories, dramatizes what happens when we take for granted that clichés are only dead, empty expressions" (113).

Just as Harris suggests that we take more seriously O'Connor's characters' use of clichéd language, I argue that we should more often take seriously the characters who deploy such language; indeed, I agree with Harris's observation that O'Connor is "a keen observer of the politics of everyday conversation" (113). According to Harris, O'Connor's "depiction of Georgia does not simply pay allegiance to its traditions. It records the tensions in those traditions," specifically those that O'Connor observes at Andalusia. Harris points out that not only O'Connor's fiction but also her letters show her to be "[e]ndlessly fascinated by her mother's conflicts with her hired help" (113). More importantly, these farm stories allow O'Connor to "closely stud[y] . . . the way each party in the master-servant relationship uses language to negotiate differences in social power" (111). However, these tensions are not simply of a two-dimensional hierarchy of power. In her stories (as in real life), in their roles as sole proprietors, the women who run these farms are independent, yes, but also vulnerable.

Their vulnerability is heightened by their status as single women in the midcentury rural South. The women who run the farms are divorced or widowed; the only surviving marriage bonds in these stories are among the workers.[7] Whether Asbury's mother in "The Enduring Chill" or Mrs. McIntyre in "The Displaced Person," these single women are ultimately responsible for their farm's continued operation, on which a number of people depend for their living, and their preoccupation with the materialistic demonstrates an important rejection of a pastoral mode of representation.

"The Life You Save May Be Your Own," for example, depicts the mundane tasks of farm life such as putting a new roof on the garden house or building a new hog pen.[8] And unlike earlier writers of the rural South, from Caldwell to Faulkner, the agricultural South about which O'Connor was writing in the 1950s was undergoing great changes in farming practices, changes which made farmwork less pastoral as it required farm owners to adopt a more specifically professional approach to their work. By the time that O'Connor was writing, "extension agents and the farm press encouraged farm families to think of themselves as multi-generational farms as opposed to the previous attitude that farming was simple sustenance for the family group. We see this style of life change from *farming* to *agribusiness*" (Faber 122, emphasis in original). Such a shift from *farm* to *business* requires a similar shift in roles for women on these farms. In order to survive, they must reject traditionally feminine characteristics of domesticity and nurturing in favor of "masculine" traits such as pragmatism and rationality; this shift away from domesticity and femininity mirrors a larger economic shift.

However, given the sociohistorical context of the midcentury, rural South within which O'Connor was writing (and her mother was working), such a pursuit of financial survival cannot escape the double bind of gender expectations. I cannot conceive of a credible female character who might be judged favorably in such circumstances. As Bernard explains, "On one hand, her women are defying southern tradition by assuming male roles. Indeed, they overcome the challenge of running a farm, but as mothers, they fail miserably in story after story. . . . For while it is true that O'Connor allows her female protagonists to defy male ethics, we see that they will eventually be punished for doing so" (77). Indeed, Bernard observes that "O'Connor's farm mothers adopt masculine values in order to succeed, pushing their feminine 'weaknesses' aside, and in the process, alienating themselves from their children" (72). Not only do they alienate their children but also the rest of their community in their constant struggle to keep their farms in business.

The resulting alienation between these mothers and their children causes much of the conflict that arises in many of O'Connor's stories. I agree with Bernard's argument that "O'Connor's fictional mothers should not be seen as heartless predators. Although not easily likeable—O'Connor's characters rarely are—they and their children are victims of circumstance. Neither Regina nor the mothers in this collection can fully be blamed for their fractured families" (77). Indeed, given the circumstances of midcentury, rural life, it is fair to characterize characters such as Mrs. Crater in "The Life You Save May Be Your Own" or Mrs. Hopewell in "Good Country People" as women who "indulge but do not nurture, collude with patriarchy but do not compensate this collusion with affection or mutual support" (Bernard 74). Caught in the double bind of traditional gender expectations combined with the material realities of midcentury agribusiness, the ways in which these characters attempt to make ends meet while maintaining some semblance of compliance to gender roles, these characters find it impossible to fully succeed in either realm.

This is not to say that characters such as Mrs. McIntyre in "The Displaced Person" are without fault; I don't deny that she is ultimately a flawed, narcissistic, bigoted character. Typically, such characters are read without any sympathy; as Bernard explains succinctly, "All of her characters are guilty of something—generally pride, or one of its derivatives" (75). However, I argue that the instability and vulnerability that characters such as Mrs. McIntyre claim to experience be read as genuine, rather than dismissed as hyperbolic or hysterical complaint. In the opening to "The Displaced Person," for example, I suggest reading the description of Mrs. McIntyre as one of a woman desperate to deny her own vulnerability:

> Mrs. McIntyre was coming down the steps of her house to meet the car. She had on her largest smile but Mrs. Shortley [the wife of the dairyman], even from her distance, could detect a nervous slide in it. These people who were coming were only hired help, like the Shortleys themselves or the Negroes. Yet here was the owner of the place out to welcome them. Here she was, wearing her best clothes and a string of beads, and now bounding forward with her mouth stretched. (194–95)

While Mrs. Shortley interprets Mrs. McIntyre's appearance to greet the new hired help as revealing Mrs. McIntyre to be overly concerned with appearances, I suggest we might also notice the emphasis on strain in the passage, "bounding forward with her mouth stretched." While Mrs. McIntyre certainly is flawed, she is also under pressure to make her farm produce. It is significant that both "The Displaced Person" and "Good Country People" open with a white female worker observing the white female farm owner's behavior, reading her skeptically from a position of insecurity. In these stories, both sides claim financial insecurity—and I suggest that both sides have valid points. In "The Displaced Person," Mrs. Shortley fears that her husband (who is admittedly lazy and who frequently smokes in the milk house, a dangerous practice) will lose his job; Mrs. McIntyre, the owner, fears not having the resources to keep the farm going.

Considering that the source of the skeptical reading of Mrs. McIntyre is Mrs. Shortley, I propose that we be less hasty in fully accepting this biased reading. I find it curious that both readers and critics tend to take Mrs. Shortley's description of Mrs. McIntyre uncritically. For example, Harris's analysis of Mrs. McIntyre's language assumes the generally accepted, skeptical reading of Mrs. McIntyre, that

> To further buttress her self-presentation as victim, Mrs. McIntyre draws on clichés from the authoritative repertoire of her beloved first husband, the late Judge, a respected figure in the community: "I've been running this place for thirty years . . . and always just barely making it. *People think you're made of money. I have the taxes to pay. I have the insurance to keep up. I have the repair bills. I have the feed bills.*" It all gathered up and she stood with her chest lifted and her small hands gripped around her elbows. "Ever since the Judge died, . . . I've *barely been making ends meet* and *they all take something when they leave. The niggers don't leave—they stay and steal. A nigger thinks anybody is rich he can steal from* and that *white trash thinks anybody is rich who can afford to hire people as sorry as they are.* And *all I've got is the dirt under my feet!*" (294, emphasis mine)[9]

In Harris's explication of this passage, she discusses the ways in which Mrs. McIntyre adopts such cliché use from her late husband, the Judge, "[copying] his habit of speaking as if he were penniless. Whereas the Judge may have spoken ironically at times, Mrs. McIntyre seems to believe her own clichés, presenting herself to her hired help as if she were the victim in the employer/employee relationship" (112). While I certainly don't want to suggest that Mrs. McIntyre is actually in a state as vulnerable as that of her workers (nor do I want to suggest that we feel sympathy for her race- and class-based prejudices and outright bigotry), I do want to bring attention to the fact that running a farm was an uncertain endeavor, and that perhaps the litany of complaints about money we see in these stories should be taken as more than comic relief.

For much of the story, Mrs. McIntyre's vision of the world seems to come down to one enormous balance sheet. Before the Guizacs arrive, "There had been a great deal to do to get ready for them because they didn't have anything of their own, not a stick of furniture or a sheet or a dish, and everything had to be scraped together out of things that Mrs. McIntyre couldn't use any more herself" (196). They make curtains out of feed sacks because "Mrs. McIntyre said she could not afford to buy curtains" (196). When the priest admires the peacock, Mrs. McIntyre replies, "Another mouth to feed" (198). Three weeks after the arrival of the Guizacs, Mrs. McIntyre is able to buy a new machine; she says that Mr. Guizac "would save her twenty dollars a month on repair bills alone" because he is so "thrifty and energetic" as well as an "expert mechanic, a carpenter, and a mason [. . .] She said getting him was the best day's work she had ever done in her life. He could work milking machines and he was scrupulously clean. He did not smoke" (201). He also catches Sulk (one of the black farmworkers) presumably stealing a turkey, which he reports to Mrs. McIntyre. She tells the black man who has worked the farm longer than she has been there, "What you colored people don't realize . . . is that I'm the one around here who holds all the strings together. If you don't work, I don't make any money and I can't pay you. You're all dependent on me but you each and every one act like the shoe is on the other foot" (217). While Mrs. McIntyre's complaints here could be written off as another example of what Harrison interprets as her self-presentation of victimhood, I believe that there is enough truth to them that they should not be so easily dismissed. There is a complex irony beneath Mrs. McIntyre's statement about the farm: while it is true that her workers are dependent on her for their pay, she is also quite dependent on her workers for her survival. Neither side seems able to fully comprehend the interdependent nature of the farm.[10]

Conventional readings of Mrs. McIntyre and others that dismiss these women as merely bossy and overbearing misunderstand the complexity of the interdependence that exists between the owners and the workers on the farm. We see this in "Greenleaf," for example, when Mrs. May thinks to herself, "she had been having shiftless people's hogs root up her oats, their mules wallow on her lawn, their scrub bulls breed her cows. If this one was not put up now, he would be over the fence, ruining her herd before morning—and Mr. Greenleaf was soundly sleeping a half mile down the road in the tenant house" (312). I certainly see reflections of Regina Cline O'Connor in Mrs. May in this story:

> She was a country woman only by persuasion. The late Mr. May, a businessman, had bought the place when land was down, and when he died it was all he had to leave her. The boys had not been happy to move to the country to a broken-down farm, but there was nothing else for her to do. She had the timber on the

place cut and with the proceeds had set herself up in the dairy business after Mr. Greenleaf had answered her ad. . . . . Over the years they had been on her place, Mr. and Mrs. Greenleaf had aged hardly at all. They had no worries, no responsibilities. They lived like lilies of the field, off the fat that she struggled to put into the land. When she was dead and gone from overwork and worry, the Greenleafs, healthy and thriving, would be just ready to begin draining Scofield and Wesley. (319)

Mrs. May feels quite alone and overwhelmed by her responsibilities, reflecting Flannery O'Connor's comment about how taking on Andalusia might add to her mother's worries. We see similar worries expressed by Asbury's mother in "The Enduring Chill" as well:

When she looked out any window in her house, she saw the reflection of her own character. Her city friends said she was the most remarkable woman they knew, to go, practically penniless and with no experience, out to a rundown farm and make a success of it. "Everything is against you," she would say, "the weather is against you and the dirt is against you and the help is against you. They're all in league against you. There's nothing for it but an iron hand." (321)

In all of these examples, the women who run the farms do so out of necessity and without any substantial background in farm management or business. Rather, they rely on their strong wills, common sense, and keen intelligence in order to learn what they need to survive. These character traits are necessary in the face of physical and financial vulnerability as well as uncontrollable forces such as market changes and the whims of Mother Nature. Lacking physical prowess, technical ability, or the privileges that accompany masculinity, their very real vulnerability is generally unacknowledged. It is their intent to convince others of their shared precarious state which drives their frequent litanies of complaint. Unfortunately, the invisibility of so many of these forces cause their complaints to often be dismissed as hyperbole.

To be fair, all of these characters are, to varying degrees, narcissistic, thoughtless, overbearing, and bigoted. But I'd like to suggest that perhaps there's less of an ironic undertone than we generally read in the narrator's description of Mrs. McIntyre in "The Displaced Person":

But she had survived. She had survived a succession of tenant farmers and dairymen that the old man himself would have found hard to outdo, and she had been able to meet the constant drain of a tribe of moody unpredictable Negroes, and she had even managed to hold her own against the incidental bloodsuckers, the cattle dealers and lumber men and the buyers and sellers of anything who drove up in pieced-together trucks and honked in the yard. (218)

Rather than read this as an ironic statement of Mrs. McIntyre's own self-aggrandizement (which I acknowledge is a valid reading), I suggest this alternately be read as a more general ironic statement toward the midcentury agrarian (and Agrarian) trend in southern fiction. In particular, I argue that these "incidental bloodsuckers, the cattle-dealers and lumber men and the buyers and sellers of anything who drove up in pieced-together trucks and honked in the yard" provide a pragmatic commentary on a Faulknerian vision of such characters, such as V. A. Ratliff in the Snopes trilogy.

It is important to recognize that O'Connor's farm stories are not those of the Compsons and the Snopeses—Faulknerian epics which W. J. Cash characterized as "the romantics of the appalling," in which "the essence of romanticism is the disposition to deal in the more-than-life-sized, the large and heroic, the picturesque and vivid and extravagant" (378). The difficulties that O'Connor's farms face, while vivid, eschew any characterization of the rural South which might qualify as romantic, even a "romantics of the appalling." Rather, I believe that these works articulate a significant counter-Agrarian trajectory in midcentury southern fiction. And while it is true that O'Connor does write from a place of generally unexamined race and class privilege, it is also true that her depictions of southern life lack any sense of romantic nostalgia.

Ultimately, I am arguing that O'Connor's farm stories represent an important turn away from nostalgic visions of a pastoral South which so much of the narrative of traditional southern studies drew upon and which New Southern Studies has worked to critique. As author Alice Walker describes in her essay "Beyond the Peacock," explaining her own appreciation of O'Connor's fiction, O'Connor's stories contain white people without a "whiff of magnolia in the air" as well as "black folks without melons and superior racial patience." Identifying O'Connor as "for me the first great modern writer from the South" (52), Walker gestures toward what I am ultimately arguing here: O'Connor's fiction in general, and her farm stories in particular, should be considered an important sea change in the development of southern literature. Rather than simply using the rural setting to provide a southern sense of place, O'Connor's rural settings should be understood to provide a significant context of financial and other material difficulties which encourage us to reconsider the farm women who populate them. By taking more seriously the challenges they face, we gain a deeper understanding of their struggles toward grace.

NOTES

1. Throughout this article, I refer to the two women as "Regina" and "Flannery" for the purpose of clarity, not out of any disrespect for either.

2. In my usage, lowercase "agrarian" refers to rural, farm-based living, while capitalized "Agrarian" refers specifically to the cultural criticism of those who identify with the Agrarian movement, with its foundation in the 1930 publication *I'll Take My Stand*.

3. See also *Mystery and Manners*, 192, 283.

4. See "Flannery and Her Mother" for my account of how visiting Andalusia changed my understanding of Flannery's relationship with Regina.

5. It is true that the reading I am suggesting here is also one based on biography. Though my reading does begin with a different understanding of Flannery's relationship with Regina than most, my focus is less on how this biographical aspect of the author's life appears in her fiction than it is on how this might change our understanding of characters such as Mrs. Asbury. In other words, if Flannery understood that running a farm meant constant financial anxieties, then we should not be so quick to dismiss her characters in her work who express such anxieties as hyperbolic or comic relief.

6. See "Andalusia."

7. However, even these bonds generally follow the unsentimental tradition of farm novels in which marriage bonds are founded more on practicality than romance.

8. See "The Life You Save May Be Your Own" (176–77).

9. These characters' use of cliché is frequently noted by scholars, such as Bernard, who sees this as part of their complying with the southern code (74).

10. Perhaps only the Guizacs, whose life experience provides them a broader perspective on such things, are able to more fully grasp the nature of the farm's workings.

WORKS CITED

"Andalusia." *Andalusia Farm: Home of Flannery O'Connor*. 2014.

Bernard, Gretchen Dobrott. "Flannery O'Connor's Fractured Families: Mothers and Daughters in Conflict." *Revista de Estudios Norteamericanos* 10 (2004): 71–82.

Brown, Melissa, and Lane O. Ely. "Dairy Industry." *New Georgia Encyclopedia*. 2 August 2016.

Caruso, Teresa. "Introduction." *"On the Subject of the Feminist Business": Re-Reading Flannery O'Connor*, edited by Teresa Caruso, 1–8. New York: Peter Lang, 2004.

Cash, W. J. *The Mind of the South*. 1941. New York: Random House, 1991.

Donahoo, Robert. "O'Connor and *The Feminine Mystique*: 'The Limitations That Reality Imposed.'" *"On the Subject of the Feminist Business": Re-Reading Flannery O'Connor*, edited by Teresa Caruso, 9–28. New York: Peter Lang, 2004.

Donaldson, Susan V. "Introduction: The Southern Agrarians and Their Culture Wars." *I'll Take My Stand: The South and the Agrarian Tradition*, by Twelve Southerners. 1930. Baton Rouge: Louisiana State University Press, 2006. ix–xl.

Faber, Becky. "Women Writing about Farm Women." *Great Plains Quarterly* 18 (Spring 1998): 113–26.

Gooch, Brad. *Flannery: A Life of Flannery O'Connor*. New York: Little, Brown and Company, 2009.

Miller, Monica Carol. "Flannery and Her Mother." 17 October 2014. *Andalusia, Home of Flannery O'Connor*.

O'Connor, Flannery. "The Displaced Person." 1953. *A Good Man Is Hard to Find*. New York: Library of America, 1988. 285–327.

O'Connor, Flannery. "The Enduring Chill." 1965. *Everything That Rises Must Converge*. New York: Library of America, 1988. 547–72.

O'Connor, Flannery. "Greenleaf." 1965. *Everything That Rises Must Converge*. New York: Library of America, 1988. 501–24.

O'Connor, Flannery. Letter to Regina O'Connor. 1 February 1947. Flannery O'Connor papers, Stuart A. Rose Manuscript, Archives, and Rare Book Library, Emory University.

O'Connor, Flannery. Letter to Regina O'Connor. 3 February 1947. Flannery O'Connor papers, Stuart A. Rose Manuscript, Archives, and Rare Book Library, Emory University.

O'Connor, Flannery. Letter to Regina O'Connor. 8 February 1947. Flannery O'Connor papers, Stuart A. Rose Manuscript, Archives, and Rare Book Library, Emory University.

O'Connor, Flannery. Letter to Sally and Robert Fitzgerald. 20 September 1951. *Letters.* New York: Library of America, 1988. 890.

O'Connor, Flannery. Letter to A. 5 August 1955. *Letters.* New York: Library of America, 1988. 946.

O'Connor, Flannery. "The Life You Save May Be Your Own." 1953. *A Good Man Is Hard to Find.* New York: Library of America, 1988. 285–327.

Owsley, Frank Lawrence. "The Irrepressible Conflict." *I'll Take My Stand: The South and Agrarian Tradition.* 1930. Baton Rouge: Louisiana State University Press, 2006. 61–91.

Ransom, John Crowe. "Reconstructed But Unregenerate." *I'll Take My Stand: The South and Agrarian Tradition.* 1930. Baton Rouge: Louisiana State University Press, 2006. 1–27.

Vernon, Zachary. "The Enfreakment of Southern Memoir in Harry Crews's *A Childhood*." *Mississippi Quarterly* 67, no. 2 (Spring 2014): 193–211.

Vernon, Zachary. "Romanticizing the Rough South: Contemporary Cultural Nakedness and the Rise of Grit Lit." *Southern Cultures* 22, no. 3 (2016): 77–94.

Walker, Alice. *In Search of Our Mothers' Gardens: Womanist Prose.* New York: Harcourt Brace Jovanovich, 1983.

Westling, Louise. "Flannery O'Connor's Mothers and Daughters." *Twentieth Century Literature* 24, no. 4 (Winter 1978): 510–22.

PART 3

STRANGE BEDFELLOWS

Mystery and Myth: Friedrich Nietzsche, Flannery O'Connor, and the Limiting Power of Certainty

WILLIAM MURRAY

At first glance, the philosophies and writings of Friedrich Nietzsche and Flannery O'Connor might seem fundamentally unrelated or at odds with each other. After all, they hailed from different continents, lived in different centuries, and throughout their lives maintained different beliefs about religion. Despite these obvious differences, though, they promote a surprisingly similar discourse on the power and purpose of art. They both understood art as having the ability to dismember and reshape a culture's static worldview, and they saw a reintroduction of stories or myths, capable of reintroducing mystery, as being vital to their civilization's health.[1] While O'Connor rarely mentions Nietzsche, the southern author was aware of the German philosopher's work, and through her writing, she seems to be engaging in a conversation of sorts with him.

The conversation she has, however, is one that largely takes place in the margins. In her library, she had a copy of F. C. Copleston's *St. Thomas and Nietzsche*, as well as Erich Heller's *The Disinherited Mind in Modern German Literature and Thought* (Kinney 25, 128). She also references Nietzsche twice in letters (*HB* 90, 334)[2] and once in a review of Denis de Rougemont's 1963 book *The Christian Opportunity* (*PG* 168), but she avoids any overt or extended discussions of his philosophy. This relatively light engagement with Nietzsche, along with their clear differences, has largely led scholars either to ignore the similarities between the two authors or to pit them against one another as natural enemies. When we look at O'Connor's "A Good Man Is Hard to Find" (1953) together with Nietzsche's *Birth of Tragedy* (1872), however, we can begin to understand how O'Connor's work not only engages with early Nietzsche, but also how these two very different authors shared and promoted similar views on art and culture.

Exploring the similarities between O'Connor's and Nietzsche's writing also adds to our understanding of how both authors can be read outside the categories in which they are typically confined. O'Connor's fiction is often bracketed off as fitting neatly within the classifications of Catholic, gothic, or regionalist art, and particularly, scholars have grappled with how to engage with her Christian beliefs. O'Connor's work is unavoidably Catholic,[3] and critics such as Terry Teachout have long argued that the "American intellectual community [that] has lately become almost entirely secularized ... will necessarily result in only a partial appreciation of her work" (57, 58).[4] Understanding O'Connor's writing in dialogue with non-Catholic thinkers, like Nietzsche, diffuses some of the inherent tension that emanates from the author's seemingly narrow faith, and it also chips away at the idea that one must understand Catholicism in order to appreciate the full power and message of her stories. Ultimately, this reading of O'Connor's fiction outside the borders of religious writing should help alleviate Teachout's concern that "O'Connor's faith [might] cause the brilliance of her art to fade in an age of increasingly militant secularism" (58). Putting O'Connor's stories in conversation with *The Birth of Tragedy* also can help us better understand Nietzsche's philosophy, which is often erroneously reduced to a dark form of nihilism or a militant attempt at deicide. Just as O'Connor is subject to being categorized as solely a "religious" author, Nietzsche, too, is frequently cordoned off as categorically opposed to the spiritual, and by reducing these two authors to their belief or disbelief in a deity, it becomes easy to ignore their larger claims about art and culture.

Henry Edmondson's book *Return to Good and Evil: Flannery O'Connor's Response to Nihilism* (2002), which is the only extended treatment of the relationship between Nietzsche and O'Connor, exemplifies the temptation to read these authors as diametrically opposed to each other. The book casts Nietzsche and O'Connor as promoting fundamentally different beliefs, where Nietzsche argues for a brand of soulless nihilism and O'Connor endorses a worldview that affirms transcendentally defined Good and Evil. As Edmondson argues in his preface, O'Connor believed "that despite Nietzsche's brilliance in recognizing the weaknesses of Western civilization, he failed to offer anything of constructive value to replace what he sought to overthrow. Quite the contrary, a distillation of Nietzsche's thoughts yields little more than a dangerous product of crude sex, raw power, and aimless destruction" (xii).[5] Whether O'Connor really felt this way about Nietzsche or not is beyond the purview of my chapter, but when we consider *The Birth of Tragedy* alongside O'Connor's "A Good Man Is Hard to Find," I believe we can clearly see that both texts envision a similar form of "constructive value" that could be introduced into Western civilization through art's ability to reveal the inexplicable. While Edmondson largely dismisses *Tragedy* as a book promoting sexual hedonism and the destruction of morals, which stands opposite O'Connor's sense of morality (25–28, 41), a fuller reading of Nietzsche's text suggests that he, like O'Connor, promotes a reintroduction of mystery, through myth or art, into a world dominated by Socratic rationalism.

To better understand O'Connor's and Nietzsche's similar views, it is important first to step back and grapple with Nietzsche's often-vexing *The Birth of Tragedy*. The text, importantly, is Nietzsche's first published book, and as such, it is not a full representation of his philosophy; however, as he explains in the introduction for the 1886 republication, the book represents not only a "first work . . . in the bad sense of the term," but also "a book which has *proven* itself, I mean one which has in any case measured up to the 'best of its time'" (5; emphasis in the original). The arguments in *Tragedy* are, in places, tortuous, and it is easy to see why Nietzsche viewed the book as less mature than his later writings. As his translator Walter Kaufmann puts it, "*Tragedy* is badly overwritten and murky" (3). Despite the aesthetic faults and the occasional lapses in logic, though, both Nietzsche and generations of readers have recognized *Tragedy*'s enduring brilliance. Douglas Smith, for instance, defends it as a "complex but compelling book" that "deals with much more than the origins of Greek classical drama. It engages with some of the major philosophical and aesthetic questions of its day and continues to provide a framework for approaching the analysis of cultural phenomena" (xxxvi).

When we look more closely at *Tragedy*, we can see that Nietzsche has at least two clear ambitions for the text: first, he traces the rise and fall of Dionysian art in ancient Greece, and second, he explains how Germany's current artistic and cultural moment has experienced a similar decline in Dionysian influence. Through the first half of *Tragedy*, Nietzsche establishes how the Greeks married Dionysian disorder to an Apollonian sense of structure through the genre of tragedy, which ushered in a golden age of art. Eventually, however, through the ascendency of Socratic rationalism, the Dionysian element was excluded and art lost its revolutionary and dangerous edge. Nietzsche argues that after Greek culture subdued the wild passions of the Dionysian, it began only to promote a version of Apollonian art and discourse that left behind mystery in favor of a sense of absolute knowledge. Nietzsche envisions the Socrates, who was brought to life by Plato, as embodying the "optimistic" belief that logic and reason could lead to a final and complete Truth, which Nietzsche argues destroys the balance between knowledge and mystery. As he explains, "Let us consider the consequences of the Socratic principles: 'Knowledge is virtue; sin is the result of ignorance; the virtuous man is the happy man': in these three basic forms of optimism lies the death of tragedy" (78). Nietzsche goes on to write:

> The optimistic dialectic drives *music* out of tragedy with the whip of its syllogisms: that is, it destroys the essence of tragedy, which can only be interpreted

as a manifestation and transformation into images of Dionysian states, as visible symbolizations of music as the dream-world of intoxication." (79; emphasis in the original)

In other words, as societies begin to "optimistically" believe in their own ability to attain perfect Truth, there is a corollary diminishing of art's intoxicating and transformative power.

Nietzsche then concludes *Tragedy* by arguing for a rebirth of Dionysian influence in Germany, which should take place under the auspices of "Socrates the maker of music" (93). In this newly formed art, which marries Socrates and music, the Apollonian and Dionysian reach a synthesis between defined order and unbound mystery. Nietzsche saw Richard Wagner's music as having the power to reintroduce this Dionysian sense of dismemberment to their Apollonian dominated culture. He hoped his friend's operas could unseat the fixed "optimism" he saw dominating Germany's art, and while Nietzsche eventually moved away from believing that Wagner could achieve this end, he maintained throughout his life a deep sense that the certainties espoused by science and mainstream religion posed a threat to both art and the larger culture of his homeland.

Although O'Connor remained a faithful Catholic, she, like Nietzsche, sought a similar reintroduction of disorder and mystery into her culture. Her tactics for introducing this disruption have often been criticized as grotesque or morbid,[6] but O'Connor consistently articulated that the violence in her stories was a part of a larger attempt to "shock" readers beyond the safe conformities of midcentury America.[7] Both Nietzsche and O'Connor, then, believed artists have the capability to unsettle their audiences, which could push them toward a re-association with mystery. As Nietzsche explains, the audience of true tragic art undergoes "dismemberment, the proper Dionysian suffering" as they shed their old allegiance to cold logic and reason (59). O'Connor concurs with this vision of violent dismemberment in her speech "Novelist and Believer" (1963), where she argues that art should move audiences beyond their safe environment of comfort and stability. She explains, "For the last few centuries we have lived in a world which has been increasingly convinced that the reaches of reality end very close to the surface, that there is no ultimate divine source . . . that the mysteries of life will fall before the mind of man" (*MM* 157–58). O'Connor goes on to point out that art, like faith, should challenge these certainties, and "If the novelist is doing what as an artist he is bound to do, he will inevitably suggest that image of ultimate reality as it can be glimpsed in some aspect of the human situation" (158). She continues, pointing out that in an America that had become "dulled" and unfeeling (160), the novelist must "jar the reader into some kind of emotional recognition" of "awe and mystery" (*MM* 162).

In O'Connor's fiction, her characters almost always are jarred awake and shown "ultimate reality" through undergoing some act of violence,[8] and while this violence certainly can be unsettling at times, it reliably serves to illuminate some greater mystery or hidden truth. As she explained to the Georgia Writers' Association, "I have found that violence is strangely capable of returning my character to reality and preparing them to accept their moment of grace. Their heads are so hard that almost nothing else will work" (*MM* 53–54). For O'Connor, violence is closely linked with the revelation of mysterious Truth, which is hidden from her hardheaded subjects. These claims about the potentially constructive power of artistic violence are, again, very much in tune with Nietzsche's assertions about the effect of Dionysian art. He writes in *The Birth of Tragedy* that "the most expensive marble, man, is kneaded and hewn, [by] the chisel-blows of the Dionysian Artist," which leads to "the Eleusinian Mysteries calling: 'Do you fall to your knees multitudes? World do you sense the creator?'" (23). The language is different, of course, but both authors essentially argue that art must commit violence if it is to introduce mystery into a static culture rooted in logic and science.

Both O'Connor and Nietzsche argued this artistic violence was necessary because mere logic was not enough to reveal the totality of human experience, and we can see their shared rejection of unchecked scientific rationalism in one of O'Connor's rare mentions of Nietzsche. After hearing about genetic modifications to chickens, which made them unable to fly, O'Connor wrote to her struggling pen pal Elizabeth Hester, "This is a generation of wingless chickens, which I suppose is what Nietzsche meant when he said God was dead" (*HB* 90). As Ralph Wood points out, we can see in this "ever so revealing" phrase that "O'Connor rightly refused to demonize Nietzsche. Like Heidegger after him, Nietzsche was not engaged in a shouting match with the Almighty. He was protesting the massive vacancy of soul that, largely unrecognized, characterizes modern religious life in the West" (179–80). O'Connor, in this letter, is staking out a position where she seems to be agreeing with Nietzsche's sentiment in *The Birth of Tragedy*, where he states, "without myth every culture forfeits its healthy, natural creative force [and] only myth can rescue all the forces of imagination" (23). The wingless chickens, unable to fly, then resemble those without myth who lack the imagination to see beyond the ground to which they have been confined.

While O'Connor certainly would not have identified her fiction as illuminating a Christian "myth," at least not in the sense which that word is often used to signify something couched in falsehood, she did affirm that her stories and novels were aimed at helping provide access to the inexplicable. O'Connor, in other words, uses her fiction to reassert the traditional function of myth, which is to use the recognizable world in order to reveal something larger and beyond immediate comprehension.[9] As she explains in the essay

"The Church and the Fiction Writer," good art attempts to "eliminate mystery while another part tries to rediscover it" (*MM* 145), or as she puts it later in the same text, "When fiction is made according to its nature, it should reinforce our sense of the supernatural by grounding it in concrete, observable reality" (148). O'Connor's fiction, like myth, uses what can be comprehended in the material world to point toward something that cannot be understood or explained by mere intellect and reason. Truth, for O'Connor and Nietzsche, then, exists beyond mere signification or explanation and could only be approached through something like myth, which confronts the gap between the known and unknown. Therefore, while O'Connor may have differed from Nietzsche on who or what God is,[10] both authors were united against cultures that did not take seriously the way myth or art could reveal monstrous and mysterious realities lurking beyond human certainty.

O'Connor's desire to reintroduce this sense of mystery into her world of Socratic rationalism can clearly be witnessed in one of her most anthologized short stories: "A Good Man Is Hard to Find."[11] In the story, O'Connor sets up an interaction between two opposing societal forces, which are brought to life by the grandmother and an escaped outlaw named the Misfit.[12] Almost immediately, O'Connor identifies the grandmother as being associated with the Socratic belief that all could be deciphered and understood. As the family travels to Florida, the grandmother busies herself by educating the other travelers. She tells Bailey, her son, the speed limit and where the police officers like to hide; she educates her grandchildren, June Star and John Wesley, about Georgia's geological formations; and she offers the entire car lessons on the crops that line the highway (GM 11). Throughout the family's trip, she works as a tour guide and teacher for the younger generations, and when John Wesley complains about the South, calling Tennessee "a hillbilly dumping ground" and Georgia "a lousy state too," the grandmother is incensed. She tells them, "In my time . . . children were more respectful of their native states and their parents and everything else. People did right then" (12). Through her lessons and claim of knowing what is "right," she asserts her fixed worldview as being grounded in an unshakable and clearly defined Truth that should not be questioned.

The grandmother's certainty that she has a clear and stable vision of the world is further established as the family passes an African American child with no pants. When the grandmother sees the boy, she exclaims, "Wouldn't that make a picture now?" and after June Star comments on the oddity of the child not wearing any pants, the grandmother informs her, "Little niggers in the country don't have things like we do. If I could paint, I'd paint that picture" (12). The grandmother, here, using racist language reiterates a racist view of the world as a fixed and stable hierarchy, and she wishes that world could be frozen as an immobile "picture" or "painting," forever reminding her that she inhabits a class above the poor boy. Nietzsche characterizes this obsession with fixed images as being an important part of the Apollonian dominated worldview. He writes, those who ignore Dionysian influences regard "even the fury of raging Achilles as nothing more than an image, whose raging expression he enjoys with that dreamer's pleasure in appearance—so that he is protected by this mirror of appearance from unification and fusion" (36). Like the Apollonian, who is unmoved by angry Achilles and, therefore, cannot reach unification, the grandmother is blissfully unperturbed by the deeper, troublesome connections between African American poverty and the plantation she wishes to visit. She is simply content looking into a "mirror of appearance" and seeing only a pretty picture (36), which, for her, remains safe and unconnected to the larger, violent realities that underlie that image.

The grandmother's obsession with maintaining and preserving the image of the past as a fixed part of her identity builds as the family travels toward Florida, and in her fixation with history, we can again see how she is connected to Nietzsche's definition of the "myth-less" Apollonian. Nietzsche describes "the myth-less man" as someone who "remains eternally hungering among all the bygones, and digs and grubs for roots, though he have to dig for them even among the remotest antiquities" (122). The grandmother centers her life on the certainties she finds in the "bygones" of her past, and we can see her share these sentiments not only in her persistent attempts to convince the family they should break off their trip and go someplace connected to their "roots," but also in her conversation with Red Sammy, the proprietor of a barbecue restaurant.

In their conversation, the two form a chorus lamenting the passing of better times. Their nostalgia for the past, though, is couched in a great deal of irony, as they unwittingly demonstrate the racism and sexism that plague American history. Sammy and the grandmother, however, are deeply convinced their version of reality is unquestionably true, and they seem wholly unaware of any contradictions in their assertions or that other views could possibly exist. They plunge forward, armed with a sense of blind conviction in their claims about themselves and the plight of the modern world. At one point, the grandmother lauds Sammy as a "good man," and he responds, "Yes'm I suppose so" (15). Here, Sammy and the grandmother feel as if goodness can clearly be known and ascribed, and later when the grandmother blames Europe for America's problems, Sammy tells her, "it was no use talking about it, she was exactly right" (16). In their exchange, the two characters revel in a kind of shorthand where assumptions are recast as facts and there is "no use" in discussing differences in opinion. Their dialogue, which is rooted in a national history of injustice and conservatism, exhibits, then, a steady and false confidence in their own ability to discern and reveal Truth, making them like the Apollonian artists or Socratic philosophers who naively believed they could unmask and expose the uncertainties of the world.

After leaving Red Sammy's, the grandmother again feels a hunger for the "bygones" of history, and she finally convinces her family, by telling them they might find a hidden treasure, to leave the highway in search of a plantation from her youth. In this departure from the safety of the highway, though, she unwittingly allows for an introduction of Dionysian terror into her family's safe and structured environment. The first intrusion into her serene view of the world is the "horrible thought" that the plantation house she claimed was in Georgia is actually in Tennessee (18). This crack in the sense that her views on history and place are stable and verifiable causes the grandmother to accidentally liberate the cat, Pitty Sing, who, finally free from his containment, works as another force of disruption and attacks her son Bailey. While trying to separate from the cat, Bailey drives the car into a ravine where it flips once before coming to rest in a ditch. The family's world, then, is literally flipped by the crack in the grandmother's sense of certainty, but despite her revelation that she does not truly know the past, the grandmother clings to a fixed view of herself as a lady living in an orderly world. The grandmother's hat, "still pinned to her head," suggests her view of herself as a respectable woman remains intact (19).[13] It is battered and damaged but still in one piece, providing her a bit of reassurance as she tries to reorder her senses.

The hat, however, cannot withstand the intrusion of the Misfit, and O'Connor uses its eventual destruction to further symbolize the grandmother's crumbling sense of self. After the wreck, the grandmother unsuspectingly flags down the Misfit's car, and when he emerges, she cannot contain her Apollonian desire to unmask and know. She blurts out, "You're the misfit! . . . I recognized you at once!" and he responds by informing her, "it would have been better for all of you, lady, if you hadn't of reckernized [*sic*] me" (22). The Misfit's lightly veiled threat causes Bailey to turn on the grandmother, saying something "that shocked even his children" (22), and the impact of his attack, along with the realization that they have encountered the outlaw, starts the final collapse of the grandmother's façade of respectability. Her once-ordered world, where she saw herself as a proud matriarch of an honorable southern family, is thoroughly damaged by these forces. The grandmother, nonetheless, stubbornly maintains the illusion that she is a lady and people are defined by the quality of their blood. She tells the Misfit, as he approaches them with his gun, "You wouldn't shoot a lady would you? . . . I know you're a good man. You don't look a bit like you have common blood" (22). Despite her pleas and reasoning, though, the Misfit goes on to murder the entire family, and O'Connor signals the impact of this violent disruption by having the brim of the grandmother's hat come off in her hand (23).

Still, as the Misfit kills each member of the family, feeding them to the "line of woods [which] gaped like a dark open mouth" (21), the grandmother refuses to understand that she is in the presence of a force that will eventually destroy her preconceived notions of reality. It is not until he finally turns the gun on her that she realizes monsters do exist, and it is here, next to the "mouth" of the woods, staring into the Misfit's red-eyes (29), that the grandmother recognizes her own failure to see the world as it is. O'Connor marks the grandmother's revelation, which carries her from the dream world of certainty to the world of wakefulness, mystery, and monsters, as being a movement away from individualism and toward a sense of inexplicable unity. As Nietzsche puts it, the reintroduction of the Dionysian leaves individuals feeling "reunified, reconciled, reincorporated, and merged with his neighbor . . . genuinely one" (23). Nietzsche and O'Connor, then, link individualism to the false security offered by Socratic optimism, and to fix this overconfidence, they both call for a disruption that can lead to an understanding of human unity.

Throughout O'Connor's story, the grandmother resists this sense of unity and instead obsesses over her own individual and limited view of the world. She talks about her politics, her past boyfriends, her view of manners, her memories of the past, and her understanding of the social hierarchy; however, when she is forced to face the monstrous Misfit, the grandmother is finally able to see him and shifts from these myopic obsessions to a comprehension of the universal. O'Connor makes it clear that truly seeing the Misfit means understanding the kinship or unity between the outlaw and the old lady. She writes, the grandmother "saw the man's face twisted close to her own . . . and she murmured, 'Why you're one of my babies. You're one of my own children!'" (29). It is in this moment that the grandmother, through the guidance of the twisted and monstrous face, understands that she is unified with and directly related to the broader, violent world, which to that point she had chosen to ignore. As Lila N. Meeks explains, "When she reaches out to this criminal, this twisted murderer, when she calls him 'one of my babies,' she is reunited with her creator" (21). Jessica Hooten reiterates this point, writing, "the grandmother . . . loses her earthly life, but in the last moment when she renounces her individualism, she may also be finding spiritual life" (200). The old lady's acceptance of a new reality, where monsters and mysteries are part of the family, allows her to break free from the structured "truths" that were the sources of her racism and isolation. Her realization and death, then, symbolize the dissolution of the organized and self-obsessed outlook that dominates her sense of reality for the majority of the story. As a result of this freedom, she is reunited with her "creator," which again echoes the language of Nietzsche, as he asks those who have experienced the Dionysian, "Do you fall to your knees multitudes? World do you sense the creator?" (23).

The grandmother's reunification with the mysterious "creator" relies on this final moment of clarity, where she realizes that she is symbolically akin to a "monster." While the story's seemingly dark conclusion often causes some trepidation, it falls in line with our previous discussion of O'Connor's relationship with fictive violence as a positive force. In the closing lines of "A Good Man Is Hard to Find," O'Connor makes her views on the old lady's revelation clear by leaving readers with an image of the grandmother, who is dead but at peace, "smiling up at the cloudless sky" (29). In her fiction, letters, and lectures, O'Connor consistently frames this sort of violence as showing readers some hidden, universal aspect of themselves. As she explains in a discussion at Hollins College, speaking about the grandmother's death, "violence is never an end in itself. It is the extreme situation that best reveals what we are essentially" (*MM* 113). In other words, O'Connor argues that artistic violence is a necessary component in showing individuals some essential aspect of shared humanity, and this view of violence as being strangely capable of showing that which relates us, closely resembles the way Nietzsche explains the intrusion of Dionysian art into the Apollonian world. He writes:

> The effect aroused by the Dionysian . . . seem[s] 'Titanic'; and 'barbaric' to the Apollonian Greek: while at the same time [he is] unable to conceal from himself the fact that he was inwardly related to those fallen Titans and heroes. Indeed, he was obliged to sense something even greater than this: his whole existence, with all its beauty and moderation rested on a hidden substratum of suffering and knowledge, which was once again revealed to him by the Dionysian. (32)

What Nietzsche's text suggests here is that while the Dionysian may appear barbaric and foreign to the Apollonian, it serves an important function in awakening the self to the "substratum of suffering and knowledge" that unites humanity. Like the grandmother, who when confronted by the Misfit is first repulsed then realizes she is figuratively related to him, audiences, when confronted by Dionysian art, eventually realize that there is a deeply ingrained relationship between themselves and the larger world that stretches beyond logical and safe explanations. More clearly, without acknowledging the monstrous and the "Titanic," which resides universally in humanity, there would be no reversal, no understanding of grace, and, perhaps most importantly, no revelation of a greater communal oneness for the grandmother.

Finally, when we consider O'Connor alongside Nietzsche, we can see how she uses her art and faith not to bludgeon or coerce readers toward a particular and clearly defined answer; rather, like the German philosopher, she promotes an inexplicable sense of mystery that extends beyond visible comprehension. Her work, therefore, avoids crusading for a narrow set of values that are singularly aligned with any one doctrine or any final version of Good and Evil. She, instead, illustrates how confrontations with the limits of knowledge can lead to freedom and transcendence, and while these confrontations may be violent, akin to Dionysian dismemberment, O'Connor suggests that such radical realignments are necessary when humanity becomes too convinced of its own ability to know and understand all facets of life. Put simply, by looking at both authors' larger claims about art and culture, we can see how Nietzsche and O'Connor transcend the narrow categories into which they are often placed, and more than that, we can also recognize their still relevant message that art is often our best tool in combating accepted and calcified knowledge.

NOTES

1. I use myth here and throughout the essay, largely, according to its first definition, which is a story "typically involving supernatural beings or forces, which embodies and provides an explanation, etiology, or justification for something such as the early history of a society, a religious belief or ritual" ("myth"). For both authors, art performs the function of "myth," in that it helps embody or explain something beyond immediate human comprehension.

2. The first letter, written July of 1955, draws a connection between wingless chickens and Nietzsche's statement that God was dead (*HB* 90). The second letter was written May of 1959, and in it she informs her friend Dr. Spivey that she was reading Heller's book and specifically references the chapter on Nietzsche (*HB* 334). In the review she recommends Denis de Rougemont's 1963 book *The Christian Opportunity*, which is a text that rebuts post-WWII interpretations of Nietzsche's claim that "God is dead." Rougemont, however, is not interested in engaging directly with Nietzsche or his philosophy; rather, the book centers on other writers who are attempting to move past God.

3. In this chapter, I do not mean to suggest there is no value in reading O'Connor as a Catholic writer, and this chapter could easily be written putting her Thomistic- and Maritain-influenced aesthetics in conversation with Nietzsche's philosophy. The reason I avoid dwelling on these influences, though, is I want to illustrate how her work can be read beyond the Catholic tradition. There has been an abundance of great work that focuses on how her work is impacted by her faith, and for more information on how her art is influenced by Thomistic and Maritain aesthetics, see Susan Srigley's *Flannery O'Connor's Sacramental Art* (2004) and Rowan Williams's *Grace and Necessity* (2005), respectively.

4. Davis J. Leigh echoes Teachout, writing, "to understand suffering as a transformative experience in the stories of O'Connor *requires* insight into her framework of Christian faith" (365; emphasis added).

5. Edmondson admits that not everyone agrees with his characterization of Nietzsche as a devout nihilist (xii), and he also claims that O'Connor was not interested "in a debate with Nietzsche or any other philosopher" (3); however, throughout the book he argues that Nietzsche's views were indeed deeply nihilistic and therefore antithetical to O'Connor's belief in Good and Evil.

6. Specifically, I am thinking here of Mab Segrest's insightful essay "Southern Women Writing: Toward a Literature of Wholeness," in which she characterizes O'Connor's fiction as being obsessed with "images of deformity and despair" (29): however, O'Connor's work since the first reviews of *Wise Blood* has been characterized as grotesque and disturbing (, Butcher 3, Goyen 4, Rosenfeld 19).

7. In her talk "The Fiction Writer & His Country" O'Connor told the audience, artists of faith engaging with "modern life" must, at times, "make your vision apparent by shock—to the hard of hearing you shout, and for the almost-blind you draw large and startling figures" (33–34).

8. We can see examples of violence coupled with transformation in many of O'Connor's works beyond "A Good Man Is Hard to Find." For instance, the gouging of Hazel Motes's eyes

in *Wise Blood* (1952), the gorging by the bull in "Greenleaf" (1956), and Harry Ashfield's drowning in "The River" (1955). In all of these examples, the act of violence is linked to the character's moment of grace or possible enlightenment.

9. Her views appear to echo C. S. Lewis's, who wrote about what he called the "True Myth," a term he borrowed from his friend J. R. R. Tolkien. Lewis explains, "Therefore it [myth] is true, not in the sense of being a 'description' of God (that no finite mind could take in) but in the sense of being the way in which God chooses to (or can) appear to our faculties" (427–28).

10. In *Tragedy,* we can see Nietzsche's views on the God he wishes to kill, as he claims that God "exiles art, *each and every* art, to the realm of *lies*—that is he denies, damns, condemns it" (Nietzsche 9; emphasis in the original). This view of the Christian deity is revisited in his later work *The Gay Science* (119–20, 199).

11. O'Connor links "A Good Man Is Hard to Find" to tragedy, which Nietzsche argued best captured the balance between Dionysian and Apollonian art, in an address entitled "On Her Own Work." In this speech she says that the story "should elicit from you a degree of pity and terror," and she also points toward the idea that the plot follows the basic structure of a tragedy so that "any element of suspense will be transferred from its surface to its interior" (*MM* 109).

12. An interesting note is that Erich Heller, in a book that O'Connor read, *The Disinherited Mind* (1952), writes that Nietzsche is "an eternally cheated misfit" (81).

13. In the beginning of the story the grandmother references that she chose her outfit (including the hat) so that "In case of an accident, anyone seeing her dead on the highway would know at once that she was a lady" (11).

WORKS CITED

In the text, I use (GM) to mean "A Good Man Is Hard to Find," (*MM*) to mean *Mystery and Manners*, (PG) *The Presence of Grace*, and (*HB*) to mean *Habit of Being*.

Butcher, Fanny. "A Good Man Is Hard to Find, and Other Stories (Book Review)." *Chicago Sunday Tribune*, 3 July 1955, 3.

Edmondson, Henry T. *Return to Good and Evil: Flannery O'Connor's Response to Nihilism*. Lanham, MD: Lexington Books, 2002.

Goyen, William. "Wise Blood (Book Review)." *New York Times* (Early City Edition), 18 May 1952, 4.

Heller, Erich. *Disinherited Mind: Essays in Modern German Literature and Thought*. New York: Farrar, Straus, and Cudahy, 1957.

Hooten, J. "Individualism in O'Connor's 'A Good Man Is Hard to Find.'" *Explicator* 66, no. 4 (2008): 197–200.

Kaufmann, Walter. "Translator's Introduction." *The Birth of Tragedy and the Case of Wagner. Translated with Commentary by Walter Kaufmann*. New York: Vintage Books, 1967.

Kinney, Arthur F., and Flannery O'Connor. *Flannery O'Connor's Library: Resources of Being*. Athens: University of Georgia Press, 1985.

Leigh, Davis J. "Suffering and the Sacred in Flannery O'Connor's Short Stories." *Renascence: Essays on Values in Literature* 65, no. 5 (2013): 365–79.

Lewis, C. S. *They Stand Together: The Letters of C. S. Lewis to Arthur Greeves (1914–1963)*. Edited by Walter Hooper. London: Collins, 1979.

Meeks, Lila N. "Flannery O'Connor's Art: A Gesture of Grace." *Flannery O'Connor's Radical Reality*, edited by Jan N. Gretlund and Karl-Heinz Westarp, 18–26. Columbia: University of South Carolina Press, 2006.

"myth, n." *OED Online*. Oxford University Press, January 2018. Web. 22 February 2018.

Nietzsche, Friedrich Wilhelm. *The Birth of Tragedy*. Translated by Douglas Smith. New York: Oxford University Press, 2000.

Nietzsche, Friedrich Wilhelm. *The Gay Science: With a Prelude in German Rhymes and an Appendix of Songs*. Edited by Bernard Williams. Translated by Josefine Nauckhoff. Cambridge: Cambridge University Press, 2011.

O'Connor, Flannery. *A Good Man Is Hard to Find*. New York: Harcourt Brace Jovanovich, 1983.

O'Connor, Flannery. *The Habit of Being: Letters Edited and with an Introduction by Sally Fitzgerald*. Compiled by Sally Fitzgerald. New York: Farrar, Straus and Giroux, 1979.

O'Connor, Flannery. *Mystery and Manners: Occasional Prose*. Compiled by Sally Fitzgerald and Robert Fitzgerald. New York: Noonday, 1970.

O'Connor, Flannery, *The Presence of Grace, and Other Book Reviews*. Athens: University of Georgia Press, 1983.

Rosenfeld, Isaac. "To Win by Default." *New Republic* 127, no. 1, 7 July 1952, 19.

Segrest, Mab. "Southern Women Writing: Toward a Literature of Wholeness." *My Mama's Dead Squirrel: Lesbian Essays on Southern Culture*. Ithaca, NY: Firebrand, 1985. 19–42.

Teachout, Terry. "Believing in Flannery O'Connor." *Commentary* 127, no. 3 (March 2009): 55–58.

Wood, Ralph C. *Flannery O'Connor and the Christ-Haunted South*. Grand Rapids, MI: Eerdmans, 2005.

Flannery O'Connor and the Fascist Business: Plurality and the Possibility of Community

ALISON STAUDINGER

The word "fascist" comes with such baggage that I wonder if thinking about any author in its light is illuminating or useful—at the same time, its continued (if convoluted) resonance suggests we must. The point shouldn't be to label so-and-so a fascist, although important work has been done to evaluate actual practicing fascists, including covert collaborators, particularly among the modernists. Flannery O'Connor is decidedly not an "actual fascist,"[1] but neither the term, nor its aesthetics,[2] are distant from her writing. Just as modernism has been reevaluated from its initial reception as staunchly antifascist to admit the fascist tendencies within, so too is the relationship between American culture, art, and fascism ripe for reappraisal. Flannery O'Connor intervenes at the heart of this debate; her writing makes clear the attractions of fascism as it also critiques the work of mass ideology. In responses to literary modernism, liberal democracy, and Catholic universality there is the temptation to bisect aesthetics and thought and identify wholly with the world of modernity, progress, and faith. In this view, fascism functions merely as the shadow-self of ideology, conservatism, and unthinkingness—rather than of democracy, progress, and liberality. In contrast, O'Connor's fiction mockingly indicts American fascist impulses and imagery—and perhaps gestures toward some of them in the Church, if not Christ. Yet, her characters themselves have no technology for overcoming these impulses, and instead wait for an eschatological awakening (in a world where fascism threatens us in the short term, this may not be enough). However, the precise refusal of O'Connor to foreclose alternative readings of this eschatological moment itself holds open the space for radical pluralism, which at least some thinkers suggest is antifascist. Although O'Connor's work to build a community across deep divides in her life is less evident in her fictional worlds, which contain

few examples of characters engaging across difference, I argue that the fleeting moments of grace, read as a secular eschaton, provide a starting point on
which we could imagine building such communities.

In this essay, I explore the role of banal, everyday fascism in O'Connor's
fiction, correspondence and aesthetic practice, using an Arendtian understanding of totalitarianism, buffered with other political theories of fascism,
to illuminate the particular contribution of O'Connor to the question of
fascism in the United States. While O'Connor avoided direct public commentary on what she called "the fascist business," her work and correspondence
evidence a deep engagement with it (*HB* 97). In particular, she seems to interpret fascism as a radical denial of human plurality. She rejects this denial in
her artistic practice, fiction and nonfiction, and friendships, but rarely, especially not when considering racial inequality, portrays an earthly community
that could embrace plurality. This community requires responding to these
"fugitive" moments of democracy and building institutions on them—and it
rejects the naturalization of race that both civil rights integration and segregationist exclusion can perpetuate. Ultimately, she offers a subtle portrait of
the attractions of fascism for Americans, and in her resolute commitment to
pluralism, even when her own tendencies are anti-pluralist, suggests that it
is in the reader's response to the texts, rather than the text themselves, that
resistance seems possible.

Increasingly, O'Connor is read as a political writer.[3] Although she claimed
to have written only one "topical" story—the treatment of bus integration in
"Everything That Rises Must Converge" (*HB* 537), this was an exaggeration.
Her fiction, in context and content, along with a voluminous correspondence
and a well-stocked library, betray her political savvy. O'Connor herself connected her own grotesque style to politics—writing in a letter that a televised
debate of candidates for governor was a "classical exhibition of Georgia politics" that couldn't have "been better" if she had "written it herself" (*HB* 483).
This typical wryness around electoral politics even extended to the assassina-
tion of John F. Kennedy, whose candidacy she had supported; O'Connor wrote
that it would "take all the wind out of the sails of Southern politics, which has
been operating exclusively on a 'damn the Kennedys!' basis . . ." (*HB* 550). She
understood the hyperbole of politicians and recognized that civil rights were
important to understanding southern politics. Yet, she did not concern herself
with racial issues, and was "shockingly naïve" at best "and insulting" at worst
in her understanding of the civil rights movement at least before 1963 (Whitt
89, 90). Still, her fiction explores concepts with deeply political resonance, particularly, themes of fascism and democracy—showing that American political
culture is vulnerable to fascism because of its white-supremacist roots.

Robert Brinkmeyer's *The Fourth Ghost: White Southern Writers and
European Fascism 1930–1950* explores this terrain, connecting fascism (the

eponymous fourth ghost) to the anti-industrial call for southern renewal epit-
omized by the Agrarians. Although O'Connor did not read *I'll Take My Stand:
The South and the Agrarian Tradition* until 1964, late in her life, she worked
with many of its authors. Jon Sykes Jr. argues that O'Connor offers an alternative, eschatological route out of the Agrarian narrative of southern degeneracy,
but he also identifies race as a "troubling lacuna" in her move toward "authentic religion" (41). But the haunting question of Brinkmeyer's study, "what
does the authoritarianism and the racial politics of European Fascism, and
most particularly that of Nazi Germany, have to do with southern culture?"
(209) applies beyond 1950, when his study ends (and is not addressed in his
O'Connor book). Bacon suggests that a shift from "brown" to "red" fascism
occurs after World War II ends and proceeds to consider O'Connor primarily in relation to fears of communist invasion. However, O'Connor's own
discussion of the term, along with her occasional use of fascist imagery, suggests that she is still working through questions about "brown" fascism—and,
indeed, often in tandem with racial questions, as Brinkmeyer suggested.

Here, I want to consider fascism in two ways; one, as a political stance and
the other as literary practice. In terms of political fascism, I follow O'Connor's
own engagement with Hannah Arendt, who helped create what has been
called the "totalitarianism industry," constructing a replacement for ideas like
authoritarianism and fascism because, for Arendt, they were insufficient for
explaining the regimes during and after World War II. Although totalitarianism, too, has since lost its precision of meaning, Arendt's use is similar to
O'Connor's, and for that reason appropriately illuminating, particularly in
that Arendt's commitment to "radical plurality," an idea I will return to in
the conclusion, pushes the boundaries of O'Connor's antifascism. Arendt
writes *Origins of Totalitarianism* in the late 1940s on the Nazi *and* Soviet
regimes, yet only really makes the case for their similarity when she added
a section on "Ideology and Terror" in the second edition published in 1958.[4]
For Arendt, totalitarianism is an unprecedented government which "crystal-
ized" in Europe after anti-Semitism and colonial capitalism, along with other
modern processes, made people "superfluous" and lonely. These isolated individuals, lacking a community in which they can act together politically, are
vulnerable to mass movements and, ultimately, to propaganda and rhetoric
which replaces reality with ideological clichés. Although Arendt suggests any
ideology will do, Nazi racism is her clearest example, as anti-Semitism provides a ready narrative of what (exclusion and genocide) needs to happen
for fascist regeneration of the homeland as well as a powerful basis on which
to encourage collective distrust and further stamp out human spontaneity
and freedom. While fascism perhaps requires a more precise definition than
Arendt's Totalitarianism, and I do not want to collapse them utterly, my sense
is that O'Connor's own understanding of fascism is fundamentally Arendtian:

it tempts lonely, modern individuals because it removes the painful need to engage with reality and substitutes a premade set of ideas, and fascist pedagogy itself is one of force and domination, not persuasion or openness.

David Carroll offers an excellent working definition for thinking about literary fascism, arguing that literary fascism is:

> not the application of fascist ideology to literature, a form of determination from the political "outside"; rather, it concerns the "internal" relations of fascism and literature. In a sense, literary fascism exploits the totalizing tendencies implicit in literature itself and constitutes a technique or mode or fabrication, a form of fictionalizing or aestheticizing not just of literature but of politics as well, and the transformation of the disparate elements of each into organic, totalized works of art.

Along with the possibility for "totalizing," I also understand literary fascism to happen at the level of the "everyday" experiences of characters and in the way that literature is, as Kaplan says, "open to the use of the entire community" and "banal" (43).[5] The connection between fascism and aesthetics, made most famous by Walter Benjamin in *The Work of Art in the Age of Mechanical Reproduction*, where he defines fascism as the aestheticization of politics, finds possible literary expression in both the content, form, and style of a work—and the relationship of the work, author, and reader. In O'Connor, I argue that, while various temptations of fascism are explored in the experiences of characters, an ultimate refusal to close off interpretation or to totalize is a doubly antifascist gesture.

FASCISM ONE: POLITICAL STANCES

That O'Connor thought seriously about fascism is clear in her correspondence with where we find both the germ of the idea that Americans, northern and southern, are problematically vulnerable to racialized thinking as ideology and the way in which O'Connor understands fascism in an Arendtian way as forced ideology. Her engagement with her friends and readers shows a deep commitment to building a community that accepts radical difference and a rejection of the "use of force." As Gordon and other readers of her correspondence held in the *Flannery O'Connor Collection* at Georgia College & State University have suggested, O'Connor's most directly political letters are to New Yorker and playwright Maryat Lee on the subject of race. Although we do not have Lee's half of the correspondence, it seems clear that the two writers took exaggerated postures representing the "bleeding heart liberal" and the "dirty old southland," and O'Connor never directly defends herself against the charge that she is a racist or seems to take offense that Lee must have suggested as much. Instead, these letters are full of racial epithets, jokes, and opinions that even her defenders describe as a "numbness to the evil that blacks suffered in the segregated South" (Wood "Morals" 1076). To a contemporary ear, her lack of defense and almost campy racism in some places is surprising.

O'Connor responds very differently to an accusation of fascism in another set of correspondence, suggesting a serious concern with this topic. She defends herself when called a "fascist," in an early letter from Betty Hester. Hester and O'Connor's correspondence, which would continue throughout O'Connor's life, gains its initial energy from this accusation and O'Connor's response. This exchange begins an epistolary friendship at the "heart of the Georgia writer's massive postal exchanges" wherein O'Connor explores her deepest commitments (Wood "Sacramental" 147). That the question of fascism originates this friendship is no mistake, because it is deeply important to O'Connor's worldview and fiction. In this correspondence, O'Connor reframes fascism as a possible orientation an author could have to a reader but defends herself against the charge.

Their correspondence on fascism extends from August through October of 1955; it is likely (we don't have her letters) that Hester first accused the author of portraying fascism in her fiction,[6] given that O'Connor responds in a letter on 28 August:

> But if it [fascism] does mean a doubt of the efficacy of love and if this is to be observed in my fiction, then it has to be explained . . . by what happens to conviction (I believe love to be efficacious in the loooong run) when it is translated into fiction designed for a public with a predisposition to believe the opposite. (*HB* 97)

Her initial definition is "a doubt of the efficacy of love," at least in the short term—and in the rest of the letter she defends her art as expressing a "tolerantly realistic" Christianity which, therefore, does not wait for love's efficacy. The image she uses as an analogy is Thomas Aquinas's famed run-in with a prostitute, whom he supposedly chased off with a hot-poker. O'Connor is Aquinas and the poker her art—she later plays with this image, in farcical duplicate, in "The Comforts of Home" where Thomas fends off with a chair the "nimpermaniac" Sarah Ham, who appears in his bedroom at night (*CS* 384). But here, her defense is no farce.

Fascists may indeed doubt the efficacy of love but the phenomenon is more commonly defined in terms of its racist hyper-nationalism, mass mobilization, imperialism, patriarchal masculinity, and romantic narrative. O'Connor's strange definition focuses most directly on how fascism attempts to convince people. Rather than applying the pedagogy of "love," which seeks to persuade the beloved without domination, O'Connor admits a shared tendency with fascists toward shock, in line with what she says elsewhere about her methods.

This must not have satisfied Hester, who it seems refuted O'Connor's re-definition with aid of a dictionary. In O'Connor's next letter to Hester, from 6 September 1955, she writes:

> I looked in my Webster's and see it is 1948, so you are years ahead of me in your vocabulary and I'll have to concede you the word. But I can't concede that I'm a fascist . . . I see it as an offense against the body of Christ. I am wondering why you convict me of believing in the use of force. (*HB* 99)

The "conceding" suggests that Hester objected to O'Connor's first definition of fascism as a doubting of love. O'Connor's library held a 1925 printing of Webster's at the time of her death, not a 1948—so it is unclear whether the latter one was lost (Kinney). The 1925 version did include an "addenda" where fascism was defined as "a (political) group, a club" with a reference to its literal meaning in Italian of bundle, while "Fascista" was defined as those who acted "with violent means when necessary" to subdue "radical elements." Latter versions of Merriam-Webster defined fascism as "[a]ny program for setting up a centralized autocratic national regime with severely nationalistic policies exercising regimentation of industry, commerce, and finance, rigid censorship, and forcible suppression of opposition."

O'Connor seemed to find accusations about "the use of force" troubling, perhaps most of all because they implicated the Church, also, with employing "forcible suppression of opposition." O'Connor implicitly recognizes that antifascism requires persuasion by means *other* than force. She, in fact, argues that her relationship to faith has been on this model; she wrote on 2 August that her faith was deeply freeing, and yet without "blueprint" (92). Saying that "the Church can force no one to believe," this earlier comment about faith prefigures her rejection of the "use of force." O'Connor takes the charge of fascism as an indictment of using force on behalf of the Catholic church—a charge that she denies. Interestingly, her use of the term "convict"—to suggest that Hester has already declared her guilty—both points to the seriousness of the debate and to the way that actual fascists, particularly at the Nuremberg trials, were held to account for ideological crimes including the use of propaganda and mass political manipulation. Although Arendt would not publish *Eichmann in Jerusalem*, which O'Connor read and praised, until 1963, the linkages between a fascist lack of political judgment which Arendt sees in Eichmann are already present in her earlier work and in O'Connor's strange understanding of fascism as pedagogical force.

In contrast to the "conviction" that Hester has apparently rendered, O'Connor implies that any "force" she employs is part of a just war she makes on her readers for the purposes of theistic art, but this bellicose pedagogy stops short of requiring them to adopt her worldview. She also calls

[Louis-Ferdinand] Céline a "REAL fascist" in a 24 September letter (*HB* 1050). By this she seems to mean a political rather than artistic one, given that the French author had published three virulently anti-Semitic pamphlets in support of the Nazis in the 1920s. Later, O'Connor calls fascism "opprobrious" and hopes that Hester will "relieve [O'Connor] of the burden of being a fascist" (*HB* 100), pointing even more fully to the way this accusation rankled.

The heart of this tension is that O'Connor realized that a theological horizon shares with fascist ones a commitment to a set of comprehensive doctrines and dogma. This is expressed in many places, but perhaps nowhere more directly than in her treatment of the doctrine of the incarnation, which she states is "the ultimate reality" (*HB* 60), both in her fiction and in the famous Mary McCarthy dinner party. For O'Connor, even Catholic dogma was a tool for freedom rather than a restrictive limitation on thought. This type of religious commitment was under fire from the secular political class—as the 1951 "Religion and the Intellectuals" symposium in *Partisan Review* expressed, or even more directly in Sinclair Lewis's bestselling *It Can't Happen Here*, which imagined an alternate, fascist future for the United States where a charismatic politician defined religious freedom as "allegiance to the New Testament."

While this was a fictional critique of American religious demagogy, the REAL American fascist right adapted Christian symbols and narratives to their purposes, including the jeremiad excoriating the fallen world. These symbols were twisted—as with the use of Christ motifs to portray Adolf Hitler as a transcendent figure, although of course also some American Christians, and Catholics, were sympathetic to either nativist right-wing movements, European fascism, or both. Richard Steigmann-Gall argues that nativist fascism, although overlooked in many histories, was a powerful interwar force that was fundamentally American, led by figures including William Dudley Pelley, Gerald Winrod, and Gerald L. K. Smith. Robert Paxton argues that the Ku Klux Klan might be the protypical fascist movement. And Kevin Spicer has argued in several books that Christians, especially Catholics, are susceptible to anti-Semitism and its political mobilization for collaboration in the Holocaust. In fact, Kathleen Lipovski-Helal identifies "The Displaced Person" as one place where O'Connor struggles with the relationship of Catholicism to anti-Semitism and the Holocaust. O'Connor's response to Hester's accusation may also stem from this very real association of Christianity with white-supremacy groups.

Even more common was use of eschatological imagery in these movements. Many American fascists wanted to revitalize or replace a liberal society of decadence undermined by materialism and luxury, symbolized often by the Phoenix's rise from ashes (Griffin). And while O'Connor's imagery serves a different purpose, it also draws on the eschatological: fires, grace-striking, sunsets the color of blood. Even the peacock, which O'Connor lovingly describes in "The King of the Birds" and associates with the transfiguration in "The Displaced Person," shares a common history with the phoenix as a symbol for Christ—and fascism.[7] Perhaps it is this shared well of imagery and worldview that makes O'Connor vulnerable to the charge, and ultimately thank Hester for raising this fascist business, saying that this exchange serves to "clarify what I think on various subjects or at least to think of various subjects and is all to my good and to my pleasure—" (HB 103). She also may have recognized that illiberal ideologies were alive and well in the community in which she lived and have been part of the American political culture from the start (Smith). She welcomes the chance to distinguish her method from that of the fascists, no matter their common use of symbols, and in this, too, invites a democratic ethos of contestation and reason-giving over force.

O'Connor rejects the notion that religion serves as an ideology that prepares one for fascism. In this she echoes the work of theologians who extended worries about American fascism into critiques of scientific methodology. For example, Eric Voegelin makes this the heart of his (negative) review of Arendt's The Origins of Totalitarianism.[8] He follows scholars who argued that "totalitarianism has greatly profited from that value-emptiness which has been the result of positivism and relativism in the social sciences" (Brecht qtd. in Purcell 181). O'Connor said much the same thing in her letters, calling nihilism a poison gas that can make you "the stinkingest logical positivist" if you aren't careful (HB 97). Such an argument was central for Reinhold Niebuhr, who also suggested that internal signs of totalitarianism were present in American secularization and hubris (Bacon 68). In these readings, totalitarianism (which becomes emptied of the notion of force and instead focuses on individual fear) emerges not from too rigidly held values but instead from value pluralism and liberal individualism. In this category also belongs the connections O'Connor makes frequently between the gas chambers and sentimentality, which have been powerfully explored in previous scholarship, and certainly are prominent in her fiction as well as writing like the famous introduction to The Memoir of Mary Ann.[9]

By the time O'Connor and Hester leave the subject of fascism in their letters, O'Connor has sought to redefine antifascism as nonideological methods of instruction, but also to suggest that the Church, and, therefore, truly religious art, is both absolutely universal ("the ultimately reality") and yet different from fascism because of how it is taught. To see whether this is a persuasive defense against the charge—the conviction—of fascism, we need to turn to her fiction and to "literary fascism" as well as the political.

FASCISM TWO: BANALITY AND THE EVERYDAY

While O'Connor's politics may not rise to the level of REAL fascism, does she use "force" on her readers? Gary Ciuba, after considering this same exchange on fascism, argues that "[a]lthough O'Connor's fiction generally works to reveal rather than conceal sacred violence, she occasionally romanticized such force" (157) as in her famous defense of her "startling figures" as a method. While it is the violence that many remember from O'Connor's fiction, few of the deaths are outright murders—and none are described with much blood. Instead, it is the very calm use of stokes, goring, suicide, murder, and betrayal as a vehicle for the violent alteration of consciousness that unsettles. It is this riot of imagery that causes Hawkes to assert that O'Connor is of the devil's party. Yet, since O'Connor tells us that these moments should be interpreted as moments of grace, and expressions of the reality of Christ-in-the-world, the more alarming possibility is that O'Connor wants to force readers to, at the least, consider that she writes "from the standpoint of Christian ortho-doxy" (*MM* 32), although she knows very well that the New Critics will ignore this. She knows even more directly that her audience is unlikely to start from the assumption that her fiction is Christian and acknowledges to Hester in the same exchange of letters discussed above that "[y]ou are right that I won't ever be able entirely to understand my own work or even my own motivation" (*HB* 92). Taking this as an invitation to reconsider O'Connor's politics beyond her own claims about them, I consider how the "use of force" is linked to ideological thinking in O'Connor's fiction, particularly for every day, banal, citizens.

The fascist use of force is as a method of ideology, not violence, and so it is not the portrayal of murderers like Singleton, in "The Partridge Festi-val" or the Misfit, in "A Good Man Is Hard to Find," where we find fascist leaders of the ideal type. Only Mark Fortune of "A View of the Woods" is a clear fit, particularly for totalitarian leadership as characterized in Hannah Arendt's work as the attempt to erase humanity in the fascist subject. Fortune demands that his granddaughter Mary replicate his values and even appear-ance such that "the spiritual difference between them was slight" (*CS* 336). Fortune remains locked in his own perception of the world even as his senses provide external evidence to the contrary—just as Arendt defines ideology as "isms which to the satisfaction of their adherents can explain everything and every occurrence by deducing it from a single premise" (*OT* 468). For Fortune, this premise is the project of American progress and bound up in patriarchal and capitalist frameworks. The fascist leader, in the Arendtian ver-sion of totalitarianism, portrays himself as conduit for forces and eternal laws greater than himself. Fortune is the American version, channeling "progress" and the "highway . . . supermarket . . . gas station . . . motel . . . [and] drive-in picture-show" that it will bring (337). Musing that "all men were created free and equal," he commits to selling "the lawn" in front of his family's house because "it was his duty to sell the lot . . . he must insure the future" (349).

At the climax of the story, when his granddaughter rejects his unthinking commitment to progress, she exposes that his pedagogy of force has failed. Her defiance is both about her love of the titular view of the woods and the lawn that provides it and her rejection of his bloodline in her claim to be "pure Pitts," her father's surname (355). In her alternative "view," she rejects him two-fold—both his ideology of blood-purity and the antidemocratic premise of a single view. Fortune is more than mere patriarch because he wants perfect reproduction of his ideology.[10] Even his murder of his granddaughter is por-trayed as an expression of external forces, so that "with his hands still tight around her neck, he lifted her head and brought it down once hard against the rock that happened to be under it" (CS 355). It is not right to call this acci-dental, as Mark Fortune's very identity premised this violence (including his willingness to permit the physical abuse of his granddaughter by her father), yet the purpose of his force was persuasion, not death. After he kills her, he sees not his dead beloved granddaughter but a "conquered image" with "no look of remorse on it" (CS 355). He tries the method of force, but is stymied by the unwillingness, even in death, of his granddaughter to meld her view to his own, displaying the hopelessness of ideological domination.

While no other O'Connor characters so directly exercise this method of "persuasion," others indulge in bellicose fantasies of erasing ideological plu-rality and ignore any evidence that contradicts their viewpoints. Mrs. Shortley, in "The Displaced Person," daydreams of a war between "dirty" foreign words and good, clean, American ones, prompting a fabricated prophecy that does not occur in the Bible where she says it does (Roos 288). Both Calhoun and Mary Grace in "The Partridge Festival" insist on assigning "real guilt" for the murders at the festival, repeating their pet theories even as various towns-people offer evidence that refutes them, until they are finally confronted with the "fact" of the murderer himself (CS 427). Many, perhaps even most, of O'Connor's characters seem to live in worlds separated from those they interact with—parents and children especially. While these estrangements certainly have emotional and religious valences, they also signal that these characters inhabit the lonely "desert" that Arendt worries makes us ripe for either the gas chamber or the executioner's chair.

In this "desert," it is no surprise that characters display little resistance to fascist imagery, suggesting the vulnerability of American political culture and thought and its often-traumatized citizens. Rufus Johnson, of "The Lame Shall Enter First," is the object of do-gooder Sheppard's reform efforts. Yet, O'Connor associates him with a hybrid and sexualized American/Nazi fas-cist imagery. Johnson's first act as resident in Sheppard's house is to enter the room of his deceased wife, while Sheppard's horrified son Norton watches in thrall of this violation. Johnson puts on the dead woman's corset and dances a burlesque while singing a modified cover of "Shake, Rattle and Roll" (by Joe Turner but, covered by Elvis and Bill Haley, and often called the first song of rock and roll). This performance links the United States through its pre-mier musical art form with an erotic fascism, as the narrator comments that

Rufus Johnson's hair was "swept . . . to the side, Hitler fashion" (*CS* 455). John-son, like Fortune, uses force (he tells us that one kick of his "monstrous" and symbolic boot convinces others "not to mess" with him) (*CS* 453), to compel obedience—but also seduction. Norton serves Johnson. While it is likely that Johnson is meant by O'Connor to display the attractions of Satan, he also demonstrates why suffering American youth, like Norton, might be attracted to fascism, especially when the alternative (his father, the teacher) has his own forceful, albeit liberal, pedagogy.

The attractions of fascism are also the attractions of community where there is none. The working-class boys from "A Circle in the Fire" who travel from a city to a rural farm they will eventually set afire have a deep camara-derie with one another. They say the same lies "at once in loud enthusiastic voices" and temporarily construct their own mini-society in the woods at the farm (183). Their masculine camaraderie is hostile to the female farm inhabi-tations, and the entire story carries the ultimately unrealized threat of rape against the women at the farm. While the young girl in this story seems to rec-ognize this threat, practicing her own militaristic, antifascist responses to the potential violence in the trees—her mother instead refocuses her fear through the lens of her own ideology, connecting the boys to the fascist threat and to race relations, telling her daughter to be happy they don't live "in a develop-ment" and are not "Negroes," "in iron lungs," or "Europeans ridden in boxcars like cattle" (*CS* 190). These amalgamation of the "threat" of the poor, Black, and foreign—rather than the fascist band in her own woods, makes possible the eventual explosion of fire at the farm, which, in addition to the biblical reading, could also be read alongside the burning of the Reichstag. If Arendt is right that ideology and loneliness means we seek comfort in strict ideology and even violent community, that ideology and (militarized) community can be turned against us, and prevent us from correctly interpreting threats to our political community and those who might take advantage of them.

Along with these few outright fascists and their followers are many banal bystanders, some of whom profess antifascist views, but do nothing to under-mine the actual institutions that produce strict hierarchies, of race and gender most directly. In this, they unthinkingly enforce biopolitical distinctions between life that is precious and life that is expendable. This is most blatant in "The Displaced Person," when three members of the farm community watch a tractor crush a refugee and kill him. To preserve the shaky Jim Crow color line, the outsider who threatens miscegenation must be eliminated, because he exposes the way that segregation unsettled, rather than confirmed, racial difference and whiteness (Taylor 2012). The policeman who delivers the fatal blow to Hazel Motes in *Wise Blood* is similarly operating on a logic of consti-tutive exclusion and views the homeless and the mentally ill as noncitizens. Motes is seen as a vagabond and thus is outside of the political community and eligible for elimination. O'Connor's other character "types"—such as the farm-matriarch, the northern-intellectual, and even the anti-southern-belle—although they fall in different places on the political spectrum, share a rigidity when it comes to possessing a sense of who "counts."

O'Connor seems to identify fascism not with disorder (as proto-fascist Mrs. Shortley does, fearing the "ten billion of them pushing their way into new places over here"), but with order and rationality (*CS* 200). It is characters who desire such order who end up accidentally killing others or watching them die, because they refuse to develop judgment and instead overlay their ideologies over reality. This has implications for the question of race in her fiction. Although O'Connor's claims to offer a "plague on everybody's houses as far as the race business goes" (*HB* 539), it is more accurate that O'Connor finds in both southern racism and northern racial progressivism the same bad logic which perceives membership in the national political community as the same as membership in the ranks of humanity. This move (for racists, the desire is to exclude nonwhites from both while the liberal goal is inclusion) is problematic because it polices the boundaries of the political body and the edges of the human as if they are identical qualities. Nationality and humanity become identical in a fascist regime such that to be nonnational means to be expendable.

In short, O'Connor explores the attractions of fascism as a powerful social relation, especially between disempowered masculinities like those of working-class white men and offers the comfort of a consistent *answer* to any question put to it. Hannah Arendt's argument about ideology and totalitarianism starts from a premise that the "traditions"—like religion and philosophy—which provided a framework in which social and political life was intelligible were lost in World War II—and in this vacuum of tradition, isolated individuals are vulnerable to dictators and their ideology. O'Connor, with perhaps more of an intent in turning her readers eyes toward these lost traditions, writes about the same process that makes fascism possible, both in terms of perpetrators and victims. Its attractions notwithstanding, the commitment to ideology here in O'Connor is often a commitment to the nationalist project of limiting the reach of rights to those in the same political community, often at the expense of racial outsiders (and even in the hands of reformers, by collapsing the distance between human rights and legal rights). This has important implications for American political thought and development, which has too often accepted unthinkingly the idea that the South is the home of racism and the North of progress.

Through addressing the problem of fascism in her work, O'Connor offers an implied critique of the sometimes equation of Jim Crow racism with Soviet totalitarianism. Robert Brinkmeyer shows that it was not only northern leftists who "began noting similarities between the political and social orders of the South and those of Fascist countries" (3), but southern thinkers and writers also explored this question. Regionalism, which often opposed centralization and even capitalism, "appeared to draw from the same irrational thinking and loyalty as Fascist ideologies" and denied universalisms (12). Southern capacity for fascism was nowhere more evident than in Jim Crow segregation, a connection that would animate many a cold warrior critic of the South as well. This was despite the persistent and structural racism in the North, particularly through redlining and housing discrimination, police violence and surveillance, and *de facto* segregated education systems. At the same time, authors, many of them southern, associated the threat of totalitarianism with the urban, capitalist, and conformist social world which was itself an oversimplified reduction of life in the North.

O'Connor's fiction takes sides in the debate about fascism by suggesting that *both* the traditionalist southern and progressive northern approaches to social change and political belonging potentially lead to totalitarianism and that the trick would be creating an alternative to either route. While most of the figures discussed above as part of the fascist apparatus read as "southern" and "conservative," the progressive liberals in her fiction are just as bad. They are "politically correct" in the sense of pronouncing liberal platitudes about the unity of man while treating others with condescension or, worse perhaps, as mere data points for their social scientific research. Sheppard, Ashbury, Calhoun, Hulga, Julius, and Mary Grace all fall into this pattern to some extent. Many of them seek "reform" in some way— quite explicitly in the case of Sheppard, who volunteers at a reformatory. Their reforms aim at the mores and traditions of the South, such that Ashbury describes it as a "slave's atmosphere" (*CS* 364), while Calhoun hopes to write an exposé of Partridge's society and Hulga thinks she can "see there is nothing to see" (*CS* 288). All of them seek to instruct others—to produce an "enduring chill" so powerful that it will convert others to their ideological views. In this they practice force in the same way as seemingly very different characters, who stand for southern recalcitrance. For example, Mr. Head, who believes that he was a "suitable guide for the young," demands, for example, that young Nelson learn race, and immediately use it to draw distinctions between "a man" and "a nigger" on behalf of his rural homeland and in rejection of the "blended" ways of the city where he was born (*CS* 252). Even more conservative foils are no more self-aware. While they attempt less forcibly to reform the world around them, they participate in a cliché-ridden conformity and cannot critically judge their political worlds. They are the figures in O'Connor's fiction, farm matriarchs and maiden aunts, who repeat folk sayings and set up ill-fated blind dates for their angry nephews. Like the central figure in Hannah Arendt's *Eichmann in Jerusalem*, they are simply unable to think beyond the ideologies handed to them.

FASCISM THREE: RACE AND REAL FASCISM

If O'Connor's fiction displays the temptations of fascism and either employing or succumbing to the "force" of ideology—where are we left on the question of O'Connor and fascism? On one hand, she successfully illustrates that both North and South are open to ideological thinking, just as Arendt argues that Totalitarianism is present in both Russia and Germany. This would suggest that antifascist practice would require the cultivating of communities that offer the space to practice the development of political judgment, just as Arendt argues for communities rooted in the "right to have rights"—including to be seen and heard as a human. However, despite their insights, both thinkers fall short of imagining this community across racial difference. O'Connor does not depict it in her fiction at all, and instead we have to infer from her own personal practices that she values the opportunity to develop political judgment in community. It has been argued that she was one of the "[r]eligious figures who failed to celebrate capitalist society—setting themselves in opposition to the cultural status quo and making a rival claim for the allegiance of U.S. citizens" (Bacon 63). But to say that her fiction made a "rival claim" is a bit unfair, as her stance is not one of the positive doctrine of Christianity, but the absolutely and ultimately negative doctrine of the Incarnation, in the sense of negative theology. A negative theology avoids making direct (positive), claims about the nature of God, often framing the divine as beyond human perception and characterizes the thinking of mystics who inspired O'Connor. Although as a practicing Catholic she accepted Catholic dogma, which could be understood to make up the positive content of religion, as a fiction author, she leaves open the absolute transcendence of God as totally beyond human understanding. This negative doctrine demands that her stories are open to the reader's own worldviews, even as O'Connor herself proposes a theological reading.

Her rejection of pedagogies of force is a similarly negative tactic. In her own correspondence, O'Connor creates a vibrant political community where religious and political questions, especially as they are worked out in aesthetics, are debated powerfully. O'Connor's own reconsideration of topics like fascism, race, and art occurs in dialogue, not solitary contemplation. That correspondence that raised the "fascist business" is itself a powerful reminder of the role that Hester and Lee, among myriad correspondents, did to help O'Connor "at least to think of various subjects," which is exactly the type of civic work of which most of her characters seem incapable because of their lack of political community.

That O'Connor had no African American correspondents testifies to the limitations of a democratic practice hemmed in by hierarchy. Although, as Rachel Watson argues in her essay in this collection, it is racialized thinking that often leads O'Connor characters, such as Ruby Turpin and Mrs. Short-ley, to images of the Holocaust, this critique of racialized hierarchies did not extend to a willingness on O'Connor's part to confirm these hierarchies in her own world. Farrell O'Gorman argues persuasively that O'Connor's fiction rejects eugenics in her commitment to a natural order that requires us to recognize how "the poor and the ill [are] always with us" (201) because we are all essentially poor when separated from God, but the same argument cannot be extended to her black characters, which as we've seen are both spatially and epistemologically separated from white characters. The point here is not to beleaguer the question of race, but to suggest that her own fiction opens up tantalizing possibilities for rejecting the dichotomy of inclusion or exclusion in the "back-slapping gum-chewing hiya-kid nation" (*HB* 552). O'Connor's linkage of both northern liberalism and southern exceptionalism with ridged and ideological thinking, which I have labeled fascist, implicates the American project with the biopolitical one of managing and creating populations, most importantly in this historical context on the basis of race. O'Connor's fiction implies that American political order is premised on constitutive exclusions from the start and will not be fixed through the slow work of progressive inclusion. Race is not, as the American Creed would have it, a failure to consider the pre-political status of race in the democratic polity. Instead, the very work of creating race as a political fact is the work of creating American democracy—displayed in O'Connor's fiction, but never theorized in her nonfiction writing and correspondence. While not all of the characters I discussed above as portraying the attractions and dangers of fascism do so to protect the racialized lines of the national body, they all cede to the state the power to draw such lines.

Race is the most important tactic for managing population in the United States and in O'Connor's fiction. That she plays with the artificiality of race is well known, most directly in "The Artificial Nigger," which is a twisted travelogue of a grandfather and grandson, Mr. Head and Nelson, and their visit to Atlanta. Along with the titular statuary figure whose appearance closes the story, we begin "The Artificial Nigger" with an encounter on a train where it is clear that young white Head cannot recognize race, having taken literally the idea of "black" people (*CS* 255). Greif deftly argues that the story exposes the vanity of "too much pride, and that of failing to see that material incarnations and physical objects never escape, but only advance, divine truths" (219). He suggests that any other reading is there to tempt racial moralists. However, before the final image, the text also engages questions of the democratic polity and belonging. "Social death" is not only about the ignorance of white Americans, but the spatialization of that ignorance in our urban planning (Patterson). In this story, Nelson and his grandfather are lost, first in a black neighborhood where Nelson asks a woman how to "get back to town" and, "after a minute she said, 'you in town now'" (261). While Nelson was geographically incorrect in his assumption that black neighborhoods were not part of Atlanta, he identifies correctly their distance from social and political power. This assumption causes the pair to get even more lost, because they assume that their passage into a white neighborhood will lead them to the center of the city, when instead it is the suburban periphery. They attempt to use racial categories to organize their journey home, but their own "wages of whiteness" are not paying high dividends because the city is reorganizing around a new core. This core is perhaps best represented by the attraction not of racial hierarchy, but of the black woman to whom Nelson feels an erotic yet maternal attraction. "He suddenly wanted her to reach down and pick him up and draw him against her and then he wanted to feel her breath on his face. He wanted to look down and down into her eyes while she held him tighter and tighter" (CS 262). Yet Nelson ignored this desire, and as he hurries away his face is "burning with shame" (Ibid.). A recognition of this new core *and* of the development it would take to reach across difference could form the first steps toward a possibility of a more democratic community, in O'Connor's fiction, but also in racially fraught America—but are inaccessible for those still working off old segregated maps.

This missed opportunity for coalition building across difference is evident in O'Connor's famous reluctance to offer any window into the interiority of black characters (Walker). This is despite her willingness to comment on the interiority of white characters who inhabit very different identity positions from O'Connor, suggesting she viewed race as a particular and fundamental, if constructed, difference. She explains this by claiming that the "negro is isolated" (Whitt), into a separate world—in what seems to be an unknowing redeployment of W. E. B. Du Bois's idea of the "veil" between the black and white worlds, or where we might also find a "social death" which Orlando Patterson argues differentiated the situation of enslaved people from indentured servants. She makes the mistake of naturalizing this division, when instead even her work points to a "specific political theory of race" produced within the political realm rather than prior to it and therefore a product of democracy rather than its anti-thesis" (Olson xiii). O'Connor is willing to speak for and through white characters of any class or gender—but portrays the split between the black and white "worlds" as absolute. So, although her fiction displays a critique of such ideologies, she as an actual person, like all of us, was still susceptible to such thinking. While O'Connor doesn't offer a way out of the racial problem, and in her correspondence suggests that she thinks that nothing can be done, her fiction makes clear that the American problem of race is deeply rooted—but not only for southerners.

RECONSIDERING FICTION AND THE MOMENT OF GRACE

So, is O'Connor a fascist? Although she rejects it in her correspondence as the "use of force," her fiction shows how the desire for fascism, at least microfascism, is present in a wide range of ideologies and that the supposed dichotomy of totalitarian oppression and democratic equality is overdrawn. O'Connor's struggle to engage in or portray community across difference in her fiction suggests that defending America against fascist thinking is incredibly difficult as long as racial ideology is prevalent. This is a similar issue to the one Arendt raised with her "banality of evil" thesis, which suggested that those innocent bystanders are fundamentally "unable to think." Arendt died before completing her work on developing this ability to think, which was less about intellectualization, and more about reflective political judgment. O'Connor, indeed, models for us her personal practice of democratic dialogue with her friends, as well as her commitment to open interpretation of her fiction, even when it goes against her wishes—but provides few such models in her fiction.

In the spirit of her invitation to discovery, I would also like to reconsider the famous O'Connor moments of grace as possible connections to democratic life. O'Connor herself connects them to grace in reference to the death of the grandmother in "A Good Man Is Hard to Find"—which interestingly follows the grandmother's outreach toward a fellow human whom she claims as her own rather than other. Edward Kessler focused on these moments as providing the "language of apocalypse," suggesting that the metaphor "as if" used in many of these moments points to the eruption of the imaginary into the world. Yet, as John Roos argues with reference to Kessler, we should avoid "assuming that O'Connor was simply an apocalyptic writer whose characters plunge into the realm of grace in an unquestioned and unquestionable fashion" (286). He identifies "Revelation" as providing one glimpse into O'Connor's vision of the well-ordered polity. What if we extended this democratic vision back into other "moments of grace," although most recipients lack the human communities or skills to build on these fugitive experiences? In O'Connor's fiction, there are moments that suggest the possibility of the development of reflective judgment. For example, Ruby Turpin, who arguably displays the most fascist-leaning tendencies of all in her dreams and fantasies of ordering types of people, changes during "Revelation." After a chance encounter with a nihilistic enemy, armed with a "human development" textbook, she spends most of the story pursuing the question of whether she could be "a warthog and me both." In a parody of the Socratic encounter with the Delphic oracle, she asks everyone she meets how this could be true—she enacts a Socratic pedagogy and really seeks to learn. Unlike O'Connor's other fascist-minded housewives, she lets this contradictory statement unsettle her assumptions. After asking her husband and her black farmhands, she even asks her pigs to weigh in, unsettling the divide between human and animal which was previously so neatly drawn.

While hardly a full-throated "deliberative democrat," Ruby Turpin does pursue a reflective and communal practice. Deliberative democracy, popularized as a critique of participatory or electoral democracy, "affirms the need to justify decisions made by citizens and their representatives" and thus makes inquiry and reason-giving central to the democratic process (Gutmann and Thompson 3).While O'Connor completes Turpin's inquiry with a vision of a heavenly parade, featuring all classes of people and the appearance that "even their virtues were burned away," this is *Turpin's* interpretation of the event and which need not be read as a literal vision of heaven (*CS* 508). What might Turpin's exploration of identity have developed into if she had a friend or interlocutor to help her explore them? The absent figure in many O'Connor stories is not one of rational judgment or the anti-grotesque, but the friend who sees grotesquerie and still affirms, as in Arendt's gloss on Augustine: "I want you to be" (*LSA*). Such a friend would listen closely to Ruby, rather than force their own worldview upon her, and such a friend would respect her through opposition and discovery.

Few of O'Connor's other "moments of Grace" come with this much dispositional work and few, if any, provide much sense of their communal possibilities. But, reading Ruby's final vision as a revelation for a necessary development of an earthly practice through which class and racial ordering will be upended and where possible futures are contained in that moment suggests the possibility of reading it as a secular eschaton. In this, and the other moments of grace, there is no penetration into the interiority of the experience and, with the notable exception of Mrs. Shortley, little ability for the reader to understand or see beyond such experience. Only those within the space of the eschaton can see such possible futures; it is a place of epistemological privilege, in keeping with the frequent use of "seeing" verbs. Although O'Connor offers no stories which tell us how to proceed from a fleeting experience of radical equality toward any sort of earthly institutions, such points (read against her religious intent) gesture toward the type of "fugitive democracy" that political theorists like Sheldon Wolin have argued characterize its appearance in a time of neoliberalism and what he calls "inverted totalitarianism." Wolin's concept of democracy is "a project concerned with the political potentialities of ordinary citizens, that is with their possibilities for becoming political beings through the self-discovery of common concerns and of modes of action for realizing them" (100). In a world characterized by constrictive hierarchies, bureaucracies, economic imperatives, and technocracies, expressions of this possibility of agency are fleeting and must be grasped when available. "Fugitive democracy," as an episodic phenomenon, is "a crystallized response to deeply felt grievances or needs," whose power "lies in the multiplicity of modest sites . . . and in the ingenuity of ordinary people" (Wolin "Vision" 602–5). One key characteristic of these moments for ordinary people, he argues, is their suspension of the linear time encompassed in the bureaucratic and neoliberal alternatives instead of those within the moments of fugitive democracy.

It is these moments of grace reconsidered in combination with her own practices of friendship that establish O'Connor as an antifascist writer, albeit one who struggled to fully conceptualize or realize the implications of her own critique of hierarchy in her treatment of race. She encourages us to engage interlocutors, including literary characters, whose plurality demands that we "at least . . . think of various subjects," and avoid thoughtless capitulation to ideological rigidity. To advance this sort of democratic practice against fascism may take more institutional work on the part of readers who seek to establish communities of deep affirmation of difference and rejection of state biopolitical management of populations, but it may start with fleeting moments of a democratic eschaton.

NOTES

1. These include Louis-Ferdinand Céline, Ezra Pound, Martin Heidegger, and Robert Brasillach, as well as more complicated figures like Paul de Man and even Gertrude Stein. For considerations of the impact of their "actual fascism" on their art, see especially chapter 7 in Carroll; Morrison and Knowles.

2. Importantly, critics have moved away from identifying modernity with antifascism and instead recognize a "fascist modernity" with an expanded canon including women (Carlston) and "pop" writers (Kaplan). These explorations of a "fascist imagination" (Dasenbrock) often center on the gendered politics of fascist desire, whether through eroticized representations of what Susan Sontag identified (and Michel Foucault decried) as "fascinating fascism"—or through exploration of the idea that "people have a sexual, as well as material, interest in their political life" (Kaplan 23). Frost situates this in the American context, suggesting that even "anti-fascist, democratic culture has substantial, unacknowledged libidinal investments in fascism that need to be explored" (15).

3. Not least because of work in Rath and Shaw, Hewitt and Donahoo's, and Edmondson's collections—and political theorist Jerome Foss's recent book.

4. Many have argued that she crafted her arguments around Nazi fascism and only added in the Soviets as an afterthought, perhaps as part of the broader turn toward Cold War anticommunism. As Richard King has noted, "by linking Nazi Germany with Stalin's Soviet Union as totalitarian regimes, her book tended to dilute the importance of race and anti-Semitism in the historiography of totalitarianism" (46). I think this same tendency is visible in O'Connor's understanding of fascism, although perhaps for different reasons.

5. Kaplan distinguishes her use of banal from Arendt's—whom she argues defines away the core problem of fascist aesthetics by understanding its banality to be a lack of thinking—and instead draws on Walter Benjamin's use of the same term. I think that Arendt's work as a whole understands banality in a more capacious way, rooted in a denial not only of thinking but of radical plurality, so I am comfortable combining them here.

6. Hester's first letter itself is lost to us, unless it emerges as part of William Sessions's forthcoming *Stalking Joy: The Life and Times of Flannery O'Connor*, an autobiography that may benefit from Sessions access to Hester's literary estate as executor as well as unique access to O'Connor's.

7. St. Augustine wrote that Peacocks were immortal and the phoenix myth is eternal life.

8. See Bell for a compelling reading of Voegelin, Arendt, and O'Connor in dialogue with each other and contemporary questions of ethics via Badiou.

9. Although, connections between masculinity and fascism, played with most memorably by Sylvia Plath in "Daddy," are clear in feminist scholarship, which finds "the exaggerated masculinity of fascism is based on a fantasy of virility and patriarchal domination" (Woodley 218).

WORKS CITED

Arendt, Hannah. *Love and Saint Augustine*. Chicago: University of Chicago Press, 1958. (*LSA*)

Arendt, Hannah. *The Origins of Totalitarianism*. New York: Harcourt, Brace and Company, 1951. (*OT*)

Arendt, Hannah. *The Human Condition*. Chicago: University of Chicago Press, 1958. (*HC*)

Bacon, Jon Lance. *Flannery O'Connor and Cold War Culture*. New York: Cambridge University Press, 1993.

Bell, Vikki. "On the Critique of Secular Ethics: An Essay with Flannery O'Connor and Hannah Arendt." *Theory, Culture & Society* 22, no. 2 (2005): 1–27.

Brinkmeyer, Robert H. *The Fourth Ghost: White Southern Writers and European Fascism, 1930–1950*. Baton Rouge: Louisiana State University Press, 2009.

Carroll, David. *French Literary Fascism: Nationalism, Anti-Semitism, and the Ideology of Culture*. Princeton, NJ: Princeton University Press, 1998.

Carlston, Erin G. *Thinking Fascism: Sapphic Modernism and Fascist Modernity*. Palo Alto, CA: Stanford University Press, 2000.

Ciuba, Gary M. *Desire, Violence and Divinity in Modern Southern Fiction: Katherine Anne Porter, Flannery O'Connor, Cormac McCarthy, Walker Percy*. Baton Rouge: Louisiana State University Press, 2007.

Dasenbrock, Reed Way. "Wyndham Lewis's Fascist Imagination and the Fiction of Parnoia." In *Fascism, Aesthetics, and Culture*, edited by Richard J. Golsan. Lebanon, NH: University Press of New England, 1992.

Edmondson, Henry T., III, ed. *A Political Companion to Flannery O'Connor*. Lexington: University Press of Kentucky, 2017.

Foss, Jerome C. *Flannery O'Connor and the Perils of Governing by Tenderness*. New York: Rowman & Littlefield, 2019.

Frost, Laura. *Sex Drives: Fantasies of Fascism in Literary Modernism*. Ithaca, NY: Cornell University Press, 2002.

Gordon, Sarah. "Maryat and Julian and the 'Not So Bloodless Revolution.'" *Flannery O'Connor Bulletin* 21 (1992): 25–36.

Greif, Mark. *The Age of the Crisis of Man: Thought and Fiction in America, 1933–1973*. Princeton, NJ: Princeton University Press, 2015.

Griffin, Roger. *The Nature of Fascism*. New York: Psychology Press, 1993.

Gutmann, Amy, and Dennis Thompson. *Why Deliberative Democracy?* Princeton, NJ: Princeton University Press, 2009.

Hewitt, Avis, and Robert Donahoo, eds. *Flannery O'Connor in the Age of Terrorism: Essays on Violence and Grace*. Knoxville: University of Tennessee Press, 2010.

Kaplan, Alice Yaeger. *Reproductions of Banality: Fascism, Literature, and French Intellectual Life*. Minneapolis: University of Minnesota Press, 1986.

Kessler, Edward. *Flannery O'Connor and the Language of Apocalypse*. Princeton, NJ: Princeton University Press, 1986.

King, Richard H. *Arendt and America*. Chicago: University of Chicago Press, 2015.

Kinney, Arthur F. *Flannery O'Connor's Library: Resources of Being*. Athens: University of Georgia Press, 2008.

Knowles, Adam. *Heidegger's Fascist Affinities: A Politics of Silence*. Palo Alto, CA: Stanford University Press, 2019.

Lipovski-Helal, Kathleen. "Flannery O'Connor, the Holocaust, and the Evolution of Catholicism." *Lit: Literature Interpretation Theory* 21, no. 3 (August 2010): 205–22.

Morrison, Paul. *The Poetics of Fascism: Ezra Pound, T. S. Eliot, Paul de Man*. New York: Oxford University Press, 1996.

O'Connor, Flannery. *The Complete Stories*. New York: Farrar, Straus and Giroux. 1971. (*CS*)

O'Connor, Flannery. *The Habit of Being: Letters of Flannery O'Connor*. Edited by Sally Fitzgerald, Reprint edition. New York: Farrar, Straus and Giroux, 1988. (*HB*)

O'Connor, Flannery. *Mystery and Manners: Occasional Prose*. Edited by Robert Fitzgerald and Sally Fitzgerald. New York: Macmillan, 1969. (*MM*)

O'Gorman, Farrell. "O'Connor and the Rhetoric of Eugenics: Misfits, the 'Unfit,' and Us." In *A Political Companion to Flannery O'Connor*, edited by Henry T. Edmondson III, 199–221. Lexington: University Press of Kentucky, 2017.

Olson, Joel. *The Abolition of White Democracy*. Minneapolis: University of Minnesota Press, 2004.

Patterson, Orlando. *Slavery and Social Death*. Cambridge, MA: Harvard University Press, 1982.

Paxton, Robert O. *The Anatomy of Fascism*. New York: Vintage Books, 2004.

Purcell, Edward A. *The Crisis of Democratic Theory: Scientific Naturalism and the Problem of Value*. Lexington: University Press of Kentucky, 2013.

Rath, Sura Prasad, and Mary Neff Shaw, editors. *Flannery O'Connor: New Perspectives*. Athens: University of Georgia Press, 1996.

Roos, John. "Political Community in 'The Displaced Person.'" In *A Political Companion to Flannery O'Connor*, edited by Henry T. Edmondson III. Lexington: University Press of Kentucky, 2017.

Smith, Rogers. "Beyond Tocqueville, Myrdal, and Hartz: The Multiple Traditions in America." *American Political Science Review* 87, no. 3 (1993).

Spicer, Kevin P. *Hitler's Priests: Catholic Clergy and National Socialism*. DeKalb: Northern Illinois University Press, 2017.

Steigmann-Gall, Richard. "Star-Spangled Fascism: American Interwar Political Extremism in Comparative Perspective." *Social History* 42, no. 1 (2017): 94–119.

Sykes, Jon D., Jr. "Flannery O'Connor and the Agrarians: Authentic Religion and Southern Identity." In *A Political Companion to Flannery O'Connor*, edited by Henry T. Edmondson III. Lexington: University Press of Kentucky, 2017.

Taylor, Alan C. "Redrawing the Color Line in Flannery O'Connor's 'The Displaced Person.'" *Mississippi Quarterly* 65, no. 1 (2012): 69–81.

Walker, Alice. "Beyond the Peacock: The Reconstruction of Flannery O'Connor." *In Search of Our Mothers' Gardens: Womanist Prose*. New York: Houghton Mifflin Harcourt, 2004.

Whitt, Margaret Earley. "The Pivotal Year, 1963: Flannery O'Connor and the Civil Rights Movement." In *A Political Companion to Flannery O'Connor*, edited by Henry T. Edmondson III, 79–98. Lexington: University Press of Kentucky, 2017.

Wolin, Sheldon S. *Fugitive Democracy: And Other Essays*. Princeton, NJ: Princeton University Press, 2016.

Wolin, Sheldon S. *Politics and Vision: Continuity and Innovation in Western Political Thought* (Expanded Edition). Princeton, NJ: Princeton University Press, 2004.

Wood, Ralph. "Sacramental Suffering: The Friendship of Flannery O'Connor and Elizabeth Hester." In *A Political Companion to Flannery O'Connor*, edited by Henry T. Edmondson III, 145–74. Lexington: University Press of Kentucky, 2017.

Wood, Ralph. "Flannery O'Connor's Racial Morals and Manners." *Christian Century* 111, no. 33 (16 November 1994): 1076.

Woodley, Daniel. *Fascism and Political Theory: Critical Perspectives on Fascist Ideology*. London: Routledge, 2009.

"Herself but Black": Richard Wright, Flannery O'Connor, and the "Near Enemy" of Civil Rights

RACHEL WATSON

I felt that a right more immediately deeper than that of politics or race was at stake; that is, a human right, the right of a man to think and feel honestly.[1]

In a letter to Elizabeth Hester on 1 September 1963, referring to Eudora Welty's fictionalized account of the recent murder of Medgar Evers, O'Connor wrote: "The topical is poison. I got away with it with 'Everything that Rises' but only because I say a plague on everybody's house as far as the race business goes." Two weeks later, she wrote to Hester again: "I am reading *Eichmann in Jerusalem* [...] . Anything is credible after such a period of history. I've always been haunted by the boxcars, but they were actually the least of it. And old Hannah [Arendt] is as sharp as they come."[2] O'Connor started drafting the short story "Revelation" soon after.

It would appear from this letter that, for O'Connor, something about totalitarianism allowed it to transcend the comparatively "topical" matter of American racial injustice—and that, in turn, race inequality did not stand up as worthy material for lasting fiction. But since O'Connor frequently invoked the "manners" of the Jim Crow South in her most ambitious work, it would be more precise to say that for her there was a *right* way and a *wrong* way of using that kind of material. The wrong way would be to recognize the reproduction of racial injustice in the United States as merely "topical," by mistaking its significance as a matter of violence occurring between types of individuals (e.g., the irrational white southerner and the moral black man). When O'Connor says that she puts a "plague on everybody's house as far as the race thing goes," the moment suggests a certain self-awareness of the kind of "equality" Alice Walker noticed in O'Connor's work many years ago: "[H]er black characters, male and female, appear equally shallow, demented, and absurd [as the whites]."[3] But I suggest that we also take it as way of understanding racial hierarchy in O'Connor's later work as eschewing the "topical" mode of its representation, and dramatizing it instead as an instance of a particularly dangerous form of sin. This form of sin takes on a misplaced faith in what Hannah Arendt called "the delusion of human omnipotence through organization": a mode of being that sought eternal truths in the appearance of the social order, a spiritual mistake that both O'Connor and Wright saw as evidence of an American vulnerability to authoritarian rule.[4]

What O'Connor was not willing to extend to any of her characters, regardless of race, was the cheap form of *pity* she saw circulating in postwar liberalism, and which she found especially dangerous in the shadow of the totalitarian threat presumed by the Cold War. Richard Wright made resonant declarations against literary and political invocations of pity throughout his career, perhaps most famously when he described the development of *Native Son* as reflecting his ambition to never again write a story that would make a banker's daughter cry:

> When the reviews of that book began to appear, I realized that I had made an awfully naive mistake. I found that I had written a book which even bankers' daughters could read and weep and feel good about. I swore to myself that if I ever wrote another book, no one would weep over it; that it would be so hard and deep that they would have to face it without the consolation of tears. It was this that made me get to work in dead earnest.[5]

For Wright, to provide the "consolation of tears" was the very worst kind of work literature could do in response to the illnesses of American political and social life. Such "weeping" made the experience of reading literature a phony catharsis, pacifying the very tensions that he wanted to see instead break wide open into social change.

And as O'Connor saw in Hannah Arendt, pity had a similarly "disastrous" effect when evoked as a guiding principle for politics and public discourse. For Arendt, *love* was not something that could be shared between the abstractions of groups, but only in the private lives of individuals—away from the power and influence of the state. Anything political that appeared as such was a dangerous kind of false "feeling" imposed upon individuals who were objectified, and instrumentalized, for its purpose. For Arendt, the political significance of Eichmann's disabled conscience was not its lack of sympathy, but rather the fact that it stemmed from an inability to imagine a point of view other than his own: not a failure of feeling, but of "rational imagination." It was Eichmann's inability to engage with *reality* as it existed outside of the product of his own mind that presented the worst danger.[6] If enough people share such an affliction, Arendt suggested, one therein has the substance of a "racial bureaucracy"—a totalitarian state.

One might say that a variant of Eichmann's affliction is what dooms many of the most famous characters in the works of both O'Connor and Wright. For Ruby Turpin of "Revelation," one example among many, the hard facts of reality are all but invisible to her—even when they are flying toward her forehead—because Ruby is incapable of seeing outside of her own self-fabricated view of the social world that surrounds her.[7] And in but one example of many from Wright's work, his most famous protagonist, Bigger Thomas, is marked by a relentlessly limited and starving vision. From childhood forward, Bigger's sense of the forces that shape his world never clarify into much more than great white storms of fear and rage; other than a fleeting moment of friendship, he cannot see other people as much more than vague obstacles in his path. And even demonstrations of liberal pity have the unintended effect of both objectifying him and precipitating his dramatic acts of murder. Though Ruby Turpin and Bigger Thomas appear to exist on opposite sides of the social plane, the gothic harshness of their stories suggests that they share a similar kind of affliction and that they were created by authors who diagnosed their readers with the same kind of disease.

For both Wright and O'Connor, literature that was to do any good in the world had to be of a kind that would dislodge readers' self-serving assumptions and provoke the kind of sharp and unexpected confrontations with reality that might reveal the dangers of conceding to American hegemony. One might say that both authors aimed to dramatize what Arendt suggested was the truest enemy of an authoritarian regime's racial bureaucracy: the "factuality of the real world," as the only force able to "ward off" the "fictitious world of totalitarianism."[8] O'Connor understood secular society as, in the words of St. Paul, "ruled by sin and death," a condition of entropy well masked by postwar culture and prosperity. For Wright, the world of Jim Crow similarly cultivated a mass delusion, one that aimed to make a regime of violence and exploitation appear both "natural" and "ethical." Though Bigger's limited view has been imposed upon him by forces outside of his control, and Ruby's narrow mindset is more self-serving, both characters appear as figures whose self-generated interpretations of the social world, and their place in it, make them not just ignorant, but explicitly vulnerable to the allure of authoritarian rule. As such, we might understand Ruby Turpin as a "native daughter" as much as we read Bigger Thomas as a "native son."

In a less abstract set of similarities, both authors also described being deeply influenced by Henry James, Edgar Allan Poe, and Nathaniel Hawthorne. The influence appears in both form and content: Gothic elements emerge unexpectedly and decisively in the modern world (whether a monstrous prophet from the side of a road, or a boy sitting as a "living corpse" in his own sentencing hearing) and frame the stories' spiritual stakes. In particular, the narcissism of false sympathy appears throughout the work of both O'Connor and Wright, as does a shared anxiety regarding the kind of damage such "feeling" might either cause outright or quietly legitimate. As if to actively thwart common circuits of readers' pity, both authors made a point throughout their careers to present some of the worst candidates for salvation, and through them ask readers to confront what it means to be worthy of the highest gifts: love, forgiveness, compassion, justice. In other words, in the fictional worlds of both Richard Wright and Flannery O'Connor, grace is purposefully not reserved for the nice guys.

In this essay, I consider a few protagonists from O'Connor and Wright that share similarities along these lines. The comparison, I suggest, allows us to see how two sets of problems that we associate with each writer, and presume to be mutually exclusive, are more properly understood as intertwined— problems of the spirit and problems of politics. For both writers, one of the greatest moral evasions of modern life was the belief in individual supremacy, rooted in a "faith" that one was fundamentally right about—and fundamentally alone within—the universe. Although the symptoms of this affliction often appeared as violence, intolerance, and even misplaced pity, for both authors its broader consequences also revealed a political significance, particularly evident in scenes that connect these despairing individuals to shadowy figurations of the recent Holocaust. Such common thematic ground between two otherwise quite different authors might suggest that a "reconsideration" along these lines would be warranted for both. Wright's persistent spiritual preoccupations tend to be diminished by the force of his naturalist, "social protest" reputation and overt political commitments. And in an inverse way, O'Connor's spiritual commitments tend to overshadow the political significance of her themes and aims. But in both authors' work, I suggest, one can find efforts to put these realms of human experience into conversation, even reconciliation, with one another, frequently dramatized through scenes of racial and economic hegemony, and the social world that constituted its stage.

As Timothy Caron has shown, critical work on Flannery O'Connor and race tends to resolve itself in one of two ways. In the prevailing set of attitudes, by what Caron calls the "True Believers," critics interpret O'Connor's black characters as serving to "point the way to heaven" for the whites, with the story of salvation relegating the historical and material realities of the Jim Crow South similarly in service to it.[9] These critics tend to read O'Connor the way they presume she wanted to be read herself, "embody[ing] the views of the author" by "us[ing] religion to deflect racial concerns." The other set of critical approaches to race in her work also avoids making it center stage, though by subsuming it to interpretations driven by critical theory. Caron's work shows how both approaches fall short of addressing the full significance of O'Connor's approach to race, and in doing so inadvertently shore up a pervasive dehistoricization of it. Building on Toni Morrison's famous critique of American literature and American literary criticism, Caron names this thematic system "theological whiteness."[10] As Caron and others have shown, O'Connor's general disposition regarding the dismantling of *de jure* and *de facto* Jim Crow was, in the polite term of the day, that of a gradualist.[11] But if "embodying the views of the author" produces limited readings on the positive side, it produces another set of limitations on the other.

For O'Connor's protagonists, the fatal sin that most often brings about their violent redemption is pride. Such characters presume too much knowledge about the world and hold too much certainty of it, emerging as both ridiculous and complacent, vulnerable and oppressive, too ignorant and too smart for their own good as a result. But more than this, they have in common a tendency to subscribe to a sense of reality that squarely, and often hilariously, denies the truth staring them in the face. Not only wrong in what they think they see, such characters are "seeing" what they want to believe true for the unconscious sake of reinforcing maladaptive egos—or what today might be called their "personal identities." Such characters' insistence on producing and maintaining the conditions necessary for this false sense of self often leads to their violent, and transformative, encounters with grace. Events that might appear as accidents, or even random crime, or a combination of both, usually culminate at the end of a causal chain that begins with a grasping ego: a grandmother who not only refuses to admit that she's gotten her family lost, but also that she snuck her cat into the picnic basket and thus accidentally gets them all killed. And in the worlds of O'Connor and Wright, grasping egos need hierarchical order.

For many of these characters, belief in their own entitlement appears as more than just laughable ignorance, but as the outward symptom of a deeper spiritual affliction. The combination of superiority and inheritance that gives them a sense of position and belonging within the broader social fabric depends upon a naturalized hierarchy: for example, a "faith" in the rewards due them for being white in a raced society. In this light, O'Connor's depiction of secular identity itself bears out Toni Morrison's description of how black figures function in white American literature (and white American literary criticism) generally. O'Connor's white characters do not "see" black people as they actually are, but instead as an "Africanist presence": projected desire for the coherence of their own illusory sense of identity, persistently demonstrating the fact that "the subject of the dream is the dreamer."[12]

By dramatizing racism as a matter of self-serving fantasy, race appears in O'Connor's fiction as more than "topical," and more than what might be accounted for by speculations regarding the personal attitudes of its author.[13] Instead, O'Connor's later work depicts *race* as not a matter of individual racists and their victims, but as an ongoing matter of ideology: a set of flexible beliefs and practices that attach to, and gain their coherence from, structurally specific relations of power. This depiction of how race *works* (not simply what race *is*) emerges as a rebuke of the social order writ large—not only of the Jim Crow South, but of the assumptions of cultural pluralism that undergird the comparatively liberal northern view as well, through which gestures of sympathy only objectify the other by projecting fantasies of superiority onto it. The "damage thesis" of postwar liberalism that cast black individuals as pathologized victims of white racism is nowhere to be found in O'Connor— as Walker noted, black characters in her work are usually just as ridiculous and flawed as the whites. As a result, in O'Connor's work there is no operating concept of *race*, or belief in racial difference, separate from its defining mechanism: *racism*.

As such, instead of hewing to a "damage thesis" story regarding race in America, O'Connor's later work shows how badly the white people need to believe in racial hierarchy, and how dangerously poor they are for subscribing to the delusion. And by yoking such delusions to a desire for authoritarian power, as O'Connor does in her 1964 story "Revelation," her work shows how understanding oneself as located in a social order that naturalizes hierarchy creates a hall of mirrors, in which delusions beget delusions. When these white characters feel such hierarchies slipping away, the destabilizing of their "faith" in race appears as the action of grace itself, and brings the possibility for understanding themselves outside of a structure that depends upon essentialized inequality.

In this sense, commitment to *identity* emerges in O'Connor's work a lot like the critique of pity: as a false virtue, or near enemy, that appears in response to a genuine, but unmet, spiritual need. In the case of pity, that genuine spiritual need is an unsentimental acknowledgment of the reality of oneself and others. In fantasies of identity, the genuine spiritual need it seems to address is similar: that of understanding oneself as an individual among other individuals, all granted equally the unearned gift of God's grace. When the living God is not called upon for this kind of socially situated self-understanding, and grace is not understood as the condition that grounds political equality, racial ways of being stand in as a clever—and disastrous—counterfeit. In this respect, racial ideology appears in O'Connor's work as neither "topical" nor as a metaphor for the spirit that serves to "deflect" racial matters. Rather, it appears in its true form: as a mystifying, pervasive set of beliefs that mask a broadly shared spiritual affliction—a delusional commitment to naturalized social hierarchies that had potentially terrifying political consequences.

In 1964, O'Connor described the dangers of a liberal sympathy in no uncertain terms in the "Introduction to the Memoir of Mary Ann":

> In this popular pity, we mark our gain in sensibility and our loss in vision. If other ages felt less, they saw more, even though they saw with the blind, prophetical, unsentimental eye of acceptance, which is to say, of faith. In the absence of this faith now, we govern by tenderness. It is a tenderness which, long since cut off from the person of Christ, is wrapped in theory. When tenderness is detached from the source of tenderness, its logical outcome is terror. It ends in forced labor camps and in the fumes of the gas chamber.[14]

In the context of 1964, one of the most violent years of the civil rights movement, to claim that "we govern by tenderness" seems especially striking, if not brutally nonsensical. But such false "tenderness" whose "logical outcome is terror" helps to illuminate the unexpected appearance of boxcars and gas ovens in the midst of Ruby Turpin's otherwise pluralist social vision from "Revelation":

> Sometimes Mrs. Turpin occupied herself at night by naming the classes of people. On the bottom of the heap were most colored people, not the kind she would have been if she had been one but most of them [. . .] But here [after trying to sort the heap according to essentialized traits] the complexity of it would begin to bear in on her, for some of the people with a lot of money were common and ought to be below she and Claud and some of the people who had good blood had lost their money and had to rent and then there were colored people who owned their homes and land as well. There was a colored dentist in town who had two red Lincolns and a swimming pool and a farm with registered white-face cattle on it. Usually by the time she had fallen asleep all the classes of people were moiling and roiling around in her head, and she would dream they were all crammed in together in one box car, being ridden off to be put in a gas oven.[15]

Here, Ruby Turpin's ordinary race and class prejudices, as demonstrated in the social microcosm of the doctor's office, give way to reveal their true stakes, and her true nature: a "race bureaucrat" in disguise.[16] In the violent order of the South, Ruby Turpin seems relatively mild as racists go, and she even applauds herself inwardly for preferring "niggers" to "white trash." After all,

Turpin does not exactly deny black individuality: "'There's a heap of things worse than a nigger,' Mrs. Turpin agreed. 'It's all kinds of them just like it's all kinds of us.'"[17]

But when Turpin uses the phrase "heap of things" to describe human society, it signifies more than a regional turn of phrase. Here, it is her *will to racialize* that stands out, and how such racializing sees both herself and others as a variety of elaborately marked objects. In the context of a fracturing Jim Crow regime, Turpin tries to refine the "natural" social hierarchy by essentializing the markers of wealth and poverty in addition to those of race itself. In her self-soothing, Turpin creates bureaucratic order out of an apparent social chaos, and organizes herself into place in the midst of a stratified, dehumanized "heap." The third-person narration allows us to see both the totalitarian character of this habit of mind, and Turpin's moral obliviousness to its implications. She privately applauds herself for being a good Christian, for having the correct feelings of sympathy for the classes and kinds who, according to her, deserve it. Turpin was even feeling an "awful pity" for the ugly college student Mary Grace, and a joyful gratitude for her own God-given and well-deserved spot in the social hierarchy, just moments before Mary Grace chucked a copy of *Human Development* at her forehead.

For Ruby Turpin, the social organizing of the passage above works to lull her to sleep, until the hard facts of reality intrude and show how the growing economic power of African Americans—not just political or legal power in the form of individual rights—undermines what is otherwise a solid hegemonic "faith" in the racial order of the Jim Crow South. The disintegration of her vision at this point suggests how economic redistribution threatens the illusory cohesion of racial thinking. And when her desire for holding on to that order persists, its true moral character is revealed: boxcars to the gas ovens. Despite having outwardly demonstrated all the proper "feelings" for others, Ruby Turpin's racial beliefs reveal an Eichmann within—a fact about her that would not surprise Mary Grace one bit. And it is the fact of growing economic power across the color line that intrudes upon her fantasy and breaks apart her delusions of racial hierarchy. Here, O'Connor betrays a surprisingly leftist political critique, in which racial inequality is revealed as merely functioning as an evasion and enforcement of class difference.

In a more conscious prayer preceding this, Turpin asked God that "if he must make her black, make her a neat clean respectable Negro woman, herself but black." The phrase is comical in part because it emblematizes the deeper narcissism at work in all forms of racializing, in which one "sees" a world created out of one's own desires for an order of essentially stable, distinct groups. Here, quite directly, the subject of the dream is the dreamer. That is to say, O'Connor's story suggests that to be committed to a racializing view of humanity is to be doomed to a delusional view not unlike the critique of pity.

And if we understand Turpin's racial ideology as masking desire for the kind of totalizing power reflected in the Holocaust, the stakes of such narcissism feel extremely high. As her argument with God shows, what Turpin clings to more than anything is the power that inheres in the hierarchy itself, regardless of its terms, even if she's on the bottom of the heap: "Call me a wart hog from hell. Put that bottom rail on top. There'll still be a top and bottom!"[18] It is not hard to see how this desire might express itself as both reinforcement of the racial order and as liberal pity—two sides of the same coin.

The beliefs of the putatively fascist nemesis of Richard Wright's *The Outsider* (in the character of Herndon, a former Texas oil tycoon) earn a description from a communist that makes Herndon's way of being in the world sound a lot like that of Ruby Turpin:

> All of his arguments boil down to this: God made him and his kind to rule over the lower breeds. And God was so kind and thoughtful as to arrange that he be repaid handsomely for it. Of course, he has conceived this God of his in the image of a highly successful oil or real estate man, just a little more powerful and wonderful than he is. [. . .] Herndon is quite anxious to collaborate with God by shouldering a rifle, if necessary, and helping to defend what God has so generously given him. Herndon feels that God was absolutely right in giving him what he's got, but he does not completely trust God's judgment when it comes to his keeping it.[19]

As Mark Christian Thompson has shown, Herndon's fascism is marked more by capitalism and racism than explicit devotion to an authoritarian ideology.[20] As such, when the characters in Wright's novel find themselves drawn to grand narratives, including the doomed protagonist, the particulars of the ideologies matter far less than how they function for wielding a totalizing power. For Wright's Herndon and O'Connor's Turpin, the "fascist" god that legitimates racial hierarchy is the same false god that legitimates the economic inequality of capitalism—a god who shapes reality as they want to perceive it, totally, and who is conceived, more or less, in their own image. In this respect, both Wright and O'Connor suggest a relationship between the danger of authoritarian power and the naturalizations of racial hierarchy and class inequality. What appears as a spiritual problem in O'Connor's work has clear political implications; the same kind of problem that appears in Wright's work as a matter of politics also has a distinctly spiritual cast. And the resistance to imagining equality, framed as a commitment to socially ascribed forms of group identity, appears as a spiritual failure with political consequences.

After her revelation over the hog pen, Turpin's vision suggests a different view of social organization from her pluralist dream. In this procession of souls toward heaven, Turpin can still acknowledge the outward signs of social difference—she is not rendered color- or class-blind—but also "could see by their shocked and altered faces that even their virtues were being burned away."[21] Turpin's vision seems to be watching as worldly social order falls away to reveal the truth of Pauline equality below its surface. Here, the socially marked self is not simply discarded, but transformed, through a recognition of other "selves" in coordination with it—even hogs.[22] The dynamic dramatizes a kind of encounter in which compassion for others is not a matter of moral sentiments or "feeling," but an ontology based on human equality, ordained by the Creator at the level of the spirit, and thus transcending all notions of difference stemming from worldly identity.[23] In the grips of such delusion, the world of others is merely experienced as an endless series of *things*, or functions, rather than the mutually constitutive, and real, encounter of what theologian Martin Buber called the "I-Thou." This theological framework defines the living hell that afflicts so many of both Wright's and O'Connor's protagonists, particularly the ones who cling to the ideological demands of their own personal omniscience: the consequences of a false reality based on vanity and its self-serving objectifications of others.[24]

In this light, O'Connor's flawed protagonists might be read—as Wright's often are—as exorcising O'Connor's own artistic and spiritual fears and as expressing a knowledge of her own limitations.[25] But they also suggest a different way of understanding the significance of racial ideology in her work. As a pathologically narcissistic (that is to say, *vain*) set of projections, the function of American racism appears in her work as an *ur*-figure for the sin of pride, and engenders the same kind of alienation from God. Two of her most casually racist characters, Ruby Turpin from "Revelation" and Julian's mother from "Everything That Rises Must Converge," share a resonant perspective on the world, in which everyone they encounter—even those closest to them— appear more or less as objects that exist for the sake of shoring up their own fragile sense of identity. As such, the affliction they share reflects an existential state of pride: a failure to see themselves as they are, but also a failure to see and love others.[26] But when the boxcars appear as the true message of Ruby Turpin's dream, it also suggests that for O'Connor the political stakes of such a failure amount to no less than the potential rise of a totalitarian state.

In the final sentencing hearing of Richard Wright's *Native Son* (1940), the prosecutor argues for Bigger Thomas to receive the death penalty, and justifies it with an allegiance to human omnipotence that one would not be surprised to find in an ill-fated O'Connor character: "I say that the law is holy because it makes us human!"[27] But when Boris Max counters this argument by insisting on Bigger Thomas as a victim of structural constraints, he refuses what is for

Wright a crucial point: that Bigger needs to be an intentional individual in order to be a moral agent, to be fully *human*. Instead, Max repeatedly presents Bigger as a "living corpse." In this sympathetic but necessarily dehumanizing defense, Max claims that the structural violence that makes him a product of his environment has also rendered Bigger incapable of free will or moral choice, or even of seeing others as individual human beings.[28] Bigger's climactic "I am" moment seems to confirm this lack, the sign of a moral vacuum that reveals Bigger to be the harbinger of fascism that Wright intended: "I didn't want to kill! [. . .] But what I killed for I *am*!"[29] And while Boris Max was not exactly wrong in his sympathetic account, his recoil from Bigger's self-assertion shows that in his materialist analysis of Bigger's life, Max did not account for the depth of "horror" that such spiritual violence could produce.

Despite Wright's fame as a "naturalist" writer, this kind of spiritual concern regarding the preservation of moral agency persisted throughout his work and often served as a warning regarding the consequences of systemic violence that might strip an individual of his basic freedom to choose good or evil. Like O'Connor's work, in Wright's fiction, not only do the overt racists get called to task, but even the liberal "sympathizers" may find themselves stuffed into a furnace. In *Native Son*, the only two characters who do not dehumanize Bigger through either overt violence or liberal pity also offer the only two perspectives that recognize him as both an equal and a fully individuated other: Jan, in his gesture of friendship, and Wright himself as the implied narrator. As in O'Connor, this careful, unsentimental third-person point of view also makes possible the coordination of both spiritual and political realms, and suggested an author unwilling to finally admit the irrelevance of the former to the immediacy of the latter.

For Wright, the deprivation of moral agency was a prophetic kind of violence, one that produced a landscape of "moral horror." Such a world gave birth to "native sons" like Bigger Thomas, figures who could be either black or white, and who stood as a cautionary tale regarding the authoritarian threat: "Bigger Thomas would loom as a symbolic figure of American life [. . .] the prophecy of our future."[30] In the same essay, Wright alludes to the spiritual dimension of these concerns: "I felt that a right more immediately deeper than that of politics or race was at stake; that is, a *human* right, the right of a man to think and feel honestly."[31] In the concluding passage, Wright articulates what would remain an artistic motivation for the rest of his career. Here, he cites not only the modern malaise of "spiritual hunger" as providing his sense of urgency, but also indicates the same three authors whose influence most shaped the work of fellow southerner Flannery O'Connor:

> But we do have in the Negro the embodiment of a past tragic enough to appease the spiritual hunger of even a James; and we have in the oppression of

the Negro a shadow athwart our national life dense and heavy enough to satisfy even the gloomy brooding of a Hawthorne. And if Poe were alive, he would not have to invent horror; horror would invent him.[32]

In the same essay, Wright also discusses the desperation produced by a market-driven society which he saw as creating a dangerous degree of inequality, one that engendered a widespread sense of "exclusion" from political life, and thus produced fertile ground for the seeds of an authoritarian regime. The "prophecy" demonstrated by Bigger Thomas was symptomatic of a national sickness, one that appeared as both racial violence and the naturalized forces of the market.[33]

Well after *Native Son*, and after WWII, Wright's work continued to depict American hegemony as producing an alienated population vulnerable to the allure of authoritarian power. Despite the philosophical obsessions of Cross Damon of *The Outsider*, like many of O'Connor's doomed-and-chosen protagonists, Damon remains blind to his own fatal weaknesses right up until his mortal end. After finally being captured by police for a variety of crimes, including the brutal murder of at least three people, Damon reveals an image of himself as a man who subscribes to a demonstrably false humility: "I'm the kind of man who simply cannot feel that kind of godlike imperiousness to impose my will on others."[34] The violence and desperation of the prior five hundred pages certainly suggest otherwise.

Early on, an underground train derailment gives Cross Damon a chance to fake his own death and start a new life, free of social and familial obligations. Though Damon appears revitalized by the terrifying turn of events, the narrator describes the scene that generates it as one of both physical and moral horror. In the wreck's jumble of bodies and body parts, a gruesome iteration of a totalitarian "heap" resonates, as human dignity and individuality is obliterated in a train car that, like Ruby Turpin's bedtime fantasy, resonates with real events from the recent Holocaust. The physical violence of the scene aligns with a moral vacuum as well, as Damon coolly strategizes how best to use the bodies of the dead and injured to climb out and free himself: "If the man was dead, then any action he took to free himself was right [. . .] He panted with despair, regarding the man's head as an obstacle; it was no longer flesh and blood, but a rock, a chuck of wood to be whacked at until it was gone [.]"[35] After multiple acts of violence against what he assumes are corpses, Damon frees himself from the train car, but his ensuing attempts at life render questionable whether there is a meaningful difference between him and the bodies he leaves behind, or the manner by which he left them.

The distinction between authoritarian ideologies in the story that follows, whether communist or fascist, is merely an arbitrary matter of the particular social world in which the "alienated man" finds himself. When Cross Damon is later analyzing why such figures appeal to him so deeply, he unconsciously diagnoses his own spiritual affliction in identifying theirs. Speaking to a local leader of the Communist Party chapter, Damon explains: "What these sincere people [those who believe that the Cold War is an ideological battle] do not realize is that Communism and Fascism are but the political expressions of the Twentieth Century's atheistic way of life."[36] A few pages later, through the free indirect voice of the narrator, we see Damon analyze himself in the course of analyzing his oppressors, just below the level of consciousness:

> They would never credit him with as much freedom to act as they had. A certain psychological blindness seemed to be the hallmark of all men who had to create their own worlds . . . All other men were material for them; they could admit no rivals, no equals; other men were either above them, or below them.[37]

The assessment describes his ideological enemies, but it also recalls the jumble of bodies that marked his escape from the train car and thus his self-generated rebirth. Here, Damon reveals his own driving desire for a man-made hierarchy—a version of Turpin's driving desire to still have a "bottom and a top"—as a fundamental inability to admit something like human equality. The problem of equality then appears both in Wright and O'Connor as a fundamentally *spiritual* failure that manifests as a *political* disaster: when the human hunger for God attaches itself to the false idols of authoritarian rule.

Damon's drive to—godlike—create himself anew demands more forms of violence, as he continues to encounter the world of others not so unlike his experience in the train car: a series of objects, defined and sorted by his projections as either functional or obstacle in relation to his freedom. Like O'Connor's protagonists—even the self-consciously "Christian" ones, like Ruby Turpin—Cross Damon lives according to a belief in the authoritarian article of faith: "human omnipotence." In this novel, what appears to be a self-determined individual is revealed instead as having the soul of a bureaucrat. When Damon finds the district attorney won't charge him due to lack of evidence, that which he consciously feared most turns out to have been his driving wish all along: to be assumed into the juridical scheme, organized into the power and apparatus of the state. When he finds himself finally, formally excluded from this power, he is thrown into a spiritual wilderness.

Like Ruby Turpin coming to terms with her essential "hog" nature, both characters are pushed to their crisis points when they must face the fact that the power they unconsciously desire—whether the expressions of a powerful state or a powerful market—cannot "organize" them into it after all. Their commitments to such false gods produced a delusional sense of reality—and in turn made them ripe for totalitarian seduction, without even knowing it. But the very impossibility of realizing what they want also made them ideal candidates for the transformative gift of grace. For Cross Damon, the crisis of *not* being thrown in jail for murder unexpectedly evokes in him a sense of urgent obligation toward a woman who bears no blood relation to him at all, but who was generous to him, and who stood to lose the fragile economic stability that she had gained. It was en route to helping her—not himself, nor even his own family—when his unexpected final moments clarified the epiphany.

As he lay dying on the sidewalk, vengefully murdered by a Marxist, Damon expresses this revelation in a merging of his Christian mother's words with the chapter's epigraph from Nietzsche, when he "sees" that in order to be truly alive in the world one must remain an open potential in communion with all of humanity, "a promise":

> "The search [for what an individual life may be worth] can't be done alone," he let his voice issue from a dry throat in which he felt death lurking. "Never alone ... Alone a man is nothing ... Man is a promise that he must never break ... "[38]

Damon's revelation at death appears as an effort to recuperate his mother's Christianity into a political ethic. In other words, Damon emerges in the end as having been deeply "Christ-haunted" all along: a blinded intellectual, both saved and killed by the intervention of grace. Damon's revised politics are not built on familial, racial, or any kind of "blood" tie, but on active compassion for others who have no socially determined relationship to him, a bond that exceeds "identity" and thus might be extended to all humans in need. When the realization appears to him just before he dies on the street from gunshot wounds, one cannot help but think that Damon might have been a good person—if someone had been there to shoot him every day of his life.

In sum, both authors' later work appears to pose a set of resonant questions, one being whether a politics based on equality and individual rights can be enforceable without a spiritual authority grounding one's sense of identity in a moral universe. As such, both authors demonstrate a shared sense of the aim and urgency of fiction, in which the special task of the writer might not be to assert equality by engendering sympathy for others of different class or racial status, but instead to tell the kind of disturbing stories that could wrench their audience away from the fantasies of identity that produce *difference* in the first place. In Christian terms, such dramas of authority demonstrate how the world of man can be mistaken for the order of the divine; in political terms, it might be understood as the operations of ideological hegemony.

Though Wright's narrators did not betray the same kind of wry humor as O'Connor's, both chose the ironically distanced third-person voice, often focalized through select—and benighted—protagonists. This form allowed them to dramatize the most liminal and ambivalent aspects of consciousness and power in modern life: the dynamic between externalized authority and its refraction as internalized dictates; the way hegemonic "common sense" works by seeming so natural and "obvious" it can barely be "seen" by its hosts (and its victims); and the violence required to disrupt an ordinary individual's grasp on such deeply embedded delusions. And in a shared desire to put the spiritual realm into conversation with the political imagination, one sees a similarly shared anxiety regarding how "rights" discourse might manifest itself in a social world that remains committed to a belief in the racialized subject and the kind of inequality upon which such a structure depends. Without what Arendt called a "benevolent guarantor" of rights-based identity, both O'Connor and Wright show in their fiction how a facsimile of such divine authority might arrive to fill the vacuum, (mis)identified either as the forces of the market, or as the technocratic wisdom of the postwar state. And for both writers, it appears that when concepts of self and other are "detached from their source" in the political realm, "the logical outcome is terror."

NOTES

1. Richard Wright, *Native Son and "How Bigger Was Born"* (New York: Harper Library of America, 1993), 449. Emphasis in original.

2. Flannery O'Connor, *The Habit of Being*, ed. Sally Fitzgerald (New York: Farrar, Straus and Giroux, 1979), 537, 539.

3. Alice Walker remarked on this aspect of O'Connor's work as well: "[A]nd her black characters, male and female, appear equally shallow, demented, and absurd. That she retained a certain distance (only, however, in her later, mature work) from the inner workings of her black characters seems to me all to her credit, since, by deliberately limiting her treatment of them to cover their observable demeanor and actions, she leaves them free, in the reader's imagination, to inhabit another landscape, another life, than the one she creates for them. This is a kind of grace many writers do not have when dealing with representatives of an oppressed people within a story, and their insistence on knowing everything, on being God, in fact, has burdened us with more stereotypes than we can ever hope to shed." From "Beyond the Peacock" in Alice Walker, *In Search of Our Mother's Gardens* (New York: Harcourt, 1983), 52.

4. Hannah Arendt, *The Origins of Totalitarianism* (San Diego: Harvest Books, 1968), 387–88.

5. Wright, *Native Son*, 454.

6. See Deborah Nelson, "Suffering and Thinking: The Scandal of Tone in *Eichmann in Jerusalem*," in *Compassion: The Culture and Politics of an Emotion*, ed. Lauren Berlant (New York: Routledge, 2004), 219–44. See also "Chapter 2: Hannah Arendt: Irony and Atrocity," in Deborah Nelson, *Tough Enough: Arbus, Arendt, Didion, McCarthy, Sontag, Weil* (Chicago: University of Chicago Press, 2017).

7. I am grateful here for Marshall Bruce Gentry's reading, which suggests as much regarding Ruby Turpin by claiming that her "revelation" is wholly manifested from within herself. The question also came up for me during July 2014, when I was fortunate enough to participate as a summer scholar in the NEH Summer Institute "Reconsidering Flannery O'Connor." There, I

was delighted to have the opportunity to pose my questions regarding Turpin and totalitarianism to Bruce Gentry and Robert Brinkmeyer in person; the conversations that followed were some of my favorites that month (among many), and informed my thinking for this essay immensely, as has their scholarship: Robert Brinkmeyer Jr., *The Fourth Ghost: White Southern Writers and European Fascism, 1930–1950* (Baton Rouge: Louisiana State University Press, 2009), as well as *The Art and Vision of Flannery O'Connor* (Baton Rouge: Louisiana State University Press, 1989); and Marshall Bruce Gentry, *Flannery O'Connor's Religion of the Grotesque* (Jackson: University Press of Mississippi, 1986).

8. Arendt, *The Origins of Totalitarianism*, 387. For Arendt, and one might argue for O'Connor and Wright, the reverse threat is also true: "Factuality itself depends for its continued existence upon the existence of the nontotalitarian world" (388).

9. Nicholas Crawford, for example, writes: "In O'Connor's short fiction, we find a recurring pattern: a white protagonist on a journey of return, whose encounter with an African American character signals a failure of personal and social self-reckoning; and it is this failure, this impasse, that sparks the need for deliverance through spirituality." Nicholas Crawford, "An Africanist Impasse: Race, Return, and Revelation in the Short Fiction of Flannery O'Connor," *South Atlantic Review* 68, no. 2 (Spring 2003): 1–25.

10. Timothy Caron, "'The Bottom Rail Is on the Top': Race and 'Theological Whiteness,' in Flannery O'Connor's Short Fiction," in *From inside the Church of Flannery O'Connor: Sacrament, Sacramental, and the Sacred in Her Fiction*, ed. Joanne Halleran McMullen and Jon Parrish Peede (Macon, GA: Mercer University Press, 2007), 140–66. In the same essay, Caron briefly pairs the two stories I'm discussing here: "Revelation" of 1964, and "Everything That Rises Must Converge" of 1961, and departs from the dominant critical view by claiming that they both ought to be read primarily as stories about racial ideology in the Jim Crow South.

11. Caron's work more broadly demonstrates that "O'Connor's theology led her to advocate a 'go-slow' policy on issues such as racial integration. She believed the South's pre–Civil Rights 'manners' were sufficient to shepherd the region through the tumultuous 1950s and 1960s and felt that the racial justice would be meted out in heaven if not in her lifetime in Georgia." Caron, "'The Bottom Rail Is on the Top,'" 147–48. Regarding O'Connor's "gradualism," also see Ralph C. Wood, "Where Is the Voice Coming From? Flannery O'Connor on Race," *The Flannery O'Connor Bulletin* 22 (1993–1994).

12. Toni Morrison, *Playing in the Dark: Whiteness and the American Literary Imagination* (Cambridge, MA: Harvard University Press, 1990). Also see Nicholas Crawford, "An Africanist Impasse," regarding a relationship between Morrison's argument and O'Connor's work with black character figuring as functions in stories of white redemption and homecoming.

13. For those few critics who have been willing to depart from the two approaches Caron identifies, and to, in a nutshell, call her work out as racist, this has certainly been the dominant mode, as demonstrated by Caron's own conclusions. The biographical tendency has only intensified since the availability of her archival letters, which were selected and edited by Sally Fitzgerald for *The Habit of Being* collection in part as an effort to soften O'Connor's expressions of offensive and derisive attitudes toward black people and efforts toward black equality.

14. O'Connor, *Mystery and Manners*, 227. Despite O'Connor's critical stance in relation to liberalisms of the day, the attitude above resonated with one expressed ten years prior by Lionel Trilling in his national bestseller *The Liberal Imagination* (1950), asserting an Arnoldian perspective on the moral value of literature for a liberal society. Both authors would see the political attitude of pity as an objectifying, even "coercive" position: "Some paradox of our natures leads us, when once we have made our fellow men the objects of our enlightened interest, to go on to make them the objects of our pity, then of our wisdom, ultimately of our coercion. It is to prevent this corruption, the most ironic and tragic that man knows, that we

stand in need of the moral realism which is the product of the free play of the moral imagination." Lionel Trilling, "Manners, Morals, and the Novel," from *The Liberal Imagination* (New
York: New York Review of Books, 2008), 221–22.

15. O'Connor, *Collected Works*, 636.

16. Here I am borrowing the concept from Hannah Arendt, *The Origins of Totalitarianism*,
186, and more generally 185–221.

17. Ibid., 640.

18. O'Connor, *Collected Works*, 653.

19. Wright, *The Outsider* (New York: Harper Perennial, 1993), 264–65.

20. Mark Christian Thompson, "Richard Wright's Jealous Rebels: Black Fascism and
Philosophy," in *Black Fascisms: African American Literature and Culture between the Wars*
(Charlottesville: University of Virginia Press, 2007), 143–70. In Thompson's provocative reading
of the allure that various forms of fascism held for certain twentieth-century African American
writers, Wright appears to be an exception, insofar as, for Thompson, *The Outsider* reveals that
Wright held a more circumspect relation to the appeal of a racial nationalism than some of
his peers. I would go further and say that much if not most of Wright's work was dedicated to
using literature to precisely fight against the appeal of authoritarian ideology, beginning most
famously with *Native Son*, but appearing as a commitment that persisted in various forms
throughout the rest of his career.

21. O'Connor, *Collected Works*, 654.

22. "There is neither Jew nor Gentile, neither slave nor free, nor is there male and female, for
you are all one in Christ Jesus." Galatians 3:28, NIV.

23. As other scholars have shown, this also theologically aligns O'Connor's depictions of
the social world with Martin Buber's theory of the "I-Thou" encounter. As Maurice Friedman
noted in his 1955 essay on the relationship between psychoanalytic theories of personality
and Buber's theology of the "I-Thou" and "I-It" relations—an essay that O'Connor read and
noted for its usefulness in her fiction—the fundamental "insanity" of modern life appears as
a relentless projection of the "I" as an "It" into the real world. As Christina Bieber Lake has
noted, O'Connor read this essay by Friedman and found it instructive for her practice of writing. O'Connor wrote marginally the word "fiction": "Particularly important in this relationship
is 'seeing the other' and 'making the other present,' which is not, as we have seen, a matter of
'identification' or 'empathy,' but of a concrete imagining of the other side which does not at the
same time lose sight of one's own." Lake is quoting Maurice Friedman, "Healing through Meeting: Martin Buber and Psychotherapy," *CrossCurrents* 5, no. 4 (1955): 297–310, 297.

Further, *love* for Buber was "a cosmic force": not a feeling, but a state of being, one that
becomes "actual" only in the "unique" and equalizing force of the "I-Thou" encounter. "Exclu-
siveness comes into being miraculously again and again—and now one can act, help, heal,
educate, raise, redeem. Love is responsibility of an I for a You: in this consists what cannot
consist in any feeling—the equality of all lovers, from the smallest to the greatest [.]" The
remaining passage refers directly to Christ: "and from the blissfully secure whose life is circumscribed by the life of the beloved human being to him that is nailed his life long to the cross of
the world, capable of what is immense and bold enough to risk it: to love *man*." Martin Buber,
I and Thou, preface and translation by Walter Kaufmann. Kindle e-book, Location 811–2. For a
more comprehensive consideration of O'Connor in relation to Buber, specifically concerning
the story "Revelation" and the spiritual significance of the Holocaust, see George Piggford, "A
Dialogue Between Above and Below: Flannery O'Connor, Martin Buber, and 'Revelation' After
the Holocaust," *Flannery O'Connor Review* 13 (2015): 90–91.

24. As Lake also claims in her discussion of an early story, "The Crop," O'Connor staged this
relation of encounter as reflecting the ideal relation between "artist and hero." When such an

encounter fails, as it does in the work of the writer protagonist of "The Crop," Lake reads the shortcoming as a sign of O'Connor's spiritual take on the act of fiction writing itself: such that a failure to be honest in one's gaze and evocation of a character, drawing them as a projection of one's own self-affirming fantasies, is not just a failure of aesthetics but also a "failure to love." Christina Bieber Lake, "The Violence of Technique and the Technique of Violence," in *Flannery O'Connor in the Age of Terrorism: Essays on Violence and Grace*, ed. Avis Hewitt and Robert Donahoo (Knoxville: University of Tennessee Press, 2010), 25–39, 33.

25. During her time at the Iowa Writers' Workshop, O'Connor confronted this danger of self-worship in the pursuit of knowledge, and cast it in increasingly literary terms. In an undated entry from her prayer journal, she writes: "Dear God, I cannot love thee the way I want to. […] I do not know you God because I am in the way. Please help me to push myself to the side." And later in the same passage: "Please do not let the explanations of the psychologists about this make it turn suddenly cold." Flannery O'Connor, *A Prayer Journal* (New York: Farrar, Straus and Giroux, 2013), 3.

26. Here I am borrowing the phrase from Lake, ibid.

27. Wright, *Native Son*, 408.

28. Ibid., 392–93.

29. Ibid., 429.

30. Wright also directly cited a desire to avoid engendering literary sympathy as his early inspiration for writing *Native Son*: "When the reviews of that book [*Uncle Tom's Children*] began to appear, I realized that I had made an awfully naive mistake. I found that I had written a book which even bankers' daughters could read and weep and feel good about. I swore to myself that if I ever wrote another book, no one would weep over it; that it would be so hard and deep that they would have to face it without the consolation of tears. It was this that made me get to work in dead earnest." Richard Wright, "How Bigger Was Born," 447, 454.

31. Ibid., 449. Emphasis in original.

32. Ibid., 462.

33. "I made the discovery that Bigger Thomas was not black all the time; he was white, too, and there were literally millions of him, everywhere. […] I sensed, too, that the Southern scheme of oppression was but an appendage of a far vaster and in many respects more ruthless and impersonal commodity-profit machine." Ibid., 441.

34. Wright, *The Outsider*, 517.

35. Ibid., 95.

36. Ibid., 491.

37. Ibid., 495.

38. Ibid., 585. The final book of the novel begins with a quote from Nietzsche: "Man is the only being who makes promises" (501). And earlier in the novel, his mother pleads with him: "'Son, can't you deny yourself sometimes and not hurt others?' she begged of him humbly; she was again, in the evening of her life, supplicating the fateful world of man. 'You're destroying yourself. I know you believe in your own pleasure, but must you hurt other people? […] Life is a promise, son; God promised it to us and we must promise it to others. Without that promise, life's nothing,'" Ibid., 28–29.

WORKS CITED

Arendt, Hannah. *The Origins of Totalitarianism*. San Diego: Harvest Books, 1968.

Brinkmeyer, Robert, Jr. *The Fourth Ghost: White Southern Writers and European Fascism, 1930–1950*. Baton Rouge: Louisiana State University Press, 2009.

Brinkmeyer, Robert, Jr. *The Art and Vision of Flannery O'Connor*. Baton Rouge: Louisiana State University Press, 1989.

Buber, Martin. *I and Thou*, preface and translation by Walter Kaufmann. Kindle e-book, Amazon Digital Services, 2011.

Caron, Timothy. "'The Bottom Rail Is on the Top': Race and 'Theological Whiteness' in Flannery O'Connor's Short Fiction." In *From Inside the Church of Flannery O'Connor: Sacrament, Sacramental, and the Sacred in Her Fiction*, edited by Joanne Halleran McMullen and Jon Parrish Peede, 140–66. Macon, GA: Mercer University Press, 2007.

Crawford, Nicholas. "An Africanist Impasse: Race, Return, and Revelation in the Short Fiction of Flannery O'Connor." *South Atlantic Review* 68, no. 2 (Spring 2003): 1–25.

Friedman, Maurice. "Healing through Meeting: Martin Buber and Psychotherapy." *CrossCurrents* 5, no. 4 (1955): 297–310.

Gentry, Marshall Bruce. *Flannery O'Connor's Religion of the Grotesque*. Jackson: University Press of Mississippi, 1986.

Lake, Christina Bieber. "The Violence of Technique and the Technique of Violence." In *Flannery O'Connor in the Age of Terrorism: Essays on Violence and Grace*, edited by Avis Hewitt and Robert Donahoo, 25–39. Knoxville: University of Tennessee Press, 2010.

Morrison, Toni. *Playing in the Dark: Whiteness and the American Literary Imagination*. Cambridge, MA: Harvard University Press, 1990.

Nelson, Deborah. "Suffering and Thinking: The Scandal of Tone in *Eichmann in Jerusalem*." In *Compassion: The Culture and Politics of an Emotion*, edited by Lauren Berlant, 219–44. New York: Routledge, 2004.

Nelson, Deborah. *Tough Enough: Arbus, Arendt, Didion, McCarthy, Sontag, Weil*. Chicago: University of Chicago Press, 2017.

O'Connor, Flannery. *The Habit of Being*. Edited by Sally Fitzgerald. New York: Farrar, Straus and Giroux, 1979.

O'Connor, Flannery. *Mystery and Manners: Occasional Prose*. Selected and edited by Sally and Robert Fitzgerald. New York: Farrar, Straus and Giroux, 1969.

O'Connor, Flannery. *A Prayer Journal*. New York: Farrar, Straus and Giroux, 2013.

Piggford, George. "A Dialogue Between Above and Below: Flannery O'Connor, Martin Buber, and 'Revelation' After the Holocaust." *Flannery O'Connor Review* 13 (2015): 90–91.

Thompson, Mark Christian. *Black Fascisms: African American Literature and Culture Between the Wars*. Charlottesville: University of Virginia Press, 2007.

Trilling, Lionel. "Manners, Morals, and the Novel." In *The Liberal Imagination*. New York: New York Review of Books, 2008. 221–22.

Walker, Alice. *In Search of Our Mother's Gardens*. New York: Harcourt, 1983.

Weil, Simone. *Waiting for God*. New York: Putnam, 1951.

Wood, Ralph C. "Where Is the Voice Coming From? Flannery O'Connor on Race." *Flannery O'Connor Bulletin* 22 (1993–1994).

Wright, Richard. *Native Son and "How Bigger Was Born."* New York: Harper, Library of America, 1991.

Wright, Richard. *The Outsider*. New York: Harper, Library of America, 1993.

Inscrutable Zoot Suiters and Civil Rights Ambivalence in Flannery O'Connor and Toni Morrison

ALISON ARANT

Flannery O'Connor's "The Barber" (1947) and Toni Morrison's *Home* (2012) both feature moments when characters see—or perhaps, more accurately, fail to see—African American men wearing zoot suits. In O'Connor's short story, Rayber, the white main character, looks out a window and sees three young black zoot suiters strolling by outside. They stop and lean against the window, and Rayber perceives them not as a presence on the sidewalk but rather as an absence, "making a hole in the view" (20). In Morrison's novel, the protagonist, Frank Money, a black veteran of the Korean War, has a similarly illusory meeting with a zoot suiter. He sees "a small man wearing a wide-brimmed hat. His pale blue suit sported a long jacket and balloon trousers. His shoes were white with unnaturally pointed toes," but the man disappears, leaving no indentation on the leather seat he appeared to occupy (27).

These encounters with spectral zoot suiters seem to be minor events in both texts, but they introduce tensions central to the cultural moment when these works are set—O'Connor's 1940s, just after World War II, and Morrison's 1950s, just after the Korean War. In these decades, the participation of people of color in US wars abroad heightened the visibility of their exclusion from economic, political, and legal rights at home. This obvious double standard renewed ongoing questions regarding what the promises of the United States could mean for people of color. In this essay, I put the zoot suit in its historical context and argue that in both works, inscrutable zoot suiters function as a way of engaging the fears, promises, and limits associated with the struggle for black rights in the mid-twentieth century. The zoot suit has had a range of shifting meanings over time, and thus it resists simple resolution through one single interpretation. I suggest that these texts use the zoot suit's indeterminate status strategically, as a way to explore ambivalent responses to the prospect of racial integration.

Double-mindedness about an integrated society is a feeling shared by protagonists in both works, albeit for very different reasons. For O'Connor's Rayber, the "hole" made by the zoot suiters represents an integrationist reality both too inevitable and too upsetting to actually see. Although it is clearly just, it also indexes a loss of white status. For Morrison's Frank Money, the phantom zoot suiter underscores the irony of black soldiers fighting for a country that has yet to recognize black humanity. Frank internalizes a measure of army loyalty in order to escape his dead-end hometown, but his experiences of combat and return disrupt his sense of morality and his relationship to his masculinity. In reading these texts together, I do not mean to suggest that the ambivalence manifest in O'Connor's work is equivalent to that in Morrison's. It is not. Rather I want to explore the range of meanings attendant on the zoot suit in these texts. By not resolving the meaning of the zoot suit and the tensions it evokes, O'Connor's and Morrison's stories highlight ongoing questions about whether black rights can become a reality and how the struggle affects black people who demand their rights. Considered together, these texts suggest that the effects and momentum of white ideology are more extensive than they seem, persisting even among those who recognize the justice and necessity of black rights.

This essay reconsiders Flannery O'Connor in two ways. First, I introduce the zoot suit as a new context for engaging O'Connor's fiction, one that helps us reexamine her evolving views on the civil rights debate. As I will later discuss, zoot suits appear both in O'Connor's "The Barber," as well as in an unpublished work titled "A Place of Action," which she wrote as an undergraduate student. Putting this unpublished text in conversation with her published work extends the trajectory available to O'Connor's readers, and it demonstrates how O'Connor's later story consciously critiques the stereotypical thinking her earlier story employs. Together these texts show some development in O'Connor's thinking about the political valences of the zoot suit as her focus shifts from a preoccupation with black criminality to a later engagement with the depth of white attachment to the racial hierarchy.

Second, my essay puts Morrison's novel in conversation with O'Connor's fiction. As Beauty Bragg pointed out in 2008 in a special feature on race and gender ideologies in *Flannery O'Connor Review*, critics have tended not to put O'Connor's fiction in dialogue with that of other southern black writers besides Alice Walker (58). While Toni Morrison is not a southern writer in the conventional sense, her work certainly exhibits a sustained engagement with the US South, both as a setting for some of her fiction and as an essential part of understanding the history of black people in the United States. Timothy P. Caron, Nicholas Crawford, and others have used Morrison's *Playing in the Dark* as a theoretical lens for reading O'Connor, and yet there are very few critical studies that consider how the fictional works of these two writers speak to each other. In showing how both writers engage the zoot suit and its attendant anxieties, I hope my essay can in part address that gap.

The zoot suit often gets referred to as an enigma, both in the era of WWII and more recently.[1] It is simultaneously hyper-visible and inscrutable, rife with meanings that continually shift across time and subcultures. It originates in African American culture, with early adopters including Malcolm X in his days as a young hustler prior to his incarceration, conversion, and rise to prominence (51). It also becomes associated with Chicanos and especially the pachuco subculture Luis Valdez depicts in his 1979 play *Zoot Suit* and the 1981 film of the same name (Peiss 3). Meanwhile for those who came of age in the '90s, the phrase "zoot suit riot" evokes not the historical events of 1943 but rather the 1997 hit single by the Cherry Poppin' Daddies, a ska-swing band originally out of Eugene, Oregon. An association with youth culture is a persistent link in these various contexts, but pinning down the politics of the zoot suit is more difficult. Though some scholars try to resolve these tensions and establish definitive interpretations of the zoot suit, my essay works from the premise that its indeterminacy makes up an important part of its meaning for O'Connor and Morrison. Here I will give a brief history of the zoot suit's origin and outline some of the valences most relevant to O'Connor's and Morrison's fictional representations of it, including its indecipherability.

One variable in the zoot suit's interpretive range was who wore it. Though it begins with African Americans, the zoot suit was also popular among other people of color, including Mexican Americans, Filipinos, and Japanese Americans. On the most basic level, a zoot suit is usually brightly colored, featuring broad shoulders, a long-cut coat, and high-waisted pants that balloon through the thigh and tapper at the ankle. Accessories often include a wide-brimmed hat and a long watch chain. The name comes from the jive of jazz culture and the hep cats who spoke it, language Cab Calloway cataloged in 1944 when he published *The Hepster's Dictionary*. Calloway included an entry for the word "zoot" and for its most famous application—the zoot suit. According to Calloway, "zoot" is an adjective meaning "exaggerated," and the zoot suit is "the ultimate in clothes; the only totally and truly American civilian suit" (qtd. in Peiss i). Calloway's emphasis on the excessive aspect of the zoot suit demonstrates the ways in which it disrupts conventional categories of menswear and the familiar modes of race and masculinity, as I will later show.

Calloway's emphasis on the zoot suit's civilian status also signals one of the symbolic meanings attached to it: the zoot suit was read as unpatriotic in the early 1940s, a discursive strand that affects Morrison's black veteran in *Home*. After the United States entered into WWII in December 1941, fabric rations took effect, especially limiting the manufacturing of all clothing containing wool. Stuart Cosgrove writes, "the War Production Board drew up regulations for the wartime manufacture of what *Esquire* magazine called 'streamlined suits by Uncle Sam'" (154). One way that good citizens could support their troops and country was to avoid excessive fabric use, making zoot suits prohibited. The 1945 edition of Richard Wright's *Black Boy* demonstrates this patriotic logic, featuring a dust cover with an advertisement on the inside flap that exhorts readers to buy war bonds, not fancy clothes. Supposedly written by Richard Wright, this ad does not mention zoot suits by name, but it does reveal the binary of clothes vs. country: "Don't be a dude: All dressed up and nowhere to go. Dudes usually get into trouble. And you'll get into trouble—inflation—if you spend war dollars unnecessarily. [. . .] So pull off your 'Sunday Best'—shed your dollars—and buy war bonds." Here the ad's language aligns sartorial restraint and civic-mindedness against the foppery of the dude bound to imperil himself and his country through extravagant clothing.

For other observers, the zoot suit signified racialized criminality, an interpretation that fueled a series of conflicts between zoot suiters and military men in June 1943. Known as the "zoot suit riots," these clashes took place in Los Angeles where white sailors and soldiers attacked Mexican Americans and African Americans in zoot suits, stripping them of their coats and jackets. Justifications for the soldiers' actions emphasized ideas of race-based criminality associated with the zoot suit. Surveying the mainstream press coverage that followed these fights, Luis Alvarez writes, "During that week of the riots, headlines from Washington, D.C., Chicago, Atlanta, and elsewhere blared, 'Zoot-Suiters Again on Prowl as Navy Holds Back Sailors,' 'Los Angeles' Zoot War Called "Near Anarchy,"' and 'Army, Navy Promise to Halt Zoot Riots'" (190). Such coverage framed the zoot suit as a visible sign of growing gangsterism and moral decline and associated it with racialized "others." Agnes E. Meyer's work for the *Washington Post* demonstrates: "Obviously letting the Navy beat them [zoot suiters] up is only going to increase the solidarity of this spontaneous if perverted youth movement," she wrote in 1943 (B1). Even as some press coverage like Meyer's in part faulted the actions of military personnel, the stigmas associated with the zoot suit shape popular interpretations of these events. Though no one was killed in the Los Angeles riots, more than one hundred people were hospitalized with injuries, and similar waves of racial violence connected to zoot suits subsequently occurred in Texas, New York City, and Detroit (Peiss 1).

Interpretations of the zoot suit, however, were not wholly negative. Though some strains of the discourse figure the zoot suit as a sign of criminality, others register its capacity to signal powerful self-determination, if not outright political subversion. Pointing to the relatively small body of evidence used to support the zoot suit's supposed antiestablishment politics, Kathy Peiss asserts that the archive reveals more about how zoot suits were interpreted by onlookers than about what they signified to those who wore them at the time (10). However, in Luis Alvarez's interviews with former zoot suiters named Perry and Maria, he notes a persistent thread of "self-valorization" in their explanations of what attracted them to the style:

> Amidst growing concerns among the mainstream media, city officials, and the general public that zoot suiters undermined the war effort with their outrageous costumes and makeup, sexually loose and violent behavior, and general lack of respect for authority, "feeling good" and "looking good" were no trivial matter. For Maria, Perry, and others the zoot was more than just cloth cut and stitched together. It was also part of an outlook on and approach to life that helped them claim dignity in a society that routinely dehumanized them. (3–4)

I am persuaded by Peiss's claim that scholars have made too much of the zoot suits' purported capacity to signal self-conscious rejection of middle-class values (9). At the same time, I agree with Alvarez's assertion that looking and feeling good could afford affirmation to young people of color who were marginalized by increasing wartime xenophobia and ongoing racial segregation, both in the military and in the United States more generally. Still, this range of meanings attributed to the zoot suit demonstrates how it disrupts conventional frameworks and remains difficult to interpret.

Among African American newspapers and magazines, contributors debated whether zoot suits indexed probable race progress or decline as black people sought new economic opportunities and expanded civil rights. For those committed to respectability politics, the zoot suit signified a threatening indifference to social norms. A. L. Holsey, a representative of the Tuskegee Institute and the National Negro Business League, argued that black zoot suiters were dangerously prioritizing "pleasure seeking spots" over "the economic welfare of the group" (qtd. in Peiss 83). Yet to Ed Peterson, another contributor to a black newspaper, zoot suits "embody the new freedom of thought" even if they are "extremely ugly" (qtd. in Peiss 149). Writing in the *Defender*, Private Clifton Searles took a third position. Disrupting the discursive binary between soldiers and black zoot suiters, he saw the Los Angeles riots as acts of aggression against black soldiers in particular, as Peiss writes:

> He pointed the finger at white supremacists' violent opposition to racial progress, especially the presence of African Americans in the military. The attacks were "directly aimed at Negro Yanks," who were "fighting the world over so that men may wear any type of clothing they care to; speak that which is on their minds, and ride on or in anything they can pay to ride." (150)

In reading the zoot suit as evidence of freedoms that should be distinctly American, Searles signals the interpretive breadth associated with the zoot suit, which also, paradoxically, came to represent a form of patriotism. In the 1943 film *Stormy Weather*, black stars including Cab Calloway and Lena Horne feature in the film's climax, which is set in a USO cabaret. Peiss writes, "when the announcer calls out 'everybody dance,' zoot suiters and servicemen fill the frame, symbolically unifying home front and battle ground" (95). Thus the zoot suit signifies a range of meanings, some of them contradictory, around what it means to be American in the mid- to late 1940s and '50s.

In the spring of 1943, eighteen-year-old Mary Flannery O'Connor was also thinking about zoot suits, particularly in their associations with black consumers and violence. As a sophomore student in Miss Hallie Smith's Advanced Composition course at Georgia State College for Women, she wrote a number of short, descriptive exercises and character studies (Gooch 102). One slightly more developed story titled "A Place of Action" features at least one African American zoot suiter. Less than two full pages in length, "A Place of Action" is imagistic and removed, relying heavily on conversation written in dialect from unnamed African American characters.² The story takes place after dark outside a corner store where a group of young black people have gathered to window shop and have fun. O'Connor's dialogue blends admiring comments about the clothes in the window with a female character's repeated request that the story's male zoot suiter quit bothering her. When he persists, she presumably stabs him, and she and the others leave him, bleeding out on the sidewalk as police sirens sound in the distance (file 4i).

O'Connor's "A Place of Action" exhibits what I consider a form of double vision regarding the zoot suit. In other words, the story simultaneously offers two images of one scene, demonstrating a rudimentary variation on the zoot suit ambivalence that is realized more fully in O'Connor's "The Barber," as I will later show. On the most obvious level, the first image is made up of racist stereotypes, from its opening generalization about the way black people smell to its tragic/comic shorthand and use of hyperbolized black sexuality and interpersonal violence. This first image reads like a racially phobic morality tale, presenting what happens when young black people congregate and get showy new clothes.

At the same time, the story introduces a much subtler second image, one where vision itself, the mechanism that would seem to reveal race difference, is not to be trusted. In the story, the black characters are drawn to eye-catching objects in a storefront window, and yet the very act of seeing is unreliable, both for the characters and for the narrator. O'Connor describes the distorting effects of the display lights, making imitation items appear to be genuine and blended materials seem to have a single source. In her descriptions, the story's most flashy elements are uncertain, calling into question the story's stylized representation of black consumerism and criminality. "A Place of Action" ends with the same distorting light from the shop window shining on the entire scene. The group of young black people almost vaporizes into nothing, leaving just the streetlight shining down on the dead body of the zoot suiter. O'Connor's language in the story's final line denotes unreliability regarding what the scene actually reveals (file 4i). This second image of uncertain vision in a small way questions the overt racism of the story. Even as the text rehashes derogatory associations about black people that were common at the time, it also second-guesses the accuracy of vision itself. My point in suggesting this reading is not to excuse the story's racial bias; instead, what interests me here is the way the story manifests a process of drawing on racially prejudicial ideology and then perhaps questioning the rightness of that participation. I read this story as a failed attempt by the writer to see past ingrained white assumptions evoked by the zoot suit to recognize the complexity of the black people associated with it. In my reading of it, the story can neither relinquish that first stereotyped image, nor can it leave intact the notion that this vision is accurate.

Four years after writing "A Place of Action," O'Connor returns to black zoot suiters in her short story "The Barber." Written in 1947, it was one of six stories that made up her thesis at the Iowa Writers' Workshop.[3] I argue that O'Connor's subsequent engagement with the zoot suit demonstrates some development in her thinking associated with it. Specifically, her later story suggests an increased awareness of the mixed feelings the zoot suit evokes for white onlookers. Whereas "A Place of Action" seems unconsciously to employ a double vision that both images racially caricatured black zoot suiters but then questions the accuracy of that image, "The Barber" self-consciously narrates its main character's experiences of a similar kind of ambivalence. Amid a debate about the politics of racial integration and in response to the sight of black zoot suiters, Rayber, O'Connor's white protagonist, has a more explicit form of double vision. His dual responses contradict each other as he simultaneously recognizes the justice of black rights and recoils from the prospect of their actualization. Though he can agree with black rights in the abstract, the material evidence of economic and social gains for black people disturbs him.

In narrating his ambivalent response, the story indexes the intensity and persistence of racial prejudice even on the part of those who acknowledge the horrors of white supremacy. "The Barber" has received limited critical attention, most of it focusing, as Sarah Gordon notes, on "the early satire of the liberal intellectual, a theme that dominated [O'Connor's] later work" (2). However, my focus on the zoot suit disrupts this standard interpretation. By reading "The Barber" alongside "A Place of Action" and in the context of the zoot suit discourse of the 1940s, the story emerges as more than a send-up of liberal hypocrisy. Rayber, a white university professor, obviously does fail to live up to the integrationist politics he attempts to articulate. The text repeatedly shows him condescending both to George, the story's most developed black character, and to the white men in the barbershop who have less education than he does. Rayber also clearly tries to use his "good" politics to bolster his sense of intellectual superiority. Nevertheless, analyses that conclude with the liberal satire thesis fail to account for the way Rayber at times seems trapped by racist thoughts and feelings that persist despite his recognition of their wrongness. Through Rayber, the story explores the unnerving way a deep attachment to white supremacy can coexist with an intense awareness of its myths and dangers.

The story's opening establishes Rayber's double-mindedness about black rights as he chats with his barber while getting a shave. Rayber mentions the name of his preferred candidate in an upcoming election and in response the barber asks, "You a nigger-lover?" (15). O'Connor writes, "Rayber started in his chair. He had not expected to be approached so brutally" (15). Rayber's shock at the barber's question could stem from a sense of decorum around offensive language or an impulse toward self-protection rather than convictions about respect for black people; even so, his thoughts register an awareness of and discomfort with the violence of the barber's language. At the same time, his verbal response signals his reluctance to be seen as an advocate of black rights: "'No,' he said. If he had not been taken off-balance, he would have said, 'I am neither a Negro- nor a white-lover" (15). The scene makes it clear that Rayber is both disconcerted by the barber's blatant racism but also not about to directly challenge his derogatory language.

O'Connor repeatedly represents Rayber's attempts to make the case for racial integration as an experience of disgust, signaling his simultaneous recognition of the rightness of race equality and repulsion at the notion of it: "As much rot as it was, the whole asinine conversation stuck with him the rest of the day and went through his mind in persistent detail after he was in bed that night. To his disgust, he found that he was going through it, putting in what he would have said if he'd had the opportunity to prepare himself" (18). Though Rayber attributes his frustration to the ridiculousness of the barbershop debaters, his fixation with the conversation and his concurrent compulsion and revulsion toward actually working out the argument demonstrate a double-mindedness about the prospect of racial integration. He both feels compelled to itemize the arguments for race equality and repulsed by the need to do so.

Throughout the series of barbershop visits recounted in the story, O'Connor repeatedly uses the language of blindness or obstructed vision to describe moments that involve Rayber's mixed feelings about racial integration. The first of these occurs when another barbershop customer challenges Rayber's stated support for race mixing:

"Listen," the man said, "you can talk all you want. What you don't realize is, we've got an issue here. How'd you like a couple of black faces looking at you from the back of your classroom?"

Rayber had a blind moment when he felt as if something that wasn't there was bashing him to the ground. George came in and began washing basins. "Willing to teach any person willing to learn—black or white," Rayber said. He wondered if George had looked up. (19)

Rayber has two contradictory responses to this image of racial integration, rendering him momentarily blind. First the image of black faces in his classroom seems to upset Rayber. His sense of being beaten down suggests he feels degradation, possibly connected to a loss of white status attendant on racial integration. Though Rayber experiences the idea as an attack, he also senses that this violence has no source, coming from "something that wasn't there" (19). This suggests that perhaps he perceives a threat to white supremacy even as he rejects the notion at a surface level. His second response is to explicitly articulate his willingness to teach anyone regardless of race, a statement he makes despite his negative feelings about the idea of a mixed-race classroom. The impetus for his affirmation of racial equality seems to be the arrival of George, a black employee of the barber's, whom he apparently wants to impress. Rayber's conflicting impulses to recoil from and to recognize black people make him temporarily blind, unable to accurately perceive other people and his surroundings.

In depicting Rayber's ambivalence regarding race equality, O'Connor returns to the image of the black zoot suiter that figures in her early experimental story, "A Place of Action."

Here, however, O'Connor consciously articulates the double vision of a white spectator whereas in "A Place of Action," she seems to unconsciously participate in it. In other words, my claim is that the move O'Connor unknowingly enacts in writing "A Place of Action" is similar to the move she knowingly writes for Rayber in "The Barber"—one where the spectator's race biases obstruct the visibility of black zoot suiters. For Rayber, the sight of three black men in zoot suits represents a reality both too inescapable and too disconcerting to behold:

Three colored boys in zoot suits strolled by on the sidewalk. One dropped down on the pavement so that only his head was visible to Rayber, and the other two lounged over him, leaning against the barbershop window and making a hole in the view. Why the hell can't they park somewhere else? Rayber thought fiercely. (20)

Even as Rayber recognizes these figures as zoot suiters, they appear to him not as a presence but as an absence, a "hole in the view." In perceiving them as a negative, he fails to actually see their existence as real people in his community. His resentment of their presence, manifest in his desire for them to "park somewhere else," coexists with his verbal attempt in the barbershop to make the case for the right of black people to equally inhabit all spaces. Rayber, however, manages to hide from himself the nature of this blinding contradiction.

In illustrating Rayber's ambivalence regarding integration, O'Connor also shows how, surprisingly, Rayber makes use of the barber. Rather than recognizing his own deep internalization of antiblack biases, Rayber displaces his frustration, fear, and guilt onto the barber. Just before he makes the case for black rights, O'Connor writes, "Rayber felt as if he were fighting his way out of a net" (25). The image of the net signals the degree to which Rayber's attachment to a status quo of white supremacy traps him even as he seeks to reject that premise. He and the barber appear as political opponents, yet in many ways Rayber seems to share the barber's prejudices; even the similarity of "Rayber" and "barber" subtly links them.

The story's ending—where Rayber presents his argument for integration and then assaults the barber and runs from the shop—appears incongruous apart from considerations of his ambivalence regarding race equality. In articulating his reasons for affirming civil rights for black people, Rayber's aggression toward and identification with the barber reach a breaking point. O'Connor writes, "The barber shook Rayber's grip off his shoulder. 'Don't get excited,' he said, 'we all thought it was a fine speech. That's what I been saying all along—you got to think, you got to . . .' He lurched backward when Rayber hit him, and landed sitting on the footrest of the next chair. 'Thought it was fine,' he finished" (25). For the first time, readers, and apparently Rayber himself, hear the similarities between Rayber and his purported opponent, who continues to offer affirmation even after Rayber hits him. Here the text underscores the similarity between the integrationist and the segregationist. Furthermore, the text suggests that Rayber's violent outburst stems not from anger regarding differences of opinion but rather from two-fold disgust at having made a case for integration and at identifying with those who oppose it. Finally Rayber is horrified to be his own opponent as he both recognizes and rejects the prospect of black social equality.

In returning to the image of black men in zoot suits that O'Connor first used in "A Place of Action," "The Barber" reveals more than just the hypocrisies of white liberals. It shows the disconcerting persistence of white ideology, even in the thinking of people who recognize, at least on some level, its fraudulence and brutality. Furthermore, it implies that the systemic and generational benefits associated with whiteness are not easily dismantled or relinquished, even on the part of those who may recognize the necessity of such changes. The zoot suit, with its shifting range of interpretive possibilities, offers an apt image for exploring these tensions since it can signify black freedom, creativity, pride, and resistance, along with a host of white fears in response to those prospects.

Where the spectral zoot suiters in O'Connor's work reveal white ambivalence toward black rights in the post-WWII era, the ghostly zoot suiter in Toni Morrison's *Home* demonstrates the inscrutable intersections of blackness and masculinity in the United States after the Korean War. Morrison's protagonist is Frank Money, a black soldier whose very existence upsets the discursive binary that framed white military personnel in opposition to zoot-suited people of color. Frank's experiences of growing up in the US South, enlisting in the army, facing combat in Korea, and coming home afterward demonstrate a range of tensions around the meaning of masculinity, blackness, patriotism, and citizenship. In the novel, Morrison uses what Jan Furman calls a "dual-voiced narrative" that "signals the psychological effects of war and racial violence on masculine self-identity in 1950s America" (231). On the page, this means the novel contains two different and sometimes contradictory points of view. One comes from a third-person narrator and the other comes from Frank in the first person; Frank's sections, however, frequently question and dispute the perspective of the novel's third-person narrator. This dual technique underscores the contradictions that Frank must navigate as a soldier and a black man in a context that refuses to recognize the humanity and manhood of black men, contradictions the novel manifests using the figure of the zoot suiter.

In order to show the significance of Frank's repeated encounters with the otherworldly man in the zoot suit, it is necessary to understand how Frank's context shapes his relationships to blackness and masculinity, subjects that receive complex treatment in Morrison's novel. Here my examinations of blackness and masculinity in *Home* are by no means exhaustive, but I outline several of the elements most relevant to my study of the zoot suit, beginning with the tensions affecting black servicemen. Though African Americans since the early twentieth century had questioned the rhetoric that connected military service to civil rights, this debate especially intensified after 1950, when black people served in the military in disproportionate numbers (Phillips 4). In Morrison's novel, Frank, a modern Odysseus figure, must navigate the pitfalls of the nation's discriminatory status quo on his journey home. He returns from the Korean War—the country's first with a supposedly integrated military—and faces bias in the nation's public spaces, police encounters, and housing policy. For example, in his journey, Frank uses "Green's traveler's book" (22–23). Officially known as *The Negro Motorist Green Book*, this guide published, annually from 1936 to 1964, provided black travelers with the names of hotels, restaurants, and auto repair shops where they could safely receive service (Loewen 227). Additionally, while he is traveling, Frank meets Thomas, a young black man with an arm paralyzed from police brutality he experienced as an eight-year-old (Morrison 31). The novel also illustrates the discriminatory housing practice known as redlining when Lily, Frank's girlfriend, consults a realtor. Despite having a substantial down payment for a house she would like to buy, Lily encounters "restrictions," a euphemism for a policy that forbids people "of the Ethiopian [. . .] race" from using or occupying the property (73). Incidents like these make up the everyday backdrop of Frank's journey from the Pacific Northwest to the South as he seeks his sister and wrestles with his identity after the war.

Despite the destructive effects of combat, Frank internalizes a measure of loyalty to the military that makes him downplay its discriminatory practices. Readers learn that Frank and his friends, Mike and Stuff, enlist in the army out of camaraderie and a desire to escape Lotus, Georgia (16). The stasis and apathy of Lotus, which conjure the mythic lotus-eaters of Homer's *Odyssey*, drive Frank and his friends into the service. As Frank says, "*At least on the field there is a goal, excitement, daring, and some chance of winning along with many chances of losing*" (83, italics in original). Having enlisted, however, Frank also believes in the military, which puts him at odds with some black people. For example, upon his return from Korea, Frank receives help from the pastor of an AME Zion church, who points out the double-standard facing black soldiers: "An integrated army is integrated misery. You all go fight, come back, they treat you like dogs. Change that. They treat dogs better" (18). Frank's response demonstrates a degree of defensiveness regarding the army: "Frank stared at him, but didn't say anything. The army hadn't treated him so bad. It wasn't their fault he went ape every now and then. As a matter of fact, the discharge doctors had been thoughtful and kind, telling him the craziness would leave in time. They knew all about it, but assured him it would pass" (18). Here Frank's thoughts show how he retains a positive view of the military by taking sole responsibility for his unstable mental health. The doctors' knowledge of his problem—what would today most likely be diagnosed as post-traumatic stress disorder—suggests it is connected to his time in combat.

Frank's experiences also trouble his relationship to manhood. As a boy, Frank witnesses multiple acts of violence and emasculation white people carry out against black men, from the burial of a man killed by his own son in a white-enforced fighting ring (4, 137–40) to the mutilation and lynching of a neighbor man who defies the KKK (9–10). These events demonstrate both the expendability of black men's lives within contexts of white power and how black men are punished for the same acts of self-assertion that get associated with white masculinity. In a more positive vein, Frank's ability to nurture and protect his younger sister makes up a healthy aspect of his male identity (4). In fact, it is only his desire to help Cee that could prompt Frank's return home. He states, "*Only my sister in trouble could force me to even think about going in that direction. Don't paint me as some enthusiastic hero. I had to go but*

I dreaded it" (84, italics in original). As this quote demonstrates, Frank also rejects notions of heroic masculinity. His experiences of postwar survivor's guilt (15), financial reliance on his girlfriend (78–79), and the temptation to sexually exploit a young Korean girl undercut his relationships to his manhood and to morality itself. In explaining why he shot the Korean girl in a horrified response to his arousal at her proposition of trading food for oral sex, he asks: "*What type of man is that?*" (134). Through these and other experiences, the novel probes the ways in which war and racial hierarchy shape and constrain Frank's sense of what it means to be a good man.

Frank's questions about the meaning of masculinity and morality crystalize around the man in the zoot suit, and the figure's indecipherability signals the very difficulty of resolving such tensions. As Frank travels cross-country from Washington State to Georgia, he is initially "more amused than startled" by the zoot-suited man who sits surprisingly close to him on the train (27); however, after their first encounter, the zoot suiter also haunts Frank, appearing though "no indentation was left in the leather seat" (27). I read this spectral recurrence as evidence of the zoot suit's status as an enigma that embodies questions like *What does it mean to be a good citizen? Should a black man be a solider for a country that grants him second-class status?* and *What does it mean to be a good man?* Although the zoot-suited man never speaks, when Frank encounters him a second time, he reads the man's outfit as evidence of an attempt to define black masculinity amid the political climate of the zoot suit riots:

> He had heard about those suits, but never saw anybody wearing one. If they were the signals of manhood, he would have preferred a loincloth and some white paint artfully smeared on forehead and cheeks. Holding a spear, of course. But the zoot-suiters chose another costume: wide-shoulders, wide-brimmed hats, watch chains, pants ballooned up from narrow cuffs beyond the waist to the chest. It had been enough of a fashion statement to interest riot cops on each coast. (34)

Frank's rejection of the zoot suiter's wardrobe seems to stem from its width, inflation, and capacity to attract police attention. In contrast to this model of hyperbolized masculinity, Frank imagines and prefers its minimalist opposite: loincloth, spear, and face paint.[4] Both models, however, carry racialized connotations overdetermined by the white gaze, imagining the black man as either a showy criminal or a primitive savage. Frank's preference for the latter demonstrates the difficulty of navigating these intersections of blackness and masculinity where the available models are not without attendant costs.

In his third apparition, the ghostly zoot suiter remains inscrutable. He appears only to Cee as she and Frank respectfully rebury the remains of the black man whose hasty interment they accidentally witnessed as children:

"Who's that?" Cee pointed across the water.

"Where?" Frank turned to see. "I don't see anybody."

"He's gone now, I guess." But she was not sure. It looked to her like a small man in a funny suit swinging a watch chain. And grinning. (144)

For Jan Furman, the zoot suiter's final appearance is "confident and prophetic," offering a hopeful signal that the struggles of the 1940s and '50s will culminate in the civil rights progress of the 1960s and 1970s (240); however, I disagree with this reading. In the post–Korean War moment, the symbolic power of the zoot suit gestures more toward the past than toward the future, and its debated meanings make it ever difficult to pin down. Instead I argue that Cee's uncertainty about who she saw and whether he's gone is in fact the point of the zoot suiter's final appearance—to underscore difficulty, irresolution, indeterminacy.

By not resolving the significance of the zoot suit, Morrison finally challenges readers to sit with its tensions. Although its meaning may be inscrutable, the questions it raises are clear: *To whom and what are you loyal? What does it mean to be self-determined? What does it mean to be a man? Who counts as an American?* Frank and Cee finally inter the body of the black man killed in the white fighting ring and put up a marker that reads "Here Stands A Man" (145). In doing so, they recognize the dead person's status as a man; however, their context remains one that continually denies the personhood of black people, making the notion of home continually vexed.

In conversation, these fictional works by Toni Morrison and Flannery O'Connor are instructive in both their similarities and differences. In "The Barber" and in *Home*, O'Connor and Morrison both foreground the enduring effects of white ideology in ways that complicate simple narratives of social progress. As both Rayber and Frank engage the prospect of integration in new ways, they also encounter new levels of ambivalence in their feelings toward themselves, toward other members of their same race groups, and toward members of other race groups. These feelings crystalize around the zoot suit, an object that raises questions of criminality, patriotism, masculinity, pleasure, excess, and freedom. In representing the tensions their protagonists feel, O'Connor and Morrison both demonstrate that one is not simply a racist or not, a patriot or not, a citizen or not. In other words, Rayber is not nearly as free of racial prejudice as he claims to be, neither is Frank as unified in his feelings of loyalty to the army as he might think he is, nor is he as assured of his citizen's rights as the government might promise he is. Of course racism, patriotism, and citizenship all have their most visible forms, but they are also intertwined here with white ideology that naturalizes itself and persists in shaping people's lives even as narratives of race progress proliferate.

Though O'Connor's and Morrison's texts both demonstrate the lingering persistence of white ideology, each author explores these effects with a different level of personal implication and on a different scale. In writing "A Place of Action" at the age of eighteen and "The Barber" four years later, O'Connor seems to first employ derogatory depictions of African Americans, then to question the rightness of those perceptions, and lastly to self-consciously describe a white character's experience of a residual attachment to white supremacy despite recognizing its wrongness. This trajectory seems to suggest at least the start of a process of self-examination in considering her personal participation in white ideology. In terms of scope, these works of O'Connor's focus more on individuals than systems, an approach that seems to carry throughout her later work as well, where matters of personal salvation seem to supersede questions of justice on earth (Caron 138). By contrast, the approach Morrison takes in *Home* highlights the systemic nature of white power, which affects Frank, along with his girlfriend who encounters redlining, the boy injured through police brutality, and the preacher, who questions how the army treats black soldiers. Morrison's work makes clear that institutional forces bolster white ideology on a scale that transcends the attitudes and actions of individuals. Furthermore, Morrison's fiction and nonfiction demonstrate her position as someone who has lived with and indexed the effects of white ideology, which distorts the humanity of white people and people of color. Thus Morrison's fiction tells the other side of O'Connor's story, taking the analysis further than O'Connor could in showing what it means for black people to live in systems of white power.

The zoot suit evokes mixed feelings for both O'Connor's Rayber and Morrison's Frank; however, these ambivalences are by no means equal. Where one stems from an unwanted attachment to the ideology of whiteness, the other stems from an awareness of how this ideology can both promise and withhold black citizenship and hurt those who seek to claim it.

In the work of Flannery O'Connor and Toni Morrison, zoot suits demonstrate how specific contexts affect the very act of seeing. Their stories suggest that perception itself is not automatic or neutral, but rather highly mediated by the characters' environments, histories, and beliefs. Together these texts show the effects of white ideology, which lingers both in individual minds and in social systems that purport to be free of it.

NOTES

1. For example, in an unsigned editorial Ralph Ellison published in 1943 in the *Negro Quarterly*, he refers to it as a riddle (301), and in June of the same year, Agnes E. Meyer referred to the zoot suit as "mysterious business" in an article in the *Washington Post* (B1). Similarly, Kathy Peiss's 2011 book traces what she calls its "enigmatic career."

2. At the time of this writing, the story remains unpublished, and without permission to quote from the work, my reading must rely on paraphrase.

3. It was first published posthumously in the *Atlantic*, vol. 226, no. 4, in October of 1970 with the permission of Robert Fitzgerald and was later included in *The Collected Stories* (1971).

4. In imagining the zoot suit in contrast to a spear and loincloth, Morrison's novel evokes Ralph Ellison's *Invisible Man*, where the titular character sees three black zoot-suited men who appear "outside of historical time" (440) and later encounters Ras the Destroyer as a spear-flinging "Abyssinian chieftain" (556). Like O'Connor's and Morrison's characters to some degree, Ellison's invisible man cannot decide how to interpret the zoot suiters (Kim 46). See Heidi Kim's chapter "*Invisible Man*, Invisible Subjects: History and Race Erased in the Early Cold War" in her book *Invisible Subjects: Asian America in Postwar Literature* (New York: Oxford University Press, 2016), 19–49.

WORKS CITED

Alvarez, Luis. *The Power of the Zoot: Youth Culture and Resistance during World War II*. Berkeley: University of California Press, 2008.

Bragg, Beauty. "Intersections: Race and Gender Ideologies, Flannery O'Connor and Alice Walker." *Flannery O'Connor Review* 6 (2008): 56–58.

Caron, Timothy P. "The Bottom Rail Is on the Top." In *Inside the Church of Flannery O'Connor: Sacrament, Sacramental, and the Sacred in Her Fiction*, edited by Joanne Halleran McMullen and Jon Parrish Peede, 138–64. Macon, GA: Mercer University Press, 2008.

Cosgrove, Stuart. "The Zoot-Suit and Style Warfare." *Critical Encounters with Texts: Finding a Place to Stand*, edited by Margaret Himley and Anne Fitzsimmons, 151–64. London: Pearson, 2005.

Crawford, Nicholas. "An Africanist Impasse: Race, Return, and Revelation in the Short Fiction of Flannery O'Connor." *South Atlantic Review* 68, no. 2 (2003): 1–25.

Ellison, Ralph. "Editorial Comment." *Negro Quarterly* (Winter–Spring, 1943): 301.

Furman, Jan. "Telling Stories: Evolving Narrative Identity in Toni Morrison's *Home*." *Toni Morrison: Memory and Meaning*, edited by Adrienne Lanier Seward and Justine Tally, 231–42. Jackson: University Press of Mississippi, 2014.

Gooch, Brad. *Flannery: A Life of Flannery O'Connor*. New York: Back Bay Books, 2009.

Gordon, Sarah. *Flannery O'Connor: The Obedient Imagination*. Athens: University of Georgia Press, 2000.

Loewen, James W. *Sundown Towns: A Hidden Dimension of American Racism*. New York: New Press, 2005.

Meyer, Agnes E. "Zoot-Suiters—A New Youth Movement." *Washington Post*, 13 June 1943, B1.

Morrison, Toni. *Home*. New York: Vintage Books, 2012.

Morrison, Toni. *Playing in the Dark: Whiteness and the Literary Imagination*. New York: Vintage Books, 1992.

O'Connor, Flannery. "The Barber." *The Complete Stories*. New York: Farrar, Straus and Giroux, 1971. 15–25.

O'Connor, Flannery. "A Place of Action." Unpublished manuscripts. Flannery O'Connor Collection. Georgia College Library, Milledgeville, GA.

Peiss, Kathy. *Zoot Suit: The Enigmatic Career of an Extreme Style*. Philadelphia: University of Pennsylvania Press, 2011.

Phillips, Kimberley L. *War! What Is It Good For?: Black Freedom Struggles and the U.S. Military from World War II to Iraq*. Durham: University of North Carolina Press, 2012.

Wright, Richard. *Black Boy*. New York: Harper, 1945.

X, Malcolm, and Alex Haley. *The Autobiography of Malcolm X*. New York: Grove Press, 1965.

Silence, Scalpels, and Loupes: Reconsidering O'Connor as Sylvia Plath's Contemporary

LINDSEY ALEXANDER

They were silent as thieves hiding. . . .
The large boy looked up and stared at her. "Jesus," he growled,
"another woman."
—"A CIRCLE IN THE FIRE"

I intended to write an essay about why men read Flannery O'Connor's work but don't read Sylvia Plath's work. Now, I'm not saying that men do not critique or review Plath's work. They critique, often leaving hardly any accomplishment or shine left.[1] As a writer who is also a woman, I have been left to wonder at which women's books get picked up, which cast off, which "rediscovered," and why; but of course, during the midcentury, for Plath and O'Connor, men remained the gatekeepers.

A half-century later, men are the sometime gatekeepers; sometime nuisances.[2] In my brief career as a writer, I've seen my share. Recently, after a reading from my award-winning book, a man (who did not take the time to introduce himself) asked me about the single poem I offered an explanation for—about the foreign word I had defined; he then gave me a pointer on readings: *Don't explain so much—the audience will be more intrigued.* Seeing my face, he repeated several times it was "just a suggestion." On the way out the door, he asked a bookstore employee how *he* could read there soon.

These kind of men bore me,[3] and I am tired of them interrupting my work, my thoughts, and my days.[4]

Their responses to a woman's creative work, however, are exactly why I'm interested in the question of why one woman writer's work is acceptable and another's is not. They are why I am interested in mining the personal alongside the literary, rather than following traditional forms.[5]

"Reconsidering" can be mulling over something again in the same way but more deeply, and it can mean thinking newly about an old topic.[6] In this case, I choose the latter. To fully reconsider O'Connor, we must reconsider our methods of inquiry. Other modes of thinking (writing is, after all, thinking), even, yes, more creative and personal ones,[7] must be included.

After all, the same writing and same methods of inquiry will likely lead to the same conclusions.[8] That, in itself, seems worth reconsidering.

To this end, to figure out why cishet[9] men tend to read O'Connor and resist Plath, I've decided to focus on comparing O'Connor's and Plath's careers as women writers, their presence in or absence from their own work, the impact of biography on their reputations, and their peculiar vision. I use reader responses, biography, and yes, personal experience to make my case. Both reader responses and biography are by nature anecdotal; they also seem to me the best way (short of conducting a years-long survey) of showcasing these points. If someone does not accept the first two as convincing, I doubt anything will convince them of The Veracity and Wisdom of My Anecdotal Life (a contender for the title of my memoirs). But if the lives of women writers (including even our canonical ones) are floated as mere anecdote—that's kind of the point, isn't it?

Reconsidering O'Connor alongside Plath in these terms may illuminate how female authors are received by male readers and why. I will also examine silence and absence in O'Connor's work: What parts of the work and author are unknowable? I'm not talking about thrown-out letters or drafts that weren't carbon copied. I'm talking about admitting what we'll never know: the loss that evades publicity and afterlife. Women writers, and their work, must justify why they chose such an unseemly vocation. With women writers, readers subconsciously search for biography to justify their inheritance: where is the talent from? where is it stored? was it earned? did it hurt people in their personal lives? Essentially—were they worthy? And if they were worthy, how can we explain this? O'Connor is crowned with masculinity, and Plath is seen as someone who gave her life to the cause of art. However, masculinity is what lures the bulk of heteronormative men as readers, a sort of homoerotic pied pipering, an unspoken, convincing literary drag show. Call the writer Flannery—not Mary. With female identity absent, O'Connor passes what Lili Loofbourow calls "the male glance," the tendency of consumers and scholars to read genius into the work of "white cis straight" men and to exclude women's work from having much, if any, at all. ("The further you move away from white masculinity, the more points of view you have to juggle," Loofbourow writes, and I think of O'Connor's "Judgment Day," a white male character carving glasses from wood, lens-less, so a black male character can see him better.) Plath's gender performance is markedly more feminine, her womanliness more "present," and, therefore, receives a cursory male glance. As

Loofbourow writes in her seminal essay "The Male Glance," "When we look at a girl story, most of us go a tiny bit stupid."

Readers tend not to go as stupid as usual when looking at an O'Connor story though. Is this because hers aren't considered "girl stories" or because she has unlocked some method of making stories by a girl attractive to men?

How we view O'Connor's and Plath's biographies as ones of excess or abstinence, too much or not enough, forges these readerships. Maybe male readers must feel they have space, that a female author must absent herself—they manspread across the literary landscape, the reader encroaching on the writer in the whitespace of the page; whereas, where femininity is present, it is—solely by its mere existence—perceived as an overpresence, a woman large and not crossing her legs, one who uses the full width of her armrest. By overpresence, I simply mean "an acknowledged presence," which unfortunately can be felt as an overpresence when the author is a woman. Female writers cannot be "enough" or "just right" on their own;[10] instead they must be "promoted" to a certain masculinity or relegated to the disrespect most women's work traditionally receives in America. In being seen as "not enough" of a woman in her life (despite the dresses, the women's college, and general propriety), O'Connor was granted ascendancy, more-than femaleness: maleness. Plath, in being "too much" of a woman in her life (a red-lipstick-loving married mother who had a premarital sex life and who wrote about the lives of young women), was penalized and stamped with less-than status.

Biography isn't and shouldn't be considered irrelevant to art—this type of New Criticism has protected art and artists from social and moral obligation. (Indeed, it's not just similarity in style and disparity in readership but similarity in biography, too, that struck me in reconsidering O'Connor and her work alongside Plath and Plath's.) Instead, I'm asserting how heavily biography is applied to art is gendered.[11] In our culture, in this lifetime, for instance, a woman artist's romantic subplot is a necessity to her work in a way that a man's is not. By comparing how these two women's biographies are applied to their work—leaning into narratives of romance and illness (which, in our culture, are often understood as narratives of dependency)—rather than of prowess, discipline, and savvy—we, literature's consumers (reviewers, scholars, and other readers), reveal (surprise!) ourselves. We, not women artists, are the naked emperors we seek. Yet we gawk and stare, myopically, in want of fig leaves.

BEGINNINGS

O'Connor grew up in Savannah, Georgia, eavesdropping on the gamblers and passersby in the square near the cathedral, telling grim tales on the lip of the bathtub, training her chicken to walk backward in the backyard, and marking up children's books with snide reviews. Plath also grew up on the coast, though in Massachusetts.

Their fathers died within three months of each other. Plath, age eight, lost her father in November 1940 to complications from diabetes. In February the following year, at age fifteen, O'Connor lost her father to lupus. The relationships these women formed with their mothers influenced their careers and their writing.

Both attended women's colleges close to their respective homes and mothers. O'Connor worked as a cartoonist for a student paper at Georgia State College for Women. The fall following graduation, she headed to Iowa to study journalism on a fellowship (Gooch). She switched into the Writers' Workshop soon thereafter. She graduated from the Workshop, sold *Wise Blood*, and made her way to the East Coast.

Plath began her career at a summer internship at *Mademoiselle*. This was a trial run of her big plan, which was to move to New York (as was O'Connor's) and make a living working at a magazine, becoming a famous writer. She interviewed Elizabeth Bowen, posed for the college edition of *Mademoiselle* holding an upside-down rose, and by the end of the summer had a nervous breakdown. Plath took time off from Smith College before completing her degree and receiving a Fulbright, which brought her to England.

Health issues also derailed O'Connor from the path she presumed was hers to take. After attending Yaddo, living in New York City, and nannying for Robert and Sally Fitzgerald, a literary couple, in Connecticut, a lupus diagnosis meant returning home to Milledgeville and her mother, Regina.

In England, Plath met fellow poet, Ted Hughes, whom she went on to marry.

LIVING THE DREAM

While the stereotyped Plath is one who writes in a tear, madness-inspired genius guiding her through pages and pages, her actual writing habits prove far duller and more dutiful. Balancing paid and creative work, then alone time to write once married, then child-rearing, Plath had to be intentional about how and when she'd get writing time in. In the early days of her marriage, this meant a writing schedule of four to six hours that she shared with Ted; after their children were born, they traded shifts (Middlebrook 92). They shared space and paper, typing up drafts on the backs of each other's work. Even this use of paper—re-using the backs of pink Smith memoranda and of discarded drafts—belies a writer who was methodical, not maniacal.

As for O'Connor, she is mythologized, fitting her reputation for faithfulness and discipline, as writing two hours a day, even when she was symptomatic and nearing death, sneaking work into the hospital in her final months. This alongside the posthumous publication of *Mystery and Manners*, which *Publishers Weekly* called a "handbook" for the craft of writing (qtd. in Moran 88), has made her the subject of numerous listicles on writing habits and tips.

Whom from O'Connor's camp would it serve to contradict this holy image, to bring to her "habitus of writing" a spoonful of doubt? I can't think of one. Yet, as O'Connor herself notes in her introduction to *A Memoir of Mary Ann*, "Stories about pious children tend to be false" (*Collected* 822).

Unlike Plath, O'Connor never became a wife or had a man whom her life and livelihood can be attributed to; Robert Fitzgerald and Robert Giroux aided her career and reputation, but, being un-husbanded, the art itself is hers to own. This escape from marriage allows her an unconventional life, and this life, absent man, may allow male readers aware of her biography to forget her gender—virginity and single womanhood being things to suffer, making her maybe a better artist, or at least an impenetrable one.[12]

Plath, on the other hand, *was* a wife, and the wife of a fellow writer at that. *Ariel*, especially, is tied up with motherhood and romantic love. Despite Plath's overpresence, it may be some readers feel an absence without Hughes's presence to stand in. Hughes was her trusted reader. He shared his network with her. However, Hughes is given credit for her work's acclaim, and through his collection *Birthday Letters*, Hughes offers the lens through which (presumably he believed) we should see her life and work.[13]

Lucky for us, O'Connor and Plath shared a lens, and it was not Hughes's. It was a loupe, the magnifying lens of a surgeon.

STYLE

Intentionality and precision, having each word on the cutting edge, many laughs blunt and ugly, link O'Connor's and Plath's styles. Certainly, O'Connor and Plath shared a certain (bloody) sensibility. They revised furiously, leaving much more out than in, off the page than on.[14] They sculpted their best work ruthlessly, blasting away any unnecessary facet, creating unbreakable rocks of image and story and musicality. It isn't just midcentury efficiency; it's an assault on the senses, particularly the eyes and ears.

I think of them both as eyes with brains. These eyes glare at the mothers in O'Connor's work and at the protagonists—often men who think they're smarter than their mothers. Plath sets her gaze on just about any character in *The Bell Jar*. It was first published in England under a pseudonym—in part because of how hurtful it might be to readers clearly identified in the book, including her mother, Aurelia (Winder 247). When it was published in America, it did not go over well among the women with whom she spent the summer of 1953. Laurie Totten, a fellow *Mademoiselle* intern from Plath's cohort, took this away from her reading:

> In *The Bell Jar* it is obvious to me now that Sylvia did not particularly like people.... It is ironic that she chose the title *The Bell Jar* to symbolize how she felt being the subject of medical scrutiny. I believe she was the one who was the observer of people, and obviously others came up short of her expectations. (Winder 247)

To be fair, it would be hard not to take any piece of fiction personally if you found yourself portrayed therein. But this idea is pervasive. Plath, Elizabeth Hardwick wrote for the *New York Review of Books* in 1971, "has the rarity of being, in her work at least, never a 'nice person'" (qtd. in Malcolm 31). However, Plath was also seen as a good listener and conversationalist, qualities that typically correspond to liking people: "if you spoke at length with Sylvia she'd inevitably coax out a funnier, smarter, more curious version of yourself," said a fellow 1953 *Mademoiselle* intern (Winder 136). This sounds a little charitable and a little like O'Connor in her letters, drawing others out, responding to senders she didn't know, and striking up friendships. Both had a tendency to skewer those people in fiction—a fault that is our fortune.

Goodreads reviewers repeatedly categorize O'Connor's work by its "'darkness'" (Moran 169); they also accuse her characters "and by extension, her work" of being "'unlikable'" and the work as being "'difficult'" (170).

Is it coincidence that niceness and likability are the words used to critique women's work and women? No.[15]

O'Connor may be granted masculinity when she's done well—she may even win over male readers; but readers' negative criticism still judges her as it would other women.

Still, Totten did pick up on something that applies to both O'Connor's and Plath's work, which is an eye of "medical scrutiny." It could be that the intimate look they had of Western medicine, really into their own bodies and minds as they were understood in their time—as misfiring, misbehaving, "being ugly" (Miller)—gave them a mode of looking and a sharpness to their writing—a loupe for magnification and a scalpel for incision. In the healing that grace provides, nothing can be spared. And no one.

They learned to wield their words as scalpels to excise images from the world around them—eyeglasses from wood; the moon over a tree; poppies and a naked, then tattooed back—and then paste them into manuscripts. They excavate the world's uglinesses from its cracked ribs and produce tumors, which they plop into jars, which they offer us. What we receive is bold, collaged, geometric, putrid, brightness muted, suspended, stunning. Curious readers might also wonder what these images and instances have been removed from; quick-minded, we fill in with our imaginings, which, less interesting, are mostly limited to biography.

Biography swallows Plath's work in a way that it does not totally O'Connor's, not to say biography doesn't affect O'Connor's—it does. We fans travel to her homes in Savannah and Milledgeville; we traverse the pond and the dairy farm and feel we aren't traipsing through scene but *setting* and *The Past*. We try to place apocrypha and gossip in the periphery, but as humans our delight in it often brings it into focus. Much of what we know about O'Connor is an invasion of privacy if it's even true at all. Brad Gooch's highly readable biography is guilty of this. No doubt that Gooch devotes a whole chapter to "The Bible Salesman" partially because a romantic plot is necessary for every book about a woman. In this chapter, he includes anecdotes from an interview with Erik Langkjaer, the man on whom the Bible salesman in "Good Country People" is presumed to be based. Perhaps most cruelly (and with whom to corroborate, more than a half-century after the fact?), Gooch shares Langkjaer's detailed account of kissing O'Connor: "'I had a feeling of kissing a skeleton, and in that sense it was a shocking experience'" (251). This story is doubly convenient, as it paints O'Connor as un-sexed and sickly. Also included: the gratuitous story her professor Paul Engle tells and Gooch relays about O'Connor being unable to convincingly write a love scene (126), which at best reads as a major breach of trust between student and teacher, and at worst, a male professor taking a female student to his car to explain sex. Yet, what the story is meant to convey is O'Connor's "'lovely lack of knowledge'" (Ibid.). These stories and their popularity say much more about us as readers than O'Connor as a person or a writer.

Our understanding of O'Connor as a devout virginal misanthrope (neutered, homely, crippled Flannery) allows us to leave her somewhat outside the stories, as we view her life as an absence of life—an absence of romance, sex, ability, religious moderation, and most joy (though not all—*no pleasure but meanness*). In 1966, one reviewer went so far as to call her "'the only true ghost writer'" (qtd. in Moran 87). Ghosts, skeletons: Posthumously, her life is spoken of as if she were only undead.

Plath—sensual, physical, gluttonous, furious, inspired, wild—we view as an overabundance of life, biographically speaking. Winder notes Plath's favorite word was "vital" (xi),[16] and so maybe this is why we drag her back into her fiction and poetry.[17] Robert Lowell wrote the original introduction to *Ariel*,[18] and Plath's daughter, Frieda Hughes, wrote the introduction to the latest edition. Though Frieda Hughes is a poet, it's safe to say that if she weren't Plath's daughter, she wouldn't have been considered for this task.[19] As one might expect, Plath's role as a mother (or truer to stereotype: as a troubled, selfish, absent mother), not as a writer, is primary.

It's possible to read O'Connor without once thinking the writer is a woman, while many women are drawn to Plath's writing precisely because of its undeniable feminine energy—"And I eat men like air" ("Lady Lazarus" 17).

This overtly threatening femininity[20] differs from O'Connor's quiet (though inherent) threat of control: Hazel Motes may be at the wheel committing vehicular homicide, but it's O'Connor making the car go.

The Bell Jar may prove threatening not because of any direct threat toward men but because it focuses solely on the female perspective. Romantic interests pulse through the book, but the protagonist finds herself ultimately disinterested or dissatisfied in these relationships—not to mention being fitted for a diaphragm, hemorrhaging after sex, and surviving daily life at a women's fashion magazine.[21] The male glance shies away from such matters. Plath, with her loupe, does not.

Ironically—given her reputation as being too much—as the title of Janet Malcolm's *The Silent Woman* suggests, Plath's absence also dictates a large part of her legacy. A distinct voice—"Love set you going like a fat gold watch" ("Morning Song")—is often remembered by her voicelessness. In recounting a story Olwyn Hughes, Ted Hughes's sister, told her about a conflict with Plath, in which Plath left without a word, Malcolm posits "it is Plath's silence that unnerves Olwyn. . . . [I]t is Plath's (Medusan) speechlessness that is the deadly, punishing weapon" (49).[22] Plath's silence includes her suicide, but the silence that scares is not the one of a dead person but of a person who refuses to explain her work. The overpresence of Plath's speakers[23] contrasts with her silence concerning how we should interpret her work; biography, personal writings, and rumor fill in gaps.[24]

Thus far O'Connor generally has gotten the last word in explaining her own work, dictating much of its interpretation: *Mystery and Manners* is used as a decoder ring for understanding her fiction, as are some of her letters. Having the last word, ownership, has a male quality to it—not that women don't desire these things, just that they aren't usually allowed them. As you'll see, even my own argument is tinged with a conceptualization of how O'Connor's work functions that she gave us: "violent grace." Is O'Connor given the last word because she's assigned a modicum of maleness and male readership? Is she assigned maleness and male readership because she got the last word?

At any rate, in 1965, a writer praised her work thusly: "Though feminine in spirit, Miss O'Connor writes with a firm masculine hand. No story would identify her sex" (qtd. in Moran 77).

O'Connor is given this masculine promotion, which begs a question of intentionality: Did O'Connor aspire to masculinity? Did she use her scalpel to cut part of herself out of her writing? Her work (like all artists') was the result of a team effort—mainly of women, but with some influential men. Men constructed the training she received. Katherine Hemple Prown makes a compelling argument that the Workshop turned O'Connor from a writer who wrote about strong women into one who, questioning her role as a woman writer, allied herself with the Agrarians, adopting their "masculinist" style

(4–5). The official teachers and ultimate judges were men. This not to mention the patriarchy of Catholicism.

O'Connor wrote in third person, an illusion of absence, another potential entry point for male readers to forget that they might be engaging with a woman's work. Third person works like a gender eraser. This may be more palatable for male readers: O'Connor is hidden in third person and drag. I'm not saying men do not want to read *about* women—O'Connor's stories are filled with women. I'm saying it's possible they don't want to read *like* a woman. *She* not *I.*

This technique, this style (akin to the "Cool Girl" archetype[25]) in which a woman artist makes herself invisible to placate men (wittingly or no), that erases gender from authorship, is an inherently feminine one. That's the glitch—and the trick. Women now know this. While this may appear seamless from the audience, an artist erasing herself from her work is an act of self-harm. To reach male readers, the violent price of their grace may be at the woman writer's expense in O'Connor's case.

To become what (what, not who) she became, O'Connor had to give up which parts of her identity? As an almost negative shape of Plath, let us reconsider the absence of O'Connor, and "violent grace" being for the benefit of male readers. The violent act itself, however, is the woman artist's disappearing act, which she performs within her own work. To consider absence as a form of violence is a bit of an abstraction, but think of the violent grace in "Parker's Back" that Sarah Parker bestows on Obadiah Elihue by shutting her door to him, by disappearing. Only then is he able to utter his name. What we experience is the male suffering (because O'Connor has chosen to focus on the man's experience rather than the woman's in this story); however, the woman is left without her counterpart, and she, despite her rigidity, might also be hurting (at least suffering an idolatrous fool). O'Connor's own gender erasure may be to enlarge her readership, or may be a sacrifice so men can receive her grace. Divinity in place of femininity—its own troublesome barter. Then there's the matter of her name—going by Flannery instead of Mary, which "often caused her to be mistaken for a male writer" (Gooch 129).

Disappearing one's self from the text gains cishet male readership for O'Connor; being overly present—consider the robust voice of *The Bell Jar* or the confidence of line and speaker in *Ariel*, and thus overtly subjective—doesn't win Plath straight male readership. More likely, it precludes it.

Plath's reverse approach, being more front-and-center with her identity as a woman on the page, is perceived as an aggressor, violent, and, conveniently, mad. Her mere presence, an admission of a feminine perspective within the text, is experienced as an overpresence by male readers.

But did Plath aspire to masculinity? Yes and no.

"Being born a woman is my awful tragedy," she wrote in July 1951 (*The Unabridged Journals* 77). "From the moment I was conceived I was doomed . . . to have my whole circle of action, thought and feeling circumscribed by my inescapable femininity." She considers being born a woman a tragedy. But this identity, and the work that springs from it, is beyond her control—"inescapable." Her most memorable poems and *The Bell Jar* are written in first person; their speaker is inescapably feminine.[26] The first person announces that a particular viewpoint is worth reading. *I* am worth your attention. Maybe this, as least as much as content, including "women's issues," more than the quality of writing, is why Plath's work captures women readers, especially young women readers, and not male readers. For girls and women, to step into this first-person writing can prove an initial step, or a further one, into embracing their own personhood.

For some reason, young women's praise makes any work un-literary, un-intellectual, as Alana Massey writes:

> [Young girls] like what they like for good reason. They seek to build kingdoms out of their favorite people and things, and there is a certain subset of girls, even today, who have made Sylvia their icon-elect. . . . Public derision is directed at girls . . . because we assume that such unsubtle devotion is the result of juvenile obliviousness, rather than bold and certain admiration. (39)

Or it could simply be that omniscience is read as a level of objectivity and masculinity as the default mode of objectivity; in its professed unknowing, subjectivity is presumed weaker, and thus feminine.[27] In that case, (even close) third-person narration is stronger than first-person.

Could this be why O'Connor's own ideas about writing are used to frame her creative work, while Plath's biography and letters, and her husband's criticism, are used to explain hers? Is Plath's work seen, in first person written by a woman, as incomplete?

Ironically, O'Connor's absence via third person allows men to hear her—"to the hard of hearing you shout, and for the almost-blind you draw large and startling figures" ("The Fiction Writer and His Country" 34). This calls for cartoons and sometimes cartoonish characters and situations. It calls for turning down the treble of femininity to blast the bass men are attuned to hearing; for third, not first.

POSTHUMOUS REPUTATION

O'Connor and Plath, like many artists, are perceived largely as sufferers. In *Creating Flannery O'Connor*, Moran gives ample evidence of critics' need, from the time of her death, to use her disease as a context through which to understand the quality of her work, or "*to explain away* O'Connor and to account for the strangeness of her art" (86, emphasis mine)—to erase her from her success. Citing reviewers who comment on her "'terrible affliction'" (71), Moran says the idea that "her illness was somehow responsible for her art ... proved irresistible to many readers" (70).

When I visited Andalusia, a pair of crutches sat cloyingly against O'Connor's twin bed.

In a letter to her friend Betty Hester, O'Connor jokes about having "never been anywhere but sick" (*Habit of Being* 163),[28] but that was personal.

In "Tulips," Plath's speaker talks about water "from a country far away as health" (20).[29] The speaker, with equal prescience, notes, "Nobody watched me before, now I am watched" (19). The *I* here is easy to read as the author, but it's the speaker—and therefore, at least somewhat performative. Because mental illness and biography are entwined into the lore of being an artist, a *sign* of an artistic temperament,[30] and because so many of the mental health issues she examines, especially in *The Bell Jar*, sound less like mental health problems and more like correct reactions to a world which awarded its smartest, most privileged women MRS degrees, Plath's mental health and resulting suicide elided with the culture's need for a white feminist martyr. She had it all, and yet. The pull of Plath's mental illness, no doubt, has stolen credit for her work. Indeed, she is so overidentified with mental illness that the greater likelihood that a woman poet will experience mental illness compared to other creative professionals is named for her: the Sylvia Plath effect (Bailey).[31]

When the British government wanted to honor Plath's work with one of its commemorative plaques, they suggested putting it at the apartment Yeats had lived in, where Plath killed herself. Her daughter, Frieda, took it as evidence of Plath's death attracting more attention than her life or work:

> if I had ever been in doubt that my mother's suicide, rather than her life, was really the reason for her elevation to the feminist icon she became, or whether *Ariel*'s notoriety came from being the manuscript on her desk *when she died*, rather than simply being an extraordinary manuscript, my doubts were dispelled when my mother was accorded a blue plaque in 2000, to be placed on her home in London. . . . It was initially proposed that the plaque should be placed on the wall of the property in Fitzroy Road where my mother committed suicide. . . . English Heritage [the selection committee] had been led to believe that my mother had done all her best work at that address, when in fact she'd been there for only eight weeks, written thirteen poems, nursed two sick children, been ill herself, furnished and decorated the flat, and killed herself. (xix)

I think of this plaque's placement, and I think of O'Connor's crutches leaned up against her bed, visible almost as soon as one enters her home at Andalusia. But where else to put them?

Aren't these again ways to take away accomplishment from a female artist? Demanding she suffer eternally in our imaginations to pay for the debt of talent and servitude, of being too accomplished before the age of accomplishment would browbeat women a generation or two later? To justify her position, her voice?

Both authors published outstanding works posthumously: *The Bell Jar* and *Ariel*, and *Everything That Rises Must Converge* and *Mystery and Manners*.

In the wake of these, personal writings have also been published, muddying the waters of reputation and readership. The authors did not choose which would be their last, and this has had a lasting impact on their respective pop identities.

Habit of Being shows O'Connor as a human (certainly imperfect, as her racist correspondence, particularly with friend Maryat Lee, is included) but mainly as a scholar of theology and a diligent writer. Aurelia Plath insisted on publishing *Letters Home*, a selection of her own daughter's letters, as evidence that charges of meanness were unfounded, or that this was a literary persona—the voice was not the author (Malcolm 33). However, in trying to prove that the speaker and the author were not one and the same, she divulged the personal writings of said author. While Plath's literary prowess and suicide passed her into the hands of an all-consuming readership, as Malcolm says (too forcefully): "In exposing her daughter's letters to the world's scrutiny, Mrs. Plath not only violated Plath's writer's privacy but also handed Plath herself over to the world as an object to be familiarly passed from hand to hand" (35). Malcolm's argument relies on a slippery slope: give readers an inch and they'll take a mile; give them a few letters and you're obliged to give them the rest. This thinking, would, for instance, presume that readers will not enjoy a selected volume—they must have the collected. With the publication of *Habit of Being* and the many *Selected*s of beloved poets, this logic is undone. It also assumes a collected version of a particular set of works or correspondence (collected meaning what remains that we know of at the time), rather than a partial one, is a better representation of the truth.[32] Besides, O'Connor's selected letters were published, and like Plath's journals (which Hughes published in 1982), are equal parts literature and voyeurism; of course, we're only seeing what the estates want us to see. Letters to Regina are not included in *Habit of Being* and correspondence is redacted throughout; Hughes famously burned two of Plath's journals written toward the end of her life.

The Prayer Journal is precocious and endearing, but therein aren't the thoughts of a fully formed woman but a young woman in school during one short-lived project. *Volume 1* of Plath's collected letters lands like a thud, longer than the Bible; a future volume promises even more data to us. Biographers and memoirists march on. Scholars and fans argue for more transparency as ipso facto the truth—even as "restitution" to the writer (Wood), but what about when context is gone? What about when something "truer" further violates privacy? What about the collusion between the writer, the estates, and the readers in shaping literary personae? How do we untangle it? What about the hunger the writer and her estate create in us, the readers, for more, and about our demand for more? Doesn't that sound rapacious? Is that coincidental? Is this what is meant by labeling one's self a "voracious reader?" Doesn't that sound like the dangers of capitalism's expectations of artists?

More silence.

Different silences exist. Silence of shame, silence of shyness, which is uncomfortable, is accepted in women. Silence of self-possession, necessitating comfort with one's self, not so much. In O'Connor's biography, we are encouraged to read shyness: a late-bloomer who couldn't kiss, who lived with her mother and kindled her best friendships through letters. In Plath's, what we see as self-possession—a modern woman who took the man that she wanted, the publications she wanted, fame, and even her own life—ends in ruin. A satisfying tragedy. Her control, her agency, does her in. It can be done straight or as a morality play. It's unclear to me whether this is because of how we understand women and silence or women and physical versus mental well-being.

As the years go on and more trickles from these literary archives, the omissions that have produced our understanding may be revealed but not nullified.[33]

Of course, O'Connor's gender isn't nullified either; it can't truly be *absent* from her work. It's hidden. The question is whether the hiding's a game—and if so, whether anyone is seeking her (and who is)—or a means of survival. Could be a paradox: it's both. Third-person, biographical interpretation, a heavy hand over her own work's interpretation, and her trusty loupe have allowed her to hide while receiving male consideration.

The male glance is brief and myopic, while a loupe focuses and magnifies. "Anything that helps you to see, anything that makes you look. The writer should never be ashamed of staring" ("The Nature . . ." 84).

And me? What am I looking at? Why do I care that men like one straight white woman writer over another straight white woman writer? I must've hoped to find at the delta that magical set of qualities, the keys to that pearliest set of gates, made no doubt of poached teeth and tusks, White Writer Fame Heaven, that is, what I grew up understanding as the canon. The important questions for writers like myself to ask, then, are not "Why do cishet white male readers choose the books they read?" and "How do their tastes shape the canon?" The way is not to penetrate the canon: that is a masculine form of thinking. The way is to honor and bind the negative shape of the canon, to hold vigil for ghosts. The questions for writers come largely from the work of black, brown, and queer feminists: How has the canon colonized my imagination? My sense of self? How can I move it outside of me and move alongside it? When am I choosing disappearance and when is it being chosen for me? When is my silence limiting and when is it freeing? When can't I distinguish the difference? Why?

I'd love to have work read by all, life-changing and still of merit. Likely, that's too much to ask or I'm too much, and so I'll gladly settle for a readership and the company of a few women. In the meantime, I'll stop seeking male approval. My violent grace will be how men receive the experience of my abstention, in a wave of absences, in the small moments, the flashes, when they recognize their understanding, their own art, is lacking, but they cannot name the lack. The lack escapes them. We are the lack. We are the missing unknowable, knowable if only they'd crack open a book. Prepare for our grace. Perhaps my yes to truth is a no to those readers' truths. My violence is silent, willful, precise: I lift my scalpel, look through my loupe, and cut.

NOTES

1. See, for instance, this reader response from a woman with an advanced degree about a man's condescending attitude toward her respect for Plath's work: https://noneofthatblog.wordpress .com/2016/08/22/gaslight/. For a reader response about how responses to Plath's work can be racially exclusive, read writer Vanessa Willoughby's great essay "Black Girls Don't Read Sylvia Plath."

2. But now, white women can share this gatekeeper-nuisance role, with some different undertones.

3. I cut an exhaustive list of sexism I've been the recipient of in publishing.

4. I do not claim the genius of an O'Connor or a Plath, and I am writing and living some half-century or more later, so I can only imagine how irritated and bored they must have been.

5. If you are not interested in how women writers of the past affect living women practitioners (, contemporary writers), I invite you not to read this and instead to ask yourself, "Why not?"

6. Akin to "I reckon" as "I figure" versus a reckoning.

7. Of course, I insist that all writing is personal.

8. And largely to the same full-time academic, white commentators.

9. Nathan Smith's "How Sylvia Plath's Rare Honors Thesis Helped Me Understand My Divided Self" is an excellent example of how one male writer views Plath as a "gay icon."

10. It strikes me why Goldilocks must be a little girl and not a little boy. She isn't just particular; she's wrong two out of every three attempts.

11. In her article for the *Paris Review* among the #MeToo wave (a movement activist Tarana Burke began more than a decade earlier in 2006), Claire Dederer lays out the conundrum of how we should deal with male artists' work when the man is a so-called monster. She then discusses the problem of female artists being seen as monsters for simply taking time to work. In Plath's legacy, this is plain: either monster-genius or genius with demons or unfit-mother genius. It seems interesting men who are considered genius do not have the prerequisite of monstrosity affixed as a clause onto most sentences written about them or their work.

12. I do believe this is somehow related to being sexually penetrated. In an undergraduate course on twentieth-century American literature, a cis male student raised his hand to ask our

professor why we were reading so many books by gay writers. (We'd read James Baldwin and Tennessee Williams.)

13. In 1998, *Birthday Letters* was published, and many of its poems directly take up Plath. This ensured Plath's reputation would be entwined with his own mythology and that she'd be seen as an art object rather than an artist—certainly overstepping what most family members and literary executors feel inclined to do. He gaslit a ghost and another generation of feminists. Unsurprisingly, *Birthday Letters* won many prestigious awards.

14. O'Connor essentially revises "The Geranium" from graduate school almost up until her death. Malcolm writes Plath had an "apparently limitless" tolerance for rejection of her writing, but "she herself rejected as unworthy most of what she wrote" (84).

15. Or rather, there isn't *evidence*, just *coincidence*, until one adds up all the coincidences. My argument here is necessarily refutable, but the problems lie not with the argumentation but with the world in which the argument couches itself.

16. Vitality, or living fully, rather than merely existing is considered an overpresence for women to this day.

17. This could also have to do with critics and readers feeling less confident wading into poetry's deep waters without clinging to the fun noodle of biography.

18. Both O'Connor and Plath were in Lowell's orbit.

19. This isn't to speak ill of the quality of her poems—just that typically such introductions are left to equally famous writers, contemporaries, or scholars. Frieda fits none of these categories.

20. The threat of an actual maneater!

21. I do not remember men's coming-of-age experiences keeping my class from being assigned *A Separate Peace* or *Catcher in the Rye*. Teenage girls are tough; they have seen some things.

22. And poetry is mostly silence. Think of the whitespace a poet might take up in a single page.

23. In poetry, "speaker" refers to the first-person narrator of a poem. The speaker is not quite a protagonist, as poetry often lives outside of character and plot (and time), but is still separate from (and should not be assumed to be) the poet herself.

24. Interestingly, Plath is then classified as a Confessional poet, while O'Connor is a writer who forces many a character into confession (how self-aware those confessions are varies).

25. Made famous in Gillian Flynn's *Gone Girl*. For the excerpt from the book and examples of Cool Girls, read Anne Helen Peterson's "Jennifer Lawrence and the History of Cool Girls": https://www.buzzfeed.com/annehelenpetersen/jennifer-lawrence-and-the-history-of-cool |-girls?utm_term=.ncRBEMK3aW#.juJyxoX9AN.

26. Though Plath scholar Tracy Brain notes in *The Other Sylvia Plath* scholars should attend to her "hermaphroditic" register—slipping between masculine and feminine voices—as well.

27. Another reason for combining "personal," literary, and scholarly writing.

28. O'Connor continues, "In a sense, sickness is a place, more instructive than a long trip to Europe, and it's always a place where there's no company, where nobody can follow."

29. Plath was sick *in* Europe, which might account for outsized loneliness—a foreigner far from home and health. She wrote "Tulips" in 1961.

30. In "The Enduring Chill," Asbury's sister confronts her mother: "'Asbury can't write so he gets sick. He's going to be an invalid instead of an artist'" (*Collected Works* 563).

31. Cute. The coiner of this phrase is James C. Kaufman, a professor of psychology.

32. It calls to mind WikiLeaks' publication of 2016 presidential candidate Hillary Clinton's e-mails and how information gluts can work censoriously. *New York Times* columnist and Information and Library Science professor Zeynep Tufekci argued, "In this era of information overload, censorship works by drowning us in too much undifferentiated information, crippling our ability to focus." The assumption seems to be, on Malcolm's part, if some of a woman's data is offered, all must be, which is both absurd and perhaps true for women with public lives,

as Hillary Clinton's e-mails were stolen and shared, while the forty-fifth president still has not shared his tax documents (as of today). Women who want a public life are refused a private one; this is only truer for women of color, queer women, and nonbinary people.

33. O'Connor's literary reputation has been shaped by generous editors (the Roberts—Fitzgerald and Giroux) and women (her mother, Sally Fitzgerald, Caroline Gordon), and her letters to these and other women, leading right to her current literary executor, Miss Louise Florincourt, while Plath's was carved mostly by Ted Hughes, the man who left her for another woman and has been revealed to be an abuser, and his sister. Though his sister, Olwyn Hughes, has begrudgingly dedicated her life to this literary executorship, she did so on behalf (one could assume) of her brother's reputation—not her erstwhile sister-in-law's.

WORKS CITED

Bailey, Deborah Smith. "The 'Sylvia Plath' Effect." *Monitor on Psychology* 34, no. 10 (November 2003): 42–43. American Psychological Association, http://www.apa.org/monitor/nov03/plath.aspx. Accessed 13 November 2017.

Brain, Tracy. *The Other Sylvia Plath*. New York: Pearson Education Limited, 2001.

Dederer, Claire. "What Do We Do with the Art of Monstrous Men?" *Paris Review*, 20 November 2017. https://www.theparisreview.org/blog/2017/11/20/art-monstrous-men/. Accessed 26 March 2018.

Gooch, Brad. *Flannery: A Life of Flannery O'Connor*. 2009. New York: Back Bay Books / Little Brown Company, 2010.

Hughes, Frieda. "Foreword." *Ariel: The Restored Edition*. New York: Harper Perennial Modern Classics, 2005. xi–xxi.

Kean, Danuta. "Unseen Sylvia Plath Letters Claim Domestic Abuse by Ted Hughes." *Guardian*. 11 April 2017. https://www.theguardian.com/books/2017/apr/11/unseen-sylvia-plath-letters-claim-domestic-abuse-by-ted-hughes. Accessed 13 November 2017.

Loofbourow, Lili. "The Male Glance." *Virginia Quarterly Review* 94, no. 5 (March 2018). https://www.vqronline.org/essays-articles/2018/03/male-glance. Accessed 26 March 2018.

Malcolm, Janet. *The Silent Woman: Sylvia Plath and Ted Hughes*. 1993. New York: Vintage Books, 1994.

Massey, Alana. "All the Lives I Want: Recovering Sylvia." New York: *All the Lives I Want*. Grand Central Publishing, 2017. 37–56.

Middlebrook, Diane. *Her Husband*. 2003. New York: Penguin Group, 2004.

Miller, Monica. *Being Ugly: Southern Women Writers and Social Rebellion*. Baton Rouge: Louisiana State University Press, 2017.

Moran, Daniel. "O'Connor and the Common (Online) Reader." *Creating Flannery O'Connor*. Athens: University of Georgia Press, 2016. 164–88.

Moran, Daniel. "O'Connor's Posthumous Reputation." *Creating Flannery O'Connor*. Athens: University of Georgia Press, 2016. 64–90.

Moran, Daniel. "Robert Giroux, Sally Fitzgerald, and *The Habit of Being*." *Creating Flannery O'Connor*. Athens: University of Georgia Press, 2016. 91–131.

O'Connor, Flannery. *Collected Works*. New York: Literary Classics of the United States, 1988.

O'Connor, Flannery. "The Enduring Chill." *Collected Works: Everything That Rises Must Converge Collected*. New York: Literary Classics of the United States, 1988. 547–72.

O'Connor, Flannery. *Habit of Being*. Edited by Sally Fitzgerald. New York: Farrar, Straus and Giroux, 1988.

O'Connor, Flannery. "The Fiction Writer and His Country." *Mystery and Manners*. 1969. New York: Farrar, Straus and Giroux, 1970. 25–35.

O'Connor, Flannery. "Good Country People." *Collected Works: A Good Man Is Hard to Find.* New York: Literary Classics of the United States, 1988. 263–84.

O'Connor, Flannery. "The Nature and Aim of Fiction." *Mystery and Manners*. 1969. New York: Farrar, Straus and Giroux, 1970. 63–86.

Peterson, Anne Helen. "Jennifer Lawrence and the History of Cool Girls." *Buzzfeed*, 18 February 2014. https://www.buzzfeed.com/annehelenpetersen/jennifer-lawrence-and-the-history -of-cool-girls?utm_term=.aakL3M6rvq#.xmjRZpBn6W. Accessed 26 March 2018.

Plath, Sylvia. *Ariel: The Restored Edition*. New York: Harper Perennial Modern Classics, 2005.

Plath, Sylvia. "Lady Lazarus." *Ariel: The Restored Edition*. New York: Harper Perennial Modern Classics, 2005. 14–17.

Plath, Sylvia. *Letters Home*. Selected and edited by Aurelia Plath. 1975. New York: Harper Perennial, 1992.

Plath, Sylvia. "Morning Song." *Ariel: The Restored Edition*. New York: Harper Perennial Modern Classics, 2005. 5.

Plath, Sylvia. "Tulips." *Ariel: The Restored Edition*. New York: Harper Perennial Modern Classics, 2005. 18–20.

Plath, Sylvia. *The Bell Jar*. New York: Alfred A. Knopf, 1998.

Plath, Sylvia. *The Unabridged Journals of Sylvia Plath*. Edited by Karen V. Kukil. New York: Vintage Books, 2000.

Prown, Katherine Hemple. "Introduction." *Revising Flannery O'Connor: Southern Literary Culture and the Problem of Female Authorship*. Charlottesville: University of Virginia Press, 2001.

Scholes, Robert. "Esther Came Back like a Retreaded Tire." *New York Times*, 11 April 1971. http:// www.nytimes.com/books/98/03/01/home/plath-bell.html. Accessed 13 November 2017.

Smith, Nathan. "How Sylvia Plath's Rare Honors Thesis Helped Me Understand My Divided Self: On the Poet's Understanding of Dostoevsky—and Herself." *Literary Hub*. 26 April 2016. https://lithub.com/how-sylvia-plaths-rare-honors-thesis-helped-me-understand-my -divided-self. Accessed 13 November 2017.

Tufekci, Zeynep. "WikiLeaks Isn't Whistleblowing." *New York Times*, 4 November 2016. https:// www.nytimes.com/2016/11/05/opinion/what-were-missing-while-we-obsess-over-john -podestas-email.html. Accessed 26 March 2018.

Van Duyne, Emily. "Why Are We So Unwilling to Take Sylvia Plath at Her Word?" *LitHub*. 11 July 2017, http://lithub.com/why-are-we-so-unwilling-to-take-sylvia-plath-at-her-word/. Accessed 13 November 2017.

Willoughby, Vanessa. "Black Girls Don't Read Plath." *The Hairpin*, 12 November 2014, https://the hairpin.com/black-girls-dont-read-sylvia-plath-1a8034c986b6. Accessed 10 November 2017.

Winder, Elizabeth. *Pain, Parties, Work: Sylvia Plath in New York, Summer 1953*. 2013. New York: HarperCollins, 2014.

Wood, Gaby. "Exclusive: Sylvia Plath's Unseen Letters Describe Her 1953 Suicide Attempt—'I Blissfully Succumbed to the Whirling Blackness.'" *The Telegraph*, 24 September 2017, http:// www.telegraph.co.uk/books/authors/exclusive-sylvia-plaths-unseen-letters-describe-1953 -suicide/. Accessed 13 November 2017.

PART 4

O'CONNOR'S LEGACY

Saint Flannery, Approximately: O'Connor and the Dogma of Creative Writing

ERIC BENNETT

To adopt the view of the craft of fiction that, by way of MFA programs, has dominated the last few decades of creative writing in the United States is to embrace the mantle of freedom from the thrall of premeditation. This means, not knowing. The space allotted to this chapter could be filled entirely with evidence of the devotion that contemporary creative writers pledge to ignorance. Even adjusting for false modesty, one can find the genuine pervasiveness of the sentiment overwhelming. Here's a writer from *The Eleventh Draft: Craft and the Writing Life from the Iowa Writers' Workshop* (1999): "I couldn't write knowing too much. I couldn't write knowing length, and I couldn't write knowing plot, and I couldn't write knowing more than that first instant of voice. I needed not to know" (Leebron 52). Here's another: "I had launched a novel, having no real idea of how to go about such business" (Power 78). Here's a third: "I have to slog a bit, waiting for the manuscript to start whispering in my ear" (Lashner 128). This, from our professionals.

The virtue of not knowing, according to those who pledge allegiance to the approach, lies in the receptivity it ensures. One is receptive to things as they are rather than things as an ideologue or zealot would have them. Characters must be given latitude and not handled as pawns in a plot. The complexity of the world defies any set of beliefs that one might impose. Creative writers, under this dispensation, work in fidelity to the vital and the actual and work against the sclerosis or the tyranny of the inherited, the abstracted, and the conventional. This is a modernist commitment that has evolved into stridency and purity from its adulterated origins in the nineteenth century. Henri Bergson, the idiosyncratic phenomenologist who used *fin de siècle* brain science to take aim at the cognitively deadening effect of habit, would make perfect sense of it. It is so widespread that it feels arbitrary to select spokespeople for it. Here, as one of thousands, is Jack Livings in an online interview:

> There are so many ways to spoil a good story, and writing from the top down is a great one. Starting with a political motivation or some message—for me, at least, that's a recipe for disaster. That's an essay or a position paper. Fiction is about people who might live under the umbrella of some larger political forces, for instance, which will be borne out in the way they eat their oatmeal, how they sit in a chair, what they say when someone steps on their toe. (Ford)

The novelist's concern is not political forces. It's oatmeal, chairs, and toes. That this understanding of the task of literature has been powerfully inculcated by creative writing workshops as well as the handbooks published by and for their associates, starting in the anti-intellectual atmosphere of the early Cold War, I have argued elsewhere.[1] That this understanding of the task of literature has been incalculably and bizarrely advanced by a few words from Flannery O'Connor is what I wish to argue here.

For present purposes, Stephen Koch's *The Modern Library Writer's Workshop: A Guide to the Craft of Fiction* is worth quoting at length:

> Something has moved you. You begin to write about it. You sketch. You jot down a chain of fantasies and associations. You dream the dream. You don't know what's coming; you're a vehicle for what's happening on your page, as was Flannery O'Connor when she wrote her great short story, "Good Country People." "When I started writing that story, I didn't know there was going to be a Ph.D. with a wooden leg in it. I merely found myself one morning writing a description of two women I knew something about, and before I realized it, I had equipped one of them with a daughter with a wooden leg. I brought in the Bible salesman, but I had no idea what I was going to do with him. I didn't know he was going to steal that wooden leg until ten or twelve lines before he did it, and when I found out this was going to happen, I realized it was inevitable." (8–9)

Those familiar with O'Connor will feel the violence of Koch's handling. O'Connor never conceived the act of writing in terms of being "moved" by "something." She had little interest in fantasies, associations, and dreams. She concerned herself with the hard reality of the Incarnation of Christian orthodoxy as a fact of history.[2] To the extent that her fiction struck and still strikes readers as otherworldly, it is because she perceived the Christian world as the only world and made it the subject of her fiction.

Koch's use of O'Connor, however, is typical. A secular handbook on craft, espousing no explicit or dogmatic beliefs or values, mines O'Connor's oeuvre for nuggets of wisdom that remain wise, the theory goes, once torn from the vein. Such widespread extraction has given O'Connor's choice nuggets an enduring influence, one that rivals that of her fiction. The operation reflects how shallowly O'Connor is understood and how complacent and impoverished many contemporary theories of fiction are.

Other canonical authors have suffered similar fates, but O'Connor is especially subject to such treatment, reigning as she does as Iowa's most venerable alumna. Studying in Iowa City in the late 1940s, reaching a national audience by the early 1950s, she proved almost before anybody else did that universities could help and would not harm American literature. She was a godsend to the conservative liberals of the McCarthy era who wished in one and the same gesture to institutionalize and deradicalize authorship. Paul Engle, the director of the Iowa program, touted her example, and John Crowe Ransom, the editor of the *Kenyon Review*, published her work. The Rockefeller Foundation, that lavish funder of American culture in the 1950s, effectively underwrote O'Connor's work directly.[3] Marxists had a science of history; Catholics had sacred mysteries; and O'Connor's commanding service to the doctrine of not knowing began when liberal democratic capitalists sided with mystery against dialectical materialism.

The origin story for "Good Country People," cited frequently in the handbooks,[4] is but one of a half dozen disciplinary mainstays. From *Mystery and Manners* and *The Habit of Being*, countless pedagogues have excerpted quips and rules of thumb for wide circulation. In handbook after handbook, classroom after classroom, year after year, these are the cherished ones:

> The fact is that anybody who has survived his childhood has enough information about life to last him the rest of his days. (*Mystery* 84)[5]

> The first and most obvious characteristic of fiction is that it deals with reality through what can be seen, heard, smelt, tasted, and touched. (*Mystery* 91)[6]

> I don't have my novel outlined and I have to write to discover what I am doing. Like the old lady, I don't know so well what I think until I see what I say ... (*Habit* 5)

What are the consequences when such statements float free? To make sense of the weird apotheosis, its distortion and bathos, one should distinguish between two strains of literary modernism that have remained influential from the nineteenth century through to the twenty-first. One, I have already found shorthand for: oatmeal, chairs, and toes. This is the commitment to noticing and laying bare. Social conventions, prevailing prejudices, coercive norms, and inherited poetic forms, by this practice, threaten to obscure or constrain personal authenticity and intricate truths, a living record. Big false narratives trump the veracious irreducibility of small hard details, fleshy repletion, quotidian complexity. Writers take it upon themselves to rescue what would otherwise be lost.

A genealogy of this strain, in a chapter this short, can be impressionistic at best, but examples can't hurt. The strain appears by the end of the eighteenth century in a poem like Coleridge's "The Nightingale"; rather than a melancholy bird, the speaker argues, the nightingale is a poetic convention: listen to real ones and you'll hear joy. Wordsworth and Coleridge's *Lyrical Ballads*, in fact, reflecting the initial spirit of the French Revolution as perceived by young Englishmen, presenting idiot boys, convicts, and female vagrants for sympathy, is run through with the strain. Later, it characterizes Byron's irreverence to the poetic tradition in *Don Juan*. It infuses Robert Browning's "Fra Lippo Lippi," whose eponymous hero shifts questions of beauty from heaven to earth. It accounts for much of the best French fiction from Stendhal through Flaubert into the naturalistic experiments of Zola as well as the diversity of Americans influenced by Zola, from Frank Norris to Henry James—whom, T. S. Eliot famously remarked, had a mind so fine that no idea could violate it. By the twentieth century the strain is so common to fiction from both sides of the Atlantic that it becomes virtually synonymous with the genre of the novel itself, hence all the harder even to notice. Hemingway sets the gritty details of war against its hollow rhetoric. Dos Passos exposes the ugly guts of American capitalism, unassimilable to any grand narrative. Woolf looks for what life is and finds it in colors and textures and waves. Lawrence proffers new candor in things sexual. This is modernism's audacious frankness. Joyce doesn't love outhouses, per se. He loves the freedom to be taxonomical, comprehensive.

The other strain is numinous. It refutes the materialism of the modern age by evoking in verse and prose the movements and intimations of spirit. This, too, has distinct origins in Romanticism, from Wordsworth's secluded vistas, to Coleridge's embers, de Quincy's drugs, Keats's urns, and Shelly's birds. Baudelaire is a virtual mystic, and those who follow him refine and elaborate the mysticism. Mallarmé and Rimbaud, Yeats and Stevens—the aesthetes and visionaries at century's end make a new religious faith of poetry.

The numinous and the frank can be isolated in order to be characterized, but they have intermingled from the beginning, even within single projects, as is clear in the dual mention of Wordsworth and Coleridge. Browning's Lippi, like Fra Angelico, refracts God's light through human forms; unlike Angelico, he uses prostitutes as models for Madonna. The most powerful literary works of the early twentieth century combined the frank with the numinous and made their contradictory force mutually amplifying. Proust and Joyce, Eliot and Woolf, Pound and Fitzgerald, all in very different ways, captured a world both radiant with spirit and despairing of it—ashy and dusky, sordid and meretricious. O'Connor, whose stories mingle banality and Judgment, practiced at the tail end of this moment. Numinous modernism is *not* the modernism that recent writers, on the whole, have been trained in at American colleges and universities. Where numinousness does appear in workshop writing, it almost always arises not from any broadly spiritual worldview but from recapitulations of those modernist experiments in which language itself created the last bastion of wonder and strangeness—a third- or fourth-order echo of divine intimation.[7]

Far and away, modernism's frank strain has triumphed in the classroom. But why? The long answers would fill a library. But, in brief, one might speculate that forays into laying bare accord much more readily with the democratic spirit of mass higher education than do experiments in spiritual idiolect or transcendental commonality. The earnest details and singular experiences of the thousands of lives of our students of creative writing constitute the academic data of the discipline. Such data accrue vastly, in homology with the research done in the sciences. Democratic variety proliferates and flourishes. This is largely what Mark McGurl celebrates in *The Program Era: Postwar Fiction and the Rise of Creative Writing* (which I'll return to below).

In a nation of three hundred million plus, where the permutations and combinations of identity are virtually infinite, there are always more voices to be added, always more witness to be borne. The demographic supersedes the belletristic. This feels timely in a culture whose strongest ethical commitments are to individualism but whose historical record entails discrimination, slavery, and genocide. However, the sensibility also darkly reflects our thralldom to planned obsolescence and to the atomizing commodification of everything under capitalism. To promote a career is to promote a biography—less and less to be distinguished from a brand and less and less likely to endure for longer than a fashion cycle. The world faces no impending famine of biographical subjects.[8]

The mounting reduction of all things cultural to the merely personal is a trend with implications far beyond creative writing, affecting as well the calculations of publishers and the priorities of scholars. The works of high modernism, while still read a century later, are most often read for their "real" content, their relationship to actual lives, rather than for their attempts at universalizing human experience beyond a single biography's ken.[9] Because this revolution in sensibility has made possible (if hardly complete) the democratization of literary prestige, it must be embraced, at least in part. Anybody who teaches courses in the novel finds it easier and easier to fill the syllabus with significant voices from all backgrounds as the present nears and should be grateful to behold this progress in history. Such progress would be impossible to extricate from the growth in creative writing programs—and, in fact, McGurl has made that inextricability the joy of his thesis (again, see below). America speaks for itself in its entirety more than it ever has, if still not enough, and the MFA has provided a channel.[10] Nor does it have to be the case that women of color (for instance) must write narrowly about being women of color in order to do the righteous work.[11] Yet it remains the case that the contemporary emphasis on the personal and the particular in fiction has placed us at a great remove from a mind like O'Connor's. Thus the perversity of her canonization.

The perversity appears starkly when one compares the O'Connor of the handbooks to the O'Connor who lived and wrote. We are faced with the irony that one of the most impersonal voices in twentieth century became a central spokesperson for personalistic developments she would have hated. What did O'Connor believe that her acolytes do not? Any scholar who has engaged the question of craft and faith in O'Connor will have good answers. My treatment here can only be cursory and selective. But already I have made clear that I agree with those who argue that O'Connor's Catholicism determines the meaning of O'Connor's work. Iowa might have encouraged her already terse and hard tendencies as a stylist, but it added nothing to her vision as an artist, unless it was a bluff secularism against which to react. If she learned anything from Paul Engle, it was how to hide one's contempt for one's mentor. Her most important tutors were the neo-Thomist heavyweights who shaped her understanding of modernistic numinousness.

In a 1958 review of Étienne Gilson's *Painting and Reality*, O'Connor praised the concluding pages, which posit that the "essence of the art of painting is not imitation but the creative addition of artifacts to nature" (*Presence* 57). Gilson believed that the best modern painters liberated their medium from the slavish, materialistic naturalism so important since the Renaissance, returning it, in Gilson's words, to "its primitive and true function" (57). To hold this is to hold—as Gilson and O'Connor both held—that the apparent is a distortion of the actual. The greatest artists, from this outlook, were not simply the finest naturalists or realists. They engaged in a kind of counter-distortion—the casting off of a mimesis of the merely visible. "The mechanically conceived universe of René Descartes, and all those which followed it to the end of the last century, were very different from the world in whose existence creative artists invite us to believe," wrote Gilson (298).

Artists, as such, are defined precisely by their apprehension of something beyond mere matter. O'Connor sharpened her version of this belief on Gilson and on Jacques Maritain, whose *Art and Scholasticism* counted among her great influences. "It is a Cartesian misconception," Maritain insisted, "to reduce clarity *in itself* to clarity *for us*. In art this misconception produces *academicism*, and condemns us to a beauty so meager that it can radiate in the soul only the most paltry of delights" (28). Maritain, like Gilson, found in modernist painters a pathway forward—which, in fact, was a pathway back to the holiness of medieval painting. "Gauguin," he wrote, "in affirming that it was necessary to renounce *making what one sees*, formulated a primary truth which the masters have practiced from the very beginning" (59). "For me the visible universe is a reflection of the invisible universe," O'Connor wrote to Elizabeth Hester, and this defined her practice as a writer (*Habit* 128).

Few writers writing today produce work whose shape reflects, with self-consciousness or metaphysical rigor, their reception of an invisible reality greater than our visible one. The invisible far more often exists as an obscure "over there" of the finite self. Concrete details in fiction, according to Francine Prose, are "clues to something deeper and wider and broader, to our subconscious—our squalling, impolite id bubbling thickly up to the surface" (144). Prose here perpetuates the dogma prevailing among creative writers that concrete details are foundational. Many who believe it do not go even so far as Prose in justifying these foundations. They regard it as axiomatic that specific sensory evocations are the central business of creative writing. The place to start, in other words, becomes an end.

Again and again O'Connor is cited as a voice giving authority to this dogma. Yet her emphasis on "what can be seen, heard, smelt, tasted, and touched" shares little with either Prose's or even the blander utilitarian or axiomatic defenses of detail for detail's sake. Modernist frankness, for O'Connor, as for any neo-Thomist, was worth the bother precisely because it was, simultaneously, numinous. As Rowan Williams puts it in *Grace and Necessity*, the "artist only reflects the thoughts of God as they are embodied in this actual environment" (20). Such was O'Connor's creed—a thirteenth-century elaboration of an idea from the fourth century before Christ.

Thomas Aquinas was the most systematic not to mention the most persuasive of those medieval scholars who adapted Aristotle to Christian use. He intervened against the neo-Platonism that had entered Christian thought through Augustine, that dominated the western Church for a millennium, and that shaped the work of medieval thinkers such as William of Champeaux and Bernard of Clairvaux. Unlike Plato, Aristotle had discovered the most real in the most actual—in the forms that become manifest and find perfection in the world we apprehend with our senses. To the Aristotelean affirmation of sense experience, sixteen centuries later, Aquinas added a creative, engaged, and personal God. The physical, by his account, did not spell the degradation of divine being. Rather, it played it out. The world that God made tells us so much of all that we need to know about God. Making a study of that world is a religious act for both natural scientists (as we now call them) and creative writers (as we now call them).[12]

O'Connor omits mention of God in the following passage, and one could mistake her for arguing like Livings in favor of oatmeal, chairs, and toes. Yet Thomism permeates it:

The beginning of human knowledge is through the senses, and the fiction writer begins where human perception begins. He appeals through the senses, and you cannot appeal to the senses with abstractions. It is a good deal easier for most people to state an abstract idea than to describe and thus re-create some object that they actually see. But the world of the fiction writer is full of matter, and this is what the beginning fiction writers are very loath to create. They are concerned primarily with unfleshed ideas and emotions. They are apt to be reformers and to want to write because they are possessed not by a story but by the bare bones of some abstract notion. They are conscious of problems, not of people, of questions and issues, not of the texture of existence, of case histories and of everything that has a sociological smack, instead of with all those concrete details of life that make actual the mystery of our position on earth. (*Mystery* 67–68)

O'Connor's enemies, here, are Marxists, therapists, and New Dealers. Aquinas's were Platonistic traditionalists. But O'Connor, like Aquinas, senses something fishy, foolish, and dangerous in the subordination of the creation at our fingertips to a realm of transcendence whose features are curated in secrecy by a priestly elite. O'Connor served flesh—Christ's flesh. Bearing this in mind makes "unfleshed" the most damning word in the paragraph.

A close runner-up is "reformers." As a Catholic, she took aim at the spurious illumination of a Reform religion that had, over the course of four centuries, washed out, in many quarters, to secular subjectivism.[13] But "reformers" has a much more topical force in the decade when Americans were adjusting to life under a newly expanded welfare state. FDR's brain trust, from the conservative vantage point, was a hive of abstraction and statistical calculation and sociological hubris. It probably struck O'Connor as the faculty at the University of Paris in the early thirteenth century struck Aquinas's Dominican forerunner, William of Auvergne. To the extent that social scientifically inclined liberalism infused the college classrooms under the G. I. Bill, O'Connor endured her apprenticeship in a state of chronic if silent dissent.[14]

The main difference between O'Connor and those who, for decades since her death, have misappropriated her ideas concerns above all, and quite simply, a strong belief in God. This is easiest to see in the light of a fellow believer. In *The Eleventh Draft*, Marilynne Robinson argues:

... the roots of the brain reach to the tips of the fingers and the soles of the feet.... we see and hear with the brain.... every sense and sensation retrieves for the brain the kind of thing the brain can know. Consciousness is profoundly physical, and physicality is a mental construct. We think with our whole being, continuously, because that is how we are made. (155)

Like O'Connor, Robinson omits God, and, like O'Connor, she surely is thinking of God. Robinson urges writers *to know, to think*, but to do so in cognizance of a creation that can only be grasped bodily:

> when I say writers have to think, I absolutely do not mean that they have to drift off into cerebralism, to pillow-fight with the metaphysicians. I mean they have to be faithful to everything they know, in the way that they know it, through all the nerves that feed the voracious brain. (156)

Robinson sounds more Protestant than Catholic when she expresses a fear of the "mummified idea," of "canonized thinking," of ideas "which maintain a sort of magical authority" (157). Her interest in Calvin and her affiliation with the Congregationalist Church makes this unsurprising. Her aim for her own writing, and her hope for the apprentice writer, is "to know as feeling what we can know as fact," which emphasizes feeling as O'Connor never did (161). But for O'Connor and Robinson both, knowledge—all knowledge—reflects an order originating from outside the merely human. Details are worthless without it.

Can one defend the universal interest of singular details without reference to God? Well, sure. Details provide compelling evidence of the irreducible aliveness of the person observing them. To the extent that a reader, too, is alive, she or he takes interest in those empirical testaments to another mind. It helps if the testaments are, in their empiricism, vexed.[15] As a yearning narrator is lost, so too am I. Such fiction and poetry constitute the achievement of an eloquent perdition. It is a posture of defeat rendered in good language: a bankruptcy of content and sufficiency or even surfeit of form.

David Shields, in his influential manifesto, *Reality Hunger*, has advocated for such brave literary godlessness. Autobiographical novels matter more than fanciful ones because "they narrow the gap that exists between fiction and autobiography, a gap that is artificial to begin with" (24). Aristotle's esteem for poetry as a genre superior to history (because ideal and philosophical), and his conception of character as meaningful only in terms of action—neither of these longstanding intuitions pertain in the new century. Literature's last contribution is to trace with fidelity the movements of a mind in isolation. "The lyric essay," promises Shields, "is the form that gives the writer the best opportunity for rigorous investigation, because its theater is the world (the mind contemplating the world) and offers no consoling dream-world, no exit door" (40). This amounts to a kind of writing certain of nothing but its atheism. "Reality-based art is a metaphor for the fact that this is all there is, their ain't no more" (55). Yet such writing—just like writing in service of a Christian God made flesh—establishes lower-case-I incarnation as its central value. It lives and dies by the concrete details that the mind can lay its hands on, not because they signify beyond themselves, but because they're all there is.

If the discipline of creative writing has deconsecrated O'Connor's doctrine of the senses, it has also demystified her discussion of mystery. Here is Alice LaPlante in *The Making of a Story: A Norton Guide to Creative Writing*. Like Koch, LaPlante warrants a block quotation:

> "It is the business of fiction to embody mystery through manners, and mystery is a great embarrassment to the modern mind," Flannery O'Connor told a group of college students (the text of the speech can be found in *Mystery and Manners*, a collection of her essays on writing).
>
> The mystery O'Connor is referring to is "the mystery of our position on earth," she says. What does that mean? Just that in every hour in every day, we are confronted by mysteries: by things we don't know, by things we don't understand. (63–64)

Or two:

> Although O'Connor herself viewed the world (and wrote about it) through the prism of deep religious faith, her point is also valid from a secular perspective. The "mystery" in that case would encompass all the things in the world that we don't fully understand—not just large philosophical issues, but such questions as: why was your mother so irritable at dinner? Or, what motivated your girlfriend suddenly to drop out of school?
>
> We are surrounded by such mysteries, large and small, and, as we discussed in the previous chapter, our very first responsibility as writers is simply to *notice* them. Everything follows from that. (64)

This analogy challenges a serious reader's credulity even if that reader is not among the faithful. John F. Desmond's scholarship helps limn the grounds for incredulity. Desmond performs the hard work that O'Connor's religious vocabulary requires, introducing the French philosopher and theologian, Claude Tresmontant, whom O'Connor read and reviewed for *The Bulletin*. Here, quoting Tresmontant, Desmond places O'Connor in a theological context she would have recognized:

> "Mystery today means something impenetrable to the mind, something never to be understood. To St. Paul and to the early Christian thinkers it was on the contrary the particular object of intelligence, its fullest nourishment. The *musterion* is something so rich in intelligible content, so inexhaustibly full of delectation for the mind that no contemplation can ever reach its end. It is an

eternal delectation of the mind." The crucial point to note is that mystery is intelligible; it is a proper subject of knowledge; it can be known *as* mystery. (9)

Like Tresmontant, O'Connor sets a high and rigorous bar for mystery. It's not that irritated mothers don't appear in O'Connor's fiction. They do. But the mysteries lie elsewhere.

The theme of mystery returns my argument to the matter of not knowing. The contemporary preoccupation with it reflects a faith in the unconscious mind, a belief that the human organism possesses internal sources of wisdom and creativity that are both important and difficult to tap. The authors quoted in my opening paragraph appear to regard themselves as beings with depths to be explored through a blind encounter with the blank page before them. They are both humble about their ignorance and proud of it. In both cases it signifies a complex relationship to self. Yet for O'Connor the least powerful or relevant element in the artistic process was the self. Her letters bristle with disapprobation for those who would construe religious experience and artistic labor in personal terms.

Significant to her instead were two elements that lay beyond the boundaries of the self. First was the work of art as externalized form. Like Maritain, like the Aquinas standing behind him, O'Connor considered form to be autonomous. It constituted an end in itself and made its own demands. There was right and wrong, better and less well made, according to the natural tendencies of things. Maritain insisted on it in *Art and Scholasticism*: "Making is ordered to this or that particular end, taken in itself and self-sufficing, not to the common end of human life; and it relates to the good or to the proper perfection, not of the man making, but of the work produced . . . The sphere of Making is the sphere of Art, in the most universal sense of the word" (8). I invite you to reread that quotation, for it's not a secular habit of mind to conceive of art, or much else, as semiautonomous. Yet art, says Maritain, "has an end, rules, values, which are not those of man, but those of the work to be produced" (9). O'Connor believed this too. Hence the significance of her version of the emphasis on not knowing. Her manuscripts dictated their own shape. They asked to be worked on.[16]

The second element that lay beyond the skin of the writer, for O'Connor, was God Himself, the autonomous origin of the semiautonomous good of art. His omniscience complemented the artist's ignorance. It was only appropriate for the artist not to know in a creation in which only God knew all. Reason said so, and history offered proof. Across the centuries, laborers had labored faithfully, unaware of the totality to which their efforts contributed. Maritain espouses what I assume was O'Connor's attitude toward industrious benightedness, including her own:

The cathedral builders did not harbor any sort of thesis. They were, in Dulac's fine phrase, "men unaware of themselves." They neither wished to demonstrate the propriety of Christian dogma nor to suggest by some artifice a *Christian emotion*. They even thought a great deal less of making a beautiful work than of doing good work. They were men of Faith, and as they were, so they worked. Their work revealed the truth of God, but without *doing it intentionally*, and because of not doing it intentionally. (63)

A twenty-first-century progressive wonders of course, whether Maritain is speaking for *all* cathedral builders, *some* cathedral builders, or merely the cathedral builders of a nostalgic twentieth-century imagination. But in any case, such a theory reflects a worldview shared by the young woman who could write: "Don't let me ever think, dear God, that I was anything but the instrument for Your story—just like the typewriter was mine" (*Prayer* 11). When Livings and myriad other writers disavow writing fiction with a thesis, it is not, as far as I can tell, because they believe that God is overseeing their labor. And if God isn't doing the thinking, should they be so quick to dispense with it for themselves?

Many readers will know that Mark McGurl's influential account of academically institutionalized authorship—*The Program Era: Postwar Fiction and the Rise of Creative Writing*—devotes a significant portion of its chapter on the Iowa Writers' Workshop to O'Connor. What does McGurl's argument mean for mine? For two reasons, I find it hard to respond to *The Program Era* directly. For one, McGurl classifies O'Connor's faith and art as effects rather than causes, as symptomatic rather than etiological. Such an approach has its merits but is by definition limited. What we learn about people when we take them on their own terms differs radically from what we learn about them when we take them on ours. Where literature is concerned, I find it problematic entirely to discount the former. Second, McGurl's portrait of O'Connor contains errors of fact that undermine his portrait but that feel, to me at least, tedious to clarify. Nobody likes to niggle.[17] That said, *The Program Era*'s bird's-eye view of institutionalized creative writing offers, in its way, a secular rewriting of the tale of the cathedral makers, and fleshing this out might be the least artificial way of giving McGurl his due.

The writers of McGurl's Program Era, as he describes them, resemble Dulac's "men unaware of themselves"; their accomplishment, no less collective than that of the stonemasons and gargoyle carvers of yore, exceeds the consciousness or the personal intention of any one of them. Rather than a cathedral, our MFA candidates are building an aesthetic democracy. McGurl claims that he has written "less an appreciation of individual writers and works than of the aesthetic-institutional totality they comprise" (74), and this seems right. *The Program Era*, a relentlessly affirmative text, affirms a system.

Above that system hovers no God but instead liberalism being liberalism. In 2009, when *The Program Era* appeared, liberalism still seemed destined to endure forever, and McGurl struck a utopian tone.

To the committed artist, such a vision, even in the good old days of 2009, looked at once totalitarian and deflating. To become a campus writer was to join the teeming chorus whose virtue was its profuseness. "Keep doing what you're doing, little folks!" *The Program Era* seemed to cheer. Like Shields, McGurl is skeptical of literary ambition and romantic conceptions of author-ship as well as of literary texts as somehow internally distinct from less literary ones. Unlike Shields, he shows no commitment to giving writers something they can use or do in light of this skepticism. His insights benefit above all other literary scholars. But for both theorists the idols have progressed past twilight and well into darkness—which they strangely behold and deem bril-liant. The disheartening thing about the atheism of David Shield's *Reality Hunger* (and what I am letting it represent), and of McGurl's project, is that it posits hardly any countervailing faith in human intellect—discerns no gran-deur in the possibilities for the work of the artistic mind. In its very form, as a collage of quotations torn from historical context, *Reality Hunger* shows the most meager hopes for the human, even as the human remains the sole source of aesthetic possibility. Somebody who knew deeply the thinkers that Shields quotes (Emerson and Samuel Johnson, Walter Benjamin and Robbe-Grillet) would create a very different collage. And McGurl's treatment of powerful writers from the twentieth century conveys little of their power—and scoffs at Hugh Kenner's achievement in *The Pound Era*, from which *The Program Era* facetiously takes its name.

The promise of the iconoclastic humanism that has characterized so much of modern thought, from Marx, Nietzsche, and Freud to their recent scions, is that humankind's capacity for self-knowledge and self-correction offers a heroic alternative to forms of knowledge couched in God. The legacy of secular and religious ideas and practices since 1848 is too mixed to clarify what has hurt us and harmed us most as a species that is now fully modern. With or without gods we kill each other in vast numbers. Yet it is difficult to look back on recent feats of the humanistic imagination (not only in Marx, Nietzsche, and Freud but also in Woolf, Joyce, Proust, Faulkner, Ellison, and other powerful modernist writers) and not lament the blithe resignation of contemporary creative writers who are so willing not to know—and of the scholars who applaud the small alternatives. Without putting it in such terms, they have abandoned not only the providential view of history—the religious gravitas—that the great modern iconoclasts overthrew and that O'Connor astonishingly tried to maintain, but also the faith in the mind to know itself, if only indirectly, and to order its effects, if only chaotically, that the mod-erns cherished. This modesty of self-conception, endemic to creative writing programs, has made of poets and novelists something quite trivial: custodians of the temporarily diverting details of messy, irrational, insignificant organisms, narcissistically inclined to cherish textual records made by the other organisms most like themselves.

O'Connor endowed creative writing with a popular apothegm that I have not yet quoted. You find it all over the place—in the culture of the AWP and on the pages of the handbooks: "Everywhere I go, I'm asked if I think the universities stifle writers. My opinion is that they don't stifle enough of them" (*Mystery* 84).[18] O'Connor meant, of course, that the university should strive to end rather than begin literary careers. Creative writers quote this in a spirit of happy masochism. But, in the second decade of the twenty-first century, the university does, in a different sense, stifle writers and their commentators, often quite stupidly. If it continues to do so, it should, at the very least, leave O'Connor out of it.

NOTES

1. See the conclusion to Eric Bennett, *Workshops of Empire: Stegner, Engle, and American Creative Writing during the Cold War* (Iowa City: University of Iowa Press, 2015), and "Creative Writing and the Cold War University," in *A Companion to Creative Writing*, ed. Graeme Harper (New York: Wiley-Blackwell, 2013), 377–92.

2. As long as there has been scholarship on O'Connor, there has been excellent treatment of this dimension of her oeuvre. See, for example, John F. Desmond, *Risen Sons: Flannery O'Connor's Vision of History* (Athens: University of Georgia Press, 1987), or Christine Bieber Lake, *The Incarnational Art of Flannery O'Connor* (Macon, GA: Mercer University Press, 2005).

3. For O'Connor in the context of her times, see Jon Lance Bacon, *Flannery O'Connor and Cold War Culture* (New York: Cambridge University Press, 1993). For more specifically on her place in the Cold War literary scene, see my chapter in *After the Program Era*, ed. Loren Glass (Iowa City: University of Iowa Press, 2017).

4. Here Bret Anthony Johnston makes the same point with the same passage: "Plot should come from *within* the characters, not be thrust upon them. This is an important distinction. Flannery O'Connor famously said that she didn't know the Bible salesman in 'Good Country People' was going to steal the fake leg until a few paragraphs before he did it, and it's this sense of surprise and inevitability that marks a solid plot for the writer. Instead of dragging characters toward the ending you've concocted, let them lead the way and you'll be as surprised and satisfied as the reader." See Bret Anthony Johnston, ed., *Naming the World, and Other Exercises for the Creative Writer* (New York: Random House, 2007), 159.

5. See also (for just a sampling): Pat Schneider, *Writing Alone and with Others* (New York: Oxford University Press, 2003), 6; Scott Russell Sanders, *Writing from the Center* (Bloomington: Indiana University Press, 1997), 106; Kathryn Ann Lindskoog, *Creative Writing: For People Who Can't Not Write* (Zondervan, 1989), 149; Nigel Hamilton, *How to Do Biography: A Primer* (Cambridge, MA: Harvard University Press, 2009), 155; *11 Practice Tests for the SAT and PSAT* (Princeton Review, 2013), 545.

6. See also (for just a sampling): John Huckins, *Teach through the Art of Storytelling: Creating Fictional Stories That Illuminate the Message of Jesus* (Zondervan, 2011); Zulfikar Ghose, *The Art of Creating Fiction* (Palgrave Macmillan, 1990), 60; Sarah Stone and Ron Nyren, *Deepening*

Fiction: A Practical Guide for Intermediate and Advanced Writers (Longman, 2004), 148; Olivia Bertagnolli, *Creativity and the Writing Process* (Wiley, 1982), 193; Thomas S. Kane, *Writing Prose: Techniques and Purposes* (Oxford University Press, 1981), 522.

7. Parsing the exceptions would take a monograph. A clear and heartbreaking lineage runs from Wallace Stevens to John Ashbery to someone like Ben Lerner, whose appreciation of the mysterious overtones of language is entirely demystified. "I told myself that no matter what I did, no matter what any poet did," says his fictional avatar, "the poems would constitute screens on which readers could project their own desperate belief in the possibility of poetic experience, whatever that might be, or afford them the opportunity to mourn its impossibility." See *Leaving the Atocha Station* (Coffee House Press, 2011), 38. Lerner invokes Ashbery explicitly and, like Ashbery, clings to magic in language even as he recognizes its illusiveness.

8. With his system of classification for fiction produced in writing programs—"techno-modernism," "high cultural pluralism," and "lower-middle-class modernism," Mark McGurl attempts to render this ingredient of identity at least partly aesthetic. See *The Program Era: Postwar Fiction and the Rise of Creative Writing* (Cambridge, MA: Harvard University Press, 2009).

9. Popular histories, such as Kevin Birmingham's *The Most Dangerous Book: The Battle for James Joyce's* Ulysses (2014) or Bill Goldstein's *The World Broke in Two: Virginia Woolf, T. S. Eliot, D. H. Lawrence, E. M. Forster, and the Year That Changed Literature* (2017), describe in great depth the personal and professional travails that modernists faced as they tried to write and publish but make little mention of the formidable webs of allusion that constitute their works. Mark McGurl and Lawrence Rainey render their histories of charmed institutions utterly free of magic. And whereas a Viking Critical Library edition of Joyce's *Dubliners* from 1969 included critical articles about the text's symbolic dimensions, the 2006 Norton Critical Edition maps the streets of Joyce's boyhood.

10. See Juliana Spahr and Stephanie Young, "The Program Era and the Mainly White Room" (*Los Angeles Review of Books*, 20 September 2015). With numbers and rigor, Spahr and Young illuminate how unequally distributed, across race, class, and gender, are the spoils of the MFA programs in the United States. See also Junot Díaz, "MFA vs. POC" (*New Yorker*, 30 April 2014), and Viet Thanh Nguyen, "Critic's Take: Viet Thanh Nguyen Reveals How Writers' Workshops Can Be Hostile" (*New York Times*, 26 April 2017).

11. Toni Morrison has long since settled it. But for two recent anti-autobiographical experiments of considerable power, see Chanelle Benz, *The Man Who Shot Out My Eye Is Dead* (HarperCollins, 2017), and Roxane Gay, *Difficult Women* (New York: Grove Atlantic, 2017).

12. An account of Aristotle's transformation of Christian thought that reads astonishingly like an adventure story and that will be of interest to beginners, nonspecialists, and O'Connor scholars who want to stick at least a toe into the twelfth and thirteenth centuries, is Richard E. Rubenstein's *Aristotle's Children: How Christians, Muslims, and Jews Rediscovered Ancient Wisdom and Illuminated the Dark Ages* (Orlando: Harcourt, 2003).

13. This, of course, simplifies O'Connor's relationship to Protestant Christianity and fudges on her interest in thinkers like Karl Barth (as Jordan Cofer pointed out to me).

14. O'Connor's *Prayer Journal* (New York: Farrar, Straus and Giroux, 2013) offers a brief but poignant glimpse of how out of place she felt in graduate school in Iowa City.

15. Some of the richest fiction of the twenty-first century has centered on this project of vexed, solitary, often even solipsistic or narcissistic empiricism. I have already mentioned Ben Lerner (see note 7). See also (for a sampling) W. G. Sebald's *The Emigrants* (New Directions, 1997); Teju Cole's *Open City* (Random House, 2011); Tao Lin's *Taipei* (Vintage Contemporaries, 2013); or the gazillion available pages of Karl Ove Knausgaard.

16. In the introduction to his survey of western art, E. H. Gombrich describes how artists feel guided by extrinsic imperatives even in the most "subjective" acts of creation. Artists, in his

account, are people who fuss with the things that they make until those things cease to seem objectively wrong. Gombrich offers this analogy: "Anybody who has ever tried to arrange a bunch of flowers, to shuffle and shift the colours, to add a little here and take away there, has experienced this strange sensation of balancing forms and colours without being able to tell exactly what kind of harmony it is he is trying to achieve." The folksy phenomenology stretches across a few pages and is worth reading in its entirety for non-makers interested in the artistic mind. See *The Story of Art* (Phaidon, 2006), 29.

17. Only fans of inside baseball will find the details interesting. McGurl's O'Connor is self-hating, and he bases the allegations of self-hatred on O'Connor's conflicted ties to mid-twentieth-century campaigns of social welfare and reform. His version of O'Connor on the one hand skewers psychology and sociology and the welfare state in her writing (which is true) and on the other hand has grown up attracted to progressive do-goodism informed by the social sciences (which is not). McGurl observes that "in college, O'Connor had majored not in English but in Social Studies, taking classes such as 'Current Social Problems' and 'Current Economic Problems' to fulfill the requirements for her degree," and that she "had furthermore showed up at Iowa to study journalism—another domain strongly associated with the investigations of 'social problems'—and only appealed to Paul Engle for admission to the fiction workshop a year later" (138–39).

McGurl makes three errors here. First, O'Connor's wished to be an English major at Georgia State College for Women and failed to graduate as one only because she despised a member of the English faculty whose required course she was avoiding. Social Studies was the nearest available major and a path out, not a genuine vocation. Second, O'Connor enrolled as a journalism student at the University of Iowa on the strength of her (by no means progressive) cartoons for the school paper in college. It is a real stretch to cite this as evidence of her complicity in a spirit of liberal do-goodism. One even suspects that she might have resorted to journalism school as a ruse to escape her mother and Milledgeville and go to where the writers were. Third, she did not in fact wait a year to join the writing program at Iowa. O'Connor visited Engle shortly after her arrival in Iowa City and started studying writing immediately. Paul Engle was just bad at paperwork.

18. See also (for just a sampling): Joseph McBride, *Writing in Pictures: Screenwriting Made (Mostly) Painless* (Random House, 2012), 296; Dan Simmons, *Prayers to Broken Stones* (Random House, 2011); Louis Decimus Rubin, *Where the Southern Cross the Yellow Dog: On Writers and Writing* (Columbia: University of Missouri Press, 2005), 83; Rita Mae Brown, *Starting from Scratch: A Different Kind of Writers' Manual* (Random House, 2011); Tom Monteleone, *The Complete Idiot's Guide to Writing a Novel*, 2nd ed. (Penguin, 2010); David Petersen, *Writing Naturally: A Down-to-Earth Guide to Nature Writing* (Big Earth Publishing, 2001), xiv; Richard Bausch, John Kulka, and Natalie Danford, editors, *Best New American Voices, 2008* (Houghton Mifflin Harcourt, 2007), ix; Erin Barrett and Jack Mingo, *It Takes a Certain Type to Be a Writer: Facts from the World of Writing and Publishing* (Conari Press, 2003), 88; and John Hersey, *The Writer's Craft* (Knopf, 1974), 56.

WORKS CITED

Desmond, John F. *Risen Sons: Flannery O'Connor's Vision of History.* Athens: University of Georgia Press, 1987.

Ford, Daniel. "Following the Story: 12 Questions with Author Jack Livings." *Writer's Bone*, 10 August 2015, www.writersbone.com/interviewsarchive/2015/8/10/following-the-story-12 -questions-with-author-jack-livings. Accessed on 13 June 2017.

Gilson, Étienne. *Painting and Reality*. Pantheon, 1957.

Johnston, Bret Anthony, ed. *Naming the World, and Other Exercises for the Creative Writer*. Random House, 2007.

Koch, Stephen. *The Modern Library Writer's Workshop: A Guide to the Craft of Fiction*. The Modern Library, 2003.

LaPlante, Alice. *The Making of a Story: A Norton Guide to Creative Writing*. W. W. Norton, 2007.

Lashner, William. "The Writing Life." *The Eleventh Draft: Craft and the Writing Life from the Iowa Writers' Workshop*, edited by Frank Conroy, 125–32. HarperCollins, 1999.

Leebron, Fred G. "Not Knowing." *The Eleventh Draft: Craft and the Writing Life from the Iowa Writers' Workshop*, edited by Frank Conroy, 49–56. HarperCollins, 1999.

Lerner, Ben. *Leaving the Atocha Station*. Coffee House Press, 2011.

Maritain, Jacques. *Art and Scholasticism and the Frontiers of Poetry*. Charles Scribner's Sons, 1962.

McGurl, Mark. *The Program Era: Postwar Fiction and the Rise of Creative Writing*. Cambridge, MA: Harvard University Press, 2009.

O'Connor, Flannery. *The Habit of Being*. New York: Farrar, Straus and Giroux, 1988.

O'Connor, Flannery. *Mystery and Manners*. New York: Farrar, Straus and Giroux, 1969.

O'Connor, Flannery. *A Prayer Journal*. New York: Farrar, Straus and Giroux, 2013.

O'Connor, Flannery. *The Presence of Grace and Other Book Reviews*. Compiled by Leo J. Zuber. Edited by Carter W. Martin. Athens: University of Georgia Press, 2003.

Power, Susan. "The Wise Fool." *The Eleventh Draft: Craft and the Writing Life from the Iowa Writers' Workshop*, edited by Frank Conroy, 77–84. HarperCollins, 1999.

Prose, Francine. "On Details." *The Eleventh Draft: Craft and the Writing Life from the Iowa Writers' Workshop*, edited by Frank Conroy, 133–44. HarperCollins, 1999.

Robinson, Marilynne. "Diminished Creatures." *The Eleventh Draft: Craft and the Writing Life from the Iowa Writers' Workshop*, edited by Frank Conroy, 155–62. HarperCollins, 1999.

Shields, David. *Reality Hunger: A Manifesto*. New York: Vintage Books, 2011.

Williams, Rowan. *Grace and Necessity: Reflections on Art and Love*. Harrisburg, PA: Morehouse, 2005.

Flannery O'Connor's Real Estate: Farming Intellectual Property

CAROL LOEB SHLOSS

Everyday life invents itself by poaching in countless ways on the property of others.
—MICHEL DE CERTEAU, *The Practice of Everyday Life*

The struggles between ownership and transgression, proprietorship and infringement, proper management and contamination lie at the center of Flannery O'Connor's stories about farming in central Georgia. Region, she asks us to understand, is essential to a writer's identity. We are "sustained in our writing by the local and the particular and the familiar" ("The Regional Writer" 844). Open fields, lines of trees, farm machinery, and barns clearly constitute what is familiar to her, but how to manage these assets often provides her most compelling subtext. It is not simply that rural life inhabits O'Connor's fiction, but that the very contours of inhabiting property give force and distinction to her vision. She saw well beyond the traditional categories of self and ownership: "The writer operates at a peculiar crossroads where time and place and eternity somehow meet. His problem is to find that location" ("The Regional Writer" 848).

This essay explores the meaning of property in O'Connor's work: what is its time, its place, and how does the intangible enter into its calculation? O'Connor not only wrote about land in rural Georgia, but also, at her death, her writing became a kind of property. Her fiction, her essays, and her last testament can guide us into an assessment of how she viewed individual rights of ownership, for they are haunted by their own status as objects of value, produced by labor, and circulated in an economy with a set of extraordinary rules. That is, O'Connor anticipated her works crossing the threshold of her own death; she figured the moment of their transformation from imaginative works into literary property and implicitly asked what should be their fate.

"A Circle in the Fire," written in 1954 and published in the 1955 collection *A Good Man Is Hard to Find*, creates a Georgia countryside that is not only a setting but a map of property's fate. One can read this narrative as a template of sorts, a lexicon of possible attitudes toward ownership. Taken for granted and experienced as a burden, Mrs. Cope's farm surrounds her with "rich pastures and hills heavy with timber" (234). For her, "responsibility" explains and justifies her own well-being. She presides over her estate as one presides over a hereditary kingdom, with her own superiority as the precondition and culmination of a natural order. The subsequent events in the narrative will challenge the economic, aesthetic, and political underpinnings of her unstated assumptions, transforming the wide fields of her hubris into an utterly strange and desolate landscape.

Farming in these fictive circumstances is a matter of presiding over a hierarchy; it includes various levels of hired help. While Mrs. Cope offers "prayers of thanksgiving," for all she has, her farmworker, Mrs. Pritchard, remarks, "All I got is four abscess teeth" (234). While she pulls at the nut grass, priding herself on the land's upkeep, she thinks of "her Negroes" as "destructive and impersonal" as the weeds (233). The politics of poverty never enter her mind; that the land is arbitrarily distributed is beyond imagination; to her, people are simply resources that cannot be trusted and hence they threaten continually to encroach or step out of place.

For Mrs. Cope, "plot" . . . both her land and her strategy of action . . . is predicated on the observable natural world being hers and hers alone. Before the displaced youth who set fire to the woods arrive, O'Connor articulates the resentment created by inequality and shows it to underlie the social structure she represents in narrative. Mrs. Pritchard grumbles, but accepts the hierarchy of which she is a part; the young men who arrive from the suburbs do not. They begin to subvert the "natural" procedures on Mrs. Cope's farm: they eat her food; they ride her animals; they smoke cigarettes; they refuse to be contained in the unprivileged roles that Mrs. Cope has designated for them and that she experiences as God-given. Their place in the social world comes into focus in the natural world, where one boy thinks that he and his friends are trespassing . . . treading on what is not theirs . . . and another boy makes the claim that nature cannot be owned at all.

"'She don't own them woods,' and Hollis said, 'She does too,' and that there little one he said, 'Man, Gawd owns them woods and her too,' and that there one with the glasses said, 'I reckon she owns the sky over this place too'" (243).

Through this opposition of ownership and delinquency, O'Connor demonstrates the danger of marginality and neglect; she shows that failure at the level of the social world is what causes disasters in nature. The boys burn the woods because it is the only way they have to call attention to the damage wrought by their own prior exclusion. Throughout their struggle, the woods stand impassive, the object of actions and attitudes, but never known beyond their "blue gray" silence. "A Circle in the Fire" shows human alienation to be complete, bridged neither by proprietary care . . . pulling out the nut grass . . . nor by disregard. The trees remain a brooding presence, which provokes action, but they never become a presence to be known or simply respected. "Her woods," says the "large boy" and then he burns them down (240).

We could say, then, that O'Connor's narrative examines these counter claims of ownership. "It [the place] don't belong to nobody." "'Its ours,' the little boy said" (249). With the perspective of law and custom, no counter-claims exist: the farm belongs to Mrs. Cope and the boys are trespassing. But O'Connor makes a quiet, stunning reversal by borrowing a metaphor from the book of Daniel: the boys shriek "as if the prophets were dancing in the fiery furnace, in the circle the angel had cleared for them" (251). That is, O'Connor identifies them with the divine, casting them as Shadrach, Meshach, and Abednego, who refused to worship the golden image of Nebuchadnezzar of Babylon: "King Nebuchadnezzar, we do not need to defend ourselves before you in this matter. If we are thrown into the blazing furnace, the God we serve is able to deliver us from it, and he will deliver us from Your Majesty's hand . . . we will not serve your gods or worship the image of gold you have set up" (Daniel 3:16, New International Version).

Like the prophets of the biblical story, the boys repudiate an "image of gold"; they refuse Mrs. Cope's god of entitlement, asserting an alternative to her property claims, surviving the fire and indeed thriving in its aftermath. With this allusion, O'Connor turns her narrative from the singular to the collective, effecting a critique of possessive individualism as the basis of civic society. With this metaphoric association, she achieves a radical realignment of value, suggesting that land can be "owned" by working it, by remembering it, by living on it as Powell once had. It exists in memory and in imagination, making intangible claims that haunt the grounds with as much force as Mrs. Cope's anxious, self-satisfied propriety. This is a remarkable literary turn, for it recognizes the implicit claim of the masses lying disruptively within the singularity of a legal deed. It marks the geography of O'Connor's fiction as both familiar and uncanny; it tells us that she has found a way to operate "at peculiar crossroads where time and place and eternity somehow meet" ("The Regional Writer" 848). In eternity, the earth belongs equally to all. Short of eternity, there are the private estates of people like Mrs. Cope. Here, for a narrative moment, that estate is claimed by divinity, encroachment is turned to virtue, and ownership collapses into a dubious claim, bounded not by human law, but by cosmic perspective. There are neither owners nor trespassers, for even the resources through which the boys express their dispossession are owned by someone else. To poach on land is to challenge the very idea of enclosure itself, and with it the false binarisms that ensue from these boundaries: property underlies Mrs. Cope's superiority to others, her denigration of those whose work ensures her prosperity, her sense of blessed exceptionalism. All of these preconceptions fail in this fictional universe. Mrs. Cope is leveled: "The child came to a stop beside her mother and stared up at her face as if she had never seen it before. It was the face of the new misery she felt, but on her mother it looked old and it looked as if it might have belonged to anybody, a Negro or a European or to Powell himself" (250–51).

In O'Connor's fictional universe, there is no estate to be passed down even though the next generation is represented in narrative as a dour but curious child. It is destroyed. Instead property is replaced with insight: land itself does not bestow privilege, and the privileges erroneously claimed by ownership do not endure. It takes a conflagration to "hit" Mrs. Cope with the concept of common humanity, common empathy, and the imperative to tend the earth collectively. It is only by loss that she experiences a kinship with the boys who threaten her. They are, unwittingly, instruments of extreme change.

This is not what happened to Flannery O'Connor's estate, even though we can use "A Circle in the Fire" as a kind of primer about the dangers of private property claims. Whatever she owned passed directly to her family, so that her mother, especially, could enjoy the fruits of her earnings from royalties and the few things she owned at her death. A will is, essentially, a map for the dispersal of wealth; it reallocates the "rich pastures and hills" (234) of one's life journey, leaving behind a posthumous voice to indicate who gets the barn, who gets the field, and who is granted title to the woods. Ironically, in life, it was the dour, curious child who left an estate to a "coping" parent, but we can look at the process of transmission in terms that are analogous to the ones implied by O'Connor's stories about the distribution of land. We can ask what values were inherent in shaping her estate. We can ask how O'Connor's literary imagination serves as a guide to understanding her views of intellectual property.

When Flannery O'Connor died in 1964, her will reflected her highest priorities: first, she left money for masses to be said for the repose of her soul; second, she left to her mother, Regina Cline O'Connor, "all of my royalties from books or from short fictions or from any other of my published writings, and all of my real and personal property, in fee simple, forever." Third, she designated a literary executor: "I hereby direct that no unpublished manuscript of mine be published without the written consent of Mr. Robert Fitzgerald. . . . In case of Mr. Fitzgerald's death, then submit them to my editor at the time." We note here three things that surprise no one who knew O'Connor: she gave priority to the spiritual, she was concerned to provide for the material well-being of her family, and she left the care of her literary legacy to those of her friends in New York who understood publishing. That is, she made a clear distinction between who should be the beneficiaries of her writing career, receiving its monies, and those who should make decisions about its future disposition. Robert Fitzgerald accepted this responsibility, carrying it out until his death in 1985. In March 1985, Robert Giroux, her current editor at Farrar, Straus and Giroux, accepted his place in the line of executors designated by Flannery after he received notification of Fitzgerald's death from Elizabeth McKee, who had been her agent in life and who continued to assist Regina after Flannery's death.[1]

The problem with these arrangements, for all involved, was that no one really understood what Flannery O'Connor's final distinctions meant. What was implied by giving copyright ownership to Regina O'Connor, while putting decision making about publication in the hands of Robert Fitzgerald and his successors? What kind of decision making could occur should he and the owner of the estate disagree? Was "literary executor" an advisory role or did it carry actual authority? At this point, no one even understood the status of the paper on which Flannery's manuscripts were written. They were mostly in the physical possession of Regina, who apparently hoarded them, making moot the question of quoting anything.[2] What was governing the structure of this paper estate and to what extent did it resemble the kind of real property that Regina O'Connor was accustomed to administering?

In Regina's view, the two kinds of ownership coincided: she owned land; she owned copyright. Like Mrs. Cope, she was lord of everything. The people assigned to assist were just that: consulted like Mrs. Prichard in "A Circle in the Fire." All rights remained in her hands. Copyright, although intangible, was like the air over a farm: "I reckon she owns the sky over this place too . . . owns the sky and can't no airplane go over here without she says so."

Regina O'Connor's "help" in administering Flannery's literary estate seem initially to have experienced confusion about the nature of their roles. Were they there to do more than pull at the nut grass of someone else's property? In May 1966, for example, Robert Giroux wrote a letter to Randolph Delehanty, explaining that "Publication rights to the Flannery O'Connor lecture rest with her Estate and her literary executors have authorized us to act on their behalf."[3] What was one to make of this response? Regina O'Connor was the executrix of the estate; Robert Fitzgerald was designated as O'Connor's literary executor. Who had the authority to "authorize" Robert Giroux to act on whose behalf?

In 1969, another response went out from Robert Fitzgerald to an agent at the William Morris Agency saying that he had received a manuscript by Richard Stern and Flannery O'Connor. "I reply in all haste to inform you 1. That

Miss McKee has no right to release Miss O'Connor's manuscript for publication and 2. That I, who do have this right, refuse my permission in this case. A copy of the present letter is going to Miss McKee."[4] Why the confusion? Elizabeth McKee, Flannery O'Connor's agent during her lifetime, had agreed to continue to help Regina O'Connor as a representative of the O'Connor Estate. Did her unofficial position give her authority that preceded and surpassed that of Robert Fitzgerald? Fitzgerald clearly did not believe this to be the case, but did he himself have more than an advisory role as literary executor? Did he have "rights" with regard to O'Connor's work that were independent of Regina? If Regina wanted Elizabeth McKee to "represent" the estate, as she undoubtedly did, what place in the hierarchy of gatekeepers did she occupy? As O'Connor's agent, McKee's one unambiguous role was subsidiary rights to published (not unpublished) writing, but several ambiguities surround her position. In 1967, when McIntosh, McKee and Dodds was sold to Harold Madson, Elizabeth McKee retired and was no longer officially anyone's agent. At what point did one person concede to the other? It seems that neither of them knew: Years later, in 1982, there was still misunderstanding.[5] With regard to an essay written by Marian Burns, Fitzgerald wrote to Gerald Becham at the Ina Dillard Russell Library of Georgia College: "I doubt that Miss McKee will care to make an issue of it, since the article is blameless, but if she does it is perhaps time for a clarification of her authority."[6]

Usually, as far as we can glean from formal correspondence, Flannery O'Connor's New York representatives did not "make an issue of" their respective roles: Robert Fitzgerald continued to decide what unpublished work could be published or quoted from; Robert Giroux, in turn, did the same, and Elizabeth McKee handled subsidiary rights like film and translation. All of them remained in contact with Regina O'Connor; they were friends; they functioned as a team. But they also functioned as the shapers of a legacy, deferring to Regina O'Connor and commenting among themselves about the difficulties of doing so.[7] We could say that we see people of good will operating in a dim legal zone where formal distinctions often were not clarified because personal friendships obviated the need for them.

But ambiguities persisted. As late as 1975, Rhoda F. Gamson of the Contract and Copyright Department of Farrar, Straus and Giroux was writing to Regina about the status of the estate, for she did not even know who was heir to the Flannery O'Connor Estate. What was Regina's role, once the Estate's assets were dispersed? Gamson writes, "For contractual and copyright purposes (in anticipation of our publication of *The Letters of Flannery O'Connor*), we need definite word on the current status of the Estate of Flannery O'Connor ... Has the Estate been settled and the assets distributed? If this is the case, who is the heir? If the Estate is not yet settled, are you still the Executrix of the Estate of Flannery O'Connor?"[8]

Gerald Becham, assistant director of the library at Georgia College, also had questions relating to copyright. In 1974 he wrote to Robert Fitzgerald about the status of James Tate, a frequent library visitor: "I wonder if there is not an important distinction to be made between quoting from materials that have never been published and quoting from variants of manuscripts that have been published."[9] Tate had been refused permission to quote from *Wise Blood* and its various antecedents, and the library was concerned. The value of its collection would be diminished if no one could quote from it; would Robert Fitzgerald be willing to provide a list of the materials that were prohibited? Fitzgerald responded by making a distinction that could have been challenged (a dissertation could be considered a form of publication), saying that he had not understood that Tate was only writing a dissertation; he did not regard this as a "publication" and so reversed his prior refusal.[10] He did not, as far as we know, provide a definitive list of items that could never be quoted, and thus the question—"Is there a distinction between unpublished letters, manuscripts and drafts of manuscripts?"—remained unaddressed.

While these issues remained unsorted, the fates of would-be scholars and writers were affected. We can follow the trajectory of decision making through the archives of Farrar, Straus and Giroux, Robert Fitzgerald, Sally Fitzgerald, and Robert Giroux,[11] noting, as we do so, that everyone involved in granting permission to quote treated copyright as if it were a place like Mrs. Cope's farm, a landscape identified by fences and by distinctions between inside and outside, occupant and guest, tenant and owner. The scope and nature of the farm (who was granted access to its resources) was strictly controlled.

Several scholars asked to make collections of Flannery's letters and were turned away. Not only did these refusals reflect Regina O'Connor's wishes— and she was very decided in her views[12]—but also a behind-the-scenes manipulation of who should be allowed onto the estate by those who were "hired": there by virtue of their help, but not themselves owners of property.

The idea to collect the letters apparently originated with Thomas Stritch, who wanted Regina to consider depositing all of Flannery's papers at Notre Dame. In 1966 he wrote to her saying, "I think the collecting of letters Flannery wrote others ought to start now ... some of those letters are going to get lost."[13] The very next month, Regina contacted Robert Fitzgerald to ask him what he thought of the idea. "Do you offer to pay for them or what? Who should do it? We can talk about it when you come."[14]

Apparently some informal agreement was reached soon afterward and Robert Fitzgerald solicited letters for the collection in the *New York Times Book Review*. This was not widely known, for a few months later one of Flannery's classmates at Iowa, Jean Wylder, wrote to John Farrar proposing to collect and edit the letters. Curiously, Farrar told her, "doing this book is out" because Robert Fitzgerald "has a contract with us." He then asked, "in view of his prior claim" if Jean would make copies of any letters that she had and send them on. "It would be very generous of you and much appreciated."[15] Thomas Gossett wrote asking about publishing "about 135 letters in 1972 and was again turned away, this time directly by Regina.[16]

But these refusals were, in some way, a dodge, for Robert Giroux did not even suggest a contract to Robert and Sally Fitzgerald until 1974, years after leading other scholars to believe that a collection of letters was impossible. "We continue to receive inquiries about an edition of Flannery's letters," he wrote to Robert Fitzgerald. "I wonder if the time has not come for us to contract with you and Sally to edit such a book." He had discussed the idea with Elizabeth McKee, who was "keen" for them to undertake the project; all that was needed was Regina's blessing. "If she agrees . . . I'd like to draw up an agreement along the lines of the *Mystery and Manners* contract."[17]

Years later, moves were made to prohibit other collections of letters, and these decisions continued to shape O'Connor's image. Sally and Robert Fitzgerald's sense of decorum, their "reading" of O'Connor was to remain the sole, unchallenged version of her character and priorities. Their representation of O'Connor was restricted by Regina O'Connor's scruples on one side, and on the other by their own desire to remain unhindered by competitors. In 1977, while collecting letters, Sally wrote to Robert Giroux, "Her [Regina's] excisions are often fantastic, I fear, and some of them I will restore in the final version, in the hope that she may not notice, or may have ceased to mind, or may have seen the light of reason. She is so afraid of anything personal that she has crossed out references to Henry Adams and Wyndham Lewis."[18] Sally's strategy became a cat-and-mouse game, where letters were sought and then unredacted in secret. But once she had decided upon the words to represent her subject, she actively discouraged other versions of O'Connor's life experience.

During this time, Maryat Lee wanted to publish her correspondence with Flannery and was refused permission in 1977, one year before the publication of *The Habit of Being*. Robert Giroux pointed out that being the recipient of letters meant only that pieces of paper were owned; the words and sentiments expressed remained as the property of the writer or her heirs.[19] Maryat then proposed to publish her own side of the correspondence, a new work, clearly using her own language. This project, too, was rejected (this time by Sally Fitzgerald),[20] as was, years later, Mary Lowe-Evans's 1990 proposal to bring out the O'Connor/Lee letters that had not been included in *The Habit of Being*. Here the New York literary executors guided Regina into thinking that this new (full) collection would be insignificant.[21]

A similar quiet intrigue governed the publication of any biography of O'Connor. Time and again Robert Fitzgerald withheld permission for such a project, although Robert Giroux and Elizabeth McKee frequently discussed the subject during the 1970s.[22] Leonard Melfi, who had written an authorized screenplay of "The Life You Save May Be Your Own," was the first person (of record) whom Robert Fitzgerald refused in 1964.[23] Ten years later in 1974, Mark Harris was turned away. Robert Giroux wrote, "no biographer has been chosen, and it is doubtful that the Estate will agree to authorize a biography."[24] By 1979, Robert Towers was forbidden to undertake a biography because "As you guessed, Sally Fitzgerald has been authorized by the O'Connor Estate to do the biography. She's been working on it for several years."[25]

This may have been true in an informal sense, but Sally Fitzgerald did not sign a contract with Farrar, Straus and Giroux until 1 January 1983, for she could not come to an understanding with Regina about either the terms of access to materials or control of the content of the proposed book. She also had to wrestle with the Mary Ingraham Bunting Institute of Radcliffe College, which wanted to claim copyright of the biography in exchange for financial support of the project, and, indeed, as the very precondition of granting Sally a fellowship at all.[26]

In 1978, the year that *The Habit of Being* was published, Sally had conceived of writing an O'Connor biography and submitted the proposal to Radcliffe College. It was to be a biographical study of Flannery and Regina, an inquiry into the lives of two southern women who, in Sally's words, "lived essentially without men. Their accomplishment," she said, "is self-evident." She was also confident that this study was now "possible" because Regina had agreed to make public "a very generous and illuminating collection" of O'Connor's work, where previously she had begun "to destroy any documentation of her daughter's personal life, thoughts and feelings." [27] Matina Horner, the president of Radcliffe, immediately approved a contract, which had clear but very restrictive parameters: Sally would finish this project in two years; Radcliffe would hold the copyright, would receive all royalties, and would, in turn, publish the manuscript within a designated time frame. If it didn't, the copyright would revert to Sally.

How Sally finessed her way out of her 1978 contract with Radcliffe College is not clear, but it is certain that she could not proceed as she had promised them. For one, she could not find the time needed for such a big project; she had to continue working for the Harvard Law School to earn her living; for another, Regina had been sick in the summers of 1978 and 1979 and had not been well enough to cooperate.[28] Her schedule was off track. But it is also likely that Elizabeth McKee intervened, for in 1979, Sally wrote to thank Elizabeth for "the Revised Version," and to say, "All in all, I think that they will re-consider without a war." She was also going to see Harvard's Grant Committee to "find out whether the contract I was asked to sign does not in fact conflict with Harvard's policy in such matters."[29]

It apparently took three more years to hash out the details of this project with Regina. During that time, Sally had to make clear the distinction between an "authorized" and a "definitive" biography, and to say that she was not willing to work under the restrictions imposed by authorization. "I returned from Milledgeville only a few days ago," she wrote to Elizabeth.

> While I was there I came to an agreement with Mrs. O'Connor that well satisfies me. She said for me to tell you that she agrees. So I am now ready to sign a contract, if you will work out one. . . . The change in Mrs. O'Connor's requirements regards her previously stipulated "approval" of the biography I am writing. I explained to her that this would compromise my work, since it would be assumed that I could therefore write only what she wished me to say. I told her that I was unwilling to sign such an agreement. She understood my objection, and agreed to withdraw this requirement. She will be satisfied with 33.3% of any royalties or advances on royalties or other monies. From her I will be satisfied with her cooperation and permission to quote from Flannery's writings and letters when necessary. The copyrights for any quotations from Flannery will naturally belong to her estate.[30]

She added that she had revised the title to reflect the new focus of the book. It would now be called "Mansions of the South."

There things stood for many years. Sally Fitzgerald was understood to be Flannery O'Connor's biographer and this knowledge governed responses to all other inquiries about writing O'Connor's life story. In 1982, Robert Fitzgerald died. In 1985 Robert Giroux accepted his responsibilities as the new literary executor for the Flannery O'Connor Estate,[31] and he, like Robert Fitzgerald, protected Sally Fitzgerald's "prior claim" to her position. "Mansions of the South" was due on 30 June 1984,[32] but even after it did not appear, Robert Giroux shielded it from competition.

In 1989, five years after Sally Fitzgerald's deadline, Jean Cash wrote to him asking for permission to quote from works and letters by O'Connor . . . both unpublished and published. She wanted to write "an intellectual biography." "I realize," she said, "that a problem arises because of Sally Fitzgerald's authorized biography of O'Connor. I do not feel, however, that the study I hope to produce will, in any way diminish Mrs. Fitzgerald's biography. Only she could produce a deeply personal study of O'Connor."[33] But Robert Giroux refused on all grounds, saying that, in any case, he would have to see the context in which any quote was embedded.[34]

At this point, all potential biographies of Flannery O'Connor had been held at bay for twenty-five years after her death in 1964. Both the owner of the O'Connor Literary Estate and her gatekeepers had kept out "intruders," and their vigilance had extended to would-be traditional O'Connor scholars as well. Neither Robert Giroux nor Elizabeth McKee would help Martha Stephens with her critical study, because it was considered poaching: "Because the Estate and her publishers will at some future time probably publish or authorize a book concerning the personal life of Flannery O'Connor and her publishing and agency associations during her literary career, we have adopted a firm rule that we cannot furnish such material to anyone who wants to independently publish a book about Flannery and her works."[35] In general, little could be "farmed" from this estate. Outsiders were not welcome. We could say that during these years, O'Connor scholars were considered rather like the boys in "A Circle in the Fire." Even when they stood outside the perimeter of Mrs. Cope's farm, they needed to be controlled. It was as if they were throwing rocks at a mailbox. "We're not even on your side of the road, lady" (246). But Mrs. Cope felt the need to call the sheriff. Everyone knew that the law was on the side of property.

If we step away from these individual decisions, we can see that they tend to move in a general direction that takes us away from creativity about Flannery O'Connor toward consecration of an image constructed by a very few people. Behind this sanctification lay the shrewdness and the fears that characterized Regina O'Connor's way of doing business in the world, a need for regency of the sort Mrs. Cope exercises over her land in "A Circle in the Fire": "'I cannot have this,' Mrs. Cope said and stood at the sink with both fists knotted at her sides. 'I cannot have this,' and her expression was the same as when she tore at the nut grass" (243). Sally Fitzgerald, the first person to pry physical possession of O'Connor's work from Regina's hands, sensed something of this business mentality and sensed, too, the anxiety that underlay it. "Regina is sharpening her blade," she wrote to Robert Giroux in 1977. "Her objections to letting Flannery speak in that sheaf were as nothing to her objections to the second, far more interesting, batch. Which she tore to pieces. Gutted. . . . I felt sick when I saw what she wants to do and the shell she is willing to leave." She understood that Regina's misgivings came from a deep fear of offending Protestant Milledgeville as a whole and certain people in particular. She dealt with this by a principle: Flannery O'Connor should be permitted "to be herself," and by cunning: she figured that Regina, continuing to be a good businesswoman, would respond to a generous share of royalties. Flannery O'Connor would not, she confided to Giroux, have wanted to "wound or embarrass living people . . . but Regina's scruples are not of the same kind."[36]

What would Flannery O'Connor have felt about these skirmishes over who could publish what? She never addressed the issue of copyright directly, but her attitudes toward private property of any kind can be inferred from her fiction and found, by extension, in the essays she wrote about being a writer in the South. Ironically it is the very concept of individual control of the earth that O'Connor questions in her fiction, just as it is the dominance of solitary talent that she critiques in her nonfiction writing. Indeed, she turns the tables on the hierarchy created by private ownership, time and again casting doubt on the assumption that any part of the earth can be owned. It can be borrowed and shared, but not owned absolutely. Her region included eternity, and with eternity, another perspective.

This, certainly, is true of the plot in "A Circle in the Fire." Mrs. Cope's domination of the boys fails. Insofar as they are representatives of the encroachments of the public on the private, they tell us of O'Connor's alternative perspective. When they open the bullpen, wash in the trough, ride the horses, smoke on the grounds no matter what Mrs. Cope decrees, their transgressions expose a false binarism. Rather than chastise the intruders, faulting them for interfering in private space, O'Connor gives them a wild joy as they claim that memory and love and work serve as another form of entitlement. "Listen here," the smallest boy said, "all the time we been knowing him he's been telling us about this here place. Said it was everything here. . . . Said he had the best time of his entire life right here on this here place. . . . Say, lady, you know what he said one time. He said when he died he wanted to come here" (236–37).

It is not a stretch to see a profound analogy here. For memory and love and work surely characterize the efforts of O'Connor scholars visiting the "farm" of her intellectual property. Copyright, unlike a barn or a field or a horse, has only a seventy-year detour through private property. It cannot be passed down in perpetuity. Someday it will "die" into the public domain, and the question before everyone managing the O'Connor Estate in the interim was the one facing Mrs. Cope. Could they give permission gracefully in light of other "lesser" claims to use that property? In this case, people were prohibited from quoting or even looking at work. In both situations, the result of refusal is what does not exist. To this date, it is as if the O'Connor woods had been burned. No biography exists with the full consent of the Estate; Maryat Lee's full correspondence remains unpublished; Flannery O'Connor's relationship with "Mr. G." remains unexplored.

These exclusions would have been anathema to Flannery O'Connor, who understood writing to be inherently and fruitfully an encroachment. She directly acknowledged that a writer was a poacher, someone who trespassed freely on the fields of language and custom. She called this a reliance on "region," and pointed out that the dialogic voices of fiction were essential. Mrs. Cope may have wanted the boys off her land, but the creator of the story about Mrs. Cope's stingy superiority needed to use those miscreants as well as "the help" and the African Americans of the unreconstructed South. Collectively they constituted the world of clashing values that portended and made possible a landscape that is "under the aspect of eternity" ("Catholic Novelist,"

858). "It takes a story to make a story. It takes a story of mythic dimensions, one which belongs to everybody" (859).

If literature "belongs to everybody," it belongs there in every aspect of creativity. O'Connor debunked the idea of the "isolated imagination," or the "lonely writer." The true artist, she claimed, is not a sensitive soul cut off from common experience, but someone who writes within a community: "His aim is still communication and communication suggests talking inside a commu-nity" ("The Regional Writer," 844). One writes as "part of what he writes about and is recognized as such" (845). "It is the knowledge that the novelist finds in his community" (487).

Her values could not have been more clearly expressed. Poaching is part and parcel of creativity. She openly admitted that she did it. It is hard to imag-ine that she would have agreed with the hagiography that kept her own voice from being used by others. It kept her out of the very community of voices that she recognized as her most valuable resource. Ironically, her death left her legacy in the hands of a Mrs. Cope and "help" who wanted all intruders to remain "across the road" from her writing estate. In life, she could create a parable about how the public domain haunts individual estates, challenging their isolate supremacy. In death we can imagine O'Connor walking through the borders created by her keepers; we can imagine her challenging individual possessiveness with alternative claims of fair use. We can even imagine her burning the woods to clear space for the wide fields of the public domain, the claims of the common man, and the creative commons.

NOTES

1. See Elizabeth McKee to Nancy Davis, 22 March 1985: "Robert Giroux. . . . Has agreed to make the decisions about the unpublished O'Connor material. Regina O'Connor, Executrix of The Estate of Flannery O'Connor, has confirmed this appointment." Farrar, Straus and Giroux Archives, New York Public Library.

2. See Robert Giroux to Sally Fitzgerald, 3 June 1977. "As you asked, I'm returning Regina's handwritten letter to you with all my sympathy. It's hard for her to distinguish the writer, whose work belongs to the ages, from her daughter, wrote letters to friends, 'not for the pub-lic'!" Farrar, Straus and Giroux Archives, Box 266, New York Public Library.

3. Robert Giroux to Randolph Delehanty, 10 May 1966, Farrar, Straus and Giroux Archives, Box 266, New York Public Library.

4. Robert Fitzgerald to Lois Wallace, 15 November 1969, Farrar, Straus and Giroux Archives, New York Public Library.

5. A dozen years later, in 1979, Robert Giroux confused the issue more: he considered that Elizabeth McKee was the appropriate person to consult about quotation from unpublished manuscripts. See Robert Giroux to Gerald Becham, 25 September 1979: "There is no objection to the brief quotes from Flannery O'Connor's letters in The Habit of Being on page two of Jan Gretlund's typescript, as long as credit is given. The two unpublished letters of 1963 should be cleared with Elizabeth McKee, Literary Agent for the Estate, if they have not already been."

6. See Robert Giroux to Gino Ardito, 8 November 1967: "The agent for the Estate of Flannery O'Connor is Elizabeth McKee, of McIntosh, McKee and Dodds. . . . She handles all rights, dramatic, film and television, as well as book rights." Farrar, Straus and Giroux Archives, New York Public Library.

According to Ben Camardi, Elizabeth McKee retired at the point when McIntosh, McKee and Dodds was sold to Harold Madson. Most previous clients were then represented by Don Congdon, Harold Madson, and Peter Madson. Regina O'Connor was reluctant to be passed on. "She would have no agent other than Elizabeth McKee. Hal Matson invited Elizabeth to use one of the offices and work on behalf of Flannery O'Connor." Ben Camardi to Carol Loeb Shloss, 9 April 2015. Private ownership.

See also Robert Fitzgerald to Gerald Becham, 20 May 1982. "I am often called on for permission to quote from unpublished writing by Flannery O'Connor, and I almost always grant permission. I am surprised that Marian Burns applied to Elizabeth McKee and not to me. I think her article is excellent and should be published. For a long time I have been under the impression that my permission was enough permission in these cases. I suggest that the Georgia Bulletin go ahead and publish the Burns article. I doubt that Miss McKee will care to make an issue of it, since the article is blameless, but if she does it is perhaps time for a clarification of her authority."

7. See Robert Giroux to Maryat Lee, 23 February 1976. "I'm glad you're doing a piece on Flannery for the Georgia College Bulletin. If there is anything in it, which Regina might take umbrage, my avuncular advice is to take it out. The Fitzgerald release (which you must give me time to get) ordinarily insures Regina's release too, but legally she has the final say, no matter what the literary executors might wish or recommend, during her lifetime."

8. Rhoda F. Gamson to Regina O'Connor, 15 January 1975. Farrar, Straus and Giroux Archives, New York Public Library.

9. See Gerald Becham, assistant director of the library, Georgia College to Robert Fitzgerald, 6 February 1974: "I am turning to you for clarification on two important points with reference to the use of the Flannery O'Connor manuscripts. Mr. James Tate, who has spent approximately four months of research time on the manuscript of *Wise Blood* in connection with his doctorate at Columbia University, has been denied permission to quote from early versions of the manuscript. I wonder if there is not an important distinction to be made between quoting from materials that have never been published and quoting from variants of manuscripts that have been published?

"Not having seen Mr. Tate's letter requesting permission, I am assuming that he did not make it clear that he was interested in tracing the development of *Wise Blood* from its genesis to its published form—a subject by its nature requiring quotation.

"You as literary executor of course have the sole right to make decisions, but if there has not been a misunderstanding in this particular instance should we not be in a position to forewarn scholars.

"This brings me to my second point. If it has been pre-determined which materials may not be quoted from, would you be willing to give me a written statement listing these manuscripts? At the present time, for instance, we have a scholar of established reputation who is interested in working on 'Why Do The Heathen Rage.' What should I tell him?

"If early manuscripts can never be quoted, the value of the collection for serious students of OC will be greatly reduced. Your assistance in clarifying this use of the mss will be greatly appreciated."

10. See Robert Fitzgerald to Gerald Becham, 20 February 1974. "My understanding of my duty to Flannery O'Connor is that before any of her unpublished writing is published, I should be consulted and may either give or withhold permission. When Miss McKee referred the

Tate's request to me, she seemed averse to the publication of early draft material of *Wise Blood*. As I trust Miss McKee's judgment in such matters, I concurred. But it is clear to me from your letter that publication is not in question, at present at least. Unless and until it is in this and every case, I do not think that I need be consulted."

11. Elizabeth McKee gave her correspondence with Flannery O'Connor to Robert Giroux, who in turn made copies for Robert Fitzgerald and Regina O'Connor and sent one back to Elizabeth McKee. Three Xerox files should exist, but the fate of these letters remains unknown. They appear neither in the Farrar, Straus and Giroux archives, nor in the bequest of O'Connor materials to the Georgia College Library, nor in the list of Harold Matson clients housed in the Columbia University Rare Books and Manuscript Collection. See Robert Giroux to Regina O'Connor, 6 January 1971. "Elizabeth McKee turned over to me all of Flannery's correspondence with her from June 1948 to May 1964. I have since had copies made of all the letters, one set of which I sent to Robert Fitzgerald, another to Elizabeth McKee, and a third which I am keeping. . . . I must say that I consider it extremely generous of Elizabeth to make a gift of the original letters to the Estate. While the right to publish the contents of these letters would always remain with the Estate, they have an additional value as original manuscripts signed by Flannery. That is why I am sending this package by certified mail.

"These letters also make a very interesting story in themselves of Flannery's publishing career. They have great bibliographical interest, because they pinpoint so precisely the dates of composition of individual stories and of their publication in magazines. They will make an important segment of Flannery's papers when you present them to her college." Farrar, Straus and Giroux Archives, New York Public Library.

12. See, for example, Richard Ziegfeld to Regina O'Connor, 18 May 1979. "I have received a letter from Elizabeth McKee indicating your reluctance to allow me to work on the relationship between your daughter and Mr. G. I understand your desire to make certain that *Habit of Being* sells in both hardback and paperback as well as it possibly can. Moreover, I respect the fact that ultimately you are the person who should make a decision about access to the unpublished letters . . . from Flannery to Mr. G. Should what I have to say in the balance of this letter not persuade you to reconsider my request, rest assured that I will not bother you about the issue again." Regina's answer to Elizabeth McKee, forwarded to Robert Giroux, 24 May 1979. "I think this letter speaks for itself. The answer is NO."

13. Thomas Stritch to Regina O'Connor, 23 February 1966, Farrar, Straus and Giroux Archives, Box 266, New York Public Library.

14. Regina O'Connor to Robert Fitzgerald, 27 March 1966, Farrar, Straus and Giroux Archives, Box 266, New York Public Library.

15. John Farrar to Jean W. Wylder, 16 January 1967, Farrar, Straus and Giroux Archives, Box 266, New York Public Library.

16. Thomas F. Gossett to Robert Giroux, 8 December 1972: "After Miss O'Connor's death, we asked Mrs. Edward O'Connor for permission to publish the letters, but she was adamantly opposed and—so far as I know—still is." Farrar, Straus and Giroux Archives, Box 266, New York Public Library.

17. Robert Giroux to Robert Fitzgerald, 24 July 1974, Farrar, Straus and Giroux Archives, Box 266, New York Public Library.

18. Sally Fitzgerald to Robert Giroux, 18 May 1977, Farrar, Straus and Giroux Archives, Box 267, New York Public Library.

19. Robert Giroux to Maryat Lee, 21 April 1977. "Perhaps I should point out that it's to Regina alone, as owner of the publishing rights, to give permission for the use of Flannery's letters. The recipients of the letters own the pieces of paper, but the words and their use for

publication belong to Flannery's estate. This is an aspect of copyright law that few people are familiar with—understandably, since it is a complicated distinction."

20. Sally Fitzgerald to Maryat Lee, 21 February 1977, Farrar, Straus and Giroux Archives, Box 267, New York Public Library.

21. Regina O'Connor to Elizabeth McKee, 26 October 1990. "I have your letter of October 18 concerning the request of Dr. Mary Lowe-Evans for permission to publish the unpublished letters of Flannery to Maryat Lee. I respect your judgment after reading the letters that they are not as important as those already published and I agree with Bob Giroux's disinclination to grant publication rights. Therefore, I would appreciate your advising Dr. Lowe-Evans that permission cannot be granted to publish these letters."

22. Elizabeth McKee to Robert Giroux, 28 April 1972, re the possibility of a biography of Flannery O'Connor: "We both agree that Robert Fitzgerald would not be the proper writer." Farrar, Straus and Giroux Archives, Box 267, New York Public Library.

23. Leonard Melfi to Robert Giroux, 28 September 1964. "I am planning on writing the biography of the late Flannery O'Connor, and I felt the best person to tell this to would be her publisher.... (I made a screen play of 'The Life You Save May Be Your Own'... Flannery O'Connor gave her permission and then later on her approval)." Farrar, Straus and Giroux Archives, Box 267, New York Public Library.

24. Robert Giroux to Mark Harris, 25 September 1974, Farrar, Straus and Giroux Archives, Box 267, New York Public Library.

25. Robert Giroux to Robert Towers, 13 March 1979, Farrar, Straus and Giroux Archives, Box 267, New York Public Library.

26. See Matina Horner, Contract with Sally Fitzgerald, undated. "Your manuscript and all research materials prepared in connection with it shall be the property of the College which shall have the sole right to publish them or to make alternative arrangements for their disposition. The College shall not be obliged to identify any publication of this material as an Institute for Independent Study monograph. The College alone shall hold the copyright to the work and you hereby assign such copyright to the College. It is understood that royalties on any publication contracted for by the College shall be paid to the College until such time as the College has received an amount equal to the expenses incurred by the College on the project. In computing such expenses the amount of the grant and the amount awarded to you as expenses shall not be included. Any royalties or other payments in excess of the amount expended by the College on the project shall be divided equally between you and the College." Farrar, Straus and Giroux Archives, Box 267, New York Public Library.

27. See Sarah M. Fitzgerald. "Project: Flannery and Regina: Biographical Study of Flannery O'Connor and her Mother." Unpublished Manuscript, Farrar, Straus and Giroux Archives, New York Public Library.

28. See Sally Fitzgerald to Elizabeth McKee, 24 September 1979. "I have been unable to obtain a release from the other obligations. I have told them that, due to Mrs. OCs two illnesses, this summer and the summer of 1978, I shall not be able to meet the time deadline. I offered to resign the fellowship on this account, but they don't want me to do that." Farrar, Straus and Giroux Archives, Box 104, New York Public Library.

29. Sally Fitzgerald to Elizabeth McKee, 14 December 1979, Farrar, Straus and Giroux Archives, Box 104, New York Public Library.

30. Sally Fitzgerald to Elizabeth McKee, 24 May 1982, Farrar, Straus and Giroux Archives, Box 104, New York Public Library.

31. See Elizabeth McKee to Nancy Davis, 22 March 1985. "Robert Giroux... has agreed to make the decisions about the unpublished O'Connor material. Regina O'Connor, Executrix of

The Estate of Flannery O'Connor, has confirmed this appointment." Farrar, Straus and Giroux Archives, New York Public Library.

32. See contract drawn up by Elizabeth McKee, updated. First installment of $15,000 ($5,000) due 1. Upon signing (15 January 1983). Future installments due 2. Upon submission of the manuscript, and 3. Upon publication date. Special note included in the contract: "Regina O'Connor authorizes this biography and agrees to cooperate in providing access to needed information. Author agrees to pay to O'Connor 1/3 of all monies due her through McIntosh, McKee and Dodds. Farrar, Straus and Giroux agrees to see further copies of the Work to O'Connor at a discount of 40%." Farrar, Straus and Giroux Archives, Box 104, New York Public Library.

33. Jean W. Cash to Robert Fitzgerald, 14 February 1989. Farrar, Straus and Giroux Archives, Box 267, New York Public Library.

34. Robert Giroux to Jean Cash, 18 May 1989. Farrar, Straus and Giroux Archives, Box 267, New York Public Library.

35. Elizabeth McKee to Martha Stephens, 9 April 1970. Farrar, Straus and Giroux Archives, Box 266, New York Public Library.

36. Sally Fitzgerald to Robert Giroux, 2 May 1977. Farrar, Straus and Giroux Archives, Box 104, New York Public Library.

ARCHIVES

Farrar, Straus and Giroux Archives. New York Public Library.

Robert Fitzgerald Archives. The Beinecke Rare Book and Manuscript Library, Yale University.

Sally Fitzgerald Archives. Stuart A. Rose Manuscript, Archives, and Rare Book Library, Emory University.

WORKS CITED

Coombe, Rosemary. *The Cultural Life of Intellectual Properties: Authorship, Appropriation and the Law*. Durham, NC: Duke University Press, 1998.

O'Connor, Flannery. *Collected Works*. Ed. Sally Fitzgerald. New York: Literary Classics of the United States, 1988.

Saint-Amour, Paul. *The Copywrights: Intellectual Property and the Literary Imagination*. Ithaca, NY: Cornell University Press, 2010.

Saint-Amour, Paul, ed. *Modernism and Copyright*. New York: Oxford University Press, 2010.

Afterword

Observing the composition and production of this book fills me with gratitude, and I trust that readers will indulge me as I insert here a few thank-yous
relating to "Reconsidering Flannery O'Connor," the 2007 and 2014 National
Endowment for the Humanities Summer Institutes for College and University Teachers, which we hosted in Milledgeville at Flannery O'Connor's alma
mater, now called Georgia College. Because the NEH Institutes inspired the
editors of this volume to collect these articles, I would like to share the story of
why and how the NEH Institutes came about, review a few of the struggles and
successes, and share a few thoughts about the future of O'Connor scholarship.

When I moved to Milledgeville in 2003 to take on the editorship of the
Flannery O'Connor Review, I was already thoroughly in awe of O'Connor.
Persuaded though I am that she was not a saint, I am grateful to Flannery
O'Connor for being such a very good writer and for writing in her will that
Georgia College was fit to house her papers. I was very lucky that my pre-
decessor, Sarah Gordon, was so very supportive as I started producing the
Review, working near the major library for the study of O'Connor and begin-
ning to teach at least one course each year about O'Connor's works.

And still, there were challenges. Even at Georgia College, there used to be
talk about our nearly having completed the work of figuring out O'Connor.
Although it was clear to me in 2003 that O'Connor stories were being
reprinted in just about every anthology being used in the United States to
introduce freshman college students to the wonders of serious literature, there
also seemed to be a danger that O'Connor was starting to be pigeonholed in
ways that made her seem less than central to the mainstream of American
literature. Would she continue to be included on the reading lists for upper-
division courses, and would she matter to professors planning graduate
courses on the latest trends? Another challenge came from the opening to
tourists of Andalusia, O'Connor's farm home just north of Milledgeville, at
just about the time I arrived. Overall, then, I thought we needed to find ways

to make O'Connor more widely popular. I realize, and celebrate, the signs that O'Connor's value on the literary stock market is continuously increasing: the selection of O'Connor's *The Complete Stories* as the best book ever to win the National Book Award, the appearance in *PMLA* of an article on O'Connor's *Wise Blood*, the translation of O'Connor into Arabic and into Mandarin Chinese, the founding of an O'Connor Society in Japan, and the scholarly conferences about O'Connor hosted in various European countries.

I have asked myself what Flannery O'Connor would want me to do, but more significantly (I'll admit), I have asked myself what I think O'Connor needs. These questions led me to make some grand generalizations (to myself) about the state of O'Connor scholarship in 2003. She was famous as a Great Writer of Southern Gothic, of course, and it was easy for me to agree with O'Connor that using the label of Southern Gothic was not a good way to help O'Connor's fame grow. Even though O'Connor preferred and accepted the term "grotesque" as a descriptor for her fiction, and even though I had written a brilliant book about O'Connor's profound use of the grotesque in her art, it was easy to believe that we needed to move on to something fresher.

The big issue was what to do about O'Connor's fame as the Greatest of American Catholic Writers. O'Connor coached her literary friends and her public audiences to look for religious mystery and theological insight in her works. She successfully made Catholicism her brand, and whenever I visit the dozens of Georgia College Library shelves devoted to books on O'Connor, I find myself surrounded by scholarly work relating O'Connor's fiction to her religious philosophy and her dogmatic commitments. Much of this work is very learned, and some of it is quite good. When I started my job at Georgia College, I was close to believing that O'Connor scholars had very nearly completed the work of figuring out O'Connor as a Catholic writer. While I no longer think we will ever finish figuring out O'Connor as a Catholic writer, I believe O'Connor wanted to be taken seriously, first and foremost, as a writer, and, therefore, I defined my mission as working to expand O'Connor studies beyond the southern and beyond the Catholic.

For a long time, I have realized that, in addition to people from English departments, people from all sorts of academic departments find O'Connor fascinating: art, creative writing, education, environmental science, film studies, history, museum studies, philosophy, political science, psychology, religion, sociology, theater, women's studies, and more. So one thing I can do is to invite more people from outside English to study her seriously. They might want to use their academic specialization to say something more about O'Connor as southerner or O'Connor as Catholic, and that is fine with me. The other major strategy I can use to promote O'Connor is to encourage English teachers to apply to O'Connor the approaches they use with the rest of the world of literature: asking questions about race, class, and gender;

producing cultural studies, disability studies, psychoanalytic studies; relating O'Connor to science, to money, to genre literature, to authors with whom we had never considered her to have anything in common. In this volume, you see that editors Alison Arant and Jordan Cofer, summer scholars in the 2014 Summer Institute on O'Connor, have succeeded in collecting and polishing a variety of fresh and inspiring readings of O'Connor—of just the sort that I think is of most service to O'Connor.

Now for the story about how the O'Connor institutes came to be. Linda Watson Kaufman, who used to be in charge of directing grant writing at Georgia College, told me that Georgia College really *must* apply for a grant for a summer institute. I and my colleague John D. Cox got busy drafting and redrafting and redrafting a proposal, making good use of the advice from the Georgia College community as well as the advice from the tolerant and thoroughly professional staff at the NEH. John Cox and I lived with our application for about a year before the official submission. Watson Kaufman provided the invaluable service of persuading people in offices all over campus to be flexible about their usual procedures in order to make it possible for us to pull off the gathering. Our twenty-four participants in 2007 (one of whom, Doug Davis, is a contributor to this volume) came to Milledgeville to experience life in a residence hall throughout the month of July, during which they attended seminars with visiting O'Connor experts, heard guest lecturers, went on field trips, and, perhaps most importantly, worked for a week with O'Connor's papers in our Special Collections section of the library. The results of the 2007 Institute have been strong: five books, dozens of articles, over a hundred conference presentations. The results were so strong that the record of scholarly production from the 2007 group became a major argument for why we should receive a second, even larger grant for a 2014 Summer Institute. One of the participants from 2007, Robert Donahoo of Sam Houston State University, became my excellent codirector for 2014. The vast majority of the articles in this volume are by summer scholars who participated in the 2014 Summer Institute, and I am sure they join me in thanking all the Georgia College people who made the NEH project successful. I'll name a few: Nancy Davis Bray and the entire staff of Special Collections in the Georgia College Library; Robin Lewis, Donna Douglas, and Jennifer Watkins of the grants office at Georgia College; and our imaginative and tireless student assistants Laura Martin and James Owens.

As I recall all the help I received, I would be remiss if I did not mention some of the (O'Connoresque?) episodes that kept us all on our toes. We had our fair share of illness and accidents for speakers and participants and family members and close friends. We had so many problems with automobiles that I lost count, and we had a bicycle accident in 2014 that none of us will forget. Then there are the (now) comic moments: realizing we had to buy linens for all our visitors, having a fire alarm empty the residence hall in the middle of the night, needing to install air conditioners throughout a residence hall on short notice. The NEH Institutes have given me some of the most thrilling times of my career, and I promise that most of the thrills were intellectual.

Where do we stand now? I credit the National Endowment for the Humanities with giving to the United States dozens more college teachers who are fully prepared to use O'Connor's works to enrich their classroom offerings. O'Connor scholarship is increasingly diverse, and there is every indication that O'Connor's place within the academy is secure. Georgia College has taken over the maintenance and restoration of Andalusia, so there is every reason to believe that the farm will be an increasingly valuable resource for teachers and students. After all I have experienced, I find that when I teach my course on how to be a graduate student in the field of English, it is easy to use O'Connor's stories to illustrate almost all the major approaches to contemporary literary studies. Flannery O'Connor wrote works that invite and reward continued reexamination, so I expect that we will continue to find it rewarding to reconsider Flannery O'Connor. We will find new answers to old questions, and we will find answers to brand-new questions too.

Contributors

Lindsey Alexander is the author of *Rodeo in Reverse*, winner of the 2017 New Southern Voices Prize for poetry, selected by Sean Hill. In 2014, she was a scholar at the National Endowment for the Humanities month-long institute "Reconsidering Flannery O'Connor." She also coauthored a chapter on the movie *Clueless* that appears in *ReFocus: The Films of Amy Heckerling*.

Alison Arant is associate professor and chair of English at Wagner College on Staten Island in New York City, where she teaches courses in US southern literature, women writers, African American literature, and race and music studies. She participated in the 2014 NEH Institute "Reconsidering Flannery O'Connor," and her work has appeared in *Flannery O'Connor Review, Mississippi Quarterly, Modern Fiction Studies*, and *Southern Literary Journal*, as well as the edited collection *Southern Comforts: Drinking and the U. S. South*.

Alicia Matheny Beeson is an assistant professor of English at West Virginia University at Parkersburg where she teaches courses in American literature and composition. She focuses on twentieth-century American literature, particularly women authors in the Progressive Era. She is currently working on a project regarding early twentieth-century utopian texts by American women, exploring issues of religion, domesticity, child care, and labor. She has forthcoming work in *CEA Critic* and an edited collection about women's friendships in twentieth- and twenty-first-century American works.

Eric Bennett is the author of *Workshops of Empire: Stegner, Engle, and American Creative Writing during the Cold War* and the novel *A Big Enough Lie*. His scholarship has appeared in *After the Program Era* (ed. Loren Glass), *American Literature in Transition, 2000–2010* (ed. Rachel Greenwald Smith), *Modern Fiction Studies, New Writing*, and the *Blackwell Companion to Creative Writing*. He also has written for the *New York Times, New Yorker, Chronicle of*

Higher Education, A Public Space, and *VQR*. He is a professor of English at Providence College in Rhode Island.

Gina Caison is an associate professor of English at Georgia State University where she specializes in southern literature and Native American studies. She is the author of *Red States: Indigeneity, Settler Colonialism and Southern Studies* (2018) and coeditor with Lisa Hinrichsen and Stephanie Rountree of *Small-Screen Souths: Region, Identity, and the Cultural Politics of Television* (2017). She participated in the 2014 NEH Institute "Reconsidering Flannery O'Connor," and her work has appeared in venues including *Native South, The Global South, Mississippi Quarterly, The Velvet Light Trap*, and *PMLA*. Currently, she is president of the Society for the Study of Southern Literature.

Jordan Cofer is an associate provost and professor of English at Georgia College & State University. He is the author of *The Gospel According to Flannery O'Connor* (2014) and coauthor of the textbook *Writing the Nation: A Concise Guide to American Literature from 1865–Present*. He has recently published works in the *Chronicle of Higher Education, Kansas City Star, Christianity and Literature, Southern Quarterly*, and the *Flannery O'Connor Review*.

Doug Davis is a professor of English at Gordon State College in Barnesville, Georgia, where he teaches literature and writing. His scholarly interests include Cold War cultural studies, science and technology studies, science fiction, and Flannery O'Connor. He has published essays in venues including the journals *Configurations, Southern Quarterly*, and the *Flannery O'Connor Review* on apocalyptic topics ranging from the extinction of the dinosaurs and fictions of nuclear disaster to the politics of science fiction and the fiction and thought of Flannery O'Connor. Most recently, he has guest-edited a special issue of the *Flannery O'Connor Review* on the role of science and technology in O'Connor's literature.

Doreen Fowler is a professor of English at the University of Kansas. Her latest publication is *Drawing the Line: The Father Reimagined in Faulkner, Wright, O'Connor, and Morrison* (2013), a feminist reinterpretation of the father's role in the cultural production of identity. She is also the author of *Faulkner: The Return of the Repressed*, a psychoanalytic interpretation of Faulkner's major novels; and the coeditor of eleven collections of essays on Faulkner. She has published articles on modern American fiction in such journals as *American Literature, Modern Fiction Studies, Journal of Modern Literature, MELUS*, and others.

Marshall Bruce Gentry is a professor of English at Georgia College and editor of the *Flannery O'Connor Review*. He is the author of the book *Flannery O'Connor's*

Religion of the Grotesque, editor of the volume *The Cartoons of Flannery O'Connor at Georgia College*, and coeditor of *At Home with Flannery O'Connor: An Oral History*. His articles on O'Connor's works appear in *Flannery O'Connor in the Age of Terrorism, Wise Blood: A Re-Consideration, Flannery O'Connor's Radical Reality, "On the Subject of the Feminist Business": Re-Reading Flannery O'Connor, Flannery O'Connor: New Perspectives, Southern Quarterly*, etc. Gentry is also the author of *Conversations with Raymond Carver* and served as the codirector of the NEH Institute "Reconsidering Flannery O'Connor" (2007, 2014).

Bruce Henderson is a professor of communication studies at Ithaca College, where he chaired that department and was coordinator of the Culture and Communication Program. He recently served as the Harron Family Endowed Chair at Villanova University. He is coauthor or coeditor of three books and has edited both *Text and Performance Quarterly* and *Disability Studies Quarterly*, and has been published in various journals and reference works, including *Flannery O'Connor Review*. He holds the PhD in performance studies from Northwestern University and the PhD in disability studies from the University of Illinois at Chicago.

Monica Carol Miller is an assistant professor of English at Middle Georgia State University. A participant in the 2014 NEH summer seminar in "Reconsidering Flannery O'Connor," her work focuses on the intersections of region and gender in American literature and culture. She is the current president of the Flannery O'Connor Society, secretary-treasurer of the Society for the Study of Southern Literature, and the MLA Delegate Assembly representative for Southern United States Literature, Language, and Culture division. Her monograph *Being Ugly: Southern Women Writers and Social Rebellion* (2017) examines the ways in which ugliness marks fictional characters who are excluded from traditional gender roles of marriage and motherhood. Her current projects include an analysis of images of abortion in pre-Roe American literature as well as coediting an essay collection on the Tacky South.

William Murray is a postdoctoral fellow at Baylor University where he teaches courses in American literature. His research focuses on twentieth- and twenty-first-century US literature, film/TV, and graphic novels. Will's work has appeared in journals such as *American Studies, Mississippi Quarterly, CEA Critic, Eudora Welty Review*, and the *South Carolina Review*. He is currently working on a book project that explores how post-1960 narratives (from and about the US South) protect fictions of white innocence.

Carol Loeb Shloss is a consulting professor of English at Stanford University, presently a visiting professor at the University of Pennsylvania. She is a

National Book Critics' Circle finalist for Best Biography of 2003: *Lucia Joyce: To Dance in the Wake*. She is also the author of *Flannery O'Connor's Dark Comedies: The Limits of Inference* (2011) and has published in *Flannery O'Connor Review*, *Chronicle of Higher Education*, *James Joyce Quarterly*, and others.

Alison Staudinger is an associate professor of democracy and justice studies at the University of Wisconsin-Green Bay. With primary interests in democratic theory and citizenship, she focuses on twentieth-century thinkers including Hannah Arendt, arguing for the importance of politicizing labor, including care work. Staudinger is also interested in shifting how political theory as a discipline engages literary work, particularly in response to American political development during the Cold War, civil rights era, and early deindustrialization. Her 2018 book, *Gender in the Political Science Classroom*, follows work published in *Good Society*, *P.S.: A Journal of Politics*, and *Teaching and Learning Inquiry*, among others.

Rachel Watson is an assistant professor of American literature in the English department at Howard University, and was a member of the 2014 Summer Institute "Reconsidering Flannery O'Connor." She was awarded a 2017–18 NEH Award for Faculty in support of her current book project, which considers how problems in criminal procedure and Constitutional law—particularly interpretations of the Fourth and Fifth Amendments—appear in literature of the Jim Crow and civil rights periods. Her work has appeared in journals such as *Post45*, *Peer Reviewed*, *Humanities*, *CLA Journal*, *Mississippi Quarterly*, *Sonora Review*, *Obsidian: Literature in the African Diaspora*, and the edited collection *Faulkner and Mystery*.

Index